THE LOTUS SUTRA

The Lotus Sutra

A CONTEMPORARY TRANSLATION
OF A BUDDHIST CLASSIC

Translation and Introduction by
Gene Reeves

Wisdom Publications
199 Elm Street
Somerville, MA 02144 USA
wisdompubs.org

Library of Congress Cataloging-in-Publication Data
Tripitaka. Sutrapitaka. Saddharmapundarikasutra. English.
 The Lotus sutra : a contemporary translation of a Buddhist classic / translation and
introduction by Gene Reeves.
   p. cm.
 Translated from: Miao fa lian hua jing, translated from Sanskrit into Chinese by
Kumarajiva.
 Includes bibliographical references and index.
 ISBN 0-86171-571-3 (pbk. : alk. paper)
 I. Reeves, Gene. II. Title.
 BQ2052.E5R44 2009
 294.3'85—dc22
                             2008035517

20 19 18 17
8 7 6 5

ISBN 978-0-86171-571-8   eBook ISBN 978-0-86171-987-7

Cover illustration from the Illuminated Lotus Project (detail) © Roberta Mansell.
Cover design by TLJB. Interior design by Gopa&Ted2, Inc. Set in DGP 11.5/14.5.

Please visit fscus.org.

Table of Contents

Preface

THIS NEW TRANSLATION of the Lotus Sutra is intended primarily for people who are interested in Buddhism but are not Buddhist scholars. My intention is to provide a highly readable English version of this important text. I want to make this text accessible to ordinary readers with little or no familiarity with technical Buddhist vocabulary. Several other translations are available, some better than others. For scholars interested in comparison of Sanskrit and Chinese versions, for example, the translation by the late Leon Hurvitz will be useful.

While I do my best to make the sutra accessible, I never deliberately compromise the meaning of what I find in it. There are passages in this text that I don't like and wish were not there. There are passages that are extremely difficult if not impossible to understand. There are a great many ambiguities, some intentional, some probably not. My purpose is not to eliminate or soften such passages or to settle the controversies to which they have given rise, but only to provide a version that reveals as much meaning in the sutra as possible.

My first exposure to this sutra was around 1980 when I was invited to participate in a workshop sponsored by the lay Buddhist organization Rissho Kosei-kai, which has its headquarters and the vast majority of its members in Japan. The workshop was designed to enhance interest in the Lotus Sutra among participants, but it had the opposite effect on me. I found a number of things in the text uncongenial. In succeeding years, however, I became increasingly fascinated by this sutra. And I came to think that part of what discouraged me initially was the poor choice of terms in the translation I had read.

Nearly a decade later I decided to move to Japan to study the Lotus Sutra and improve my skills in Japanese and Chinese languages. I was encouraged both by Nikkyo Niwano, the founder and then president of Rissho Kosei-kai, and by Yoshiro Tamura, the foremost Japanese scholar of Tendai thought, who had recently retired from the University of Tokyo and was teaching at Rissho University.

Tamura died within a few months of my moving to Japan, so our several joint projects had to be abandoned. But Tamura's blend of passionate, personal interest in the Lotus Sutra, combined with his profound scholarship and academic rigor, is an inspiration to me still. Nikkyo Niwano, on the other hand, was entirely lacking in scholarly, academic credentials. But he had the same sensibility as Tamura, except that whereas Tamura was primarily an academic and secondarily a follower of the Lotus Sutra, Niwano was primarily a practitioner and devotee of the sutra and secondarily one who studied the scholarship about it. I regard both of these men as my great Dharma teachers, and feel more indebted to them than I can express.

As I became more familiar with Japanese and Chinese versions of this sutra, and despite the fact that some new translations had appeared in print, I became even more convinced that a version for ordinary English-language readers was needed, one that avoided Buddhist jargon and Sanskrit terms as much as possible.

I began dabbling with a translation of my own about a dozen years ago. The first privately printed version was in 2001. Since then there have been many revisions and a few revised versions. I'm sure there will be more. Translation of any large and complex Chinese text is not something one can ever expect to get right. All one can hope for is that it will become better.

When Kumarajiva or other translators felt that they could not translate a Sanskrit word into Chinese, they transliterated it; that is, they provided a phonetic equivalent to the Sanskrit. This is one of the reasons why many Sanskrit terms have become familiar in English, terms such as "buddha," "dharma," "stupa," and so on, they are basically transliterations of Sanskrit terms. The normal procedure when translating a Chinese Buddhist text into English is to translate into English what the translator into Chinese translated and use the Sanskrit term if it was only transliterated into Chinese. This works fine, of course, for scholars already familiar with many Sanskrit terms, but less well for others. What I have done in this translation, then, is to translate into English wherever I can; that is, wherever I think there is a reasonably good English equivalent for the term in question.

Sometimes such choices are relatively easy to make. For example, the Sanskrit term *kalpa*, often left untranslated, is here rendered as "eon." Perhaps "age" would work just as well, but I can see no point in retaining the Sanskrit.

Some choices will be more controversial. The Sanskrit term *sangha* is often used in English, both in translations and in general use among English-speaking Buddhists, where it has come to mean just about any Buddhist community. For this translation, I have chosen to use "monks," since it was often used to translate "sangha" into Chinese, and "monk(s)" is what the Chinese character in this sutra literally means. Originally in India and still today in many of the Buddhist worlds of Asia, "sangha" still refers exclusively to a community of monks. Thus, to use "sangha" where the text has "monks" could be confusing or misleading. Where the text intends a larger grouping that includes monks but is not limited to them, I use "assembly" or, as is often the case in this text, "great assembly."

My decision to use the English (originally Greek or Roman) equivalents for most Indian mythological creatures will seem misguided to some. The great Buddhist and Sanskrit scholar Hajime Nakamura was the first to point out to me how closely related these imaginary creatures are. When I saw that Jean-Noël Robert used translations of these terms in his excellent translation of the Lotus Sutra into French, I decided to do the same. The Sanskrit equivalents can be found in the glossary of terms. The one exception to this practice is the term *asura*, which does not correspond very well with "titan" and appears in English-language works, translations, and dictionaries. In the case of Dharma I retain the Sanskrit, whereas others have chosen to translate it. Some translators have used "law." While I understand that choice, I think it is unfortunate. Sometimes, especially in non-Buddhist Indian usage, "dharma" does mean something like a regulatory principle, the way things ought to be. In Buddhism generally, the term has several uses, sometimes quite vague. Sometimes, especially in the Universal Sage Sutra translated here, it means something like "method." But in the Lotus Sutra the much more fundamental meaning of "dharma" is "teachings," in particular the teachings of the Buddha. Sometimes this same term refers to the fundamental truths that the Buddha realized and taught, as later interpreters have insisted. But even in such cases, the meaning of "teachings" is always retained or included. In this text, "dharma" is Buddha-dharma. Given this complexity, I think it is best to retain the Sanskrit term.

Making the situation more complicated, the term "dharma" in this and other texts has a quite different meaning, which I render as "things" and for which others have sometimes use "phenomena." These "things" are a consequence of ordinary sense experience; they are what we experience. Such things, of course, are not necessarily physical objects but can be events or even ideas. Fortunately, this use of "dharma" is almost always readily distinguishable from its use as "teaching."

In the course of doing this translation earlier versions of it have been used in classes in Tokyo, Beijing, and Chicago, and the International Buddhist Congregation of Rissho Kosei-kai has used them for study and recitation. Along the way I have received a great many comments and helpful suggestions. Two staff members of Rissho Kosei-kai— Michio Shinozaki, the president of Rissho Kosei-kai's seminary, Gaku-rin, and Yukimasa Hagiwara, now head of Rissho Kosei-kai's Dharma Missions department—read the entire manuscript and proposed many improvements.

A former student of mine, now a retired Unitarian Universalist minister, Robert Swain, worked carefully on an earlier version of the text of the Dharma Flower Sutra itself, making numerous improvements in my English expressions. Professor Brook Ziporyn of Northwestern University has reviewed and refined the translations of the opening and closing sutras, and made useful suggestions on parts of the Lotus Sutra as well. Min Yang has been very helpful in developing Pinyin versions of the dharanis in chapters 26 and 28. And three reviewers for Wisdom Publications offered many useful suggestions.

I have consulted various versions of Kumarajiva's translation into Chinese along with two frequently used Japanese versions of his translation. But the main reference text for this translation has been the three-volume version published by Iwanami Shoten with translations and extensive notes by Yukio Sakamoto and Yutaka Iwamoto. One of the great virtues of this version is that it includes on facing pages the Chinese text, a Japanese version of the Chinese, and a translation into Japanese from Sanskrit.

Despite the differences between this translation and earlier ones, I feel enormously indebted to previous translators. I have consulted and been informed by earlier translations at every point along the way. The earliest of these is the one still in use by Rissho Kosei-kai called *The Threefold Lotus Sutra*, in which the translation of the Lotus Sutra itself was done by Bunnō Katō, based in part on work previously done by W.E. Soothill. While the present version is significantly different from Katō's, I remain enormously indebted to him for initially arousing my interest in the sutra and prompting me to try to improve on his translation.

Translator's Introduction

L OTUS SUTRA" does not correspond to anything in Chinese or Japanese. The full title in Chinese is 妙法蓮華経, pronounced *Miao-fa-lian-hua jing*, and *Myō-hō-renge-kyō* in Japanese. Literally these characters mean "wonderful Dharma lotus flower sutra." Although just 法華 is sometimes found, the usual shortened title in the text itself is 法華経, pronounced *Fa-hua jing* in Chinese and *Hoke-kyō* in Japanese. In English this would be Dharma Flower Sutra. I'm uncertain about how or why this text came to be called the "Lotus Sutra" in English. I suspect it is because the first Western translation of it, in 1852 by Eugene Burnouf into French, was titled *Le lotus de la bonne loi*.

Often used as the base of statues of buddhas and bodhisattvas or held in the hands of bodhisattvas, the lotus flower may be the most common of Buddhist symbols. It is especially important in Mahayana Buddhism, where it symbolizes the bodhisattva as one who is firmly rooted in the mud of the earth and flowering toward the sky. It is a symbol of working in the world to help others to awaken while finding inspiration in a sense of the cosmos.

Thus the lotus flower and the lotus plant are important in the sutra. But more important than the plant itself, it seems to me, is its flowering. The sutra wants us to understand it as a blossoming of Buddha-dharma. Its own short title, "Dharma Flower Sutra," or even "Dharma Flowering Sutra," would thus be more appropriate than "Lotus Sutra" for the short title of this text, except, of course, for the fact that it is already well known as the "Lotus Sutra."

THE TEXT

The sutra is thought to have been translated into Chinese at least six times, the first being by Dharmaraksha (竺法護) in 286 CE. He gave it the title *Zheng-fa-hua jing* (正法華經), or True Dharma Flower Sutra. While this translation has received some attention from scholars, it has had very little influence on East Asian Buddhism or culture, as it was surpassed by the translation of Kumarajiva (鳩摩羅什) in 406, to which the title *Miao-fa-lian-hua jing* (妙法蓮華經) was given. The only other existing translation is actually a revision of Kumarajiva's version. An additional three translations found in some catalogs are no longer known to exist.

Save for a translation from Sanskrit by H. Kern, originally published in 1884 as a volume of *The Sacred Books of the East*, edited by Max Müller, all East Asian and almost all Western versions of the sutra are based on the translation by Kumarajiva, as are almost all commentaries. In fact, existing Sanskrit manuscripts are much more recent than the Chinese translations. Unfortunately, as I think is true of all translations of Buddhist texts into Chinese, the Sanskrit versions from which they were translated are lost.

There are significant differences among the existing versions, summarized well by Yoshiro Tamura in his introduction to *The Threefold Lotus Sutra*. We do not know how to explain these differences. Perhaps Kumarajiva translated very freely or had a Sanskrit version quite different from those we now possess.

The Chinese versions are usually said to be translations from the Sanskrit Saddharmapuṇḍarīka-sūtra. But while many Sanskrit texts and especially fragments of texts of this sutra have been found all over the northern part of the Indian subcontinent, they are all much more recent than existing Chinese versions.

The version in this book, like virtually all contemporary Chinese and Japanese versions, has twenty-eight chapters, though Kumarajiva's version had only twenty-seven. Sometime, probably in the fifth or sixth century, the text of what is now the Devadatta chapter was moved from the end of chapter 11 to form a separate chapter 12.

Formation of the Lotus Sutra

Traditionally the Dharma Flower Sutra has been divided into two parts. In recent times some scholars have proposed a threefold division that compliments rather than supplants the traditional division. A change of focus after chapter 9, and the fact that making copies of the sutra becomes important after chapter 9 but is not mentioned at all in chapters 2–9, have led to the conclusion that chapters 2–9, with their focus on *shravakas*, constitute an earlier version of the text, and that chapters 10–21, focusing on bodhisattvas and the practice of the bodhisattva way, were added later. Chapter 1 is seen as having been created along with this second group as an introduction to the whole in an attempt to make the two groups coherent. Finally, the last six chapters are regarded as another group, stressing the practice of bodhisattvas. Some of the chapters in this group evidently were circulated as separate sutras, perhaps before the Lotus Sutra itself was created. Though we do not know how far back such practice extends, chapter 25, "Regarder of the Cries of the World" (the *Guanyin jing* or *Kannon-gyō*), is used as a separate sutra to this day. Some regard chapter 12 as part of this third group. Compilation of the sutra probably took place within the first century of the common era. In the Mahāprajñāpāramitā-upadeśa-śastra, attributed to Nāgārjuna and supposedly written around 200 CE, there are citations from Lotus Sutra chapters up to the last. If the dating of this text is correct, it would indicate that by the end of the second century the contents of the Lotus Sutra were pretty much what we have now.

This division of the sutra into three parts can also be understood doctrinally. The first part elucidates a unifying truth of the universe (the One Vehicle of the Wonderful Dharma); the second part sheds light on the everlasting personal life of the Buddha (Everlasting Original Buddha); and the third part emphasizes the actual activities of human beings (the bodhisattva way).

While the traditional division of the sutra into two halves is useful for understanding its teachings, the division into three groups of chapters is useful for understanding the historical development of the sutra and some of the various inconsistencies in it, both doctrinal and stylistic.

The Opening and Closing Sutras

For centuries the Lotus Sutra has been closely associated in East Asia with the Sutra of Innumerable Meanings and the Sutra of Contemplation on the Dharma Practice of Universal Sage Bodhisattva, typically referred to as the "opening" and "closing" sutras, the three together being referred to as the "three-part Dharma flower sutra" and published as *The Threefold Lotus Sutra*. In chapter 1 of the Dharma Flower Sutra it is said that for the sake of all bodhisattvas the Buddha taught the Great Vehicle sutra called Innumerable Meanings (無量義經 *Wuliangyi jing*). Tradition has it that a sutra with this name was received by the monk Hui-piao (慈表) from the translator Dharma-jātayaśas (曇摩伽陀耶舍) toward the end of the fifth century. It has been taken to be a translation from a Sanskrit Amitārtha Sutra, which has been lost. There may have been an earlier translation, also now lost. Although a passage in this sutra, mentioning a truth not yet revealed after more than forty years of teaching, has been taken to be a reference to the Lotus Sutra, in fact the Lotus Sutra is not explicitly mentioned in this sutra. Virtually nothing is known of its origins or connection to the Lotus Sutra. Some believe that it may have been originally composed in Chinese.

The existing Sutra of Contemplation on the Dharma Practice of Universal Sage Bodhisattva in Chinese, *Guan-puxian-pusa-xingfa jing* (觀普賢菩薩 行法經)—often shortened to *Puxian-guan jing* (普賢 觀經) and in Japan often termed the *Zange-kyō* (懺悔經), also pronounced *Sange-kyō*, "the repentance sutra"—is traditionally believed to have been translated by Dharmamitra (曇無蜜多) in the middle of the fifth century, following two earlier translations, including one by Kumarajiva, which are now lost. In it the Lotus Sutra is explicitly mentioned, clearly indicating an intended connection. In this case, too, no Sanskrit version has been found.

A Religious Inspirational Text

There are many ways to read any important text. The Lotus Sutra has been taken to be a polemical document reflecting a conflict between conservative, classical monks and Mahayana upstarts. Its purpose would be to assert the superiority of the Great Vehicle, the Mahayana, over more conservative traditions while disparaging the smaller vehicle.

While it certainly is possible to read the Lotus Sutra this way, we know too little about the beginnings of Mahayana Buddhism and the formation of this sutra to speak confidently about that history. In any case, it certainly is not as a record of Indian Buddhist history that this sutra has been read over many centuries by the peoples of East Asia, where it has almost universally been regarded as a religious text, recited as a devotional practice, and esteemed as a source of protection from forces both natural and human, real and imagined, and where it has inspired a range of Buddhist and secular arts and served as a spiritual basis and resource for political rebellion or reform.

In short, this text has become one of the world's great religious scriptures and most influential books. It did not acquire that renown as a polemic against people or schools largely unknown to East Asian readers.

I believe we will understand this text better if we treat it as an inspirational text, rather than assuming its purpose was to give its readers ammunition against other Buddhists. Its main thrust is to encourage readers to understand themselves in certain ways. It seeks, in other words, to change human behavior by influencing the religious orientation and values of its auditors or readers.

It teaches, for example, that everyone without exception has the potential to be a buddha. This simple teaching would later develop into doctrines and theories about Buddha-nature. But in this text what we actually have is not so much a doctrine as a series of stories, narratives that appeal to the human imagination as well as to the rational mind. The story of Devadatta, for example, tells us nothing at all about the historical Devadatta, but it encourages us to understand that just as Devadatta, everywhere known to be evil, is told that he is to become a buddha, so we too, no matter how imperfect, have the potential to become a buddha. We also need to understand that this story teaches us that a buddha is one who sees the potential for good in others, even in enemies. It encourages us to realize our own capacity to be a buddha for someone else. Many other stories in this sutra are designed to move us to behave in accord with the sutra, primarily by helping others by sharing its teachings with them.

The Devadatta story is followed immediately by the very interesting story of the dragon princess, a little girl whom Manjushri Bodhisattva proclaims to be capable of becoming a buddha immediately. This story was obviously intended to persuade monks, who would have been its only early auditors and readers, that women as well as men have the potential of being buddhas, common prejudice and informed opinion to the contrary. At the climax of the story, the girl tells her two male critics, a shravaka monk and a bodhisattva, that if they look—if they really look using their spiritual eyes—they too will see her as a buddha. In other words, this story is not designed merely to criticize male assumptions, though it does do that; it also affirms the positive potential to be a buddha in the very men it also criticizes. This also means, of course, that it affirms the positive potential of both its female and its male auditors or readers.

All readers of the Lotus Sutra would be well advised to ask what the story is saying about themselves.

The sutra certainly is, however, a Mahayana text, one that champions a Mahayana Buddhist understanding of Buddha-dharma. But its claim to superiority should not be seen as opposing or excluding anyone. Quite the opposite, it affirms the equality of everyone and seeks to provide an understanding of Buddha-dharma that excludes no one.

Though we can make conjectures based on what we find in the text, virtually nothing is known about the origins of the Dharma Flower Sutra in India, as we know very little about the early centuries of the Mahayana movement of which it was an important part. It's even quite likely that it is inappropriate to think of Sanskrit as the original language of this sutra. Sanskrit was a bit like the Latin language in medieval Europe: texts originally written in a vernacular were translated into Latin or Sanskrit to give them higher status and wider appeal. While it is possible that some of the Lotus Sutra was originally composed in Sanskrit, it is very unlikely that much of it was.

Thus while it is possible, even likely, that this sutra once existed in some other Indian language or languages, there is no hard evidence for this. It's also very likely that before being committed to any written form, most if not all of the text existed in oral versions. It also seems obvious that some parts of the sutra, especially the final six chapters, and possibly chapter 12 or at least the Devadatta and dragon princess stories in chapter 12, circulated separately at least in oral form. Chapter 25, the Guan-yin chapter, has circulated separately for several centuries down to the present and is sometimes confused with the whole sutra.

Historical Significance

While the Lotus Sutra has had a fair share of critics, ranging from those who regard it as nothing more than snake oil to those who consider its influence pernicious, there can be no doubt that it has been enormously influential in East Asia from the time of its translation by Kumarajiva down to the present. In recent times it has served as a foundation for numerous Buddhist reform movements, especially in Taiwan and Japan. Today, with a revival of Buddhism in China, the sutra is widely studied and recited there as well, both by monastics and by laypeople. In Japan, where Buddhism is more sectarian than in other East Asian countries, well over fifty new Buddhist religious organizations claim to be based on the Lotus Sutra, most notably Soka Gakkai, now one of the largest Buddhist organizations in the world; Rissho Kosei-kai, which has pioneered Japanese involvement in international interfaith encounter and cooperation; and Reiyu-kai, the mother of the vast majority of new Japanese Buddhist movements and organizations.

The influence of the Lotus Sutra has not been limited to religious organizations. For many centuries it has had a major impact on East Asian culture, especially on art and politics. In the Chinese section of any major art museum one will find that a great many images are based solely on the Lotus Sutra, images such as the two buddhas sitting side by side in the stupa of Abundant Treasures Buddha, or Universal Sage Bodhisattva mounted on a white elephant with six tusks, or the burning house from the parable in chapter 3 of the sutra.

After reading it at an early age in his father's study, Japan's greatest twentieth-century storyteller and poet, Kenji Miyazawa, became devoted to the Lotus Sutra, writing to his father on his own deathbed that all he ever wanted to do was share the teachings of this sutra with others. Yet in writings published during his lifetime Miyazawa seldom if ever mentions the Lotus Sutra. He sought, rather, to display or illuminate its teachings implicitly, without explicit reference to the sutra. He wanted to embody the sutra quietly, both in his writing and in his life. This was no secret, however, in his impoverished native Iwate prefecture in the northeastern region of Japan's main island, where he was widely known as "Kenji Bodhisattva."

Much of the influence of the Dharma Flower Sutra can be attributed to its being championed by the Tiantai/Tendai and Nichiren schools and denominations. Founded by the monk Zhiyi in the sixth century, Tiantai attempted to order the huge variety of Buddhist sutras by treating the Lotus Sutra as the summation of the Buddha's teaching. This understanding of the sutra was enormously influential for many centuries, even after Tiantai as a school had largely died out. Brought to Japan among the earliest Buddhist texts to come from Korea and China, the Dharma Flower Sutra was soon established as the major spiritual protector of the nation, with monasteries and nunneries built in every province primarily for the purpose of reciting the Lotus Sutra. Mount Hiei, outside of Kyoto, soon became the headquarters of the growing Tendai denomination of Buddhism. There all the major figures in the development of new denominations of Buddhism studied the Lotus Sutra, including Dogen (1200–53), the much-revered founder of the Soto branch of Zen, who made extensive use of the Lotus Sutra in developing his own approach to Zen ideas and practice.

Among these founders of new streams of Buddhism was Nichiren (1222–82), founder of what has been called both the Dharma Flower School and the Nichiren School. Nichiren was fanatically devoted to the Lotus Sutra, at different times in his life urging study of it, extolling devotion to it, and even proclaiming the adequacy of reciting only its title. In Japan it is mainly Nichiren and related schools that carried the Lotus Sutra into modern times, giving it such a prominent place in twentieth-century Japanese culture and politics.

The sutra has also continued to attract devotees in countries of Chinese culture and language. In Taiwan, for example, it is the initial inspiration behind the nun Dharma Master Cheng Yen, the founder and head the Tsu-chi Foundation, the largest Buddhist charitable organization in the world. It is recited regularly at temples both in Taiwan and in Singapore. And in China itself it is now a prominent part of the resurgence of Buddhism, both monastic and lay. Although this sutra is not the main text for any organization, as it is for many in Japan, it is widely studied and recited regularly in temples and lay Buddhist organizations.

Though often unrecognized, the relation of the Lotus Sutra to popular East Asian devotion to Guan-yin (Kannon in Japanese pronunciation) is also an important part of this story. This bodhisattva, who embodies compassion, is easily the most popular and important Buddhist figure in East Asia, found not only in Buddhist temples of all kinds and sizes but also in Daoist and popular Chinese temples, in Shinto shrines, in ordinary homes, and increasingly in mammoth outdoor statues. The Lotus Sutra is not the only sutra in which Guan-yin appears, but it is the oldest, and more than any other it has provided a textual basis for the remarkable growth of Guan-yin devotion in China beginning in the tenth century. Consistent with the Guan-yin chapter of the sutra, "The Universal Gateway of the Bodhisattva Regarder of the Cries of the World," though certainly not always based on it, devotion to Guan-yin embodies fundamental themes of the sutra, particularly its emphasis on skillfully doing whatever is needed to help or save others, on breaking down sharp distinction between the buddha and bodhisattva ideals, on the importance of leadership by women, and especially on having Buddha-dharma infuse everyday life and popular culture, in part by fostering compassionate care for the poor.

The Fantasy Setting

Whatever else it may be, the Lotus Sutra is a storybook containing a great variety of parables and other stories, and stories-within-stories. Some of the characters are ordinary human beings, typically monks and nuns, some of them regarded as historical, such as Shariputra and his colleagues, some as fictional actors in a parable, typically a father figure, as is the physician-father who gets his dying children to take an antidote to a poison by leading them to believe he has died. Several major characters in these stories are human but not only human beings, such as the bodhisattvas Manjushri, Maitreya, and Medicine King. Other major figures who clearly are not only human also appear in these stories include Abundant Treasures Buddha and Universal Sage Bodhisattva. A large variety of gods, goddesses, and mythical creatures are also part of the setting for several stories.

The central figure in much of the text is the Buddha—Shakyamuni Buddha. Here he has supernatural powers; for example, he illuminates the infinite worlds of the universe with a light that emerges from a tuft of hair between his eyebrows. Yet the text frequently reminds the reader of the human, historical life of Shakyamuni, reminding us of key events in his life on earth: having a son and stepmother, becoming awakened under a tree, teaching ascetics at Varanasi, and so on.

Often these stories are given a vast, probably infinite cosmic setting.

Almost always in the background is the idea of vast reaches of time, divided into periods in which a buddha's teachings are alive and effective and periods in which they are merely formal, followed without enthusiasm to very little effect. Just as time is fantastically extended, so too is space. Shakyamuni lights up all the worlds on more than one occasion, in one case using that light to invite buddhas from all over the universe to come to this world to witness the presence of Abundant Treasures Buddha in his magnificent stupa, which has arrived from the distant past. Bodhisattvas travel to visit this world from other very distant worlds, and on such occasions extremely rare flowers rain down from the heavens, drums and other musical instruments make music by themselves, and the worlds, including this one, shake and tremble in the six ways that a world can shake and tremble.

To be sure, some of these fireworks have entertainment value, livening up stories. But that is not their only function.

In Kenji Miyazawa's most famous story, "The Night of the Milky Way Railroad," a young boy falls asleep and has a fantastic dream in which he and his best friend ride a very special train through the starry night, encountering a variety of strange and interesting characters and events. Eventually he realizes that the train is actually carrying souls of the dead to another world and discovers that he is the only one on the train with a round-trip ticket. He wakes up from the dream to learn that his best friend has drowned in the river that runs through their town, where a festival has been going on. And in that river he sees reflected the river that is the Milky Way, through which he has been traveling. It's a kind of epiphany, a moment in which the earthly river and the heavenly river, each with the stories of life and death associated with it, are envisioned as one. Then the boy finishes what he set out to do before falling asleep—going to the store to get some milk to take home to his mother.

That, in part, is what the Lotus Sutra tries to achieve though fantasy—moments of cosmic connectedness that enable us to carry milk home to our mothers. It seeks, in other words, to have us be inspired by a cosmic vision, one that puts our lives into a cosmic perspective and encourages us to live better, perhaps like the lotus plant itself whose roots sink deeply into the mud of the earth while its blossom is caressed by the sun.

KEY TEACHINGS

Traditionally, following Zhiyi, the sixth-century founder of the Chinese Tiantai School of Buddhism, the Dharma Flower Sutra was understood to be composed of two halves. The first, ending with chapter 14 and centered on chapter 2, the Skillful Means chapter, is called the opening half and has to do with the idea of the one vehicle of many skillful means. The second half, centered on chapter 16, the chapter on the length of the Buddha's life, has to do with how the Buddha is both everlasting and embodied in a great many forms. This twofold division is still a useful one, as it provides a convenient way of understanding key teachings of the sutra and unifying diverse parts of the text.

One Vehicle of Many Means

Often the model of the one vehicle of many means is the famous parable of the burning house found in chapter 3 of the Lotus Sutra. A father manages to get his children to abandon their play and escape from a burning house by telling them that the playthings they had long wanted—carriages drawn by goats, deer, and oxen—are waiting for them just outside the gate. But after everyone is safely outside, the father decides that he is rich enough to give each of the children a much larger and nicer carriage drawn by a great white ox. And this he does to the children's great delight.

The parable can be taken to indicate that there are four vehicles in all and that the three lesser ones are replaced by the great one. More commonly, however, the one vehicle is understood to be inclusive of the three. "Shariputra," the Buddha says in chapter 2, "with their powers of skillful means, the buddhas have distinguished three ways within the One Buddha–Vehicle." The three carriages represent three different approaches to practicing Buddha-dharma—the shravaka, the pratyeka-buddha, and the bodhisattva ways. Very little is said about the second of these three, that of monks who pursue awakening by and for themselves deep in forests in isolation from others. The first, the shravaka way, is a portrayal of traditional monks who pursue awakening in monastic communities, primarily by listening. "Shravaka" means hearer. Quite often in the text these first two ways are assimilated into a single way, such that there is a contrast between this pair, exemplified by monks who pursue the fundamentally negative goals of nirvana, putting out of passions, and such, and the third way, the way of the bodhisattva, which is basically understood to be the pursuit of awakening in interaction with others in the world.

Here there is also a basic contrast between the goal of the shravaka, which is to become an arhat, one who is worthy of offerings, and the goal of the bodhisattva, which is to become a buddha. Bodhisattvas are often called children of the Buddha because they are formed by the teachings of the Buddha. Who and what they are is more importantly a function of what they have learned from the Buddha than it is of their birth. In a sense, the Dharma they have inherited from the Buddha is more important than the genes and culture they have inherited from their parents. Much of the Lotus Sutra is a championing of this bodhisattva way, which is also the way to supreme or complete awakening. The goal of nirvana should, according to this text, be understood as a limited and inadequate goal, but nevertheless one that can lead to the bodhisattva way and thus to supreme awakening.

While the three ways can be understood as two, they can also be understood as representative of many ways. "Ever since I became a buddha," Shakyamuni says at the beginning of chapter 2, "I have used a variety of causal explanations and a variety of parables to teach and preach, and countless skillful means to lead living beings." The reason the Dharma is so difficult to understand and accept is that a great many teaching devices have been used, among them both the metaphor of the three vehicles and the reality underlying the metaphor, the three different approaches themselves. What makes everything clear, says the Buddha, is an understanding of the one vehicle of many skillful means now being revealed.

While the Lotus Sutra rejects the extreme of pure diversity and the consequent danger of nihilism through use of the one vehicle as the unity in purpose of the many skillful means, it also clearly rejects the opposite extreme of complete unity in which diversity disappears or is relegated to mere illusion. Here diversity is not lamented but regarded as a necessary consequence of the fact that living beings and their situations are diverse. And it is celebrated as the way in which a diversity of people can share the Dharma. Even when the sutra describes a future paradise, it includes shravakas as well as bodhisattvas; the diversity of approaches never disappears. In this sense, as in many others, this sutra teaches a "middle way," here a middle way between utter diversity and sheer unity.

The infinite variety of ways of teaching have the one purpose of leading all living beings to pursue the goal of becoming a buddha, a goal that everyone without exception can reach, though the time may be very long and the way far from smooth or easy. "Shariputra," Sakyamuni says in chapter 2, "buddhas of the past, through an innumerable variety of skillful means, causal explanations, parables, and other kinds of expression, have preached the Dharma for the sake of living beings. These teachings have all been for the sake of the One Buddha–Vehicle, so that all living things, having heard the Dharma from a buddha, might finally gain complete wisdom."

As in the case of the carriages in the parable of the burning house, the great vehicle can be understood as replacing the other vehicles, or as making skillful means unnecessary. There are passages in the sutra that suggest this interpretation. We might call this the narrow interpretation of the Lotus Sutra, a perspective taken by some followers of Nichiren. They insist that in the Lotus Sutra they have found the one truth in light of which all other claims, and all other forms of religion including all other forms of Buddhism, are to be rejected as false and misleading. Most of those who study the Lotus Sutra, however, understand the teaching of the one vehicle in a much more generous, inclusive way.

The one vehicle itself can be understood as nothing but skillful means. That is, without a great variety of skillful means there can be no one vehicle, since it is through skillful means that living beings are led toward the goal of being a buddha. Without skillful means the one vehicle would be an empty, useless vehicle. Furthermore, the one vehicle itself is a teaching device, a skillful means of teaching that the many means have a common purpose.

When speaking of skillful means, some contemporary interpreters of Buddhism choose to use phrases such as "mere skillful means" or "only skillful means" to indicate that teaching by skillful means is an inferior practice, something used only when one does not have something better. But this is never, I think, the perspective of the sutra itself. There, when some action is said to be a skillful means it is always taken to be something wonderful, a way by which someone, typically the Buddha or a stand-in for the Buddha, is able to save people, converting them into bodhisattvas.

Though I think this image of the one vehicle of many skillful means is the primary model for the reality of the one and the many, throughout the text a variety of other images express the theme of the reality and importance of the one and the many. On more than one occasion, for example, the many worlds of the universe are brought together into a unity. In a related image, Shakyamuni Buddha is said to have countless embodiments in other worlds, buddhas who are real in their own right yet closely tied to Shakyamuni Buddha. Similarly, buddhas of the past, present, and future are many and different, yet are somehow one in that they teach the same thing and their lives follow the pattern of Shakyamuni's. All of these images serve to affirm the inseparability of the one and the many.

One Buddha of Many Embodiments

The second half of the sutra, centering on chapter 16, can be understood as involving another one-and-many, the one Buddha of many embodiments. Throughout the sutra, but especially in the second half, there is an expressed concern over the question as to who is going to carry on Shakyamuni Buddha's teachings after his complete nirvana, his death. Various bodhisattvas promise to do so, often with an expectation that they will face strong opposition and humiliation. The most dramatic affirmation of the role of bodhisattvas in continuing to spread Buddhadharma is the story in chapters 15 and 16. Some of the bodhisattvas who have come to this world along with their buddhas in order to see Abundant Treasures Buddha in his stupa offer to remain in this world to help Shakyamuni Buddha, the buddha of this world, in his especially difficult task of teaching and demonstrating the Dharma. Shakyamuni basically responds by saying, "Thanks, but no thanks. We already have plenty of bodhisattvas of our own." Then a great host of bodhisattvas springs out of the earth. Everyone is shocked and wants to know who could have led and taught such an incredibly large number of bodhisattvas. And Shakyamuni Buddha responds that he taught them all. How such a thing could be possible, when Shakyamuni had been alive and teaching for only a relatively few years, is taken up in chapter 16.

I agree with those who understand that this great hoard of bodhisattvas includes bodhisattvas of ages to come; that is, bodhisattvas who will carry on in place of the Buddha when he is no longer available, at least no longer available as the historical Shakyamuni Buddha. Because the Buddha and his Dharma are alive in such bodhisattvas, he himself continues to be alive. The fantastically long life of the Buddha, in other words, is at least partly a function of and dependent on his being embodied in others. With the exception of the now deceased Abundant Treasures Buddha, while many different buddhas appear in the Lotus Sutra, not one is unaccompanied by bodhisattvas, suggesting that buddhas need bodhisattvas. Those who do the work of the Buddha are bodhisattvas, even when they don't know they are doing the work of the Buddha.

Thus the bodhisattvas found in the final chapters, including Guan-yin, can quite appropriately be regarded as buddhas. It is no accident that both Wonderful Voice Bodhisattva and Guan-yin, the Regarder of the Cries of the World Bodhisattva, can take on the form of a buddha when that is what is needed. Scholars may very well say that Guan-yin is not a buddha, but any devout Chinese layperson can tell you that Guan-yin is a fully awakened buddha who has chosen to continue to work in this world as a bodhisattva. Such a view is consistent with the Lotus Sutra.

Embodying the Buddha is not something limited to bodhisattvas, at least not to bodhisattvas who are recognized as such. In some ways chapter 10, "Teachers of the Dharma," is the most surprising and unconventional chapter in the sutra. There the Buddha points to a huge congregation, one that includes not only monks, nuns, laypeople, shravakas, and bodhisattvas but also a large assortment of nonhuman creatures, dragon kings, centaurs, and such, and he tells Medicine King Bodhisattva that if anyone asks what sorts of beings will become buddhas in ages to come, Medicine King should tell them that these are the ones who will do so. This chapter insists not only that all living beings have the potential to become buddhas eventually but that anyone can be a Dharma teacher now.

The idea in this sutra that everyone has the ability to become a buddha gave rise to the association of the sutra with the notion of Buddha-nature as found in somewhat later Mahayana sutras. The term "Buddha-nature" is another powerful expression of the reality and importance of the one Buddha in many embodiments. One's Buddha-nature is both the Buddha's and one's own. Consequently, anyone can develop an ability to see the Buddha in others, their Buddha-nature. Thus, to awaken is to see, to see the Buddha, or as the text often says, to see countless buddhas.

It would be a great mistake, I think, to reify this notion, turning it into some sort of substantial reality underlying ordinary realities, something that is easy to do and is often done. In the text itself, it seems to me, Buddha-nature has no such ontological status. It is mainly a skillful way of indicating a potential, a potential with real power, to move in the direction of being a buddha by taking up the bodhisattva way.

It is also a very clever way to answer the question of how it is possible for one to overcome obstacles, however conceived, along the path of becoming a buddha. If ordinary human beings are completely under the sway of passions and delusions, by what power can they break through such a net of limitations? Some say that it is only by one's own strength; one can be saved only by oneself. Others say that it is only by the power of Amida Buddha or perhaps Guan-yin that one can be led to awakening. The Lotus Sutra says that it is by a power that is at once one's own and Shakyamuni Buddha's. The Buddha really is embodied in the lives of ordinary people. He himself is both a one and a many.

Wisdom, Compassion, and Practice

While the ideas of one vehicle of many skillful means and one Buddha of many embodiments can be seen as the central teachings of the two halves of the sutra, a great many other things are, of course, taught in the Lotus Sutra, some implicitly, some explicitly. There is, for example, the important notion that the Dharma rains on all equally, nourishing all in accord with their needs. Combined with the ideas that Buddha-nature can be found in all people, that anyone can be a Dharma teacher, that all are equally children of the Buddha, and that following the bodhisattva way is not limited to those identified as bodhisattvas, one finds a powerful counter to the prevailing Indian ideas of rank and status as purely a function of birth and stage of life.

In addition to the extremely important but relatively abstract notion of following the bodhisattva way, the Lotus Sutra frequently advocates concrete practices, which are often related to the sutra itself. They are often given as sets of four to six practices, but include receiving and embracing the sutra, hearing it, reading and reciting it, remembering it correctly, copying it, explaining it, understanding its meaning, pondering it, proclaiming it, practicing as it teaches, honoring it, protecting it, making offerings to it, preaching it and teaching it to others, and leading others to do any of these things. The six transcendental practices taught especially for bodhisattvas also play a prominent and important role. But in the first chapter we find a story about a previous life of Maitreya Bodhisattva in which, as the disciple of another bodhisattva, he was called "Fame Seeker" because he was especially attracted to lucrative offerings. He read and memorized many sutras but forgot all of them and gained nothing from his reading. But, having "planted roots of goodness," he was able to meet countless buddhas and later became Maitreya Bodhisattva, the future buddha. Even more influential is the story of Never Disrespectful Bodhisattva in chapter 20. This bodhisattva did not read and recite sutras but simply went around telling everyone he met that they would become buddhas. Often despised for this, he persisted in refusing to be disrespectful to anyone. Later, after hearing the Lotus Sutra from the sky, he was able to enjoy a large following and eventually became Shakyamuni Buddha. What's most important, these stories seem to say, is not which religious practices you use but how you treat others. To do good, in other words, is to follow the bodhisattva way.

The Lotus Sutra itself ends with a chapter on the bodhisattva Universal Sage and is traditionally followed by a sutra on the contemplative methods of Universal Sage Bodhisattva. Universal Sage has widely been taken to symbolize Buddhist practice, putting Buddhist teachings to use in everyday life, making them a foundation of one's life. Manjushri and Maitreya are the two bodhisattvas who appear repeatedly in the sutra. Manjushri symbolizes Buddhist wisdom: both practical wisdom, the wisdom that solves or overcomes problems through knowledge and rational analysis, and creative wisdom, the imaginative wisdom that leads to fresh solutions to practical problems—difficulties such as helping one's son to overcome a depressing sense of inadequacy, or getting one's children to take an antidote for poison. Maitreya, along with Guan-yin, symbolizes compassion—not as just a state of mind but as the energy and drive, the inner motivation, that make it possible to work for the benefit of others as well as oneself. Universal Sage can be said, then, to symbolize the coming together in everyday life of wisdom and compassion, which can be taken perhaps as one way of expressing the heart of the Lotus Sutra.

Peace

Throughout the sutra many traditional Buddhist doctrines are mentioned and sometimes discussed, especially the four holy truths, the eightfold path, the twelve-link chain of causes and conditions, and the six transcendental practices. Thus it is possible to interpret the sutra as having the purpose of overcoming suffering. Such basically negative goals as overcoming suffering, getting rid of attachments, becoming free of faults, dispelling illusion, and so on are not to be disparaged. They do describe very important Buddhist goals. But at least for the Lotus Sutra they are not enough. Beyond them there is always a positive goal.

The positive goal of the Dharma Flower Sutra is described in several different ways. Here I have used the idea of becoming a buddha as the highest goal. Of course being a buddha is also called "supreme awakening," often translated as "enlightenment." So it might rightly be said to be the highest goal. Another very prominent term in the sutra is "joy." Over and over we are told that a result of hearing even a small part of the sutra is joy. And we are allowed to witness the great joy that comes to Shariputra when he realizes that he too is a bodhisattva on the way to becoming a buddha. Joy can be said to be the goal of the Lotus Sutra. Another equally important term is "peace." "It is not my intent," the Buddha says in chapter 3, "to lead people to extinction. I am the king of the Dharma, free to teach the Dharma, appearing in the world to bring peace and comfort to all the living." Peace can also be said to be the goal of the Lotus Sutra.

The goal of peace has inspired many people to work not just for inner peace but for peace in families, communities, nations, and the world. Peace is not the mere absence of conflict. It brings joy and happiness to living beings and gives them the strength to share their joy and happiness with others, so that all can work together to transform the world into a pure land of peace.

The Sutra of the Lotus Flower
of the
Wonderful Dharma

including the opening and closing sutras
The Sutra of Innumerable Meanings
and
The Sutra of Contemplation of the Dharma Practice
of Universal Sage Bodhisattva

The Sutra of
Innumerable Meanings

1. Virtuous Conduct

This is what I heard.

AT ONE TIME the Buddha was staying at Rajagriha on Holy Eagle Peak with a large group of great monks, twelve thousand in all. Eighty thousand bodhisattva great ones were also there. There were gods, dragons, satyrs, centaurs, asuras, griffins, chimeras, and pythons, in addition to all the monks and nuns, laymen and laywomen. There were great wheel-turning kings, minor wheel-turning kings, golden wheel-turning kings, silver wheel-turning kings, and other wheel-turning kings. There were kings and princes, ministers and people, men and women, and great elders, each surrounded by followers numbering in the hundreds of thousands. They went up to the Buddha, worshiped at his feet, circled around him a hundred thousand times, burned incense and scattered flowers. After making various offerings, they withdrew and sat to one side.

The names of those bodhisattvas included Dharma Prince Manjushri, Dharma Prince Treasury of Great Majesty, Dharma Prince Treasury of Freedom from Anxiety, Dharma Prince Treasury of Great Oration, Maitreya Bodhisattva, Leader Bodhisattva, Medicine King Bodhisattva, Lord of Medicine Bodhisattva, Flower Banner Bodhisattva, Flower Light Banner Bodhisattva, King Incantation Freedom Bodhisattva, Regarder of the Cries of the World Bodhisattva, Great Power Obtained Bodhisattva, Constantly Persevering Bodhisattva, Leader in Valuable Signs Bodhisattva, Accumulated Jewels Bodhisattva, Valuable Cane Bodhisattva, Above the Threefold World Bodhisattva, Vimabhara

Bodhisattva, Fragrant Elephant Bodhisattva, Great Fragrant Elephant Bodhisattva, Lion's Roar King Bodhisattva, Lion at Play in the World Bodhisattva, Lion's Powerful Quickness Bodhisattva, Lion's Perseverance Bodhisattva, Courageous Power Bodhisattva, Ferocious Lion Bodhisattva, Adorned Bodhisattva, and Magnificently Adorned Bodhisattva. In all, eighty thousand such bodhisattva great ones were there.

Of these bodhisattvas there is none who is not a great leader who has attained the Dharma-body. They have attained the precepts, concentration, wisdom, liberation, and insight into liberation. Tranquil and meditative, and constantly in a state of concentration, they are calm and peaceful, not attached to actions or to desires. Completely free from perversity and distractions, their minds are calm and serene, free of bias and unrestricted. They have remained this way for billions and billions of eons, and all the innumerable gateways to the Dharma have appeared to them.

Having obtained the greatest wisdom, they can understand all things deeply, completely understanding the reality of the nature and characteristics of things, clearly distinguishing their ontological status and their relative strengths and weaknesses, and make clear the revelatory quality of reality.

Moreover, knowing well the abilities, natures, and desires of all, with incantations and unobstructed eloquence, they obediently and skillfully turn the Dharma wheel of the buddhas.

First, they have small drops of moisture fall to dampen the dust of desire, and by opening the gateway of nirvana, fanning the wind of liberation, and ridding themselves of the heat of worldly passions, they bring about the cooling quality of the Dharma.

Next, raining down the profound teaching of the twelve causes and conditions, pouring it on the ferocious, intense rays of suffering—ignorance, old age, illness, death, and so on—they pour out the unexcelled Great Vehicle, soak the good roots of all the living with it, scatter seeds of goodness over the field of blessings, and everywhere bring forth sprouts of awakening. With wisdom as bright as the sun and the moon, and timely use of skillful means, they make the enterprise of the Great Vehicle prosper and grow, and lead many to attain supreme awakening quickly. Always living in the blessedness of a reality that is fine and wonderful, with immeasurable great compassion, they save the living from suffering.

They are truly good friends of living beings, an excellent field of blessings for the living. Without having to be asked, they teach living beings. They are a place of tranquil happiness for living beings, a place of salvation, a place of protection, and a place of great reliance. For the sake of living beings everywhere they become excellent leaders and teachers, great leaders and teachers. They become eyes for the blind, and ears, noses, or tongue for those who are deaf, or have no nose, or cannot speak. They restore defective organs and turn the deranged to great and correct thinking.

As the captain or admiral of a ship, they carry masses of living beings across the river of life and death to the shore of nirvana.

As a king or emperor of medicine, they analyze diseases, know well the properties of medicines, give them to all the living according to the disease, and get them to take them.

As a trainer or master trainer, they are never undisciplined. Rather, they are like a trainer of elephants and horses who never fails to train well, or like a brave lion who has authority over all the beasts and is never overcome by them.

Advanced in and enjoying the various transcendental practices of bodhisattvas, they are firm and immovable in the land of the Tathagata. Dwelling at peace in the power of their vows, they purify buddha-lands everywhere. They will rapidly attain supreme awakening. All these bodhisattva great ones have such amazing blessings.

Those monks included Great Wisdom Shariputra, Divine Power Maudgalyayana, Wisdom Life Subhuti, Maha-Katyayana, Maitrayani's son Purna, Ajnata-Kaundinya, Divine Eye Aniruddha, Precept-Keeping Upali, Attendant Ananda, Buddha's son Rahula, Upananda, Revata, Kapphina, Vakkula, Acyuta, Svagata, Dhuta Maha-Kashyapa, Uruvilva-Kashyapa, Gaya-Kashyapa, and Nadi-Kashyapa. There were twelve thousand monks such as these. All were arhats, unconstrained by bondage or faults, free from attachments and truly liberated.

At that time Magnificently Adorned Bodhisattva, the great one, realizing that everyone in the group was sitting in concentration, got up from his seat, went up to the Buddha, and with the eighty thousand bodhisattva great ones in the assembly, prostrated himself at his feet, made processions around him a hundred thousand times, scattered heavenly flowers, burned heavenly incense, and presented the Buddha with heavenly robes, garlands, and jewels of priceless value that came rolling down from the sky and gathered on all sides like clouds. Heavenly bins and bowls were filled with all sorts of heavenly delicacies, which satisfied people naturally just by their color and aroma. They placed heavenly banners, flags, canopies, and musical instruments everywhere, pleased the Buddha with heavenly music, then knelt with hands together before him and in one voice wholeheartedly praised him in verse, saying:

> He is great, the great awakened one,
> The great holy Lord,
> In him there is no defilement,
> No contamination, no attachment.

> Trainer of gods and men, elephants and horses,
> The breeze of his way
> And the fragrance of his virtue
> Permeate all.

> Quiet is his wisdom,
> Calm his emotion,
> Serene and firm his reasoning.
> His will has departed.

> His self-consciousness has been abolished,
> Making him serene.
> Long ago, he eradicated delusory thinking
> And overcame the elements, the aggregates,
> The senses, and the realms of thought.

> His body is neither existing nor non-existing,
> Neither caused nor conditioned,
> Neither itself nor other,
> Neither square nor round,
> Neither short nor long.

> It does not appear or disappear.
> It is not born and does not die.

It is neither constructed nor raised up,
Neither made nor produced.

It is neither sitting nor lying,
Neither walking nor standing still,
Neither moving nor turning over,
Neither at rest nor idle.

It does not advance or retreat,
Knows not safety or danger,
Neither right nor wrong.
It is neither virtuous nor improper.

It is neither this nor that,
Neither going nor coming.

It is neither blue nor yellow,
Neither red nor white;
Neither crimson nor purple,
Nor a variety of colors.

Born of precepts, concentration,
Wisdom, liberation, and insight,
He stems from contemplation,
The six powers, and the elements of the Way.

Springing from kindness and compassion,
The ten powers and courage,
He emerges from
The good actions of living beings.

He shows his body:

Sixteen feet tall,
Shining with purple gold,
Well proportioned,
Brilliant and very bright.

The tuft of curled hair is like the moon.
The light of the sun comes from the nape of his neck.
His curly hair is deep blue
And on the top of his head is a protuberance.

His pure eyes are like mirrors,
And work well in all directions.
His eyebrows are dark blue;
His mouth and cheeks well shaped.

His lips and tongue are a nice red,
Like a bright red flower.
His forty white teeth
Look like snowy jewels.

His forehead is broad,
His nose long and his face open.
His chest, marked with a swastika,
Is like the chest of a lion.

His hands and feet are soft,
Marked with the spokes of a wheel.
Their soles and palms are well rounded,
And the grip is firm.

His arms are long,
His fingers straight and slender.
His skin is delicate and soft
And his hair curls to the right.

His ankles and knees are exposed.
His male organ is concealed,
Like that of a horse.

His muscles are smooth.
His joints are strong.

His legs are tapered,
Like those of a deer.

His back is as resplendent as his front,
Pure and without blemish,
Untainted, like clear water,
Unspotted by any dirt.

His distinguishing thirty-two characteristics
And the eighty different attractive features seem to
    be visible,
Yet in reality, his form is neither with nor without
    features.
All visible features are transcended.

Without having features
His body has features.
This is also true of the features
Of the bodies of all living beings.

They incite joy and respect
In living beings,
Eliciting devotion, esteem,
And courtesy toward him.

By cutting off pride and arrogance,
He has acquired such a glorious body.

Now we, the assembly of eighty thousand,
Together make obeisance
To the one who has extinguished
Reflective thought and consciousness.

In the saint without attachments,
The trainer of elephants and horses,
We take refuge.

Making obeisance,
We submit ourselves to the material body of the Dharma:
Precepts, concentration,
Wisdom, liberation, and insight.

Making obeisance,
We submit ourselves to his wonderful, noble character.
Making obeisance,
We submit ourselves to the inconceivable.

His Brahma voice,
Which resonates like the eight kinds of thunder,
Fine, wonderful, and pure,
Is very profound and far-reaching.

To living beings he spreads the four truths,
The six practices
And the twelve causes,
According to their mental workings.

If one hears,
One's mind is opened,
Breaking the bonds
Of innumerable chains of life and death.

Some who hear become stream-enterers,
Once-returners, non-returners, arhats.
Some reach the state of a faultless,
Unconditioned pratyekabuddha.

Some reach the level of a bodhisattva
Free from arising and extinction.
Some obtain innumerable incantations,
Make eloquent explanations without hindrance,

Recite profound and wonderful verses,
Play and bathe in the pure pond of the Dharma,

Or display the divine power to soar and fly
And freely go in and out of water or fire.

Such are the characteristics
Of the Tathagata's Dharma wheel.
It is pure, unlimited, and inconceivable.

Making obeisance together,
We dedicate our lives
To the timely rolling
Of the Dharma wheel.

We make obeisance,
And submit ourselves to the Brahma voice.
We make obeisance and submit ourselves
To the causes, truths, and practices.

For uncountable past eons,
Through toil and suffering,
The World-Honored One has studied and practiced
All kinds of virtuous activities.

For the sake of human beings,
Heavenly beings, and dragon kings,
For all living beings everywhere,
He has given up all things hard to give up:

Goods and treasures,
Wife and child, country and palace.
Because of the Dharma
That is both for Buddhists and for non-Buddhists,

He was unsparing of himself and his possessions,
Giving his head, eyes,
Bones, and brain, everything,
As offerings to people.

He kept the buddhas'
Pure prohibitions
And never did any wrong,
Even at the cost of his own life.

Even though beaten
With swords or sticks,
Or cursed and insulted,
He never became angry.

Despite the abuse to his body for eons,
He never became weary or worn out.
He was at peace day and night,
And constantly meditating.

He studied all the ways of things,
With deep wisdom
Recognizing the capacities
Of living beings.

This is why,
Having obtained the power of freedom,
He became the Dharma king,
Free in the Dharma.

Again making obeisance all together,
We take refuge in the one
Who has done all difficult things.

2. Dharma Preaching

AT THAT TIME Magnificently Adorned Bodhisattva, the great one, with the eighty thousand bodhisattva great ones, finished praising the Buddha with this verse and said to him in unison: "World-Honored One, we, an assembly of eighty thousand bodhisattvas, now want to ask you about the Tathagata's Dharma, but wonder whether the World-Honored One will hear us or not."

The Buddha said to Magnificently Adorned Bodhisattva and the eighty thousand bodhisattvas: "Good, good! You have known well, good sons, that this is the time. What would you like to ask? Before long, the Tathagata will enter complete nirvana. After nirvana, no one will have any doubts. What is your question? I will answer it."

Then Magnificently Adorned Bodhisattva with the eighty thousand bodhisattvas said to the Buddha in unison: "World-Honored One, if bodhisattva great ones want to attain supreme awakening quickly, what gateway to the Dharma should they use? What gateway to the Dharma leads bodhisattva great ones to attain supreme awakening quickly?"

The Buddha said to Magnificently Adorned Bodhisattva and the eighty thousand bodhisattvas: "Good sons, there is a unique gateway to the Dharma that leads bodhisattvas to attain supreme awakening quickly. If a bodhisattva learns this gateway to the Dharma, he will attain supreme awakening."

"World-Honored One, what is this gateway to the Dharma called? What does it mean? How does a bodhisattva practice it?"

The Buddha replied: "Good sons, this unique gateway to the Dharma is called innumerable meanings. A bodhisattva who wants to practice and study the gateway to the Dharma of innumerable meanings should observe that all things were originally, will be, and are in themselves empty and tranquil in nature and character; not large or small, not subject to arising or extinction, not fixed or movable, and neither advancing nor retreating. Like empty space, they are non-dualistic.

"All living beings, however, make delusory distinctions: weighing whether something is this or that; whether it is a gain or a loss. Bad thoughts come to them, producing a variety of evil actions. They transmigrate within the six states undergoing all kinds of suffering and harm, from which they cannot escape during innumerable billions of eons. Seeing this clearly, bodhisattva great ones cultivate sympathy and show great kindness and compassion in the desire to extricate others from suffering. What's more, they penetrate deeply into all things.

"In accord with the character of Dharma, all things emerge. In accord with the character of Dharma, all things live. In accord with the character of Dharma, all things change. In accord with the character of Dharma, all things perish. In accord with the character of Dharma, bad things emerge. In accord with the character of Dharma, good things emerge, live, change, and perish. Bodhisattvas, observing these four modes and being thoroughly familiar with them from one end to the other, should next observe clearly that none of these things continues to live even for a moment, but emerges and perishes every moment, each emerging, living, changing, and perishing in an instant.

"After seeing this, the abilities, natures, and desires of living beings can be seen. As natures and desires are innumerable, sermons are innumerable, and as sermons are innumerable, meanings are innumerable. The innumerable meanings emerge from one Dharma. This one Dharma is characterless. Accordingly, this characterlessness manifests all characters. Neither having character nor being characterless is called true character.

"The compassion that bodhisattva great ones display after dwelling at peace in this true character of reality is clear and not in vain. They are truly capable of relieving living beings from suffering. Having given them relief from suffering, they teach the Dharma again, delighting all living beings.

"Good sons, if a bodhisattva practices well the gateway to the Dharma of innumerable meanings in this way, the bodhisattva will for certain attain supreme awakening soon.

"Good sons, such a profound and unexcelled Great Vehicle Sutra of Innumerable Meanings is truly correct in logic, unsurpassed in value, and protected by the buddhas of the past, present, and future. A host of demonic ways cannot damage it, nor can any wrong view of life and death defeat or destroy it.

"Therefore, good sons, bodhisattva great ones, if you want to attain unexcelled awakening quickly, you should practice and study the profound, unexcelled Great Vehicle Sutra of Innumerable Meanings."

At that time Magnificently Adorned Bodhisattva spoke once again to the Buddha: "World-Honored One, the Dharma preached by the World-Honored One is inconceivable. The ability and nature of living beings is also inconceivable. And the gateway to the Dharma of emancipation is also inconceivable. Though we no longer have doubts about any of the Dharma preached by the Buddha, out of fear that various living beings will be perplexed, we repeatedly ask the World-Honored One about it.

"For the more than forty years since the Tathagata attained the Way, for the sake of the living you have continued to preach—the meaning of the four modes of all things, the meaning of suffering, the meaning of emptiness, of impermanence, of no enduring self, the absence of greatness, the absence of pettiness, non-arising, non-extinction, one character, absence of character, Dharma nature, Dharma character, being originally empty and quiet, non-coming, non-going, non-appearing, and non-disappearing.

"Those who have heard it have obtained the warm Dharma, the highest Dharma, the best Dharma in the world. They have obtained fruits of a stream-enterer, fruits of being a once-returner, fruits of being a non-returner, fruits of being an arhat, and the pratyekabuddha way. They have aspired to become awakened. They have ascended the first stage, the second stage, and the third stage, and reached the tenth stage.

"In what sense is what you preached in the past, the meaning of all the buddhas, different from what you preach today? One hears that if bodhisattvas practice only the profound and unexcelled Great Vehicle Sutra of Innumerable Meanings, without fail they will soon attain unexcelled awakening. Is that true? Please, World-Honored One, out of compassion and pity for all, analyze this for the sake of living beings everywhere, and leave no doubt in the minds of all those in the present and future who hear the Dharma."

Then the Buddha said to Great Adornment Bodhisattva: "Good, good! Great and good son, you have raised good questions for the Tathagata about the subtle and wonderful meaning of the profound and unexcelled Great Vehicle. You should know that you will greatly enrich many, pleasing human and heavenly beings, and relieving living beings from suffering. This is the truth of great compassion, a truth that is not in vain. For this reason you will surely and quickly attain unexcelled awakening. You will also enable all living beings in the present and future to accomplish unexcelled awakening.

"Good sons, after sitting upright for six years under the bodhi tree at the place of the Way, I could attain supreme awakening. With the eyes of a buddha I could understand that not all the teachings could be proclaimed. Why was that? I knew that the natures and the desires of living beings were not the same. As their natures and their desires were not the same, I taught the Dharma in various ways. I used the power of skillful means to teach the Dharma in various ways. And after more than forty years the truth has not yet been revealed. This is why there are differences in the way living beings take the Way and why they do not attain unexcelled awakening quickly.

"Good sons, the Dharma is like water that washes away dirt. Just as the water in a well, a pond, a stream, a river, a valley, a ditch, or a great sea is equally effective in washing away all kinds of dirt, so Dharma water effectively washes away the filth that afflicts living beings.

"Good sons, the nature of water is the same, but a stream, a river, a well, a pond, a valley stream, a ditch, and a great sea are distinct and different from each other. The nature of the Dharma is like this. There is equal effectiveness and no differentiation in washing away the waste of afflictions, but the three teachings, the four fruits, and the two ways are not one and the same.

"Good sons, though the water washes equally well, a well is not a pond, a pond is not a stream or a river, and a valley stream or a ditch is not a sea. Just as the Tathagata, the world's hero, is free in the Dharma, all of the teachings in his sermons are like this. Though early, middle, and late teachings equally wash away the delusions of living beings, the beginning is not the middle, and the middle is not the end. Teachings at the beginning, in the middle, and at the end are the same in expression but different in meaning.

"Good sons, after leaving the king of trees, when I turned the Dharma wheel of the four truths for the five men at Deer Park in Varanasi, Ajnata-Kaundinya and the others, I taught that all things are originally empty and calm, ceaselessly changing, arising and perishing in an instant.

"When I spoke in various places during the middle period, proclaiming the twelve causes and conditions and the six transcendental practices for monks and the group of bodhisattvas, I also taught that all things are originally empty and calm, ceaselessly changing, arising and perishing in an instant.

"Now, preaching the Great Vehicle Sutra of Innumerable Meanings, I also teach that all things are originally empty and calm, ceaselessly changing, arising and perishing in an instant.

"Good sons, this is why the teachings at the beginning, in the middle, and at the end are the same in expression but different in meaning. Since the meaning is different, so too the understandings of living beings differ. And since understandings differ, so too attainments of the Dharma, of its fruits, and of the Way differ.

"Good sons, at the beginning, though I taught the four truths for those who sought to be shravakas, eight million heavenly beings came down to hear the Dharma and aspired to become awakened. In the middle, though I preached the profound twelve causes and conditions in various places for those who sought to be pratyekabuddhas, innumerable living beings aspired to become awakened or continue as shravakas. Next, though I proclaimed over many eons the practice of bodhisattvas by teaching the equality of the twelve literary forms of the Great Wisdom Sutra, and the vast Flower Garland Sutra, hundreds of thousands of monks, tens of thousands of millions of human and heavenly beings, and innumerable other living beings could remain as stream-enterers, once-returners, non-returners, or arhats in the Dharma of causes and conditions appropriate for pratyekabuddhas.

"Good sons, for this reason, it is known that while the teaching is the same, the meanings differ. Since the meanings differ, so too the understandings of living beings differ. And since understandings differ, so too attainments of the Dharma, of its fruits, and of the Way differ. Thus, good sons, from when I attained the Way and stood to teach the Dharma for the first time until I proclaimed the Great Vehicle Sutra of

Innumerable Meanings today, I have never ceased preaching about suffering, emptiness, impermanence, no enduring self, the absence of greatness, the absence of pettiness, original non-arising, present non-extinction, one character, absence of character, Dharma character, Dharma nature, non-coming, non-going, and the four modes by which all the living are driven.

"Good sons, this is why all buddhas everywhere respond to the variety of voices without a forked tongue and with one sound. Though each has only one body, they show bodies as innumerable and numberless as the sands of hundreds of thousands of millions of billions of Ganges. In each body, they display a number of similar types, countless as the sands of hundreds of thousands of millions of billions of Ganges. And in each type, they show forms as countless as the sands of hundreds of thousands of millions of billions of Ganges.

"Good sons, accordingly, this is the inconceivable and profound sphere of all the buddhas. The two vehicles cannot comprehend it, and even bodhisattvas at the tenth stage cannot reach it. Only among buddhas can it be fathomed well.

"Good sons, this is why I teach that the wonderful, profound, and unexcelled Great Vehicle Sutra of Innumerable Meanings is truly correct in logic, unsurpassed in value, and protected by the buddhas of the past, present, and future. No demonic or non-Buddhist ways can damage it, nor can any wrong view of life and death defeat or destroy it.

"Therefore, bodhisattva great ones, if you want to attain unexcelled awakening quickly, you should practice and study the profound, unexcelled Great Vehicle Sutra of Innumerable Meanings."

After the Buddha had finished teaching this, the three-thousand great thousandfold world trembled and shook in six ways, various kinds of heavenly flowers, such as the blue lotus, water lily, and white lotus, spontaneously rained down from the sky, and innumerable kinds of heavenly perfumes, robes, garlands, and priceless treasures also rained and came rolling down from the upper sky and were offered to the Buddha, the many bodhisattvas and shravakas, and to the great assembly. Heavenly trunks and bowls and other vessels filled with all sorts of heavenly delicacies and heavenly banners, flags, canopies, and musical instruments were everywhere, and heavenly music played in praise of the Buddha.

Also the Buddha-worlds in the eastern direction, as many as the sands of the Ganges, trembled and shook in the six ways. Heavenly flowers, incense, robes, garlands, and priceless treasures, heavenly trunks, bowls with all sorts of heavenly delicacies, heavenly banners, flags, canopies, and wonderful musical instruments rained down. And heavenly music was played in praise of those buddhas, those bodhisattvas and shravakas, and great assemblies. The same thing happened in the southern, western, and northern directions, in the four intermediate directions, and in the up and down directions.

At this time, thirty-two thousand bodhisattva great ones in the assembly reached the state of concentration of Innumerable Meanings. Thirty-four thousand bodhisattva great ones gained entrance through the gateway of countless and unquantifiable incantations and turned the never-retreating Dharma wheel of all of the buddhas of the three worlds.

When all the monks and nuns, laymen and laywomen, heavenly beings, dragons, satyrs, centaurs, asuras, griffins, chimeras, pythons, great wheel-turning kings, minor wheel-turning kings, kings of the silver wheel, the iron wheel, and other wheels, kings and princes, ministers and people, lords and ladies, great elders, and a hundred thousand kinds of followers together heard the Buddha Tathagata teach this sutra, they obtained the warm Dharma, the highest Dharma, the best Dharma in the world, the fruits of a stream-enterer, the fruits of a once-returner, the fruits of a non-returner, the fruits of an arhat, and the fruits of a pratyekabuddha. Furthermore, they attained a bodhisattva's stable state of non-arising, acquired one incantation, two incantations, three incantations, four incantations, five, six, seven, eight, nine, ten incantations, a hundred thousand millions of billions of incantations, myriads of incantations as innumerable as the sands of the Ganges, and they all came to turn well the never-retreating Dharma wheel. Unquantifiable numbers of living beings aspired to supreme awakening.

3. Ten Blessings

AT THAT TIME the bodhisattva great one Magnificently Adorned said again to the Buddha: "World-Honored One, the World-Honored One has taught this fine and wonderful, profound and unsurpassed Great Vehicle Sutra of Innumerable Meanings. It is truly profound, profound, profound! Why? In this assembly, all the bodhisattva great ones, all the four groups, the heavenly beings, dragons, demons and spirits, kings and ordinary citizens, all living beings, hearing this profound and unexcelled Great Vehicle Sutra of Innumerable Meanings, never fail to obtain entrance to incantations, the three teachings, the four fruits, and the aspiration for awakening. It should be known that this Dharma is truly correct in logic, unsurpassed in value, and protected by the buddhas of the past, present, and future. A host of demonic ways cannot damage it, nor can any wrong view of life and death defeat or destroy it.

"Why is this? Because to hear it just once is to embrace all the teachings. If any living beings can hear this sutra, they will acquire great benefits.

"Why is this? If anyone practices it well, they will quickly and without fail attain unexcelled awakening. If living beings cannot hear it, you should know that they lose great benefits. Even after the passing of innumerable, unlimited, inconceivable, countless eons, they will never be able to reach unexcelled awakening.

"Why? Because they do not know the great direct way to awakening, their way will be steep and very difficult.

"World-Honored One, this sutra is inconceivable. Our only wish is that out of compassion and pity for all people you fully explain the profound and inconceivable matters of this sutra. World-Honored One, from where does this sutra come? Where is it headed? Where will it live? Having such innumerable blessings and amazing powers, how does this sutra enable people to attain supreme awakening quickly?"

Then the World-Honored One spoke to Magnificently Adorned Bodhisattva, the great one: "Good, good, my good son! It is so, just as you say. Good son, this sutra that I teach is profound, profound, truly profound. Why? Because it enables people to attain unexcelled awakening quickly; because hearing it just once they retain all the teachings; because it brings great enrichment to all the living; because those who practice the great direct way do not encounter great difficulties.

"Good son, you ask where this sutra comes from, where is it headed, and where it will live. Now you should listen carefully. Good son, this sutra originally comes from the home of all the buddhas, goes toward the aspiration for awakening of all the living, and lives wherever bodhisattvas practice. Good son, this sutra comes like this, goes like this, and lives like this. Thus, having such innumerable blessings and amazing powers, this sutra enables people to attain unexcelled awakening quickly.

"Good son, would you rather hear how this sutra has ten amazing powers of blessing or not?"

Magnificently Adorned Bodhisattva said: "We want to hear!"

The Buddha said: "Good sons, first, this sutra leads a not-yet-awakened bodhisattva to aspire to awakening, leads one without human kindness to aspire to kindness, leads one with a murderous heart to aspire to great compassion, leads one who is jealous to aspire to respond with joy, leads one with attachments to aspire to impartiality, leads one who is greedy to aspire to generosity, leads one who is full of arrogance to aspire to be moral, leads one who is angry to aspire to patience, leads one who is lazy to aspire to perseverance, leads one who is distracted to aspire to meditation, leads one who is ignorant to aspire to wisdom, leads one who lacks concern for saving others to aspire to saving others, leads one who commits the ten evils to aspire to do ten good things, leads one who is willful to aspire to let things be, leads one who is prone to backsliding to aspire to never retreat, leads one who commits faulty acts to aspire to being faultless, and leads one who suffers from afflictions to aspire to detachment. Good sons, this is called the first amazing power of blessing of this sutra.

"Good sons, the second inconceivable power of blessing of this sutra is this: if living beings can hear this sutra even once, even only one verse or phrase, they will master a hundred thousand myriad meanings. Yet in an innumerable number of eons they will not be able to explain the Dharma they received and embraced. Why is this? It is because the meanings of this sutra are innumerable.

"Good sons, suppose that from one seed a hundred million seeds grow, and from each of those hundred million seeds another hundred million seeds grow, and this is repeated so that the seeds become innumerable. This sutra is like this. From one teaching a hundred thousand meanings grow, and from each of these hundred thousand meanings a hundred million meanings grow, and this is repeated so that the meanings become unlimited and innumerable. This being the case, this sutra is called Innumerable Meanings. Good sons, this is called the second amazing power of blessing of this sutra.

"Good sons, the third inconceivable power of blessing of this sutra is this: if living beings can hear this sutra even once, even only one verse or phrase, they will master a hundred thousand myriad meanings. Even though they still have afflictions, it will be as if they do not. Even though they move through birth and death, they will not know fear. They will have compassion and sympathy for all the living. They will be brave in following all the teachings.

"Just as a powerful man can easily shoulder and hold heavy things, the same is true of anyone who embraces this sutra. They can bear well the heavy treasure of unexcelled awakening and carry the living out of the way of birth and death on their backs. Even though they cannot yet save themselves, they will be able to save others. Just as the captain of a ferry who has to rest on this shore due to serious illness and inability to control his four limbs can cross over with a good solid ship that has everything needed to cross over to the other shore, one who embraces this sutra, though staying on this shore of ignorance, old age, and death due to the hundred and eight kinds of serious bodily illnesses with which he is afflicted in the five states of existence, can be saved from birth and death through practicing this powerful Great Vehicle Sutra of Innumerable Meanings as it is taught, saving living beings. Good sons, this is called the third amazing power of blessing of this sutra.

"Good sons, the fourth inconceivable power of blessing of this sutra is this: if living beings can hear this sutra even once, even only one verse or phrase, they will become brave, and, even though they cannot yet save themselves, they will save others. Together with bodhisattvas they will become part of the entourage of the buddha-tathagatas, who will always preach the Dharma to them. Hearing it, they will receive and embrace the Dharma in accord with their capacities and never oppose it. Moreover, they will teach it for people everywhere as occasion demands.

"Good sons, suppose a king and his wife have a new prince. After a day, two days, or seven days, or a month, two months, or seven months, or after he becomes a year old, or two, or seven years old, even though he would not yet manage national affairs, he would come to be revered by people and become a companion of the sons of great kings. With total affection, the king and his wife will always want to stay and talk with him. Why is this? It is because he is small and innocent. Good sons, one who embraces this sutra is also like this. The Buddha is the king; this sutra is his wife; their coming together results in the birth of their child, a bodhisattva.

"If a bodhisattva can hear this sutra, even one phrase or verse, once, twice, ten times, a hundred times, a thousand or ten thousand times, a million or ten million times, or an unquantifiable, innumerable number of times, like the number of sands of the Ganges, though not yet able to realize ultimate truth, or shake the three-thousand great thousandfold world, or turn the great Dharma wheel with a thunderous buddha-voice, this bodhisattva will be admired by all the four groups and the eight guardians of Buddhism, and great bodhisattvas will be in his entourage. Entering deeply into the secret Dharma of the buddhas, he will explain it without errors or mistakes. He will always be protected by the buddhas and especially showered with affection, because he is a beginner in learning. Good sons, this is called the fourth amazing power of blessing of this sutra.

"Good sons, the fifth inconceivable power of blessing of this sutra is this: if good sons or good daughters, either during the Buddha's lifetime or after his extinction, receive and embrace, read, recite, and copy this profound and unexcelled Great Vehicle Sutra of Innumerable Meanings, even though they still have attachments and afflictions and have not distanced themselves from affairs of ordinary men, they will reveal the way of great bodhisattvas. Extending a day to a hundred eons or shortening a hundred eons to a day, bringing joy to other living beings, they will convince them. Good sons, these good sons or good daughters are just like the son of a dragon who can make clouds appear and cause rain to fall seven days after he is born. Good sons, this is called the fifth amazing power of blessing of this sutra.

"Good sons, the sixth inconceivable power of blessing of this sutra is this: if good sons or good daughters, either during the Buddha's lifetime or after his extinction, receive and embrace, read and recite this sutra, even though they still have afflictions, they will teach the Dharma to living beings, separating them from afflictions of life and death and enabling them to cut off all suffering. After hearing it, living beings will put it into practice, and become no different from the Buddha-Tathagata with respect to the blessings of the Dharma, the blessings of the fruit, and the blessings of the Way.

"Suppose a king, due to travel or being ill, leaves the management of the affairs of the country to a prince, though the prince is only a child. Then the prince, by order of the great king, will lead all the government officials according to the Dharma and propagate good policies, so that every citizen of the country follows his orders exactly, as if the king himself were governing.

"It is the same with good sons or good daughters embracing this sutra. During the Buddha's lifetime or after his extinction, even though they themselves cannot yet live in the first stage of immobility, these good sons will teach and promulgate the Dharma as the Buddha did, and if living beings, hearing them, practice it wholeheartedly, they will cut off afflictions and attain the blessings of the Dharma, the blessings of the fruit, and the blessings of the Way. Good sons, this is called the sixth amazing power of blessing of this sutra.

"Good sons, the seventh inconceivable power of blessing of this sutra is this: if good sons or good daughters are able to hear this sutra either during the Buddha's lifetime or after his extinction, and rejoice, have faith, and gain an unprecedented consciousness; if they receive and embrace, read, recite, copy, and explain the sutra, and practice it as it teaches; if they aspire to become awakened; if they cause all good roots to sprout, show great compassion, and want to relieve all living beings of suffering; though they will not yet be able to follow the six transcendental practices, these practices will come naturally to them and they will attain acceptance of the non-arising of all things, life and death as afflictions will be instantly destroyed for them, and they will rise to the seventh level of bodhisattvas.

"Suppose a vigorous man tries to destroy an enemy for his king, and after the enemy has been destroyed, with great joy, the king gives him half the kingdom as a prize. Good sons or good daughters who embrace this sutra are like this. They are the most vigorous of all who practice the Dharma. They attain the Dharma-treasure of the six practices even though they are not consciously seeking it. The enemy of death and life will be destroyed naturally, and with the prize of an estate they will be made comfortable, realizing that the treasure of half a buddha-land is the assurance of no birth. Good sons, this is called the seventh amazing power of blessing of this sutra.

"Good sons, the eighth inconceivable power of blessing of this sutra is this: if good sons or good daughters, either during the Buddha's lifetime or after his extinction, find anyone who has received this sutra, they will make them revere and believe it exactly as if they saw the body of the Buddha, cherish and enjoy it, receive and embrace, read and recite, copy, and honor this sutra, follow and practice it according to the Dharma, firmly observing morality and endurance. At the same time, they will practice generosity and be deeply compassionate. And they will everywhere teach this unexcelled Great Vehicle Sutra of Innumerable Meanings for the sake of people.

"If anyone for a long time does not at all recognize sin or blessedness, they will be shown this sutra, and with all sorts of skillful means be firmly led to have faith in it. Through the power of this sutra, their faith will be aroused and they will convert suddenly. After having their faith aroused, they will bravely persevere, acquiring the virtues and powers of this sutra, and attaining the Way and its fruit. In this way, through the blessing of having undergone transformation, these good sons or good daughters, in their male and female bodies, will attain acceptance of the non-arising of all things, reach the upper stage, and, with bodhisattvas as their attendants, lead living beings quickly to fulfillment, purify buddha-lands, and soon attain unexcelled awakening. Good sons, this is called the eighth amazing power of blessing of this sutra.

"Good sons, the ninth inconceivable power of blessing of this sutra is this: if good sons or good daughters, receiving this sutra either during the

Buddha's lifetime or after his extinction, dance for joy, attain the unprecedented, receive and embrace, read and recite, copy and make offerings to this sutra, and everywhere explain its meaning through analysis for the sake of living beings, they will instantly destroy the heavy hindrance of sins resulting from actions in the past and become purified. They will acquire great eloquence, gradually take on the marks of transcendental practices, attain various concentrations, including very courageous concentrations, enter the great gateway of incantations, and rise to the upper stage quickly through the power of diligent perseverance. They will be embodied everywhere in all the lands of the ten directions and will save and free all the living beings who suffer greatly in the twenty-five states of existence. Such power can be seen in this sutra. Good sons, this is called the ninth amazing power of blessing of this sutra.

"Good sons, the tenth inconceivable power of blessing of this sutra is this: if good sons or good daughters, receiving this sutra either during the Buddha's lifetime or after his extinction, greatly rejoice from experiencing such an unprecedented thing, receive and embrace, read and recite, copy, and make offerings to this sutra on their own accord, practice as it teaches, and also lead many monks and laypeople to receive and embrace, read and recite, copy, and make offerings to this sutra, explain it, and practice it in accord with the Dharma, because of their powers of leading others to the practice of this sutra and to attaining the Way and its fruits, done through the power of working good-heartedly to transform others, all these good sons or good daughters in their bodies will be able to pursue innumerable teachings about incantation. As common people, from the beginning they will naturally make innumerable countless great vows and oaths, and deeply aspire to fulfill them in order to save all living beings. They will realize great compassion, thoroughly relieve the suffering of living beings, gather many good roots, and abundantly benefit all. They will extend the abundance of the Dharma and give water to the withered and dehydrated. They will generously give living beings the medicine of the Dharma, setting them all at ease, gradually elevating their views to live at the stage of the Dharma cloud. They will spread benevolence widely, always being kind and leading the living who suffer into the track of the Way. These people will be able to attain supreme awakening before long. Good sons, this is called the tenth amazing power of blessing of this sutra.

"Good sons, such an unexcelled Great Vehicle Sutra of Innumerable Meanings has extremely great divine power and is unsurpassed in value. It leads all the common people to attain sacred fruit, and forever frees them from life and death. This is why this sutra is called Innumerable Meanings. It makes the tree of blessings grow, prosper, and flourish, and it leads all the living, while at the stage of common people, to have innumerable buds of the way of all the bodhisattvas. Therefore this sutra is called 'the inconceivable power of blessings.'"

At that time the bodhisattva great one Magnificently Adorned, with the eighty thousand bodhisattva great ones, said to the Buddha in unison: "World-Honored One, the profound, wonderful, and unexcelled Great Vehicle Sutra of Innumerable Meanings preached by the Buddha is truly correct in logic, unsurpassed in value, and protected by the buddhas of the past, present, and future. It is not open to the whole swarm of demonic ways, nor can it be hurt by any of the mass of wrong views of life and death. This is why this sutra has ten such powers of amazing blessings. It is enormously beneficial for innumerable living beings, enabling all bodhisattva great ones to attain the contemplation of innumerable meanings, a million teachings about incantation, all the stages and forbearance of a bodhisattva, or to obtain evidence of the four fruits of the way of pratyekabuddhas and arhats. Out of compassion for us, the World-Honored One taught such a Dharma willingly, enabling us to obtain the great benefits of the Dharma. This is very unusual, unprecedented. It is difficult to repay the compassionate grace of the World-Honored One."

With these words, the three-thousand great thousandfold world trembled and shook in the six ways, various kinds of heavenly flowers, such as the blue lotus, red lotus, water lily, and white lotus, rained down again from the upper sky, and innumerable kinds of heavenly perfumes, robes, garlands, and priceless treasures also rained and came rolling down from the upper sky and were offered to the Buddha, the many bodhisattvas and shravakas, and to the great assembly. Heavenly trunks and bowls and other vessels filled with all sorts of heavenly delicacies naturally satisfied anyone who saw them or smelled them. Heavenly banners, flags, canopies, and musical instruments were everywhere, and heavenly music played in praise of the Buddha.

The Buddha-worlds in the eastern direction, as many as the sands of the Ganges, trembled and shook in six ways. Heavenly flowers, incense, robes, garlands, and priceless treasures rained down. Heavenly trunks and bowls, with all sorts of heavenly delicacies, naturally satisfied anyone who saw them or smelled them. Heavenly banners, flags, canopies, and wonderful musical instruments were everywhere, and heavenly music played in praise of those buddhas, those bodhisattvas and shravakas, and great assemblies. The same thing happened in the southern, western, and northern regions, in the four intermediate directions, and in the up and down directions.

At that time, the Buddha spoke to the great one Magnificently Adorned Bodhisattva and the other eighty thousand bodhisattva great ones: "You should deeply respect this sutra, practice it as the Dharma, transform everyone everywhere with it, and continue to diligently promulgate it. You should protect it carefully day and night, enabling the living to obtain the benefits of the Dharma. This is truly great kindness and great compassion. Using the divine power of your vows, you should protect this sutra and not let anyone put doubts or other obstacles in its way. Then you should have it practiced widely in Jambudvipa, and have all the living observe, read, recite, copy, and make offerings to it without fail. Because of this, you will be able to attain supreme awakening quickly."

At this time Magnificently Adorned Bodhisattva, the great one, and the eighty thousand bodhisattva great ones rose from their seats, went up to the Buddha, prostrated themselves at his feet, circled around him a hundred thousand times, and then, kneeling before him, said to the Buddha with one voice: "World-Honored One, we are pleased to have received the World-Honored One's compassion. This profound, wonderful, and unexcelled Great Vehicle Sutra of Innumerable Meanings has been taught for us. Respectfully following the Buddha's instructions, after the Tathagata's extinction we will promulgate this sutra everywhere, enabling all to receive and embrace, read and recite, copy, and make offerings to it. Please don't be worried! By the power of our vow, we will enable all the living to see and hear, read and recite, copy, and make offerings to this sutra. They will acquire the powerful, divine happiness of this sutra."

At that time the Buddha praised them, saying: "Good, good! All good sons, now you have truly become children of the Buddha. With great kindness and great compassion, everywhere you thoroughly relieve others from suffering and save them from misfortune. You are fields of blessings for all living beings. You are great and good leaders and teachers for all beings everywhere. You are great shelters for all living beings. You are great benefactors to all living beings. You always give the benefits of the Dharma to everyone everywhere."

At that time, everyone in the great assembly, fully rejoicing, paid respects to the Buddha and left, receiving and embracing this sutra.

The Sutra of
The Lotus Flower of the Wonderful
Dharma

1. Introduction

This is what I heard.

A T ONE TIME the Buddha was staying at Rajagriha on Holy Eagle Peak with a large group of great monks, twelve thousand in all. All of them were arhats, without faults, free from afflictions, self-developed, emancipated from all bonds of existence, and mentally free.

They included Ajnata-Kaundinya, Maha-Kashyapa, Uruvilva-Kashyapa, Gaya-Kashyapa, Nadi-Kashyapa, Shariputra, Maha-Maudgalyayana, Maha-Katyayana, Aniruddha, Kapphina, Gavampati, Revata, Pilindavatsa, Bakkula, Maha-Kausthila, Nanda, Sundarananda, Purna son of Maitrayani, Subhuti, Ananda, and Rahula. Such great arhats are all well known to everyone. In addition there were two thousand others, some in training and some no longer in training.

The nun Mahaprajapati was there with six thousand followers, and the nun Yashodhara, the mother of Rahula, with her followers.

There were eighty thousand bodhisattvas, great ones, all free from backsliding in the pursuit of supreme awakening. All of them had mastered incantations, taught with delight and eloquence, had turned the irreversible Dharma wheel, made offerings to countless hundreds of thousands of buddhas, planted many roots of virtue, and were always being praised by buddhas. Having trained themselves in compassion, they could enter into Buddha-wisdom, deeply understand great wisdom, and reach the other shore. Their fame had spread to innumerable worlds. And they were able to liberate innumerable hundreds of thousands of living beings.

They included Manjushri Bodhisattva, Regarder of the Cries of the World Bodhisattva, Great Strength Bodhisattva, Constant Effort Bodhisattva, Never Resting Bodhisattva, Jeweled Palm Bodhisattva, Medicine King Bodhisattva, Bold Almsgiver Bodhisattva, Jeweled Moon Bodhisattva, Moon Light Bodhisattva, Full Moon Bodhisattva, Great Power Bodhisattva, Immeasurable Power Bodhisattva, Above the Threefold World Bodhisattva, Bhadrapala Bodhisattva, Maitreya Bodhisattva, Accumulated Jewels Bodhisattva, and Guidance Bodhisattva. In all, eighty thousand such bodhisattva great ones were there.

Also there at that time were Indra, king of the gods, with his following of twenty thousand children of heaven; plus the children of heaven Rare Moon, Universal Fragrance, and Jewel Light, and the four great kings of heaven with their following of ten thousand children of heaven. There were the children of heaven Freedom and Great Freedom, followed by thirty thousand children of heaven. Brahma, king of heaven and lord of this world, was there, as was Great Brahma Shikhin, Great Brahma Bright Radiance, and others, along with their following of twelve thousand children of heaven.

There also were the eight dragon kings: Nanda Dragon King, Upananda Dragon King, Sagara Dragon King, Vasuki Dragon King, Takshaka Dragon King, Anavatapta Dragon King, Manasvin Dragon King, and Utpalaka Dragon King, each with several hundred thousand followers.

There were four chimera kings: Dharma Chimera King, Wonderful Dharma Chimera King, Great Dharma Chimera King, and Upholding the Dharma Chimera King, each with several hundred thousand followers.

In addition there were four centaur kings: Pleasant Centaur King, Pleasant Sound Centaur King, Beautiful Centaur King, and Beautiful Sound Centaur King, each with several hundred thousand followers.

There were four asura kings: Balin Asura King, Kharaskandha Asura King, Vemacitrin Asura King, and Rahu Asura King, each with several hundred thousand followers.

Four griffin kings were also there: Great Dignity and Virtue Griffin King, Great Body Griffin King, Great Fullness Griffin King, and Thus Willed Griffin King, each with several hundred thousand followers.

And King Ajatashatru, son of Vaidehi, with several hundred thousand followers was there.

Each prostrated himself at the Buddha's feet, then withdrew and sat to one side.

At that time the World-Honored One, surrounded by the four groups, was given offerings, revered, honored, and praised. For the sake of all the bodhisattvas, he taught the Great Vehicle Sutra called Innumerable Meanings, the Dharma by which bodhisattvas are taught and which buddhas watch over and keep always in mind.

Having taught this sutra, sitting cross-legged, the Buddha entered the state of concentration called the place of innumerable meanings, in which his body and mind were completely motionless. Then mandarava, great mandarava, manjushaka, and great manjushaka flowers rained down from the sky on the Buddha and the entire assembly, while the whole Buddha-world trembled and shook in six ways.

Then the whole congregation—monks and nuns, laymen and laywomen, gods, dragons, satyrs, centaurs, asuras, griffins, chimeras, pythons, humans, and nonhumans, as well as minor kings and the wheel-turning saintly kings—astonished because this had never happened before, with palms together and with complete attention, joyously looked up at the Buddha.

From the tuft of white hair between his eyebrows, one of his characteristic features, the Buddha emitted a beam of light, illuminating eighteen thousand worlds in the east, so that there was nowhere that it did not reach, down to the lowest purgatory and up to Akanishtha, the highest heaven.

In those worlds, all the living beings in the six states could be seen. Likewise the buddhas existing at present in those lands could be seen, and the sutra teachings those buddhas were preaching could be heard. Monks and nuns, laymen and laywomen, who had attained the Way through practice, could also be seen. Further, one could see bodhisattvas, the great ones, walking the bodhisattva way due to various causes and conditions, with various degrees of faith and understanding, and in various forms. Likewise buddhas who had entered complete nirvana could be seen. And one could see there stupas made of the seven precious materials, stupas that had been built to hold the remains of these buddhas after they had entered complete nirvana.

Then Maitreya Bodhisattva thought: "Now the World-Honored One has displayed a marvelous sign. But what is the cause or reason for this auspicious sign? Now that the Buddha, the World-Honored One, has entered into concentration, whom can I ask about such inconceivable and unprecedented wonders? And who will be able to answer?" Then he thought: "Here is Manjushri, the son of the Dharma-king, who has been in close contact with, and made offerings to, innumerable buddhas in the past. Surely, he must already have witnessed such rare signs as these. I will ask him."

Then the monks and nuns, laymen and laywomen, and all the gods, dragons, demon-gods, and others thought: "Whom shall we ask about this shining spiritual sign from the Buddha?"

Then Maitreya Bodhisattva, wanting to resolve his own doubts and seeing what was on the minds of the four groups of the assembly—the monks, and nuns, laymen and laywomen—as well as the gods, dragons, demon-gods, and others, asked Manjushri: "What is the reason for this auspicious and spiritual sign, emitting such a great, bright beam of light, illuminating the eighteen thousand eastern lands, revealing in detail the splendor of those Buddha-worlds?"

Then Maitreya Bodhisattva, wanting to say what he meant once again, asked in verse:

> Manjushri,
> From the tuft of white hair between his eyebrows
> Why does our leader and teacher
> Radiate so great a light in all directions?
>
> The rain of mandarava
> And manjushaka flowers
> And fragrant breezes of sandalwood
> Delight us all.
>
> For this reason
> The earth became splendid and pure,
> And this whole world
> Trembled and shook in six different ways.

At this moment the four groups
Are all full of joy,
Glad in body and in mind,
Having obtained something they never had before.

When the beam of light from between his brows
Illuminates the eastern direction
Eighteen thousand lands
Are colored in gold.

From the deepest purgatory
Up to the highest heaven,
Throughout all the worlds,
Living beings in the six states,

The directions of their births and deaths,
Their good and evil deeds and circumstances,
Their retributions, pleasing or ugly,
Can all be seen from here.

Buddhas also can be seen,
The holy masters, the lions,
Preaching sutras
That are fine, wonderful, and supreme.

Their voices clear and pure,
Sending forth soft, gentle sounds,
Teaching innumerable millions
Of bodhisattvas.

Their sacred voices are so deep and wonderful,
They make people rejoice on hearing them.
Each in his own world,
Preaches the true Dharma.

By various causal explanations
And innumerable parables,
They illuminate the Buddha-dharma
And open understanding of it to all.

If any are suffering
Or weary from age, disease, or death,
For them they teach nirvana
To bring all suffering to an end.

If any are happy,
Having made offerings to buddhas,
And are devoted to seeking the superior Dharma,
For them they teach the pratyekabuddha way.

If any children of the Buddha
Have carried out various practices,
And seek unexcelled wisdom,
For them they teach the pure way.

Manjushri,
Living here
I have seen and heard such things,
Hundreds of billions of them.

Though they are numerous,
Let me now briefly describe some of them:

In those lands I see bodhisattvas,
Numerous as the sands of the Ganges.
According to their causes and circumstances
They seek the Buddha way.

There are some who give alms of
Gold, silver and coral, pearls and jewels,
Seashell and agate, diamonds
And other precious stones,

Male and female servants,
Carriages and chariots,
Hand-drawn carriages
And palanquins adorned with jewels.

They give all these alms with joy.
Turning toward the Buddha way,
They seek to attain this vehicle,
One supreme in the threefold world and praised by buddhas.

There are also bodhisattvas
Who give precious four-horse carriages
With railings and ornate canopies
Adorning their sides and tops.

Also I see bodhisattvas
Who give their own flesh, hands and feet,
And their wives and children,
In order to pursue the unexcelled way.

Further, I see bodhisattvas
Who cheerfully and gladly give as alms
Their own heads and eyes, bodies and limbs,
In order to pursue the wisdom of the Buddha.

Manjushri,
I see various kings
Going to visit the buddhas
To ask about the unexcelled way.

Then they abandon their pleasant lands,
Palaces, ministers, and female servants,
And, shaving their beards and heads,
Put on the robes of the Dharma.

I also see bodhisattvas
Who become monks

Living alone in quiet seclusion,
Enjoying the reciting of sutras.

And I see bodhisattvas
Who with perseverance and zeal
Go deep into the mountains
To ponder over the Buddha way.

I also see them renouncing desires,
Always living in empty, quiet places,
Profoundly cultivating meditation
And obtaining the five divine powers.

Further, I see bodhisattvas
Peacefully meditating with palms together,
With tens of millions of stanzas
Praising the king of the Dharma.

Again, I see bodhisattvas,
Profound in wisdom and firm in will,
Able to question the buddhas
And receive and retain everything they hear.

And I see children of the Buddha,
Perfect in meditation and wisdom,
With innumerable illustrations
Preaching the Dharma for the multitudes.

Teaching the Dharma with joy and delight,
They transform people into bodhisattvas,
Destroying the army of the devil,
And beating the Dharma drum.

I also see bodhisattvas
Who are calm and silent.
Though honored by gods and dragons,
They take no joy in that.

Again, I see bodhisattvas
Who dwell in forests and emit a light
That saves sufferers in purgatories
And enables them to enter the Buddha way.

I also see children of the Buddha
Who never sleep
Walking through forests,
Diligently seeking the Buddha way.

Further, I see observers of the precepts,
Without flaw in their conduct,
Pure as precious jewels,
Who in this way seek the Buddha way.

And I see children of the Buddha
Dwelling in the power of patient endurance.

Though men of the utmost arrogance
Hatefully abuse and beat them,
They are able to endure all of this
In order to seek the Buddha way.

I also see bodhisattvas
Who leave behind all play and laughter
And all foolish companions,
And seek association with the wise.

Single-mindedly removing distractions,
Concentrating their thoughts while in mountain forests,
For tens of thousands of millions of years,
They seek the Buddha way.

Or I see bodhisattvas
Who offer delicacies of food and drink,
And hundreds of kinds of herbal teas
To the Buddha and the monks.

Some give fine robes and superior garments
Worth tens of millions of billions,
Or utterly priceless robes,
To the Buddha and the monks.

Some give ten million billion kinds
Of precious buildings built of sandalwood,
With all sorts of fine bedding,
To the Buddha and the monks.

Some give pure, immaculate gardens
Full of flowers and fruits,
With flowing springs and bathing pools,
To the Buddha and the monks.

Some give offerings like these,
Wonderful in every way,
Joyfully and without grudging,
Seeking the unexcelled way.

Moreover, there are bodhisattvas
Who teach the Dharma of nirvana,
In various ways teaching
Numberless living beings.

Also I see bodhisattvas
Who observe that the nature of all things
Is not dual,
But like empty space.

Again, I see children of the Buddha
With minds free from attachments,
With this wonderful wisdom
Seeking the unexcelled way.

Manjushri,
There are also bodhisattvas

Who, after the Buddha's extinction,
Make offerings to his remains.

I see children of the Buddha
Who build stupas,
Innumerable as the sands of the Ganges,
Splendidly adorning all lands.

Lofty and most wonderful
Are these stupas,
Five thousand leagues high,
And two thousand leagues in length and width.

Each of these stupas
Bears thousands of banners and flags,
Curtains decorated with jewels,
And valuable bells ringing harmoniously.

Gods and dragon-gods,
Humans and nonhumans,
With incense, flowers, and good music,
Are always making offerings.

Manjushri!
All the Buddha's children,
In order to make offerings to the remains,
Adorn the stupas splendidly.

Thereby all the lands spontaneously
Become extraordinarily wonderful and fine,
Like the king of heavenly trees
In full bloom.

The Buddha has emitted a beam of light.
With all the assembly,
I see that these lands
Are extraordinarily wonderful.

Rare are the divine powers and wisdom of buddhas.
Emitting a single beam of pure light,
They illuminate innumerable lands.
Beholding this, we gain something we never had before.

Manjushri, child of the Buddha,
Resolve the doubts of the assembly.

All of the four groups, with joyous anticipation,
Look up to you and me,
Wanting to know why the World-Honored One
Has emitted such a beam of light.

Child of the Buddha, now give an answer.
Remove our doubts and make us glad.
What abundant benefits will come from
Emitting such a beam of light?

Does the Buddha now wish to teach
The wonderful Dharma that he obtained
Seated at the place of the Way?
Is he now about to provide assurance of becoming a buddha?

He shows us all the buddha-lands,
Pure and ornate with precious things.
And we can see the buddhas of all those lands.
This cannot be for some trivial reason.

You must know, Manjushri,
That all the four groups and the dragon-gods
Are looking to you,
Wondering what you will say.

Then Manjushri said to Maitreya Bodhisattva, the great one, and to all the other great leaders: "Good people, in my view, the Buddha, the World-Honored One, now intends to teach the great Dharma, to send down the rain of the great Dharma, to blow the conch of the great

Dharma, to beat the drum of the great Dharma, and to explain the meaning of the great Dharma.

"Good people, whenever I've seen this omen from any previous buddha, after emitting such a beam of light they have always taught the great Dharma. So you can be sure that this buddha, having displayed this light, similarly intends to lead all beings to hear and understand the Dharma that everyone in the world finds so hard to believe. That is why he displayed this omen.

"Good people, a long time ago, innumerable, unlimited, inconceivable, countless eons ago, there was a buddha named Sun and Moon Light Tathagata, one worthy of offerings, truly awakened, fully clear in conduct, well gone, understanding the world, unexcelled leader, trainer of men, teacher of heavenly beings and people, buddha, and world-honored one. He preached the true Dharma in a way that was good in the beginning, good in the middle, and good at the end; a Dharma that is profound in meaning and whose words are skillful and wonderful, pure and unadulterated, perfect, flawless, and characteristic of noble practices.

"For those who sought to be shravakas he taught the Dharma of the four truths for overcoming birth, old age, disease, and death and for attaining nirvana. For those who sought to be pratyekabuddhas he taught the Dharma of the twelve causes and conditions. And for the bodhisattvas he taught the six transcendental practices to lead them to attain supreme awakening and all-inclusive wisdom.

"Then there was another buddha, also named Sun and Moon Light, and yet another buddha, also named Sun and Moon Light; and similarly there were twenty thousand buddhas all with the same name, Sun and Moon Light, and all of them with the same surname as well, Bharadvaja. You should know, Maitreya, that all these buddhas, who from the first to the last had the same name, Sun and Moon Light, were worthy of the ten epithets of a buddha and taught the Dharma in a way that was good in the beginning, good in the middle, and good at the end.

"Before the last of these buddhas had left his home, he had eight royal sons. The first was named Having Intention, the second Good Intention, the third Infinite Intention, the fourth Precious Intention, the fifth Increasing Intention, the sixth Undoubting Intention, the seventh Resounding Intention, and the eighth Dharma Intention.

"These eight princes were independently dignified and virtuous, each ruling over four great realms. All these princes, hearing that their father had left his home and attained supreme awakening, renounced their royal positions and, following him, left home. With their minds on the Great Vehicle and always observing noble practices, and having already planted roots of goodness under tens of millions of buddhas, all of them became Dharma teachers.

"At that time the Buddha Sun and Moon Light taught the Great Vehicle sutra called Innumerable Meanings, a Dharma by which bodhisattvas are taught and which buddhas watch over and keep in mind. As soon as he had taught this sutra, he sat cross-legged in the midst of the great assembly and entered the kind of concentration called the place of innumerable meanings, in which his body and mind were motionless. At this moment mandarava, great mandarava, manjushaka, and great manjushaka flowers rained down from the sky over the Buddha and the whole great assembly, while the whole Buddha-world trembled in six different ways.

"Then the congregation, the monks and nuns, laymen and lay-women, gods, dragons, satyrs, centaurs, asuras, griffins, chimeras, pythons, humans and nonhumans, as well as the minor kings and the wheel-turning saintly kings—all of this assembly—having obtained something that they had never had before, put their palms together in joy and in rapt attention looked up to the Buddha.

"Then, from the characteristic tuft of white hair between his brows, the Tathagata emitted a beam of light that illuminated eighteen thousand buddha-lands to the East, so that it extended throughout all of them, just like all these buddha-lands that we can see now.

"Maitreya, you should understand that in the congregation at that time there were two billion bodhisattvas who happily wanted to hear the Dharma. All these bodhisattvas, seeing this beam of light illuminating all those buddha-lands, and obtaining what they had never had before, wanted to know the causes and circumstances of that light.

"At that time there was a bodhisattva named Wonderful Light who had eight hundred disciples. When Sun and Moon Light Buddha arose from concentration, because of Wonderful Light Bodhisattva he taught the Great Vehicle sutra called the Lotus Flower of the Wonderful Dharma, by which bodhisattvas are taught and which buddhas watch over and keep in mind. For sixty small eons he remained seated without

getting up. During those sixty small eons the listeners in that congrega-
tion also stayed seated in their places, motionless in body and mind, lis-
tening to the Buddha's preaching as if it took no longer than a meal.
During that time no one in the congregation felt at all weary, either in
body or in mind.

"Having taught this sutra for sixty small eons to Brahma, devils, men-
dicants, brahmans, human and heavenly beings, and asuras, Sun and
Moon Light Buddha proclaimed: 'Tonight at midnight, the Tathagata
will enter nirvana without residue.'

"At that time there was a bodhisattva named Good Treasury. Sun and
Moon Light Buddha assured him that he would become a buddha, say-
ing to all the monks: 'This Good Treasury Bodhisattva will become the
next buddha. An arhat, fully awakened, his name will be Pure Body
Tathagata.'

"Having assured him, at midnight the Buddha entered nirvana with-
out residue.

"Following that buddha's extinction, Wonderful Light Bodhisattva,
having embraced the Sutra of the Lotus Flower of the Wonderful
Dharma, taught it to others for a full eighty small eons. All eight sons
of Sun and Moon Light Buddha took Wonderful Light as their
teacher, and Wonderful Light helped them to strengthen their vow to
attain supreme awakening. All these princes made offerings to innu-
merable hundreds of thousands of billions of buddhas and achieved
the Buddha way. The last of them to become a buddha was named
Burning Light.

"Wonderful Light had eight hundred disciples, one of whom was
named Fame Seeker. He was greedily attached to lucrative offerings,
and, though he read and memorized many sutras, he gained little from
them and forgot almost all of them. That is why he was called Fame
Seeker. But because he had planted roots of goodness, this man too was
able to meet innumerable hundreds of thousands of billions of buddhas,
make offerings to them, revere, honor, and praise them.

"You should know this, Maitreya. Was the Bodhisattva Wonderful
Light of that time some other person? No, it was me. And the Bodhi-
sattva Fame Seeker was you. You can see that this omen is no different
from the previous one.

"Therefore I suppose that the Buddha will teach the Great Vehicle sutra called the Lotus Flower of the Wonderful Dharma, by which bodhi-sattvas are taught and which buddhas watch over and keep in mind."

Then Manjushri, wanting to say what he meant once again, spoke to the great congregation in verse:

> I remember that in a past age,
> Unquantifiable, innumerable eons ago,
> There was a buddha, the most honored of people,
> Called Sun and Moon Light.
>
> That World-Honored One preached the Dharma,
> Saving innumerable living beings
> And countless hundreds of millions of bodhisattvas,
> Enabling them to enter the wisdom of the Buddha.
>
> The eight princes born to that buddha
> Before leaving home,
> Seeing that this great sage had left his home,
> Followed him in observing noble practices.
>
> Among the great multitude of living beings,
> That Buddha then preached from the Great Vehicle
> The sutra called Innumerable Meanings
> And extensively analyzed it for them.
>
> When the Buddha had finished preaching the sutra
> He sat cross-legged on the Dharma seat,
> In the concentration called
> The place of innumerable meanings.
>
> Mandarava flowers rained down from the sky
> While heavenly drums sounded by themselves,
> And gods, dragons, demons, and spirits
> Made offerings to the most honored of people.
>
> All the buddha-lands
> Trembled terribly at that moment.

From between his brows the Buddha emitted a beam of light
Revealing wonders rarely seen.

This beam of light illumined the eastern region
Of eighteen thousand buddha-lands,
Showing the extent to which the lives of every living being there
Was affected by their past actions.

By the Buddha's beam of light
Buddha-lands could be seen,
Adorned with many jewels
With the colors of lapis lazuli and crystal.

Also to be seen were human and heavenly beings,
Dragon-gods and satyrs,
Centaurs and chimeras,
Each making offerings to their Buddha.

Tathagatas could also be seen
Naturally achieving
The Buddha way,
Their bodies like mountains of gold.

They were very fine
And wonderful in their majesty,
As when within pure lapis lazuli
A real statue of gold can be seen.

Thus world-honored ones
Laid out the meaning
Of the profound Dharma
For the great multitudes.

In each of these buddha-lands
There were innumerable shravakas.
By the Buddha's beam of light
All these great multitudes were completely visible.

In addition there were monks
Living in mountains and forests who persevered,
Observing the pure precepts
As if they were protecting bright jewels.

And bodhisattvas could be seen
As numerous as the sands of the Ganges,
Practicing charity and patience.
All this could be seen by the Buddha's light.

Also could be seen were bodhisattvas
Who had entered deeply into various states of meditation
And were at rest, motionless in body and mind,
Seeking the unexcelled way.

And bodhisattvas could be seen who,
Knowing the tranquilly extinct character of things,
Each in his own land
Taught the Dharma and pursued the Buddha way.

Then all four groups,
Seeing Sun and Moon Light Buddha
Display his power of great divine faculties,
Asked each other with joy in their hearts:
"Why is he doing this?"

The one honored by people and gods
Then rose from concentration
And praised Wonderful Light Bodhisattva:
"You are the eyes of the world,

"The storehouse of the Dharma
To whom all turn in faith.
You alone are able to bear witness
To the Dharma that I preach."

The World-Honored One,
Having praised Wonderful Light, making him rejoice,
Taught this Dharma Flower Sutra for a full sixty small eons,
Never getting up from his seat.

This supreme and wonderful Dharma
Taught by the World-Honored One,
Wonderful Light, the Dharma teacher,
Was able to embrace fully.

When the Buddha had preached this Dharma Flower,
Causing all to rejoice,
Immediately on that very day,
He proclaimed to the multitude of human and heavenly beings:

"The principle of the true character of things[1]
Has already been taught for all of you.
Now, at midnight,
I will enter into nirvana.

"With all your hearts, make a great effort
To give up all self-indulgence.
Buddhas are very rarely encountered;
Only once in hundreds of millions of eons is one met."

Hearing that the Buddha was entering nirvana,
Every one of the children of the World-Honored One
Was full of grief and suffering:
"Why must the Buddha's extinction be so soon?"

The saintly lord, the king of the Dharma,
Then comforted the countless multitude:
"Even when I am extinct,
Do not be sad or afraid!

"This Good Treasury Bodhisattva,
Has gained full understanding

Of the flawless
True character of things.

"He will become the next buddha,
Whose name will be Pure Body.
He, too, will save
Innumerable living beings."

That night the Buddha passed away,
As a fire goes out when the firewood is completely consumed.
His remains were distributed
And innumerable stupas put up for them.

Monks and nuns,
Numerous as the sands of the Ganges,
Doubled their effort,
Seeking the unexcelled way.

This Wonderful Light, Dharma teacher,
Having kept the storehouse of the Dharma
For eighty small eons,
Proclaimed the Dharma Flower Sutra everywhere.

All of the eight princes,
Guided by Wonderful Light,
Kept firmly to the unexcelled way,
And were able to see innumerable buddhas.

Having made offerings to the buddhas
They followed them in walking the great way,
Each in turn becoming a buddha,
As one by one they had assured each other.

The last, a heavenly being among heavenly beings,
Was called Burning Light Buddha.
As leader and teacher of all the sages,
He saved innumerable living beings.

Wonderful Light, Dharma teacher,
At that time had a disciple
Who was always lazy,
Greedily craving fame and gain.

Always seeking fame and gain,
He often visited homes of noble families,
Casting aside what he had repeated and memorized,
Forgetting everything and gaining nothing from it.

Because of these things
He was called Fame Seeker.
Yet by doing good works
He too was able to see innumerable buddhas.

He made offerings to buddhas,
Followed them in walking the great way
And carrying out the six transcendental practices.
And now he has seen the Lion of the Shakyas.

Later he will become a buddha
Whose name will be Maitreya.
He will save
Living beings everywhere.

The lazy one who lived after the extinction
Of the other Buddha,
That lazy one was you.
And Wonderful Light, the Dharma teacher, was me.

Having seen Sun and Moon Light Buddha
Long ago send forth an auspicious beam of light,
I know that the present Buddha
Wants to teach the Dharma Flower Sutra.

The present sign is like the previous auspicious occurrences;
They are the buddhas' skillful means.

The present Buddha emits a beam of light
To help reveal the principle of the true character of things.

The time has come for people to understand.
With your palms together, wait single-mindedly!
The Buddha will pour the rain of the Dharma
To satisfy those who seek the Way.

If those who seek after the three vehicles
Have any doubts or regrets,
The Buddha will remove them
So that none whatever remain.

2. Skillful Means

AT THAT TIME the World-Honored One rose calmly from concentration and said to Shariputra: "The wisdom of buddhas is both profound and immeasurable, and the gateways to this wisdom are hard to understand and hard to enter. No shravaka or pratyekabuddha can apprehend it.

"Why is this? It is because every buddha has been closely associated with hundreds of thousands of billions of buddhas in the past, fully practicing the way of the immeasurable Dharma of all the buddhas. Boldly and diligently working, they have become famous everywhere, fulfilling the very profound, unprecedented Dharma and teaching it wherever opportunities arose. Yet their intention is difficult to grasp.

"Shariputra, ever since I became a buddha, I have used a variety of causal explanations and a variety of parables to teach and preach, and countless skillful means to lead living beings, enabling them to give up their attachments. Why? Because the Tathagata has attained full use of skillful means and practice of insight.

"Shariputra, the insight of the Tathagata is broad and great, profound and far-reaching, immeasurable and unobstructed. His powers, his courage, his meditation, his liberation, and his concentration have enabled him to enter into the boundless and to fulfill the unprecedented Dharma.

"By making a variety of distinctions, Shariputra, the Tathagata is able to teach with great skill, cheering the hearts of all with gentle words.

"In sum, Shariputra, the Buddha has fulfilled the whole Dharma—innumerable, unlimited, unprecedented teachings.

"But this is enough Shariputra. No more needs to be said. Why? Because what the Buddha has achieved is most rare and difficult to understand. Only among buddhas can the true character of all things be fathomed. This is because every existing thing has such characteristics, such a nature, such an embodiment, such powers, such actions, such causes, such conditions, such effects, such rewards and retributions, and yet such a complete fundamental coherence."[2]

Then the World-Honored One, wanting to say what he meant once again, spoke in verse:

> The world's heroes cannot be measured.
> Among all the heavenly beings and people of the world,
> Among all living beings,
> None can know a buddha.
>
> The buddhas' power and courage,
> Liberation and states of concentration,
> And the buddhas' other attributes,
> Cannot be fathomed by anyone.
>
> In the past I followed countless buddhas
> And fully tried their various ways,
> Their profound, fine, and wonderful teachings,
> Which are difficult to see and understand.
>
> After innumerable hundreds of millions of eons
> Pursuing all those ways,
> And gaining the fruit of the place of the Way,
> I could fully understand.
>
> Such great effects and such rewards and retributions,
> The meaning of various natures and characteristics—
> These things the buddhas of the ten directions and I
> Can now really understand.
>
> This Dharma is indescribable.
> Words must fall silent.

Among other kinds of living beings,
None can understand it,
Except the bodhisattvas,
Whose faith is strong and firm.

Even disciples of the Buddha
Who have made offerings to buddhas,
Gotten rid of all their faults,
And now live in their final incarnation,
Even such people as these,
Don't have this much power.

Even a world
Full of men like Shariputra,
Using all of their mental powers together
Could not fathom Buddha-wisdom.

Indeed, if all the worlds in the ten directions
Were full of people like Shariputra
Or any other disciples,
Filling all the worlds,
Using all of their mental powers together,
None of these people could fathom it.

If very intelligent pratyekabuddhas,
Faultless and in their final incarnations,
As numerous as the bamboos in a grove,
Filled all the worlds in the ten directions,

And single-mindedly came together
For innumerable hundreds of millions of eons
Wanting to think about the buddhas' real wisdom,
They could not understand even a small part of it.

Even if bodhisattvas who have just taken up the Way—
Who have given offerings to countless buddhas,

Have fully understood the meaning of various teachings
And been able to teach the Dharma well,

Who were as plentiful as rice, hemp, bamboo, or reeds
And filled all the worlds of the ten directions—
Even if these bodhisattvas, with complete attention
And wonderful wisdom

Were all to think together
For as many eons
As the Ganges has grains of sand,
They could not gain Buddha-wisdom.

If bodhisattvas free from backsliding,
Numerous as the sands of the Ganges,
Single-mindedly devoted themselves
To seeking and thinking together,
They too would not comprehend it.

Further, I say to you, Shariputra,
That I have already fully attained
The flawless, amazing, profound
And supremely wonderful Dharma.

Only I know its character,
As do the buddhas of the ten directions.

Shariputra, you should know
That the words of buddhas do not differ.
You should have strong faith
In the Dharma preached by the buddhas.

After the World-Honored One
Has taught the Dharma
For such a long time,
Certainly he should now teach the truth.

I say to all shravakas
And to those who seek the pratyekabuddha way
That I free them from the bonds of suffering
And enable them to reach nirvana.

Through the power of skillful means
The Buddha reveals the teachings of the three vehicles.
Though all beings have various attachments,
He leads them to liberate themselves.

At that time in the great assembly there were shravakas, arhats without faults, Ajnata-Kaundinya and others, twelve hundred in all.[3] And there were various monks and nuns, laymen and laywomen who had vowed to become shravakas and pratyekabuddhas. They all thought: "Why does the World-Honored One speak so enthusiastically about skillful means? Why does he say that the Buddha's Dharma is so profound and so difficult to comprehend, and that what he says is so difficult that not even shravakas and pratyekabuddhas can understand it? And yet at the same time he has said that there is only one principle of liberation, so that we too, with this Dharma, will attain nirvana. But now we do not know where this leads."

Then Shariputra, seeing the doubts in the minds of the four groups and not having fully understood everything himself, spoke to the Buddha: "World-Honored One, what are the reasons for you to praise so enthusiastically the buddhas' principle of skillful means and the very profound, fine, and wonderful Dharma, which is so hard to understand? Never before have I heard such teaching from the Buddha! Now these four groups are full of doubt. Will the World-Honored One please explain why you have so enthusiastically praised this very profound, fine, and wonderful Dharma, which is so difficult to comprehend?"

Then Shariputra, to say what he meant once again, spoke in verse:

Sun of Wisdom!
Great saint
And honored one!
At last you have taught this Dharma,

Saying that you yourself have gained
Strength, courage and concentration,
Meditation and liberation,
And other inconceivable attributes.

About the teachings gained on the path of wisdom
No one has been able to ask questions.
You say: "My mind is hard to fathom.
No one can question me."

Without being asked, you have taught others,
Praising the path you have taken
And that very wonderful wisdom
That all buddhas have.

All the arhats who are without fault
And those seeking nirvana
Have now fallen into a net of doubt,
Asking themselves why the Buddha has taught in this way.

Those who seek to become pratyekabuddhas,
As well as the monks and nuns,
Gods, dragons, demons, spirits, centaurs, and other beings,
Give each other perplexed looks.

They look up expectantly
To the most honored of people,
Asking: "What is this all about?
Would you please explain it to us?"

Of all the shravakas, you have said that I am first.
Yet, even with my wisdom, I cannot resolve the doubt
As to whether this is the ultimate Dharma
Or only a path for getting to it.

We who have been created by your teaching,
Put our palms together and wait expectantly,

Begging you to make wonderful sounds,
And tell the truth as it really is.

Gods, dragon-gods, and others,
Numerous as the sands of the Ganges,
Bodhisattvas seeking to become buddhas,
Some eighty thousand in number,

And wheel-turning saintly kings
Have come here from trillions of lands
With palms together and reverent hearts.
All want to hear the perfect way.

Then the Buddha said to Shariputra: "Stop, stop! There is no need to say more. If I explain this matter, all of the worlds' heavenly beings as well as human beings will be startled and perplexed."

Again Shariputra said to the Buddha: "World-Honored One, please explain it. Please explain it! Why? Because in this gathering there are countless hundreds of thousands of billions of living beings who have already seen buddhas. Their faculties are excellent and their wisdom is clear. If they hear the Buddha preach, they will be able to believe respectfully."

Then Shariputra, to say what he meant once again, spoke in verse:

King of Dharma, unexcelled in honor!
Please preach to us without reserve.
In this assembly are countless beings
Who can put their reverent faith in you.

But the Buddha again said: "Stop, Shariputra! If I explained this, all the worlds of human and heavenly beings and asuras would be startled and perplexed, and extremely arrogant monks might fall into the great pit."

Then the World-Honored One once again spoke in verse:

Stop, stop, no need to say more!
My Dharma is wonderful and hard to imagine.

On hearing it, those who are utterly arrogant
Will neither respect it nor believe it.

Then Shariputra once again said to the Buddha: "World-Honored One, please explain it. Please explain it! In this meeting there are hundreds of thousands of billions of beings like me who in previous lives followed buddhas and were transformed. Certainly they can respect and believe what you say, and thereby enjoy great peace of mind throughout the long night of time and gain abundant benefits of various kinds."

Then Shariputra, wanting to restate this idea, spoke again in verse:

Most excellent and honored of the living,
I beg you to teach the prime Dharma!
I am the oldest son of the Buddha.
Bring yourself to explain it clearly.

Countless beings in this meeting
Are able to respectfully believe this Dharma.
In previous lives the Buddha has already
Taught and transformed many like us.

With complete attention and palms together,
All of us want to hear the Buddha's words.
There are twelve hundred of us
And others who want to become buddhas.

I beg you, for their sake,
Bring yourself to explain it clearly.
If they hear this Dharma,
They will experience great joy.

Then the World-Honored One said to Shariputra: "Since you have now earnestly repeated your request three times, how can I refuse you? Now listen carefully, ponder over what I will say and remember it, for I will explain it for you clearly."

When he had said this, immediately some five thousand monks and nuns, laymen and laywomen, got up and, bowing to the Buddha, left the meeting. Why? Because their roots of sin were so deep and they were so utterly arrogant that they imagined themselves to have already attained and born witness to what they had not actually attained. Having such faults, they could not stay. The World-Honored One kept silent and did not stop them.

Then the Buddha said to Shariputra: "Now the congregation no longer has useless branches and leaves, but only firm, good fruit. It is good, Shariputra, that such utterly arrogant ones have gone. So listen carefully now. I am ready to explain it for you."

And Shariputra said: "Very well, World-Honored One, I am eager to hear you."

The Buddha said to Shariputra: "Such a wonderful Dharma as this is taught by the buddha-tathagatas only on very rare occasions, just as the udumbara blossom is seen only very rarely. You should believe me, Shariputra, in the teachings of the buddhas nothing is empty or false.

"Shariputra, the meaning of the Dharma that buddhas preach as appropriate to the occasion is difficult to understand. Why? Because we use a variety of skillful means, causal explanations, and parables to teach. This Dharma cannot be well understood through calculation or analysis. Only a buddha can really grasp it. Why is this? Because it is for this great cause alone that buddhas, the world-honored ones, appear in the world.

"What do I mean by saying it is for this one great cause alone that buddhas, the world-honored ones, appear in the world? The buddhas, the world-honored ones, appear in the world because they want living beings to open a way to the buddhas' insight, and thus become pure. They appear in the world because they want to demonstrate the buddhas' insight to living beings. They appear in the world because they want living beings to apprehend things with the buddhas' insight. They appear in the world because they want living beings to enter into the way of the buddhas' insight. This alone is the one great cause, Shariputra, for which buddhas appear in the world."

Then the Buddha said to Shariputra: "The buddha-tathagatas only teach and transform bodhisattvas. Their one purpose is to demonstrate the buddhas' insight to all beings and have them apprehend it.

"Shariputra, the tathagatas teach the Dharma for the sake of living beings only by means of the One Buddha–Vehicle. They have no other vehicles—no second or third vehicle. Shariputra, the teachings of the buddhas throughout the universe are all like this.

"Shariputra, buddhas of the past, through an innumerable variety of skillful means, causal explanations, parables, and other kinds of expression, have preached the Dharma for the sake of living beings. These teachings have all been for the sake of the One Buddha–Vehicle, so that all living things, having heard the Dharma from a buddha, might finally gain complete wisdom.

"Shariputra, buddhas who appear in this world in the future will also, through an innumerable variety of skillful means, causal explanations, parables, and other kinds of expression, preach the Dharma for the sake of living beings. These teachings are all for the sake of the One Buddha–Vehicle, so that all living things, having heard the Dharma from a buddha, might eventually obtain complete wisdom.

"Shariputra, the buddhas, the world-honored ones in all of the billions and billions of buddha-lands throughout the universe, are giving abundant benefits and peace and happiness to all living things. Through an innumerable variety of skillful means, causal explanations, parables, and other kinds of expression, these buddhas preach the Dharma for the sake of living beings. All these teachings are for the sake of the One Buddha–Vehicle, so that all living things, having heard the Dharma from a buddha, might eventually gain complete wisdom.

"Shariputra, all these buddhas only teach bodhisattvas that their purpose is to demonstrate the buddhas' insight to living beings, to enable living beings to apprehend things with the insight of a buddha, and to enable living beings to enter into the way of the buddhas' insight.

"Shariputra, I too am like those buddhas. Knowing that living beings have various desires and things to which they are deeply attached, I have taught the Dharma according to their basic nature, using a variety of causal explanations, parables, other kinds of expression, and the power of skillful means. Shariputra, this is so that they might attain the complete wisdom of the One Buddha–Vehicle.

"Shariputra, in the entire universe, there are not even two such vehicles, much less three!

"Shariputra, the buddhas appear in an evil world of five pollutions—the pollution of the age, the pollution from afflictions, the pollution of living beings, the pollution of views, and the pollution of life. When the age is in chaos, the stains run deep, and greedy and jealous living beings acquire unhealthy roots. For this reason, Shariputra, with their powers of skillful means, the buddhas have distinguished three ways within the One Buddha–Vehicle.

"Yet if any disciples of mine, Shariputra, thinking themselves to be arhats or pratyekabuddhas, neither hear nor know of these matters that the buddhas, the tathagatas, use only to teach and transform bodhisattvas, they are not true disciples of the Buddha, and not really arhats or pratyekabuddhas. Again, Shariputra, if such monks and nuns say to themselves: 'I have already become an arhat. This is my last body. I have already attained final nirvana!' And if they no longer vow to seek supreme awakening, you should know that they are extremely arrogant. Why? Because it is impossible that a monk who has already become an arhat would not believe this Dharma.

"There is only one exception—after a buddha has passed into extinction and there is no buddha present. Why? Because after a buddha's extinction it will be difficult to find people who can receive, embrace, read, recite, and understand a sutra such as this. But if they meet another buddha, they will receive decisive teachings about this Dharma.

"Shariputra, all of you should believe, understand, and embrace the words of the Buddha with all your hearts, for in the words of the buddhas, the tathagatas, there is nothing empty or false. There are no other vehicles. There is only the One Buddha–Vehicle."

Then the World-Honored One, wanting to restate this idea, spoke in verse:

> Monks and nuns full of arrogance,
> Proud laymen, and laywomen of little faith:
> In the assembly of the four groups, such people
> Were five thousand in number.
>
> Not seeing their own errors,
> Failing to observe the precepts
> And carefully defending their faults,
> These people of little wisdom have already left.

Those dregs of the assembly left
Because of the Buddha's dignity and virtue.
Such people of little merit and virtue
Are incapable of receiving the Dharma.

Now this assembly has neither branches nor leaves,
But only good, firm fruit.

Shariputra, listen carefully:
The Dharma gained by the buddhas
Is taught for the good of living beings
Through the power of countless skillful means.

What they have in their hearts,
All the ways in which they behave,
Their many kinds of desire,
The good and evil deeds of their previous lives—
The Buddha knows all of this completely.

With a variety of explanations,
Parables, and other kinds of expression,
Through the power of skillful means
He causes all to rejoice.

He teaches sutras, poetry,
Stories of disciples' previous lives,
Stories of buddhas' previous lives
And of unprecedented things,

As well as causal explanations,
Parables and similes,
Verses which repeat them,
And passages of dialogue.[4]

For those with dull minds
Who want lesser teachings,

Who greedily cling to existence,
Who, after encountering countless buddhas,

Still do not follow
The profound and wonderful way,
And are tormented by much suffering—
For them I teach nirvana.

By devising such skillful means,
I have enabled them to enter Buddha-wisdom.
I never before said,
"All of you will be able to achieve the Buddha way."

The reason why I never said this
Was that the time was not yet ripe.
But now is the right time
To teach the Great Vehicle definitively.

This Dharma of mine is of nine kinds.[5]
I adapt it to living beings when I teach them,
Keeping entry into the Great Vehicle as the basic aim.
That's why I teach this sutra.

There are children of the Buddha who are purehearted,
Who are gentle and bright,
Who in the presence of countless buddhas
Have taken the profound and wonderful way.

For such children of the Buddha
I teach this Great Vehicle sutra.
I assure such people that in the future
They will fulfill the Buddha way.

With their profound awareness of the Buddha,
And because they practice
And observe the purifying precepts,
They are assured of becoming buddhas.

Their whole bodies are filled with great joy.
Knowing their hearts and minds and their conduct,
The Buddha teaches them
The Great Vehicle.

If a shravaka or a bodhisattva
Hears the Dharma I preach,
Even a single verse of it,
Without doubt they will all become buddhas.

In all the buddha-lands in the ten directions
There is only the Dharma of one vehicle,
Not a second or a third,
Except what the buddhas teach by skillful means.

Merely using provisional expressions,
The Buddha has drawn living beings to himself,
In order to teach them
The wisdom of the Buddha.

Buddhas appear in this world
For this one reason alone,
The real reason.
The other two ways are not genuine.

After all, with a small vehicle
All living beings would never get across.

The Buddha himself dwells in the Great Vehicle,
In accord with the Dharma he has attained.
Enriched with powers of meditation and wisdom,
He uses it to liberate the living.

He himself gives witness
To the unexcelled way,
The Great Vehicle,
The universal Dharma.

If I used a lesser vehicle to transform
Even one person,
I would fall into greed—
Something that cannot happen.

Someone having faith in, taking refuge in, the Buddha
Will know that the Tathagata will never deceive,
For he has no greedy or envious desires
And is free from all the evils of the world.

That is why
In the entire universe
The Buddha alone is completely without fear.
With a body adorned with special features.

I give light to the world.
I am honored by countless multitudes,
For whom I teach
The signs of the true nature of things.

You should know, Shariputra,
I originally took a vow,
Wanting to enable all living beings to be equal to me,
Without any distinctions.

In accord with this vow of long ago
Everything is now fulfilled,
For I transform all living beings
And lead them all into the Buddha way.

Every time I meet living beings,
If I teach them only the Buddha way,
Those of little wisdom would be perplexed and confused
And would never accept my teaching.

I know that such living beings
Never put down good roots.

Firmly attached to the five desires,
They suffer greatly from stupidity and desire.

Due to their desires
They have fallen into the three evil paths.
Revolving like wheels
In the six states.

They are subject to all kinds of suffering.
Received into the womb
As tiny and frail things,
They would grow up in life after life.

Having little virtue and few blessings,
They were pressured by all kinds of suffering
And entered into a dense forest of wrong views
About existence and nonexistence and the like.

Relying on these wrong views,
Sixty-two in all,
They became deeply attached to false and empty teachings
And held on to them firmly, unable to give them up.

Their pride and arrogance were so great,
They were so full of flattery and insincerity,
Through ten million billion eons
They have not heard the Buddha's name or the true Dharma.

Such people are hard to save.
That is why, Shariputra,
For their sake I established skillful means,
Taught ways to end suffering, and showed them nirvana.

Though I have taught nirvana,
It is not truly extinction.
All things, originally and naturally,
Have the character of tranquil extinction.

When children of the Buddha
Have taken this path,
In a future life
They will become buddhas.

With the power to use skillful means,
I have revealed the Dharma of three vehicles.
Yet all the world-honored ones
Teach the one-vehicle way.

Now everyone in this great assembly
Should rid themselves of doubt.
The buddhas do not really differ in their claim
That there is only one vehicle, not two.

For countless ages in the past
Innumerable buddhas have passed into extinction,
Hundreds of thousands of billions of kinds of buddhas,
Their number beyond calculation.

All such world-honored ones,
By various explanations and parables,
And the power of countless skillful means,
Have preached characteristics of the Dharma.

All these world-honored ones
Have taught the Dharma of one vehicle,
Transforming countless living beings,
Enabling them to enter the Buddha way.

Moreover, the greatest of saints,
Knowing the deepest desires of all the gods,
People, and other beings of all the worlds,
Have used still other skillful means to clarify the highest meaning.

If any living beings,
Having encountered

Buddhas in the past,
And having heard the Dharma,

Have been generous, moral, patient, and persistent,
Practiced meditation and wisdom, and so on,
In various ways cultivating merit and virtue,
All such people have fulfilled the Buddha way.

When buddhas have passed away,
If anyone is good and gentle,
All such living beings
Have fulfilled the Buddha way.

When a buddha has passed away,
If there are those who make offerings to the remains,
Building many trillions of kinds of stupas
Of gold, silver, and crystal,

With seashell and agate,
Carnelian, lapis lazuli, and pearl
To brightly and completely adorn them
And dignify each stupa with decorations;

And if there are those who build mausoleums of stone
Or of sandalwood and aloes,
Hovenia and other wood,
Or of brick, tile, clay, and so on;

And if there are those who heap up earth
In open fields to make a mausoleum for the Buddha;
Or even little children in their play
Who gather sand and make it into stupas,

All such beings
Have fulfilled the Buddha way.

If anyone, for the Buddha's sake,
Designs and erects images
Carved with appropriate features,
They have fulfilled the Buddha way.

Some use the seven precious materials,
Or nickel, copper and bronze, lead and tin,
    and the like,
Or iron, wood, or clay, or resin and lacquer
To make or to adorn buddha images.

All such people
Have fulfilled the Buddha way.

Some paint buddha images of many colors
And adorn them with a hundred signs of good fortune.
Whether done by themselves or by employing others,
All have fulfilled the Buddha way.

Even if little children at play,
Use reeds, sticks, or brushes,
Or even their fingernails,
To draw images of Buddha,

All such people,
Gradually gaining merit,
And developing their great compassion,
Have fulfilled the Buddha way.

Just by transforming people into bodhisattvas,
They have saved countless beings.

If anyone goes to stupas or mausoleums,
To jeweled or painted images,
With flowers, incense, flags, or canopies
And reverently makes offerings;

Or if they have others perform music,
By beating drums or blowing horns or conch shells,
Or playing pipes, flutes, lutes, harps,
Mandolins, cymbals, or gongs,
Producing fine sounds and presenting them as offerings;

Or if they joyfully praise
The Buddha's virtues in song,
Even with just a tiny sound,
They have fulfilled the Buddha way.

If anyone, even while distracted,
With even a single flower,
Makes an offering to a painted image,
They will progressively see countless buddhas.

There are those who worship by prostrating themselves,
Some merely by putting their palms together,
Others only by raising a hand,
And others by a slight nod of the head.

All of these,
Honoring images in various ways,
Will progressively see countless buddhas,
Fulfill the unexcelled way themselves,

Save countless beings everywhere,
And enter into nirvana without residue,
As a fire dies out
When the firewood is all consumed.

If anyone, even while distracted,
Enters a stupa or mausoleum
And even once exclaims, "Hail to the Buddha,"
They have fulfilled the Buddha way.

People who have heard this Dharma
From one of the buddhas of the past,
While they were in the world or after their extinction,
Have all fulfilled the Buddha way.

All the world-honored ones of the future,
Uncountable in number,
These tathagatas will use skillful means
To teach this Dharma.

All of the tathagatas
By using innumerable skillful means
Save living beings,
So that they enter the buddhas' flawless wisdom.

Of all those who hear the Dharma
None will fail to become a buddha.

This is the original vow of every buddha:
The Buddha way I have practiced myself,
I want to share universally with other living beings,
That they may attain the same way.

Though buddhas in ages to come,
May teach millions and millions
Of countless gateways to the Dharma,
This will actually be for the sake of the one vehicle.

The buddhas, the most honored of people,
Know that nothing exists independently,
And that buddha-seeds arise interdependently.
This is why they teach the one vehicle.

Things are part of the everlasting Dharma,
And the character of the Dharma in the world endures forever.
Having come to know this at the place of the Way,
Leaders and teachers teach it in skillful ways.

Those who receive the offerings
Of human and heavenly beings,
The present buddhas of the ten directions,
Numerous as the sands of the Ganges,

Having appeared in the world,
For the peace and comfort
Of living beings,
Also teach the Dharma in this way.

Knowing the most tranquil extinction,
By using the power of skillful means
They demonstrate various paths.
But they are all really for the sake of the Buddha-Vehicle.

Understanding the behavior of living beings,
Their deepest thoughts,
The many things they have done in the past,
Their desires, natures, diligence, and faculties, sharp or dull,

By using various causal explanations,
Parables, and other kinds of expression,
These buddhas use skillful means
To teach appropriately.

Now, I am like them.
For the peace and comfort of living beings
I use various gateways to the Dharma
To proclaim the Buddha way.

Through the power of wisdom,
Knowing the nature and desires of living beings,
I teach them the Dharma using skillful means,
Bringing them great joy.

Shariputra,
You should understand:

With the eyes of a buddha
I see beings in the six realms

Reduced to extreme poverty,
Without merit or wisdom,
On the dangerous road
Of birth and death.

In continuous,
Unending suffering,
They are firmly rooted in the five desires
Like an ox chasing its own tail.

Blinded by greed and desire,
They are blind and can see nothing.
Seeking neither the Buddha
With his great power

Nor the Dharma,
Which can bring an end to suffering.
With deeply entrenched wrong views,
They try to use suffering to get rid of suffering.

For the sake of these living beings
I have great compassion.

When I first sat in the place of the Way,
Looking at that tree
And walking around it,
For three weeks I had thoughts such as this:

"The wisdom I have gained
Is fine, wonderful, and supreme.
But living beings with dull faculties
Are attached to pleasures
And blinded by ignorance.

"Being like this,
How can they be saved?"

Then the Brahma kings,
Indra, the king of gods,
The four kings of heaven who protect the world,
The god Great Freedom,

And all the other heavenly beings as well,
And all of their hundreds of billions of followers,
Bowing with their palms together reverently,
Begged me to turn the Dharma wheel.

Then I thought to myself:
"If I merely praise the Buddha-Vehicle,
Beings sunk in suffering
Will not be able to believe this Dharma.

"And by rejecting the Dharma through unbelief
They will fall into the three evil paths.
It would be better not to teach the Dharma
And quickly enter nirvana."

But when I thought about past buddhas,
And the power of the skillful means used by them,
I knew that the Way I have now gained
Must also be taught as three vehicles.

When I was thinking this,
All the buddhas in all directions appeared
And cheered me up with the sacred chant,
"Well done, Shakyamuni,"

And they said: "First among leaders and teachers,
Having attained the unexcelled Dharma,
You follow the example of all the buddhas
In using the power of skillful means.

"All of us as well,
Having gained this most wonderful, supreme Dharma,
For the sake of the many kinds of beings,
Make distinctions and teach the three vehicles.

"Those of little wisdom want lesser teachings,
Unable to believe that they could become buddhas.
For this reason we use skillful means,
Making distinctions and teaching about various results.

"Though we also proclaim the three vehicles,
This is only for the purpose of teaching bodhisattvas."

You should understand, Shariputra,
That when I heard the roar of the holy lions,
With their deep, pure, and wonderful voices,
I rejoiced, saying, "Hail to the buddhas."

And then I thought:
"Having come into this impure and evil world,
I too must act, as these buddhas have taught."
Having had these thoughts, I went at once to Varanasi.

Since the tranquilly extinct character of all things
Cannot be put into words,
I used the power of skillful means,
To teach the five ascetics.

This is called "turning the Dharma wheel."
Then I made distinctions
Using such words as "nirvana,"
As well as "arhat," "dharma," and "sangha."

From eons and eons ago
I have praised and taught the doctrine of nirvana—
"The miseries of birth and death are forever ended!"
This is how I usually taught.

Shariputra, you should know
I see children of the Buddha,
Bent on seeking the Buddha way—
Uncountable tens of millions of billions of them.

All with reverent hearts and minds,
Come to the Buddha,
Having already heard from past buddhas
The Dharma preached through skillful means.

Then I thought:
"The reason a tathagata emerges
Is to teach Buddha-wisdom.
This is the right time for it!"

Shariputra, you should understand
Those who are dull minded and have little wisdom,
Who cling proudly and arrogantly to appearances,
Cannot believe this Dharma.

But now, with joy and without fear,
In the midst of the bodhisattvas,
Frankly putting aside skillful means,
I teach only the unexcelled way.

When bodhisattvas hear this Dharma,
Their net of doubt will be cleared away.
The twelve hundred arhats
Will all become buddhas, every one of them.

In the same way that other buddhas,
Past, present, and future, preach the Dharma,
So too I will now teach the Dharma
That does not discriminate.

Buddhas rarely appear in the world.
They are far apart and difficult to meet.

And even when they do appear in the world,
Teaching this Dharma is difficult.

Throughout countless eons,
Hearing this Dharma is very unusual.
So those able to hear this Dharma
Are also very rare.

It is like the udumbara flower,
Which is cherished and enjoyed by all
But seldom seen by heavenly or human beings.
It appears only rarely after long intervals.

Anyone hearing the Dharma with joy and praise
Who speaks even a single word of it
Has already made an offering to
All the buddhas of the past, present, and future.

But such a person is very unusual,
Rarer than the udumbara flower.

Have no doubt,
Being king of the teachings,
I speak to the whole great assembly.
Using only the one-vehicle way.

I teach and transform bodhisattvas
And have no shravakas as disciples.

All of you should know, Shariputra,
Shravakas and bodhisattvas alike,
That this wonderful Dharma
Is the hidden core of all the buddhas.

In the evil world of the five pollutions
Only attachment to desires is delighted in.

This kind of being
Will never seek the Buddha way.

When the wicked in ages to come
Hear the one vehicle taught by the Buddha,
They will be confused and neither believe nor accept it.
Rejecting the Dharma, they will fall into evil ways.

There will also be those
Who are modest
And purehearted,
Devoted to seeking the Buddha way.

For all of these
The one-vehicle way should be praised everywhere.

It should be understood, Shariputra,
That the Dharma of the buddhas is like this.
With trillions of skillful means, in accord with what is good
They teach the Dharma.

Those who have not practiced and studied it
Cannot fully understand this.
But all of you,
Knowing that the buddhas,

The teachers of the worlds,
Use skillful means
According to what is appropriate,
Should have no more doubt.

Your hearts should be filled with great joy,
For you know that you too will become buddhas.

3. A Parable

AT THAT TIME Shariputra, ecstatic with joy, stood up, put his palms together, reverently looked up at the face of the Honorable One and said to him: "Hearing this sound of the Dharma from the World-Honored One, I am filled with ecstasy, something I have never experienced before. Why? When we heard such a Dharma from the Buddha before, we saw that bodhisattvas were assured of becoming buddhas, but not that we ourselves were. And we were very distressed at never being able to have a tathagata's immeasurable insight.

"World-Honored One, whenever I was alone under the trees in a mountain forest, whether sitting or walking, I was occupied with this thought: 'We have all equally entered Dharma-nature. Why does the Tathagata offer us salvation only by the Dharma of a small vehicle?' This is our own fault, not the fault of the World-Honored One. Why? Because had we waited to hear you teach how to attain supreme awakening, we would certainly have been saved by the Great Vehicle. But, not understanding your way of preaching by skillful means according to what is appropriate, when we first heard the Buddha-dharma we only passively believed and accepted it, pondered it, and were informed by it.

"World-Honored One, ever since then I have spent whole days and nights blaming myself. But now, hearing from the Buddha the unprecedented Dharma that I have never heard before, all my doubts and regrets are over. I am mentally and physically at ease, and happily at peace. Today, having received my share of Buddha-dharma, I realize that I really am a child of the Buddha, born from the Buddha's mouth and transformed by the Dharma."

At that time, wanting to say what he meant once again, Shariputra spoke in verse:

> Hearing the voice of this Dharma,
> I have something I never had before.
> My heart is full of joy
> And the whole net of doubt is gone.
>
> Having received the Buddha's teaching from long ago,
> I have never been denied the Great Vehicle.
> The voice of the Buddha is only rarely heard,
> But it can rid living beings of suffering.
>
> Having already freed myself of fault,
> Hearing this, I am also free from anxiety.
> Whether in a mountain valley
> Or under the trees in a forest,
>
> Whether sitting or walking around,
> I always thought about this matter
> And blamed myself completely, thinking:
> "Why have I cheated myself so?
>
> "We too are children of the Buddha
> And have entered the same flawless Dharma,
> Yet in the future will not be able to
> Preach the unexcelled way.
>
> "We will never receive
> The golden body with thirty-two characteristics,[6]
> The ten powers, or various kinds of liberation,
> Even though we are all alike in the one Dharma.
>
> "We have completely missed
> Such blessings as
> The eighty different wonderful, attractive features
> And the eighteen unique qualities."

When I was walking around alone
I saw the Buddha in the great assembly,
His fame reaching in all directions,
Everywhere bringing abundant benefits to living beings.

I thought I had been deprived of this benefit,
That I had been deceived.

All day and all night
I pondered over these things,
And wanted to ask the World-Honored One
Whether I had lost my opportunity or not.

I always saw the World-Honored One
Praising the bodhisattvas.
Therefore I thought about these things
Day and night.

Now I hear the voice of the Buddha teaching the Dharma,
The difficult to conceive and flawless Dharma,
In accord with what is appropriate,
Enabling the living to reach the place of the Way.

Once I was attached to non-Buddhist views,
And became a teacher of brahmans.
But the World-Honored One, understanding me,
Uprooted my wrong views and taught me nirvana.

Completely freed from these wrong views
And gaining proof of the emptiness of things,
I told myself that I had reached extinction.
Finally, I now realize that it was not real extinction.

If the time comes
When I become a buddha,
And possess all of
The thirty-two characteristics,

If I am revered by human and heavenly beings
And by satyrs, dragon-gods, and others,
Then will I be able to say,
"Finally I am completely extinct, with nothing remaining."

In the midst of the great assembly
The Buddha proclaimed that I will become a buddha.
Hearing such a voice of the Dharma,
All my doubts and regrets were completely removed.

When I first heard the Buddha preach this
I was frightened and perplexed,
Thinking it might be the devil pretending to be the Buddha,
Which distressed and confused me.

But when the Buddha spoke so eloquently
With various explanations and parables,
My heart was as peaceful as the sea.
Listening, my net of doubts was removed.

The Buddha teaches that in past ages
Innumerable, now extinct buddhas,
Dwelling at peace in skillful means,
Taught the Dharma.

Present and future buddhas,
Countless in number,
Also with skillful means,
Preach this same Dharma.

So too the present World-Honored One,
After his birth and departure from home,
After entering the Way and turning the Dharma wheel,
Has taught with skillful means.

The World-Honored One teaches the true way;
The Evil One has no such truth.

Thus I know for certain
This is not the devil pretending to be the Buddha.

Yet because I had fallen into a net of doubts,
I imagined it to be the doing of the devil.
But now, hearing the gentle, very fine, and wonderful
Voice of the Buddha fluently explaining the pure Dharma,

My heart is filled with joy,
My doubts and regrets
Are forever ended.
I am dwelling at peace in real wisdom.

I am confident of becoming a buddha,
Respected by human and heavenly beings,
Turning the unexcelled Dharma wheel,
Teaching and transforming many bodhisattvas.

Then the Buddha said to Shariputra: "Now in this great assembly of human and heavenly beings, mendicants, brahmans, and others, I say this: In the past, in the presence of two trillion buddhas, for the sake of the unexcelled way, I always taught and transformed you. And through-out long days and nights you have followed me and accepted my teach-ing. Since I used skillful means to guide you, you have been born into my Dharma.

"Shariputra, in the past I led you to aspire and vow to follow the Bud-dha way. But now you have entirely forgotten this, and therefore sup-pose that you have already attained extinction. Now, wanting you to recollect the way that you originally vowed to follow, for all the shravakas I teach this Great Vehicle sutra called the Lotus Flower of the Wonderful Dharma, by which bodhisattvas are taught and which bud-dhas watch over and keep in mind.

"Shariputra, in a future life, after innumerable, unlimited, and incon-ceivable eons, when you have served some ten million billion buddhas, maintained the true Dharma, and perfected the way of bodhisattva practice, you will be able to become a buddha whose name will be Flower Light Tathagata, one worthy of offerings, truly awakened, fully clear in conduct, well gone, understanding the world, unexcelled leader, trainer of men, teacher of heavenly beings and people, buddha, world-honored one.

"Your land will be called Free of Dirt. It will be level and smooth, pure and beautifully decorated, peaceful and prosperous. Both human and heavenly beings will flourish there. It will have lapis lazuli for its earth, with eight intersecting roads with golden cords marking their boundaries. Beside each road will be a row of trees of the seven precious materials, which will always be filled with flowers and fruit. Using the three vehicles, Flower Light Tathagata will teach and transform living beings.

"Shariputra, when that buddha appears, though it will not be in an evil age, because of his original vow he will teach the three-vehicle Dharma. His eon will be named Adorned with Great Treasures. Why will it be named this? Because in that land bodhisattvas will be considered great treasures. Those bodhisattvas will be countless, unlimited, inconceivable in number, beyond computation or comparison by parable or simile, such as none can comprehend who does not have a buddha's wisdom. Wherever these bodhisattvas walk, treasured flowers will receive their feet.

"These bodhisattvas will not have just begun to aspire to awakening, for all of them will have planted roots of virtue for a long time. Under innumerable hundreds of thousands of billions of buddhas they will have observed noble practices in purity, always being praised by buddhas. Constantly cultivating Buddha-wisdom, acquiring great divine faculties, knowing well the ways of all the teachings, they will be upright and genuine in character, and firm in will and thought. Such bodhisattvas as these will fill that land.

"Shariputra, the lifetime of Flower Light Buddha will be twelve small eons, not counting the time during which he is a prince who has not yet become a buddha. And the lifetime of the people of his land will be eight small eons. After the twelve small eons, Flower Light Tathagata will assure the Bodhisattva Full of Firmness of his future supreme awakening, and will say to all the monks: 'This Full of Firmness Bodhisattva will become the next buddha. A tathagata, arhat, full buddha, his name will be Flowery Feet Calmly Walking. His buddha-land will be like mine.'

"Shariputra, after the extinction of this Flower Light Buddha, the true Dharma will last for thirty-two small eons and then the merely formal Dharma will also last for thirty-two small eons."

Then the World-Honored One, wanting to restate this teaching, spoke in verse:

> Shariputra, in a future life
> You will become a buddha
> Honored for universal wisdom,
> With the name Flower Light.
>
> You will liberate innumerable living beings,
> Make offerings to innumerable buddhas,
> Master bodhisattva practice, the ten powers, and other virtues
> And attain the unexcelled way.
>
> After countless eons have passed
> You will have an eon named Adorned with Great Treasures,
> And your world, named Free of Dirt,
> Will be pure and flawless.
>
> It will have lapis lazuli for its ground,
> Roads marked off by golden cords,
> And trees of the seven precious materials
> Always bearing flowers and fruit.
>
> All the bodhisattvas of that land
> Will always be firm in mind and will,
> Having mastered
> Divine faculties and transcendental practices.
>
> Under innumerable buddhas
> They will learn well the bodhisattva way.
> Such great leaders as these
> Will be transformed by Flower Light Buddha.
>
> When that buddha is still a prince,
> He will abandon his realm, give up worldly glory,

And in his final incarnation
Leave home and attain the Buddha way.

Flower Light Buddha will remain in the world
For a lifetime of twelve small eons,
And the many people of his land
Will remain for eight small eons.

After that buddha's extinction
The true Dharma will remain in the world
For thirty-two small eons,
Saving living beings everywhere.

When the true Dharma
Has passed,
The merely formal Dharma
Will last for thirty-two small eons.

The Buddha's remains
Will be widely dispersed,
With gods and people everywhere
Making offerings to them.

These kinds of things will be
The actions of Flower Light Buddha.

That most holy and honored of people,
Most excellent and incomparable,
Is really you yourself.
You should rejoice and be glad.

When all of the four groups, namely monks, nuns, laymen and lay-women, and the gods, dragons, satyrs, centaurs, asuras, griffins, chimeras, pythons, and others—the entire great assembly—saw that Shariputra had received his assurance of supreme awakening from the Buddha, their hearts overflowed with joy and danced in ecstasy. Each took off the outer robes they were wearing and presented them as offerings to the

Buddha. Indra Devendra and Brahma, the king of heaven, as well as others, with countless children of heaven, also made offerings to the Buddha with their wonderful heavenly robes, mandarava and great mandarava flowers from heaven, and so on. The heavenly robes they had scattered remained in the sky, whirling around and around by themselves. With hundreds of billions of kinds of heavenly musical instruments, these heavenly beings made music together in the sky. And, raining down numerous flowers from heaven, they spoke these words: "In the past at Varanasi the Buddha first turned the Dharma wheel, and now he rolls the wheel again—the unexcelled, greatest Dharma wheel!"

Then all the children of heaven, to say what they meant once again, spoke in verse:

> In the past,
> At Varanasi,
> You turned the Dharma wheel
> Of the four truths.

> Making distinctions,
> You taught that all things,
> Being made of the five constituent aggregates,
> Arise and become extinct.

> Now again you turn the most wonderful,
> Unexcelled, great wheel of the Dharma,
> The Dharma that is extremely profound
> And that few are able to believe.

> From a long time ago,
> We have often heard the World-Honored One teach,
> But never before have we heard such a profound,
> Wonderful, and supreme Dharma.

> Since the World-Honored One teaches this Dharma,
> We all respond with joy.
> Shariputra, the great sage,
> Has now received the eminent assurance.

We also, in a similar way,
Certainly will be able to become buddhas,
In all the worlds
Most honored and unsurpassed.

The Buddha way
Is difficult to understand or discuss
But is taught by skillful means,
In accord with what is appropriate.

May all our meritorious deeds
In this life or previous ones,
And the blessings from seeing the Buddha,
All be devoted to the Buddha way.

Then Shariputra said to the Buddha: "World-Honored One, I now have no more doubts or regrets. I personally have received assurance of supreme awakening from the Buddha. But these twelve hundred who are mentally free, while they were at the learning stage in the past, were always taught by the Buddha, who said: 'My Dharma can free you from birth, old age, disease, and death and enable you finally to attain nirvana.' These people, some still in training and some no longer in training, being free from views of self and about 'existence' or 'nonexistence,' thought they had attained nirvana. But now, hearing something they have never heard before from the World-Honored One, they have fallen into doubt.

"Thus, World-Honored One, I beg you to give causal explanations to the four groups so that they may be free from doubt and regret."

Then the Buddha said to Shariputra: "Did I not tell you before that when the buddhas, the world-honored ones, by using causal explanations, parables, and other kinds of expression, teach the Dharma by skillful means, it is all for the purpose of supreme awakening? All these teachings are for the purpose of transforming people into bodhisattvas. But, Shariputra, let me once again make this meaning still more clear through a parable, for intelligent people can understand through parables.

"Shariputra, suppose in a village or city in a certain kingdom there was a great elder. He had many fields, houses, and servants. His house was large and spacious but had only one gateway. Many people lived in the house, one hundred, two hundred, or even five hundred in all. Its halls and rooms were old and decaying, its walls crumbling, its pillars rotting at the base, its beams and rafters falling down and dangerous.

"All over the house, at the same moment, fire suddenly broke out, engulfing the house in flames. The children of the elder, say ten, twenty, or even thirty, were in this house. The elder, seeing this great fire spring up on every side, was very alarmed and thought: 'Though I can get out safely through the flaming gateway, my children are in the burning house enjoying themselves engrossed in play, without awareness, knowledge, alarm, or fear. Fire is closing in on them. Pain and suffering threaten, but they do not care or become frightened, and have no thought of trying to escape.'

"Shariputra, this elder said to himself: 'My body and arms are strong. I can wrap the children in some robes and put them on a palette or bench and carry them out of the house.' But then he thought again: 'This house has only one gateway, and it is narrow and small. My children are young. Knowing nothing as yet of the danger, they are absorbed in their play. Probably they will be burned up in the fire. I must tell them why I am alarmed, and warn them that the house is burning and that they must get out quickly or be burned up in the fire.' In accord with this line of thought, he called to his children: 'Get out quickly, all of you!'

"Although the father was sympathetic and tried to persuade them with kind words, the children, absorbed in their play, were unwilling to believe him and were neither alarmed nor frightened. They didn't even think about trying to escape. What's more, they did not understand what he meant by the fire, or the house, or losing their lives. They only kept running around playing, barely glancing at their father.

"Then the elder thought: 'This house is already going up in a great blaze. If my children and I do not get out at once, we will certainly be burned alive. Now I have to find some skillful means to get my children to escape from this disaster.'

"Knowing what his children always liked, and all the various rare and attractive playthings and curiosities that would please them, the father said to them: 'The things you like to play with are rare and hard to find. If you do not get them when you can, you will be sorry later. A variety of goat carriages, deer carriages, and ox carriages are now outside the gate for you to play with. You must get out of this burning house quickly, and I will give you whatever ones you want.'

"When they heard about the rare and attractive playthings described by their father, which were just what they wanted, all of the children, eagerly pushing and racing with each other, came scrambling out of the burning house.

"Then the elder, seeing that his children had safely escaped and were all sitting in the open square and no longer in danger, was very relieved and ecstatic with joy. Then each of the children said to their father: 'Those playthings you promised us, the goat carriages, deer carriages, and ox carriages, please give them to us now!'

"Shariputra, then the elder gave each of his children equally a great carriage. They were tall and spacious, and decorated with many jewels. They had railings around them, with bells hanging on all four sides. Each was covered with a canopy, which was also splendidly decorated with various rare and precious jewels. Around each was a string of precious stones and garlands of flowers. Inside were beautiful mats and rose-colored pillows. Pulling each of them was a handsome, very powerful white ox with a pure hide, capable of walking with a smooth gait and fast as the speed of the wind. Each also had many servants and followers to guard and take care of them.[7]

"Why was this? Because this great elder's wealth was so inexhaustible, his many storehouses so full of treasures, he thought: 'There is no limit to my wealth. I should not give inferior carriages to my children. They are all my children and I cherish them equally. I have countless numbers of these large carriages with the seven precious materials. I should give one to each of the children without discrimination. I have so many large carriages I could give one to everyone in the land without running out. Surely I can give them to my own children.'

"Then the children rode on their great carriages, having received something they had never had before and never expected to have.

"Shariputra, what do you think about this? Is that elder, in giving equally the rare treasure of great carriages to his children, guilty of falsehood or not?"

Shariputra said: "No, World-Honored One. That elder only made it possible for his children to escape the disaster of the fire and preserve their lives. He committed no falsehood. Why do I say this? By saving their lives he has already given them a kind of plaything. How much more so when by skillful means he saved them from that burning house. World-Honored One, even if that elder had not given them one of the smallest of carriages, he would not be guilty of falsehood. Why? Because the elder, from the beginning, had intended to use some skillful means to enable his children to escape. That is the reason why he is not guilty of falsehood. How much less so, when knowing his own immeasurable wealth and wanting to benefit his children abundantly, he gave them equally great carriages!"

The Buddha said to Shariputra: "Good, good. It is just as you say, Shariputra. The Tathagata is also like this, for he is a father to the whole world. He has long ago completely gotten rid of all fear, distress, anxiety, ignorance, and blindness; has attained immeasurable insight, powers, and freedom from fear; and has gained great spiritual power and wisdom. He has fully mastered skillful means and the practice of wisdom. His great mercy and compassion never stop. He always seeks the good, whatever will enrich all beings.

"He was born into this threefold world, an old decaying burning house, in order to save living beings from the fires of birth, old age, disease, death, anxiety, sorrow, suffering, agony, folly, blindness, and the three poisons, and to teach and transform them, enabling them to reach supreme awakening.

"He sees how living beings are scorched by the fires of birth, old age, disease and death, anxiety, sorrow, suffering, and agony. Moreover, because of the five desires and the desire for wealth, they undergo all kinds of suffering. Because of attachment to desire and striving, they endure much suffering in this life and later will suffer in a purgatory, or as animals or hungry spirits. Even if they are born in a heaven, or among people, they will experience many kinds of suffering, such as the suffering of poverty and hardship, the suffering of separation from what they cherish, or the suffering from encountering what they hate.

"Absorbed in these things, living beings rejoice and amuse themselves, without knowing or seeing or being alarmed or frightened. And never being dissatisfied, they never try to liberate themselves. In the burning house of this threefold world they run about here and there, and, though they encounter great suffering, they are not disturbed by it.

"Shariputra, having seen this, the Buddha thought: 'I am the father of all living beings and should rescue them from suffering and give them the joy of immeasurable, unlimited Buddha-wisdom, so that they can find enjoyment in it.'

"Shariputra, the Tathagata also thought: 'If I used only divine powers and wisdom, setting aside skillful means, and for the sake of living beings praised only the insight, powers, and courage of the Tathagata, living beings would not be saved. Why? As long as all these beings have not escaped birth, old age, disease, death, anxiety, sorrow, suffering, and agony, and are being consumed in the burning house of the threefold world, how can they understand the wisdom of the Buddha?'

"Shariputra, even though the elder had strength in his body and arms, he did not use it, but only through carefully worked-out skillful means saved his children from the danger of the burning house and then gave each of them great carriages with precious materials. So too the Tathagata, though he has power and is free from fear, does not use these, but only by wisdom and skillful means rescues and liberates living beings from the burning house of this threefold world, teaching the three vehicles to them, the shravaka, pratyekabuddha, and buddha vehicles.

"He says to them: 'None of you should be happy dwelling in the burning house of the threefold world. Do not crave its crude forms, sounds, scents, tastes, and sensations. If you become attached to them and learn to cherish them, you will be burned up by them. You need to get out of this threefold world quickly so that you can have the three vehicles, the shravaka, pratyekabuddha, and the buddha vehicles. I now make this promise to you, and it will never turn out to be false. Just apply yourselves and make the effort!'

"The Tathagata uses this skillful means to bring people to act. And then he says to them: 'You should know that the teachings of these three vehicles are praised by sages. With them, you will be free from attachments and bondage, and will not need to rely on or seek anything else. Riding in these three vehicles you will gain flawless roots, powers, awareness, ways, meditations, liberation, concentration, and so forth. And then, enjoying yourselves, you will be able to delight in infinite peace and comfort.'

"Shariputra, if there are living beings who are wise by nature and who, following the Buddha, the World-Honored One, hear the Dharma, receive it in faith, and make a great effort, wanting to escape quickly from the threefold world and seek their own nirvana, they will be called those who take the shravaka vehicle. They are like the children who came out of the burning house to get a goat carriage.

"If there are living beings who, following the Buddha, the World-Honored One, hear the Dharma and receive it in faith, and who, seeking natural intelligence and taking solitary delight in tranquility and goodness, make a great effort to deeply understand the causes and conditions of all things, they will be called those who take the pratyeka-buddha vehicle. They are like the children who came out of the burning house to get a deer carriage.

"If there are living beings who, following the Buddha, the World-Honored One, hear the Dharma and receive it in faith, who apply themselves and make a great effort, seeking comprehensive wisdom, buddha wisdom, natural wisdom, the wisdom that needs no teacher, and seeking as well a tathagata's insight, powers, and freedom from fear, and who pity and comfort innumerable living beings, enrich human and heavenly beings, and save them all, they will be called those who take the Great Vehicle. Because bodhisattvas seek this vehicle, they are called great ones. They are like the children who came out of the burning house to get an ox carriage.

"Shariputra, the elder, seeing his children safely out of the burning house and no longer threatened, thought about his immeasurable wealth and gave each of his children a great carriage. The Tathagata does the same. He is the father of all living beings. He sees innumerable thousands of millions of beings escape from the suffering of the threefold world, from the fearful and perilous path, through the gateway of teachings of the Buddha, and thus gain the joys of nirvana. Then the Tathagata thinks: 'I have Dharma storehouses of buddhas, with immeasurable, unlimited wisdom, power, and freedom from fear. All these living beings are my children. I will give the Great Vehicle to them equally, so that no one will reach extinction individually, but all gain the same extinction as the Tathagata.'

"All the living beings who escape the threefold world are given the enjoyments of buddhas—meditation, liberation, and so forth. All are of one character and one type, praised by sages and capable of producing pure, wonderful, supreme happiness.

"Shariputra, the elder at first attracted his children with the three carriages and afterward gave them just one great carriage decorated with jewels, which was the safest and most comfortable carriage. Yet the man is not guilty of lying. The Tathagata does the same. There is no falsehood in teaching three vehicles first, to attract living beings, and afterward using just the Great Vehicle to save them. Why? Because the Tathagata has Dharma storehouses of immeasurable wisdom, power, and freedom from fear. He can give all living beings the Great Vehicle Dharma. But not all are able to receive it. For this reason, Shariputra, you should understand that the buddhas use the power of skillful means, thus making distinctions within the One Buddha–Vehicle and teaching the three."

The Buddha, wanting to restate this teaching, spoke in verse:

Suppose there was an elder
Who owned a large house,
And this house was very old,
Decaying and falling apart.

Its great rooms were in dangerous condition,
Its pillars broken and rotting at the base,
Its beams and rafters leaning and askew,
Its foundation and steps in a state of collapse.

The walls and partitions
Were cracked and broken,
Their plaster crumbling away.
The thatch was in disorder and falling off.

The ends of the eaves had slipped away,
The surrounding fences
Were crooked and falling down,
And piles of rubbish were all over the place.

Five hundred people
Were staying in that house,
With kites, owls, hawks, and eagles,
Crows, magpies, pigeons, doves,

Lizards, snakes, vipers, scorpions, centipedes and millipedes,
Newts and ground beetles, weasels, ferrets, rats, and mice.
All sorts of evil creatures
Scurried about everywhere.

There were places stinking with excrement,
Overflowing with filth,
Where dung beetles and worms
Came together.

Foxes, wolves, and jackals
Bit and trampled each other
To gnaw on carcasses,
Scattering the bones and flesh.

Because of this,
Packs of dogs,
Gaunt with hunger
And shrinking from fear,

Looking everywhere for food,
Came running to snatch and grab,
Fighting and scuffling,
Snarling and barking.

That house was frightening, extraordinary.
All over the place were goblins, ogres, and satyrs,
Evil spirits who devour human flesh,
And all sorts of poisonous insects.

Evil birds and beasts
Bore offspring,
Hatched and nursed them,
Each hiding and protecting its own.

Satyrs tried to outdo one another in seizing and eating them,
And when they had eaten their fill,

Their evil hearts became more inflamed,
And the sound of their shrieking was extremely dreadful.

Kumbhanda demons
Crouched on clumps of earth,
Sometimes springing up
A foot or two from the ground.

Wandering around here and there,
They amused themselves according to whim,
Sometimes seizing a dog by its feet
And beating it until it lost its bark,

Sometimes putting a foot
On a dog's neck,
Frightening it
For their own amusement.

Large, tall demons, naked, black, and emaciated,
Who always lived in that house
Would emit great and dreadful sounds,
Bellowing demands for food.

There were demons
With necks as thin as a needle,
And demons with heads like an ox's.
Some ate human flesh; some devoured dogs.

Their hair a mess,
Cruel and ferocious,
And driven by hunger and thirst,
They raced about shrieking and howling.

Satyrs and hungry spirits,
Evil birds and beasts
Hungrily hurried in all directions,
Peering through the windows and lattices.

Such were the perils of this house,
Terrible and horrible beyond measure.

This decaying old house belonged to a man
Who had gone out just a little earlier.
All of a sudden the house caught on fire.
And all at once the whole house was engulfed in flames.

Ridgepoles, beams, rafters, pillars
Exploded with a cracking roar
And broke, split, and fell
As walls and partitions collapsed.

The demons and spirits bellowed and wailed.
The hawks, vultures and other birds,
And kumbhanda demons and others
Were filled with fear and panic.

Unable to escape,
Evil beasts
And poisonous insects
Hid in their holes.

Pishacha demons, who also lived in the house,
Because they were weak in merit and virtue,
Were driven by the fire to cruelly attack one another,
Eating and drinking others' flesh and blood.

Jackals and similar animals
Were already dead,
And the bigger evil beasts
Fought to eat them.

Foul smoke billowed up
Filling the air everywhere.

Scorched by the fire,
Centipedes and millipedes and poisonous snakes of every kind
Scurried from their holes.
Where kumbhanda demons grabbed and ate them.

And hungry spirits,
Fire raging around their heads,
Tormented by hunger, thirst, and heat,
Rushed about confused and terrified.

Such was the state of that house,
Dreadful in the extreme,
With horrid calamities and a great fire,
With many disasters, not just a few.

At this time
The owner of the house
Was standing outside the gate,
When he heard someone say:

"A little while ago your children
Went into the house to play.
They are young and ignorant,
And engrossed in play."

Hearing this the elder was alarmed
And rushed into the burning house,
Intending to rescue the children
And keep them from being burned in the fire.

So he told his children of the many dreadful troubles,
The evil spirits and poisonous creatures,
The fire spreading all around,
One kind of suffering following another without end.

The poisonous snakes, lizards, and vipers,
The many kinds of satyrs,

Kumbhanda demons,
Jackals, foxes and dogs,

Hawks, vultures, kites, owls,
And all sorts of ground beetles and such,
Driven by hunger and thirst,
Were truly to be feared.

"This," he said,
"Is a dreadful place,
How much more so
With this blazing fire!"

But the children didn't understand.
Though they heard their father's warnings,
They remained absorbed in their games
And did not stop playing.

Then the elder
Thought to himself:
"My children are acting this way,
Adding to my anxiety and anguish.

"Right now there is not a single thing in this house to enjoy.
Yet my children, bewitched by their games,
Pay no attention to my instructions
And will be destroyed by the fire!"

Then he considered
Devising some skillful means,
And said to his children:
"I have many kinds of rare, attractive playthings—

"Wonderful, treasured carriages.
Goat carriages and deer carriages, and carriages with big oxen
Are now outside the gate.
Go out and see them!

"I have made these carriages
Especially for you.
You can play with any of them
In whatever way you like."

When the children heard him tell about the carriages,
They immediately raced each other,
Dashing out of the house to reach the open yard,
Away from the painful troubles.

Seeing his children escape from the burning house
And alive in the square,
The elder sat on a lion seat
And congratulated himself, saying:

"Now I am happy.
These children were difficult to raise.
Ignorant, young, and foolish,
They went into this dangerous house.

"Though it was full of poisonous creatures and fearful goblins,
With the raging flames of a terrible fire
Breaking out all around them,
These children stuck to their play.

"Now I have rescued them
And enabled them to escape from harm.
This is the reason, good people,
That I am now happy."

Then the children, seeing their father sitting relaxed,
Came to him and said:
"Please give us the three kinds of treasured carriages
You promised earlier by telling us:

"'If you children come out,
I will give you three carriages

And you can choose whichever you like.'
Now is the time. Please give them to us."

The elder was very wealthy
And had storehouses full of gold, silver,
Lapis lazuli, seashell and agate,
And other kinds of precious things.

He had made great carriages,
Magnificently adorned and decorated,
With railings around them,
And bells hanging on all sides.

Twisted golden cords with nets of pearls
Were spread over the top of them,
And garlands of golden flowers
Were hanging here and there.

Many-colored decorations
Were wrapped around them.
They had cushions of
Soft silk and gauze.

Over them were spread
The best quality of fine felt,
Snow-white and pure,
Worth hundreds of billions.

Great white oxen,
Sleek, sturdy, and strong,
Of handsome build,
Were yoked to the treasured carriages.

Along with numerous servants
To guard and take care of them,
The rich man gave one of these wonderful carriages
To each of the children equally.

Then the children, ecstatic with joy,
Mounted the treasured carriages
And rode around in every direction,
Playing joyfully, freely and without hindrance.

I tell you, Shariputra,
I, too, am like this.
Most honored of all the sages,
I am the father of this world.

All living beings
Are my children,
But deeply attached to worldly pleasures,
They are without wisdom.

The threefold world is not safe,
Just as a burning house
Full of all kinds of suffering
Is much to be feared.

Always there is the suffering of
Birth, old age, disease, and death.
They are like flames
Raging ceaselessly.

The Tathagata is already free
From the burning house of the threefold world.
He lives in tranquil peace,
As in the safety of a forest or field.

Now, this threefold world
Is all my domain,
And the living beings in it
Are all my children.

But now this place
Is filled with all kinds of dreadful troubles,

From which I alone
Can save and protect them.

Yet, though I have taught and warned them,
They have not believed or accepted what I said,
For they have desires
To which they are greedily attached.

Therefore I use skillful means,
Telling them of the three vehicles,
Enabling all living beings
To understand the suffering of the threefold world.

And I reveal and preach
A way of escaping from that world.
If all these children
Will just make up their minds to do it,

They can acquire the three kinds of knowledge
And the six divine powers,
And become pratyekabuddhas
Or bodhisattvas who never backslide.

Shariputra,
It is for the sake of all beings,
That by means of this parable
I teach the One Buddha–Vehicle.

If all of you
Can accept and believe these words,
You will all be able to enter
The Buddha way.

This vehicle is wonderful,
Supremely pure.
In all the worlds
There is nothing greater.

Buddhas joyfully approve of it.
All living beings
Should praise it,
Worship it, and make offerings to it.

There are innumerable thousands of millions
Of powers, kinds of liberation,
Meditations and wisdoms,
And other features of the Buddha.

If my children have this vehicle
Night and day for many eons,
They will always be able
To find enjoyment in it.

And with bodhisattvas
As well as with all the shravakas
They will be able to ride in this treasured vehicle
Directly to a place of the Way.

For these reasons,
Even if you search in all directions,
You will find no other vehicles—
Except the skillful means of the Buddha.

I tell you, Shariputra,
You and the others
Are my children.
And I am your father.

For repeated ages you have burned
In the flames of many kinds of suffering.
Yet I will liberate all of you
And enable you to escape the threefold world.

Though I previously taught
That you would attain extinction,

That was only freedom from birth and death,
Not real extinction.

What you need to do now
Is just to acquire the wisdom of a buddha.

If there are any bodhisattvas
Here in this assembly,
Let them give full attention to hearing
The true Dharma of the Buddha.

The buddhas, world-honored ones,
Use skillful means,
And all living beings transformed by them
Are bodhisattvas.

If there are people of little wisdom,
Deeply attached to clinging and desire,
For their sake the Buddha
Teaches the truth of suffering.

Then all the living will be happy,
Having gained what they never had before.
The truth of suffering taught by the Buddha
Is real and does not change.

If there are living beings
Who do not understand the roots of suffering,
Who are deeply attached to causes of suffering,
And are unable to give them up, even for a moment,

For their sake,
The Buddha
Uses skillful means
To teach the Way.

The cause of all suffering
Is rooted in greed.
If greed is extinguished
There will be no place for suffering.

The elimination of all suffering
Is called the third truth.
For the sake of this truth of elimination,
You should practice the Way.

The escape from all bonds of suffering
Is called liberation.
How can one
Become liberated?

Merely leaving what is false
Is called liberation,
But this is not yet true liberation
For it is not liberation from everything.

So the Buddha says that this person
Has not yet achieved real extinction,
Because such people have not yet gained
The unexcelled way.

It is not my intent to lead them to extinction.
I am the king of the Dharma, free to teach the Dharma,
Appearing in the world to bring peace and comfort
To all the living.

Shariputra, I teach this sign of the Dharma
Because I want to enrich the world.
Do not recklessly proclaim it
Wherever you happen to be.

If you find any who, hearing it,
Respond with joy and receive it with gratitude,

You should know that they
Will never backslide.

If there are any who believe and accept the Dharma of this sutra,
They must have already seen buddhas in the past,
Respected and made offerings to them,
And heard this Dharma.

If there are any who are able to believe what you preach,
They must have seen me
And also have seen you
And these other monks as well as bodhisattvas.

This Dharma Flower Sutra
Is taught for the sake of profound wisdom.
If people of shallow understanding hear it,
They will become confused and fail to comprehend it.

There are things in this sutra beyond the powers of
All the shravakas and pratyekabuddhas.
Even you, Shariputra, could enter this sutra only through faith.
How much more so the other shravakas.

Only because they trust the Buddha's words
Can any of the shravakas
Follow this sutra—
Not because they have any wisdom of their own.

What's more, Shariputra,
Do not teach this sutra
To the arrogant or lazy,
Or to those attached to the idea of the self.

Do not teach it, either,
To common, shallow people.
Deeply attached to the five desires,
They cannot comprehend it when they hear it.

If anyone is without faith
And slanders this sutra,
They cut themselves off
From all seeds of becoming a buddha in this world.

Or if someone scowls
And harbors doubts,
Listen, and I will tell you
How they will suffer for their sins.

Whether the Buddha is in the world
Or after his extinction,
If anyone slanders
A sutra such as this,

Or, seeing others read, recite,
Copy, or uphold this sutra,
Scorns, hates, and envies them
Or bears grudges against them,

Listen, and I will tell you
How they will suffer for their sins.

After their lives
Have come to an end
They will enter the deepest purgatory,
Staying for a whole eon.

And at the eon's end
They will be born there again,
Repeating this cycle
For innumerable eons.

When they come out of that purgatory,
They will fall into the realm of animals
And become a lean and scruffy dog or jackal,

Dark and discolored with scabs and sores
And kicked around by people.

Moreover, hated and scorned by people,
And constantly suffering from hunger and thirst,
Their bones and flesh will wither
In lives of pain and torment.

And in death they will suffer beneath tiles and stones.
Because they have cut themselves off
From the seeds of becoming a buddha,
They will have to suffer for their sins.

If they become camels or are born as asses,
They will always carry burdens on their backs,
Be beaten with sticks, think only of water and grass,
And know nothing else.

For slandering this sutra.
They will have to suffer.

Some might become jackals
Who enter a village,
Their bodies covered with sores and scabs,
And with only one eye.

They will be struck and beaten
By all the boys
And suffer pain,
At times being beaten to death.

Having died in this way,
They will be reborn
In the bodies of large, long snakes,
As long as five hundred leagues.

Deaf and stupid and without feet,
They will slither about on their bellies,
And be stung and devoured
By all kinds of insects.

Suffering day and night,
With never any rest.
Such will be their suffering
For slandering this sutra.

If they become human beings,
Their faculties will be blunt and dull.
They will be short and ugly, bent and crippled,
Blind, deaf, and hunchbacked.

Whatever they say,
People will not believe them.
Their breath will be foul smelling.
They will be possessed by devils.

Poor and menial, they will be
Ordered around by others.
Often ill and emaciated,
They will have no one to turn to.

Though dependent on others,
No one will pay attention to them.
Even if they get something worth having,
They will soon forget or lose it.

If they practice medicine
And manage to cure someone,
Other diseases will soon make the person even worse
And probably die.

If then they themselves become ill,
No one will help or care for them.

Even if they take a good medicine,
Their condition will only get worse and worse.

If others turn against them,
They will be robbed and plundered.
Their sins will be such
That they will face many misfortunes.

This kind of sinner
Will never see the Buddha,
The king of all the sages,
Preaching the Dharma, teaching, and transforming.

This kind of sinner
Will always be born in difficult circumstances,
Mad, deaf, and confused in mind,
Never hearing the Dharma.

For countless eons,
Numerous as the sands of the Ganges,
They will be born deaf and dumb
With impaired faculties.

They will always live in a purgatory,
As though playing in a garden,
Or in some other evil state
As though it were their home.

Camels, asses, pigs, and dogs
Is what they will become.
Because they slandered this sutra,
This will be their suffering.

If they become human beings,
They will be deaf, blind, and dumb.
Poverty, need, and other defects
Will adorn them.

Blisters and scurvy,
Scabs, sores, and abscesses,
All such ills as these
Will be their garments.

Their bodies will always
Smell filthy and unclean.
Deeply attached to the idea of self,
Their anger and hatred will grow.

Aflame with lustful passions,
They will consort with birds and beasts.
Because they slandered this sutra,
This will be their suffering.

Shariputra,
If I described all the sins
Of those who slander this sutra,
In a whole eon I would not be able to finish.

For this reason
I tell you especially,
Do not teach this sutra
To people who have no wisdom.

But if there are any who are clever,
Understanding and wise,
Learned and of good memory,
Who seek the Buddha way,

To such people
You may teach it.

If there are people who already have seen
Hundreds of thousands of millions of buddhas,
Planted many roots of goodness,
And been firmly and deeply committed,

To such people
You may teach it.

If there are diligent people,
Always compassionate
And never sparing
Their bodies or lives,

To such people
You may teach it.

If there are reverent people
With clearly focused minds,
Who avoid all common foolishness
And live alone along mountain streams,

To such people
You may teach it.

What's more, Shariputra,
If you see anyone
Who has given up bad friends
And associates with good people,

To such people
You may teach it.

If you see children of the Buddha
Who observe the precepts strictly,
As though they were pure, bright jewels,
Seeking the Great Vehicle sutra,

To such people
You may teach it.

If anyone is free from anger,
Upright and gentle in character,

Always sympathetic toward everyone,
And reverent toward the buddhas,

To such people
You may teach it.

Furthermore, if in the great assembly
Children of the Buddha with pure hearts
Use causal explanations, parables, and other kinds of expression
To preach the Dharma freely, without hesitation,

To such people
You may teach it.

If there are monks who seek the Dharma in every direction
For the sake of comprehensive wisdom,
And put their palms together
To gratefully accept the Great Vehicle sutra,

And receive and embrace it joyously
While never accepting
A single verse
Of any other sutra,

To such people,
You may teach it.

As one wholeheartedly seeks
The Buddha's remains,
One may seek this sutra,

And having received and gratefully accepted it,
Have no intention of seeking other sutras,
And never pay attention
To books of non-Buddhist philosophies.

To such people
You may teach it.

I tell you, Shariputra,
If I were to describe all of the kinds
Of seekers after the Buddha way,
In a whole eon I would not be able to finish.

Such people
Can believe and understand.
For them you should teach
The Wonderful Dharma Flower Sutra.

4. Faith and Understanding[8]

AT THAT TIME four men living a life of wisdom, Subhuti, Maha Katyayana, Maha-Kashyapa, and Maha-Maudgalyayana, hearing the Dharma they had never heard before from the Buddha and the assurance by the World-Honored One of Shariputra's future supreme awakening, were astonished and ecstatic with joy from experiencing such an unprecedented thing. They immediately rose from their seats, arranged their robes, bared their right shoulders, and knelt on their right knees on the ground. Putting their palms together in complete devotion, they bowed in respect, gazed up at his honored face, and said to the Buddha:

"We leading monks, old and worn out, believed that we had already attained nirvana and could go no further. So we did not seek supreme awakening. The World-Honored One has been preaching the Dharma for a long time, and all the while we have been sitting in our places, weary in body and mindful only of emptiness, formlessness, and non-action. Neither the enjoyments nor the divine powers of the bodhisattva-dharma—purifying buddha-lands and saving living beings—appealed to us.

"Why was this? The World-Honored One had made it possible for us to rise above the threefold world and gain evidence of nirvana. Besides, we are so old and worn out that when we heard of supreme awakening, with which the Buddha teaches and transforms bodhisattvas, no thought of pursuing it was attractive to us. Now, hearing directly from the Buddha that shravakas are assured of attaining supreme awakening, we are very happy. We have gained something we never before experienced.

Unexpectedly and suddenly, we have now heard this rare Dharma. We see ourselves as extremely fortunate. Without even seeking it, we have acquired something great and good, an extremely rare treasure.

"World-Honored One, we would now like to use a parable to clarify what we mean. Suppose a still-young man left his father, ran away, and lived in some other land for a long time, for ten, twenty, or even fifty years. The older he became, the poorer and more needy he became. He wandered around in every direction looking for clothing and food until, finally, by chance, he was heading toward his homeland.

"Meanwhile, the father had searched for this son unsuccessfully, and now lived in another city. His household had become very wealthy, his goods and treasures incalculable: gold, silver, lapis lazuli, coral, amber, crystal, and other gems overflowed his storehouses. He also had many grooms and servants, clerks and attendants, and countless elephants, horses, carriages, oxen, and sheep. His revenues and investments spread to other lands. There also were many merchants and traveling traders around.

"At this time the poor son, wandering through village after village and passing through various lands and cities, at last reached the city where his father was living. Although his son had been away for more than fifty years, the father always thought about him. But he had never spoken of the matter to anyone, only pondering it to himself, his heart full of remorse and regret. He thought: 'Old and worn out, I have great wealth—gold, silver, and rare treasures overflow my storehouses—yet I have no son. Someday my end will come and my wealth will be scattered and lost, for there is no one to whom I can leave it.'

"This is why he always so earnestly thought of his son. 'If I could only get my son back and entrust my wealth to him,' he thought, 'how contented, how happy I would be, with no more anxiety!'

"Meanwhile, World-Honored One, the poor son, drifting from one job to another, accidentally arrived at his father's house. Standing by the gate, he saw his father from a distance, seated on a lion seat. His feet were on a jeweled footstool, and strings of pearls worth tens of millions adorned his body. He was being revered by surrounding brahmans, nobles, and ordinary people, while attendants and servants with white fly whisks stood by on both sides. Over him was a jeweled canopy from which streamers of flowers hung down. Perfume was sprinkled on the ground, and all kinds of celebrated flowers were scattered around. And valuable things were set in rows for his approval or rejection. With such trappings, he looked majestic and distinguished.

"The poor son, seeing his father with such great power, was seized with fear and regretted that he had come to this place. He secretly thought to himself: 'He must be a king or something like a king. This is no place for me to try to earn a living. I had better go to some poor town where I can be paid for my labor, and where food and clothing will be easier to get. If I stay here long, I may be captured and forced to work.' Having thoughts of this kind, he ran away quickly.

"Meanwhile the elderly gentleman on the lion seat recognized his son at first sight. Filled with joy, he thought: 'At last I have the one to whom my stores of wealth are to be entrusted. I've always been thinking of my son but had no way to see him. Now suddenly he has come by himself. My hope is completely fulfilled. Old and worn out, I yearn for an heir.'

"Then he sent messengers to run after the son and bring him back as quickly as possible. They ran after him and grabbed him. The poor son, surprised and afraid, loudly cried out in anger: 'I have done nothing against you. Why am I being seized?' The messengers held on to him even more firmly and forced him to go back with them.

"Then the poor son thought that, although he had done nothing wrong, he was being taken prisoner and surely would be put to death. All the more terrified and desperate, he fell down in a faint. The father, seeing this from a distance, told the messengers: 'There is no need for this man. Don't force him to come. Sprinkle some cold water on his face to wake him up, and say nothing more to him.'

"Why did he do this? The father knew that his son felt inept and humble, and that his own great position would be difficult for his son. He knew perfectly well that this was his son, but, using skillful means, he didn't tell anyone that this was so.

"The messengers told the son: 'We are releasing you now. You are free to go wherever you want.' So the poor son rejoiced, having obtained what he had not had before. He got up from the ground and went off to a poor village in search of food and clothing.

"Then the rich man, wanting to entice his son back, decided to use skillful means again. Secretly he sent two men of miserable and undignified appearance after him, saying: 'Go there and visit, and gently tell the poor man that there is a place for him to work where he will be given double the normal wage. If he agrees, bring him back here and put him to work. If he asks what kind of work you want him to do, tell him that we are hiring him to remove dung, and that you will work along with him.'

"Then the two messengers went in search of the poor man and, finding him, told to him what they had been told to say. The poor son asked for an advance on his wages, and joined them in removing the dung.

"The father, seeing the son, felt both sympathy and wonder. On another day, looking through a window, he saw his son at a distance, looking gaunt, lean, and filthy from the piles of dung, dirt, and filth. Taking off his necklaces, his soft clothing and ornaments, he put on coarse, torn, and dirty clothes, smeared his body with dirt, took a pan for dung in his right hand, and in a rough manner said to the workers: 'Get to work! Don't be so lazy!' Through such skillful means he could get near his son.

"Afterward he said to the son: 'Young man, now you should stay and work here, and not go anywhere else again. I will increase your wages. And you won't have to worry about needing bowls, utensils, rice, flour, salt, vinegar, and so on. There is even an old and worn-out servant you can use if you need him. Take it easy. I'm like a father to you. You don't need to worry any more. Why? Because I am old and advanced in years, but you are young and vigorous. All the time you have been working here, you have never been deceitful, lazy, angry, or grumbling. I have never seen you display the faults of other workers. From now on, you will be like my own son.' Then the rich man gave him a new name, as he would to a child.

"Then the poor son, though pleased with all of this, still thought of himself as a humble laborer. Thus for twenty years he continued to be employed at removing dung. After that, they gained confidence in each other, and the son felt he could come and go easily. Yet he continued to live in the same place as before.

"World-Honored One, then the old man became ill. Knowing that he would die soon, he said to the poor son: 'I now have abundant gold, silver, and rare treasures filling my storehouses to overflowing. I want you to have a detailed understanding of the quantities involved, and of what should be received and paid out. This is what I have in mind and want you to do. Why? Because from now on you and I will be no different. Be careful to see that there are no careless losses.'

"The poor son accepted these instructions and took stock of all the goods—gold, silver, and other valuables—and of the various store-houses, but never expected to receive even a meal for himself. He continued to live in the place where he had lived before and was unable to get rid of his sense of inferiority.

"After some time had passed, the father saw that his son was gradually becoming more confident and accomplished, and that he despised his former state of inferiority. Realizing that his own end was near, he ordered his son to arrange a meeting with his relatives, the king, the ministers, nobles, and ordinary citizens. When they had all assembled, he said to them: 'Gentlemen, I should tell you that this is my son, my natural-born son. In another city he left me and ran away, for over fifty years enduring loneliness and suffering. His original name was so-and-so and my name is so-and-so. At that time, when I was still living in my hometown, I worried about him and looked all over for him. It was here that I suddenly happened to meet him again. This is really my son, and I am really his father. Now all of my wealth belongs entirely to my son, and all my earlier disbursements and receipts are known by this son.'

"World-Honored One, when the poor son heard these words of his father, having gained something he had never had before, he was filled with joy. And he thought: 'Without any intention or effort on my part these treasures have now come to me by themselves.'

"World-Honored One, the very rich old man is the Tathagata, and we are all like the Buddha's children. The Tathagata has always taught that we are his children. Because of the three kinds of suffering, World-Honored One, in the midst of birth and death we have borne all kinds of passionate worries. Being confused and ignorant, we enjoyed attachment to lesser teachings. Today the World-Honored One has led us to ponder over and to rid ourselves of such teachings and all the dung of diverting discussions. In the past we were diligent, and made progress in this way until we reached nirvana, which is like a single day's pay. Having attained this nirvana, our hearts were filled with great joy. We were content. We said to ourselves, 'Due to our diligent perseverance in the Buddha-dharma, we have received many rewards.'

"However, the World-Honored One, knowing from past experience that we were attached to low desires and delighted in lesser teachings, let us go our own way and did not tell us: 'You will yet have the insight of a tathagata, your portion of the treasury.' Using the power of skillful means, the World-Honored One taught Tathagata-wisdom. But following the Buddha and attaining a single day's pay of nirvana seemed such a great gain to us that we never devoted ourselves to seeking the Great Vehicle.

"Also, since we revealed and preached Tathagata-wisdom for the sake of bodhisattvas, we never aspired to it ourselves. Why was this? The Buddha, knowing that we delighted in lesser teachings, used his power of skillful means to teach us according to what was appropriate for us. But still we did not see that we are really children of the Buddha. But now we know. We realize that the World-Honored One does not hold back the wisdom of the Buddha from anyone. Why do we say this? From ancient times we were really children of the Buddha, but only took pleasure in lesser teachings. If we had had a mind to take pleasure in great things, the Buddha would have taught the Great Vehicle Dharma for our sakes.

"Now, in this sutra, the Buddha teaches only the one vehicle. Although in the past he spoke disparagingly in the presence of bodhi-sattvas of the shravakas' liking for lesser teachings, in reality he was using the Great Vehicle to teach and transform us. Therefore we say that, though we had no hope or expectation of it, now the great treasure of the king of the Dharma has come to us by itself. Since it is something that children of the Buddha should acquire, we have all acquired it."

Then Maha-Kashyapa, wanting to say what he meant once again, spoke in verse:

Today we have heard
The Buddha's voice teaching.
We are ecstatic with joy,
Having obtained what we never had before.

The Buddha teaches that shravakas
Are able to become buddhas.
This collection of unexcelled treasures
Has become ours without our seeking it.

It is like a youth who,
Immature and ignorant,
Left his father and ran away to distant lands,
Wandering about from place to place for over fifty years.

His anxious father searched for him everywhere
Until, worn out from searching,
He settled in another city, built a house there
And took pleasure in the five desires.

His home was large and expensive,
With much gold and silver,
Seashell and agate,
Pearls and lapis lazuli,

Elephants, horses, oxen, and sheep,
Palanquins, buggies, and carriages.
Field workers and servants were there,
And a multitude of other people.

His revenues and investments
Spread even to other lands.
His traders and customers
Were everywhere.

Tens of millions of billions of people
Surrounded and honored him.
He was always in the favor of the king,
And all officials and powerful families honored him highly.

For many reasons
He was surrounded by a multitude.
Such was the extent of his wealth
And the greatness of his power.

But as he became older and infirm,
He longed all the more for his son.

Day and night he wondered:
"My time to die is coming.

"My foolish son has been away
For over fifty years.
All the things in my storehouses—
What should I do with them?"

At that time the poor son
Was looking for food and clothing,
Going from city to city
And from land to land.

Sometimes finding something,
Sometimes nothing,
He became famished, weak and gaunt,
And covered with scabs and sores.

Going from place to place,
From one job to another he wandered about,
Eventually coming to the city where his father lived,
Finally reaching his father's house.

Just at that time, within his gates
The rich man had set up a great jeweled tent
And was sitting on a lion seat
Surrounded by his dependents and various attendants.

Some were counting
Gold, silver, and jewels,
Or incoming and outgoing goods,
Recording them in ledgers.

The poor son,
Seeing how eminent and distinguished his father was,
Thought: "This must be a king
Or someone like a king."

Alarmed and full of awe, he asked himself:
"Why have I come here?"
And he thought to himself:
"If I stay for long, I may be captured and forced to work."

Having thought this,
He quickly ran away
In search of some poor village,
Where he might go to work.

The rich man on the lion seat
At that time
Saw his son in the distance,
And silently recognized him.

Immediately he ordered messengers
To chase after him and bring him back.
The poor son cried out in fright,
And fell to the ground in terror.

"These men have caught me.
Surely I will be killed!
Why did I come here
To look for food and clothing?"

Knowing that his son was foolish and feeling inferior,
The rich man thought:
"He will never believe my words
Nor believe that I am his father."

So, using skillful means,
He sent some other men,
One-eyed, short, common-looking,
Unimposing men.

"Go and tell him," he said,
"You will be hired with us

To remove dung and filth,
And you will be paid double wages."

Hearing this, the poor son
Was glad, and went with them
To remove dung and filth
And clean the stables.

Through a window
The rich man always watched his son,
And thought about how he was foolish
To be pleased with such menial work.

Then the rich man,
Putting on tattered, dirty clothes,
And taking a shovel for dung,
Would go to where his son was.

Using this skillful means
To get near him,
He encouraged the son
To work hard, saying:

"I have increased your wages
And given you oil for your feet,
And plenty of food and drink
And thick warm mats for a bed."

Sometimes he used stern language:
"Get on with your work."
At other times he spoke gently:
"You are like a son to me."

Being wise, the rich man eventually allowed him
To go in and out of the house,
And after twenty years
Made him manager of the house.

He showed him gold and silver,
Pearls and crystal,
And other incoming and outgoing things.
All this to have him understand such things.

Still the son lived outside the gate,
Living in a grass hovel,
Regarding himself as poor,
And thinking: "None of this is mine."

Knowing that his son's disposition
Was gradually becoming
More open and generous,
And wanting to give him his wealth,

The father gathered together his relatives,
The king and ministers,
The nobles and ordinary citizens.
Before this great assembly

He announced: "This is my son,
Who left me and went off somewhere for fifty years.
And since I saw my son come back
Twenty years have gone by.

"Long ago in some other city
I lost my son.
I went all around searching for him,
And eventually came here.

"All that I have,
Houses and people,
I give entirely to him.
He is free to use them as he wishes."

The son thought of his earlier poverty
And feelings of inferiority,

And of how he had now, from his father,
Received such great treasures,

Along with houses and buildings
And all his wealth.
He was overjoyed at having received
What he had never had before.

The Buddha too is like this.
Knowing that we are pleased with small things,
You did not tell us before,
"You can become buddhas."

Instead you told us about
Becoming free of fault,
Fulfilling a lesser vehicle
And being shravaka disciples.

The Buddha ordered us
To preach the supreme way,
Since those who study it and put it into practice
Can become buddhas.

Having received the Buddha's teaching,
Using causal explanations, various parables,
And a variety of other kinds of expression,
We taught the unexcelled way for the sake of great bodhisattvas.

When children of the Buddha
Heard the Dharma from us,
They pondered over it day and night
And diligently studied and practiced it.

Then the Buddha
Assured them, saying:
"In future lives
You will become buddhas."

The true facts of the Dharma,
Of the secret storehouse of all the buddhas,
Could be taught only to bodhisattvas.
It was not for our sake that this essential truth was taught.

Just as that poor son,
When he came near his father,
Took care of all his possessions,
But had no desire to have them for himself,

So too, we taught
The storehouse of Buddha-dharma,
But had no will to seek it for ourselves.
We were like him.

We took the extinction of what was within
To be good enough.
Having done this,
Nothing more remained to be done.

Even if we heard
About purifying buddha-lands
Or teaching and transforming living beings,
We did not aspire to do them.

Why? Because all things are empty and tranquil
Without coming to be, without extinction,
Without being large, without being small,
Without fault, without action.

Thinking in this way, with no felt joy,
Throughout the long night
We neither sought nor were attached to
The wisdom of the Buddha.

Nor had we any desire
Or hope for it,

Believing that in regard to the Dharma
We had the ultimate.

Through the long night,
Studying and putting the Dharma of emptiness into practice,
We gained release from the threefold world's
Illness of suffering and agony.

We lived out our final lives in an incomplete nirvana.
Having been taught and transformed by the Buddha,
We thought we surely had attained the Way,
And therefore already repaid the Buddha's grace.

While we taught the bodhisattva-dharma
For the sake of the Buddha's children,
Urging them to seek the Buddha way,
We ourselves never aspired to this Dharma.

Because he looked into our minds and hearts,
We were left alone by our leader and teacher.
At first he never encouraged us
By telling us about the true gain.

Just as the rich man,
Knowing his son's sense of inferiority,
Used the power of skillful means
To soften and win him over,

Only later did he entrust him with all his wealth.
So too with the Buddha:
Displaying rare actions,
And knowing that some want little things,

He uses the power of skillful means
To soften and temper them,
And then teaches them
Great wisdom.

Today we have obtained something we never had before.
What we had not even hoped for
Has come to us by itself,
Just as that poor son obtained innumerable treasures.

World-Honored One,
We have now gained the Way and won its fruit.
In the flawless Dharma
We have attained clear vision.

Having observed the Buddha's pure precepts
Throughout the long night,
Today for the first time
We have obtained the fruit and reward.

In the Dharma of the Dharma king,
Having long observed noble practices,
We have now attained
The flawless, unexcelled great fruit.

Now we are
True shravakas.
For we will lead all beings to hear
The voice of the Buddha way.

Now we are true arhats.
Everywhere among gods and humans,
Devils and brahmans of all the worlds,
We deserve offerings.

The World-Honored One in his great grace,
Making use of rare things,
Teaches and transforms us out of sympathy,
Enriching us.

Even in countless hundreds of millions of eons,
Who could repay him?

Even if we offer our hands and feet,
Pay respect by bowing our heads,
And make all kinds of offerings,
None of us could ever repay him.

If we carried him on our head,
Or on our two shoulders,
Through as many eons as the sands of the Ganges;
Wholeheartedly revering him,

Offering him the best of food,
Countless jeweled robes,
All kinds of bedding,
And every sort of medication;

If with ox-head sandalwood
And all kinds of jewels
We built stupas,
And carpeted the ground with jeweled robes;

If we did all such things as offerings,
Through as many eons
As the sands of the Ganges,
Still we would not be able to repay him.

Buddhas have rare,
Immeasurable and unlimited,
Inconceivably great
Power of divine faculties.

Tied neither to their faults nor actions,
The kings of the Dharma,
For the sake of the lowly,
Patiently endure.

To common people attached to appearances
They preach what is appropriate.

With the Dharma,
Buddhas have the greatest freedom.

Understanding the desires and pleasures of living beings
And the strength of their intentions,
According to what is appropriate and for their sake,
They use innumerable parables to teach the Dharma.

Making use of good roots
Put down in previous lives,
Knowing who is mature
And who is immature,

And making various calculations,
Distinctions, and perceptions,
They take the way of the one vehicle,
And, as appropriate, teach the three.

5. The Parable of the Plants[9]

AT THAT TIME the World-Honored One said to Maha-Kashyapa and other great disciples: "Well done, well done, Kashyapa. You have done well at describing the real blessings of the Tathagata. Truly they are as you say. The Tathagata manifests innumerable, unlimited, countless blessings. If you described them for innumerable hundreds of millions of eons you could not finish.

"You should know, Kashyapa, that the Tathagata is the king of the Dharma. Nothing he teaches is empty. He preaches all the teachings through wise use of skillful means. All that he teaches leads to a state of comprehensive wisdom. The Tathagata sees and knows where the teachings lead. Penetrating them without hindrance, he understands the deepest workings of all living beings. Moreover, having the most thorough understanding of all the teachings, he reveals his all-encompassing wisdom to living beings.

"Kashyapa, suppose that in the three-thousand great thousandfold world, growing on mountains, along rivers and streams, in valleys and in different soils, there are plants, trees, thickets, forests, and medicinal herbs of various and numerous kinds with different names and colors. A dense cloud spreads over all of them, covering the whole three-thousand great thousandfold world, and pours rain down on all equally and at the same time. The moisture reaches all the plants, trees, thickets, forests, and medicinal herbs, with their little roots, little stems, little branches, little leaves, their medium-sized roots, medium-sized stems, medium-sized branches, medium-sized leaves, their big roots, big stems, big branches, and big leaves. Every tree, large or small, according to whether it is superior, middling, or inferior, receives its share. The rain from the same cloud goes to each according to its nature and kind, causing it to grow, bloom, and bear fruit. Though all grow in the same soil and are moistened by the same rain, these plants and trees are all different.

"You should understand, Kashyapa, that the Tathagata is like this. He appears in this world like the rising of a great cloud, and he extends his great voice universally over the world of human and heavenly beings and asuras, just like the great cloud covers the three-thousand great thousandfold world. In the great assembly he speaks these words: 'I am a tathagata, worthy of offerings, truly awakened, fully clear in conduct, well gone, understanding the world, unexcelled leader, trainer of men, teacher of heavenly beings and people, buddha, world-honored one.

"'Those who have not yet been saved will be saved; those who have not been set free will be set free; those who have had no rest will have rest; those who have not yet attained nirvana will attain nirvana.

"'I understand both the present world and the worlds to come as they really are. I am one who knows all, one who sees all, one who knows the Way, one who opens the Way, one who teaches the Way. Come to me, all you human and heavenly beings and asuras, and hear the Dharma!'

"At that moment, to hear the Dharma, innumerable tens of millions of billions of kinds of living beings come to where the Buddha is. Then the Tathagata, observing the natural powers of all these beings— whether they were keen or dull, persevering or lazy—taught the Dharma to them according to their abilities in an unlimited variety of ways, so that all rejoiced and were greatly enriched. All these living beings, having heard this Dharma, gained peace and security in their present lives and afterward were born in good circumstances, joyful in the Way and in being able to hear again the Dharma. Having heard the Dharma, they will be freed from obstacles and, according to their capacity for the teachings, will gradually enter the Way.

"It is just as that great cloud rains on all the plants, trees, thickets, forests, and medicinal herbs, and each according to its nature and kind equally receives the moisture so that it grows and develops, so too the Dharma preached by the Tathagata always has one character and flavor, namely, liberation, separation, and extinction, which amounts to the attainment of all-inclusive wisdom. When living beings hear the Dharma of the Tathagata, though they embrace, read, recite, and practice it as preached, they themselves are not aware of the blessing they have received. Why? Because only the Tathagata understands the kind, the character, the embodiment, and the nature of all these living beings, what they have in mind, what they think, and what they practice. He knows how they keep things in mind, how they think, and how they practice. He knows what teachings they keep in mind, what teachings they think about, what teachings they practice, and he knows by what teachings they attain what teachings.

"Living beings live in a variety of circumstances. Only the Tathagata sees these situations clearly and understands them without hindrance. It is just as those plants, trees, thickets, forests, and medicinal herbs do not know whether their own nature is superior, middling, or inferior. The Tathagata knows that this is a Dharma of one character and flavor, namely, liberation, separation, and extinction, an ultimate nirvana of everlasting tranquility, which ends in emptiness. The Buddha, knowing all this and observing the predilections of living beings, guides and protects them. For this reason he does not immediately teach them all-inclusive wisdom.

"Kashyapa, you and the others have something most rare—you can understand that the Dharma preached by the Tathagata is appropriate, and you can have faith in it and embrace it. Why is this so rare? Because the Dharma preached by buddhas, the world-honored ones, according to what is appropriate is difficult to comprehend and difficult to understand."

At that time the World-Honored One, wanting to say what he meant once again, spoke in verse:

> The Dharma king, breaker of ideas of being,
> Appears in this world.
> In accord with desires of living beings,
> He teaches the Dharma in a variety of ways.

> The Tathagata is highly honored
> And profoundly wise.
> Yet he has long kept silent about this matter,
> Not wanting to teach it hastily.

If the wise hear it,
They will be able to believe and understand.
But the unwise will have doubts and worries,
Perpetually missing the point.

Therefore, Kashyapa,
I teach them according to their strengths,
With various explanations,
So that they will gain right views.

You should know, Kashyapa,
It is like a great cloud
Rising over the world,
Covering everything everywhere.

A beneficent cloud full of moisture,
Lightning flashing across the sky,
And the sound of thunder reverberating afar
Bring joy to all.

The sun's rays are hidden,
And the earth becomes cool.
The cloud descends and spreads,
As if it might be touched, or plucked from the sky.

The rain falls everywhere,
Coming down on all sides,
Flowing everywhere without limit,
Reaching over the face of the earth.

Into the hidden recesses of mountains, streams, and steep valleys,
Where plants and trees grow, and medicinal herbs,
Big trees and small,
A hundred grains, rice seedlings, sugar cane, and grapevines.

All are moistened by the rain
And abundantly enriched.

The dry ground is soaked,
And both herbs and trees flourish.

By the same water that
Comes from that cloud,
Plants, trees, thickets, and forests,
According to their need, receive moisture.

All the trees,
Superior, middling, or inferior,
Each, according to its size,
Can grow and develop.

Roots, stems, branches, and leaves,
Blossoms and fruits in brilliant color,
One rain goes to all,
And all become bright and shiny.

Though their bodies, forms, and capacities
May be large or small,
The moisture they receive is the same,
Enabling each to flourish.

The Buddha is like this.
He appears in the world,
Like a great cloud
Universally covering all things.

Having appeared in the world
For the sake of living beings,
He makes distinctions in teaching
The reality of all things.

The great saint, the World-Honored One,
To human and heavenly beings
And in the midst of all beings,
Declares:

I am the Tathagata,
Most honored among people.
I appear in the world like a great cloud
To shower water on all parched living beings,

To free them from suffering
And so attain the joys of peace and comfort,
The joys of this world,
And the joy of nirvana.

Human and heavenly beings,
Give me your full attention.
Gather around
And behold the one unexcelled in honor.

I am the World-Honored One,
Who cannot be surpassed.
To bring peace and comfort to all beings
I appear in the world.

And for the sake of this assembly
I teach the Dharma, pure as nectar.
The Dharma has one flavor—
Of liberation and nirvana.

With one wonderful voice
I fluently explain its meaning,
For the sake of the Great Vehicle
Always citing causes and conditions.

I look upon all things,
Without exception, as equal.
I have no interest anywhere in favoring one over another,
Or in cherishing one and hating another.

I have no greed or attachments
And am always impartial.

At all times and for all,
I teach the Dharma equally.

As I would to one person,
So I preach it to the many.
I always preach the Dharma so.
I've never done anything else.

Going or coming, sitting or standing,
I never get weary or downhearted.
I have nourished the whole world,
Like the rain that enriches everywhere.

Eminent and humble, high and low,
Precept-keepers and precept-breakers,
Those of great character
And those who are imperfect,

Those of correct views and those of wrong views,
Quick-witted and dull-witted,
I have the Dharma rain equally on all,
Without sparing or neglecting any.

When any living beings
Staying in any environment
Hear my Dharma,
They receive it according to their abilities.

Some dwell among human and heavenly beings,
Or with wheel-turning saintly kings,
Or with Indra, Brahma, or other kings.
These are like the smaller medicinal herbs.

Some understand the flawless Dharma,
Are able to attain nirvana,
Acquire the six divine powers,
And obtain the three kinds of knowledge.

Some live alone in mountain forests,
Always practice meditation,
And become pratyekabuddhas.
These are the medium-sized medicinal herbs.

Some seek to be like the World-Honored One,
Saying, "I will become a buddha,"
They persevere and practice meditation.
These are the superior medicinal herbs.

And there are the children of the Buddha
Who completely devote themselves
To the Buddha way,
Always practicing compassion.

They are assured
That they will become buddhas
And have no doubt about it.
These are called small trees.

Some, dwelling in peace with divine powers,
Turn the irreversible wheel,
Liberating innumerable millions of living beings.
Such bodhisattvas are called large trees.

The Buddha's unbiased teaching
Is like the one rain of one flavor.

According to their capacities,
Living beings receive it differently,
Just as the plants and trees
Are all different from one another.

The Buddha uses this parable
To open and reveal by skillful means,
And with various expressions
Preaches the one Dharma.

But in the wisdom of the Buddha
This is like a drop in the ocean.
I have the Dharma rain down,
Filling the whole world.

This one-flavored Dharma is to be practiced
According to one's ability.
Just as those thickets, forests, medicinal herbs, and trees,
According to their size, grow lush and beautiful.

The Dharma of all the buddhas,
Always of the same flavor,
Causes all the worlds everywhere
To gain what they need.

Practicing it step by step,
All can gain the fruit of the Way.

Shravakas and pratyekabuddhas
Living in mountain forests in their final incarnations,
Receiving the Dharma and gaining its fruit,
Are called medicinal herbs.
Each grows in its own way.

If there are bodhisattvas who are firm in wisdom,
Deeply understand the threefold world,
And seek the supreme vehicle,
They are called small trees.
They continue to grow.

Again, those who practice meditation,
Gain divine powers,
Hear about the emptiness of all things,
Greatly rejoice,

And emit innumerable rays of light
To liberate living beings,

Are called large trees.
They continue to grow.

In this way, Kashyapa, the Dharma preached by the Buddha
Is just like the great cloud's rain of one flavor,
Which enriches human flowers,
So that each will bear fruit.

You should understand, Kashyapa:
By causal explanations
And various kinds of parables
I open and reveal the Buddha way.

This is my method of skillful means.
All buddhas do the same.
What I teach you and the others now is the utmost truth:
None has attained extinction as a shravaka.

What you are practicing
Is the bodhisattva way.
As you gradually practice and learn,
Every one of you should become a buddha.

6. Assurance of Becoming a Buddha

AT THAT TIME, after speaking these verses, the World-Honored One addressed the whole great assembly in words like these: "In a future life, this disciple of mine, Maha-Kashyapa, will go before three million billion world-honored buddhas, making offerings to them, revering, honoring, and praising them, and proclaiming the innumerable great teachings of the buddhas everywhere. In his final incarnation he will be able to become a buddha whose name will be Radiance Tathagata, one worthy of offerings, truly awakened, fully clear in conduct, well gone, understanding the world, unexcelled leader, trainer of men, teacher of heavenly beings and people, buddha, world-honored one. His land will be called Radiant Virtue, and his eon will be named Magnificently Adorned.

"The lifetime of this buddha will be twelve small eons. His true Dharma will remain in the world for twenty small eons, and his merely formal Dharma will also remain for twenty small eons. His land will be magnificently adorned, free of all evil pollution, rubble, thorns or thistles, and filthy toilet waste. The land will be level and smooth, with no high or low places, hills or valleys. The ground will be lapis lazuli. Lines of jeweled trees and golden cords will mark off its roads. It will have precious flowers scattered over it. And the whole place will be pure and clean. The bodhisattvas of that land will be innumerable hundreds of billions, and there will be innumerable shravakas. There will be no deeds of the devil there, and, though the devil and the devil's people will be there, they will all defend the Buddha-dharma."

At that time the World-Honored One, wanting to say what he meant once again, spoke in verse:

> I say to you monks
> In my Buddha-eyes I see
> That in a future life, after innumerable eons,
> This Kashyapa will be able to become a buddha.
>
> In future lives
> He will go before and make offerings to
> Three million billion
> World-honored buddhas.
>
> For the sake of Buddha wisdom
> He will observe noble practices carefully
> And make offerings to the highest
> And most honored of people.
>
> Having studied and put into practice
> All the unexcelled wisdom,
> In his final incarnation
> He will be able to become a buddha.
>
> His land will be pure,
> With lapis lazuli for ground.
> Many jeweled trees will line the roadsides,
> With golden cords marking off the roads.
>
> Those seeing it will rejoice.
> It will always be fragrant,
> With rare flowers
> Scattered everywhere.
>
> And many kinds of rare, wonderful things
> Will add to its splendor.
> The land will be level and smooth,
> Without hills or holes.

The many bodhisattvas will be countless in number.
They will have gentle dispositions,
Attain the great divine faculties,
And honor and embrace the Buddha's Great Vehicle sutras.

A multitude of shravakas, free of fault,
Will be in their final incarnations.

Children of the Dharma king
Will also be countless in number.
Even with the eyes of a god
You could not know their number.

That Buddha's lifetime will be
Twelve small eons.
His true Dharma will remain in the world
For twenty small eons.

The merely formal Dharma will also remain
For twenty small eons.
This will be the story
Of the World-Honored One called Radiance.

Then Maha-Maudgalyayana, Subhuti, Maha-Katyayana, and others, all trembling with excitement, put their palms together in rapt attention and gazed up into the World-Honored One's face, not for an instant lowering their eyes. With voices in unison, they sang in verse:

Great Hero, World-Honored One,
Dharma king of the Shakyas,
Out of compassion for us
Allow us to hear the voice of the Buddha!

Knowing the depths of our minds,
If you assure us of becoming buddhas,
It would be like being bathed in nectar,
Changing the heat to cool.

Anyone from a land of famine
Suddenly finding a king's feast,
But still cherishing doubts and fears,
Would not dare to eat right away.

Only when instructed by the king
Would they dare to eat.

So it is with us.
Reminded of the errors of a small vehicle,
We know not how to obtain
The unexcelled wisdom of the Buddha.

Though we hear the voice of the Buddha
Telling us we are to become buddhas,
We are still anxious and afraid,
Like the one who does not dare to eat.

But now if we receive the Buddha's assurance,
We will be happy and at peace.
Great Hero, World-Honored One,
You always want to put the world at peace.

Please give us your assurance,
As you would tell a starving person to eat!

Then the World-Honored One, knowing the thoughts in the minds of those great disciples, addressed all the monks: "This Subhuti, in a future life, will come before three million billion myriads of buddhas, making offerings, revering, honoring, and praising them. He will always observe noble practices and follow the bodhisattva way. In his final incarnation he will become a buddha whose name will be Famous Features Tathagata, one worthy of offerings, truly awakened, fully clear in conduct, well gone, understanding the world, unexcelled leader, trainer of men, teacher of heavenly beings and people, buddha, world-honored one.

"His eon will be called Possessing Jewels and his land named Birthplace of Jewels. The land will be level and smooth, with crystal for ground, adorned with jeweled trees, and without hills or pits, gravel, thorns or thistles, or feces. The earth will be covered with precious flowers, and the entire place will be pure and clean. The people of that land will live on jeweled terraces in rare and wonderful towers. Shravaka disciples will be innumerable, countless, beyond calculation or metaphor. The multitude of bodhisattvas will be innumerable tens of millions of billions of myriads. The lifetime of this buddha will be twelve small eons, his true Dharma will remain for twenty small eons, and the merely formal Dharma will also remain for twenty small eons. This Buddha will always dwell in midair, teaching the Dharma to the assembly and saving innumerable bodhisattvas and shravakas."

At that time the World-Honored One, wanting to say what he meant once again, spoke in verse:

You multitude of monks,
I have something to tell you now.
Give your full attention
To what I have to say!

My great disciple Subhuti
Will become a buddha
Whose name will be
Famous Features.

He will make offerings
To innumerable trillions of buddhas,
And following the practices of the buddhas,
Gradually fulfill the great way.

In his final incarnation
He will acquire the thirty-two characteristics
And be as imposing and wonderful
As a mountain of jewels.

His buddha-land
Will be unsurpassed in purity and splendor,

So that all who behold it
Will cherish and delight in it.

In its midst the Buddha
Will liberate innumerable beings.
Following his Buddha-dharma
Will be many bodhisattvas.

All of them will have keen faculties
And turn the irreversible wheel.
His land will always be
Adorned with bodhisattvas.

The multitude of shravakas
Will be beyond calculation.
All will gain
The three kinds of knowledge,

Exercise the six divine powers,
Have the eight kinds of liberation,
And possess
Great dignity and virtue.

The Dharma preached by that buddha
Will be revealed through innumerable
Divine transformations
Beyond conception.

Human and heavenly beings,
Numerous as the sands of the Ganges,
All with palms together
Will listen to and receive that buddha's words.

The Buddha's lifetime will be twelve small eons,
His true Dharma will remain for twenty small eons,
And the merely formal Dharma will also
Remain for twenty small eons.

At that time the World-Honored One once again addressed the assembly of monks and said: "Now I announce to you that this Maha-Katyayana, in future lives, will make offerings to and serve eight hundred billion buddhas, revering and honoring them. After those buddhas have passed into extinction, for each of them he will put up a stupa a thousand leagues high, and five hundred leagues of equal width and depth. These stupas will be made of the seven precious materials—gold, silver, lapis lazuli, shell, agate, pearl, and carnelian. Many flowers, necklaces, paste incense, powdered incense, incense for burning, silk canopies, flags, and banners will be given as offerings to those stupas. After this he will serve two trillion buddhas in the same way.

"Having made offerings to all those buddhas, he will complete his bodhisattva way and become a buddha whose name will be Jambunada Golden Light Tathagata, one worthy of offerings, truly awakened, fully clear in conduct, well gone, understanding the world, unexcelled leader, trainer of men, teacher of heavenly beings and people, buddha, world-honored one. His land will be level and smooth, with crystal for ground. It will be adorned with jeweled trees and have golden cords to mark off the roads. The ground will be covered with wonderful flowers, and the entire place will be pure and clean, so that anyone seeing it will rejoice. The four evil paths will not exist there— those of purgatories, hungry spirits, animals, and asuras—but the human and heavenly beings will be many, and innumerable billions of shravakas and bodhisattvas will adorn the land. The lifetime of that buddha will be twelve small eons. His true Dharma will remain in the world for twenty small eons and the merely formal Dharma will also remain for twenty small eons."

Then the World-Honored One, wanting to say what he meant once again, spoke in verse:

You multitude of monks,
Give me your complete attention.
In what I teach
There is nothing that is not true.

This Katyayana
Will give various kinds

Of excellent things
As offerings to buddhas.

After the buddhas have passed into extinction
He will put up stupas of the seven precious materials
And give flowers and incense
As offerings to their remains.

In his final incarnation
He will acquire the wisdom of the Buddha
And reach impartial, proper awakening.
His land will be pure and clean.

He will save innumerable
Trillions of living beings.
And from all the living beings of the ten directions
He will receive offerings.

The radiance of this buddha
None will be able to surpass.
His buddha-name will be
Jambunada Golden Light.

Numberless, uncountable
Bodhisattvas and shravakas,
Rejecting all ideas of being,
Will adorn his land.

Then the World-Honored One once again addressed the great assembly: "Now I say to you that this Maha-Maudgalyayana will make offerings to eight thousand buddhas, revering and honoring them. After those buddhas have passed into extinction, for each of them he will put up a stupa a thousand leagues high, and five hundred leagues of equal width and depth. These stupas will be made of a composite of the seven precious materials—gold, silver, lapis lazuli, seashell, agate, pearl, and carnelian. Many flowers, necklaces, paste incense, powdered incense, incense for burning, silk canopies, flags, and banners will be given as offerings to those stupas. After this he will serve two million billion buddhas in the same way.

"Then he will become a buddha, whose name will be Tamalapatra Sandalwood Fragrance Tathagata, one worthy of offerings, truly awakened, fully clear in conduct, well gone, understanding the world, unexcelled leader, trainer of men, teacher of heavenly beings and people, buddha, world-honored one. His eon will be named Full of Joy and his land, Mind Pleasing. The land will be level and smooth, with crystal for ground, and adorned with jeweled trees. The ground will be covered with pearls and flowers, and the entire place will be clean and pure, so that those seeing it will rejoice. There will be many human and heavenly beings, and countless bodhisattvas and shravakas. The lifetime of that buddha will be twenty-four small eons. His true Dharma will remain in the world for forty small eons and the merely formal Dharma will remain for forty small eons."

Then the World-Honored One, wanting to say what he meant once again, spoke in verse:

> This, my disciple, the great Maha-Maudgalyayana,
> After casting off this body,
> Will see eight thousand and two million billion
> World-honored buddhas.
>
> For the sake of the Buddha way
> He will make offerings to them and revere them.
> Where these buddhas are, he will always observe noble practices,
> And for innumerable eons embrace the Buddha-dharma.
>
> After those buddhas
> Have passed into extinction
> He will put up stupas of the seven precious materials
> With golden spires visible from afar.
>
> And with flowers,
> Incense, and music
> He will make offerings
> To the stupas of the buddhas.

Having gradually fulfilled the bodhisattva way,
In the land called Mind Pleasing
He will be able to become a buddha
Named Tamalapatra Sandalwood Fragrance.

The lifetime of that buddha
Will be twenty-four eons.
For the sake of human and heavenly beings
He will always preach the Buddha way.

Shravakas as numerous as the sands of the Ganges
Will have the three kinds of knowledge,
The six divine powers,
And great dignity and virtue.

Countless bodhisattvas will be
Firm in will and diligent.
In the wisdom of the Buddha
They will never backslide.

After this buddha passes into extinction,
His true Dharma will remain
For forty small eons
And the merely formal Dharma will do the same.

You, my disciples with full dignity and virtue,
Five hundred in number,
Will all receive assurance
Of becoming buddhas in the future.

About the causes and conditions
Of previous lives, mine and yours,
I am about to speak.
Listen carefully!

7. The Parable of the Fantastic Castle-City

THE BUDDHA SAID to the monks: "Once in the past, innumerable, unlimited, inconceivable and countless eons ago, there was a buddha named Excellent in Great Penetrating Wisdom Tathagata, one worthy of offerings, truly awakened, fully clear in conduct, well gone, understanding the world, unexcelled leader, trainer of men, teacher of heavenly beings and people, buddha, world-honored one. His land was named Well Made, and his eon was named Great Features.

"Monks, since that buddha passed into extinction, a long, long time has passed. Suppose for instance that someone took all of the earth in a three-thousand great thousandfold world and ground it into ink powder, and then passed through a thousand lands to the east, dropping one speck as large as a speck of dust, and again passing through another thousand lands, dropping just one speck. Suppose he proceeded in this way until he had exhausted all the ink made of that earth. What do you think? All these lands—is it possible even for mathematicians or their disciples to count all of them and know the number of all the lands visited?"

"No, it is not, World-Honored One."

"Monks, suppose the earth of all those lands through which that man had passed dropping a speck, as well as those lands where he had not dropped any, were ground into dust. Let one speck of dust be one eon. The number of eons since that buddha passed into extinction until now still vastly exceeds that number by innumerable, unlimited hundreds of thousands of billions of eons. Yet by the power of the Tathagata's insight, I observe that distant time as if it were today."

At that time the World-Honored One, wanting to say what he meant once again, spoke in verse:

I remember in a past world,
Innumerable, unlimited eons ago,
A buddha, most honored of people,
Named Excellent in Great Penetrating Wisdom.

Suppose someone used his strength to grind up
The earth of a three-thousand great thousandfold,
Completely crushing all of its parts
Into ink powder.

Then, passing a thousand lands,
He drops just one speck
And continues in that way
Until he has dropped all this ink powder.

And suppose one took all of those lands
Through which he had passed,
Where ink was dropped and where it was not,
And again completely ground them into dust.

If we take one speck to be an eon,
The number of those specks
Is exceeded by the number of eons
In which the buddha lived.

Since that buddha
Passed into extinction
An immeasurable number of eons like this
Have passed.

With unhindered wisdom,
The Tathagata remembers
The time of the extinction of that buddha

And his shravakas and bodhisattvas
As if I were seeing it now.

You monks should know
That Buddha-wisdom is pure and wonderful,
Flawless and unimpeded,
Reaching and penetrating through innumerable eons.

The Buddha told all the monks: "The lifetime of the Buddha Excellent in Great Penetrating Wisdom was five hundred and forty trillion myriads of eons. At the beginning, when that buddha, sitting at the place of the Way had destroyed the army of the devil, though he was at the point of attaining supreme awakening, the Dharma of the buddhas did not appear to him then. So for one small eon and then for ten more small eons he sat cross-legged with body and mind motionless. But the Dharma of the buddhas still did not appear to him.

"The gods of the heaven of the thirty-three gods had earlier prepared a lion seat one league high under a bodhi tree so that the Buddha might attain supreme awakening on that seat. No sooner had he sat on the seat than the kings of the Brahma heaven had many flowers from heaven rain down over an area for a hundred leagues around. From time to time a fragrant wind would come up, sweeping away the withered flowers. Then more fresh ones would rain down. This continued for a full ten small eons without interruption as an offering to the Buddha. Until his extinction the flowers rained down constantly. As an offering to the Buddha, the four kings of heaven constantly beat heavenly drums, while other gods performed heavenly music during the ten full small eons. This continued until the Buddha's extinction.

"Monks, only after ten small eons had gone by did the Dharma of the buddhas appear before Excellent in Great Penetrating Wisdom Buddha and he could attain supreme awakening. That Buddha, before he had left home, had sixteen sons, the first of whom was named Accumulated Wisdom. Each of his sons had various kinds of rare and attractive toys, but when they heard that their father had attained supreme awakening, they all threw away the things they had valued so much and went to pay their regards to the Buddha, their weeping mothers following after them.

"Their grandfather, a wheel-turning saintly king, with a hundred ministers and a hundred thousand billion people, surrounded and followed the sons to the place of the Way, all wanting to draw near to the Tathagata Excellent in Great Penetrating Wisdom and make offerings to him and revere, honor, and praise him. After arriving with heads down, they prostrated themselves at his feet, and after circling around him with palms together in complete devotion, they gazed up at the World-Honored One and praised him in verse, saying:

> In order to liberate living beings,
> The World-Honored One of great dignity and virtue
> Has devoted innumerable hundreds of millions of years
> To becoming a buddha.
>
> Your vows have been fulfilled.
> It is extremely fortunate,
> For world-honored ones
> Are very rare.
>
> At one sitting,
> Ten small eons have passed.
> Your body and arms and legs are still,
> Peaceful, and motionless.
>
> Your mind, always calm and peaceful,
> Is never distracted.
> You have reached ultimate and lasting tranquility
> And dwell at peace in the flawless Dharma.
>
> Now, seeing the World-Honored One
> Calm after attaining the Buddha way,
> We too are enriched
> And joyfully congratulate him.
>
> Living beings always suffer and agonize.
> Being blind without a leader and teacher,

Unaware of the way to end suffering,
They don't know enough to seek their liberation.

Through the long night,
Increasingly they follow evil ways,
Reducing the number of heavenly beings.
They go from darkness to darkness,
Never hearing a buddha's name.

But now the Buddha has attained the supreme,
The calm of the flawless Dharma.

Human and heavenly beings as well as ourselves
Are supremely enriched.
Thus, we all bow and offer our lives
To one of unexcelled honor.

"Then all these sixteen princes, having praised the Buddha in verse, pleaded with the World-Honored One to turn the Dharma wheel, saying together, 'World-Honored One, preach the Dharma, sympathizing with human and heavenly beings and bringing them great comfort and abundant benefits.' Repeating this in verse, they said:

Hero of the world, without equal,
Self-adorned with a hundred blessings,
You who have attained unexcelled wisdom,
We beg you to teach for the sake of the world.

Save us
And all kinds of living beings.
Make distinctions to enlighten us,
So that we may obtain this wisdom.

If we can become buddhas,
All other living beings can as well.

World-Honored One, you know
The deepest thoughts of living beings,
The paths they walk,
Their capacity for wisdom,

Their pleasures and past good works,
Their actions in previous lives.
World-Honored One, you know all this.
Now you should turn the unexcelled wheel."

The Buddha then told the monks: "When Excellent in Great Pene-
trating Wisdom Buddha attained supreme awakening, five million
buddha-lands in each of the ten directions trembled and shook in six
ways. Even the dark and secluded places in those lands, where the light
of the sun and moon never shines, were all lit up. And all the living
beings could see each other and exclaimed together: 'Where have all
these living beings suddenly come from?'

"In addition, the palaces of the heavenly beings in all those lands, even
the Brahma palaces, trembled and shook in the six ways, and great light
shone everywhere, filling all the worlds and surpassing the light of the
heavens.

"Then all the palaces of the Brahma heavens in five million billion
lands to the east were brilliantly illuminated with twice their normal
brightness. And each of those kings of the Brahma heavens thought:
'Why does this sign appear, so that our palaces are now illuminated as
never before?' Then all the Brahma kings visited each other to discuss
this matter. Among those assembled there was a great Brahma king
named Savior of All, who spoke in verse on behalf of all the Brahma
kings:

Our palaces are illuminated
As never before.
Why is this?
Let's look into it.

Is it because a great and virtuous god has been born,
Or is it because a buddha has appeared in the world,

That this great, illuminating light
Is shining everywhere in all directions?

"Then the kings of the Brahma heavens from five million billion lands, together with their palaces, each taking a robe filled with heavenly flowers, went together to the west to investigate. There they saw the Tathagata Excellent in Great Penetrating Wisdom at the place of the Way, seated on a lion seat under a bodhi tree, surrounded and revered by heavenly beings, dragon kings, centaurs, chimeras, pythons, and other human and nonhuman beings. And they saw the sixteen princes begging the Buddha to turn the Dharma wheel.

"Immediately all the kings of the Brahma heavens prostrated themselves before the Buddha, circled around him a hundred thousand times, and then scattered the flowers from heaven over the Buddha. The flowers they scattered piled up like Mount Sumeru. Flowers were also offered to the Buddha's bodhi tree. That bodhi tree was four hundred leagues tall. When they had offered the flowers, each of them presented a palace to the Buddha, saying: 'Out of compassion for us and for our benefit, we beg you to accept and use the palaces we are offering!'

"Then all the kings of the Brahma heavens, before the Buddha, with one mind and voice praised him in verse, saying:

World-honored ones are very rare
And difficult to meet.
Having innumerable blessings,
You can save everyone.

As a great teacher of human and heavenly beings,
You have compassion for the world.
All the living in the ten directions,
Everywhere are benefited abundantly by you.

We have come from
Five million billion lands,
Leaving the joys of deep meditation
In order to make offerings to the Buddha.

Due to good fortune in previous lives
Our palaces are magnificently adorned.
Now we offer them to the World-Honored One
And beg you to be kind enough to accept them.

"When the kings of the Brahma heavens had praised the Buddha in verse, each said: 'We beg you, World-Honored One, to turn the Dharma wheel, save all the living, and open the way to nirvana.'

"Then the kings of the Brahma heavens with one mind and voice spoke in verse, saying:

Hero of the world, most honored of people,
We beg you to proclaim the Dharma!
By the power of your great compassion,
Save living beings from their suffering and agony!

"Then the Excellent in Great Penetrating Wisdom Tathagata silently consented.

"Monks, then the great Brahma kings in five million billion lands in the southeast, each seeing his own palace radiant with light as never before, were amazed and ecstatic with joy from experiencing such an unprecedented thing. They all visited each other to discuss this matter together.

"At that time among those assembled there was a great king of a Brahma heaven named Great Compassion who spoke in verse on behalf of all of the Brahma kings:

What is the reason for all of this?
Why should such signs appear?
Our palaces are illuminated
As never before.

Is it because a great and virtuous god has been born?
Or is it that a buddha has appeared in the world?
We have never seen such a sign before.
We should give our full attention to looking into it.

Even if we have to go through ten million billion lands,
We will search together for the cause of the light.
It must be that a buddha has appeared in the world
To save living beings from their suffering.

"Then the five million billion kings of the Brahma heavens, together with their palaces, each taking a robe filled with heavenly flowers, went together to the northwest to investigate. There they saw the Tathagata Excellent in Great Penetrating Wisdom at the place of the Way, seated on a lion seat under a bodhi tree, surrounded and revered by heavenly beings, dragon kings, centaurs, chimeras, pythons, and other human and nonhuman beings. And they saw the sixteen princes begging the Buddha to turn the Dharma wheel.

"Then all the kings of the Brahma heavens prostrated themselves before the Buddha, circled around him hundreds of thousands of times, and then scattered the flowers from heaven over the Buddha. The flowers they scattered piled up like Mount Sumeru. Flowers were also offered to the Buddha's bodhi tree. When they had offered the flowers, each of them presented a palace to the Buddha, saying: 'Out of compassion for us and for our benefit, we beg you to accept and use the palaces we are offering!'

"Then all the kings of the Brahma heavens, before the Buddha, with one mind and voice praised him in verse, saying:

Holy lord, god among gods,
With a voice like a kalavinka bird,
With compassion for all living beings,
We now respectfully greet you.

Rarely does a World-Honored One appear,
Only once in many ages.
One hundred and eighty eons
Have passed without a buddha.

The three evil paths
Have become full,

While heavenly beings
Have decreased.

Now the Buddha
Has appeared in the world
To be the eyes
For living beings—

One to whom the world turns,
Savior of all,
Father of all,
Bringing comfort and abundant benefits to all.

Due to good fortune in previous lives,
We now meet the World-Honored One.

"After the kings of the Brahma heavens had praised the Buddha in verse, each of them said: 'Please, World-Honored One, have compassion for all, turn the Dharma wheel, and save the living.'

"Then the kings of the Brahma heavens with one mind and voice spoke in verse, saying:

Great saint, turn the Dharma wheel.
Reveal the nature of things.
Save the living from suffering and agony,
That they may obtain great joy.

When living beings hear this Dharma,
They obtain the Way or are reborn as heavenly beings.
The number of those in the evil paths is reduced,
While those who are patient and good increase.

"Then the Tathagata Excellent in Great Penetrating Wisdom silently consented.

"Monks, then the great Brahma kings in five million billion lands in the south, each seeing his own palace radiant with light as never before, were amazed and ecstatic with joy from experiencing such an unprecedented thing. They all visited each other to discuss this matter together, asking: 'What is the reason for this radiant light in our palaces?'

"Among those assembled there at that time was a great king of a Brahma heaven named Wonderful Dharma, who spoke in verse on behalf of all of the Brahma kings:

> All our palaces
> Are brightly illuminated.
> This cannot be for no reason.
> We should look into it.

> Through hundreds of thousands of eons,
> Never before has such a sign been seen.
> Is it because a great and virtuous god has been born?
> Or is it that a buddha has appeared in the world?

"Then the five million billion kings of the Brahma heavens, together with their palaces, each taking a robe filled with heavenly flowers, went together to the north to investigate. There they saw the Tathagata Excellent in Great Penetrating Wisdom at the place of the Way, seated on a lion seat under a bodhi tree, surrounded and revered by heavenly beings, dragon kings, centaurs, chimeras, pythons, and other human and non-human beings. And they saw the sixteen princes begging the Buddha to turn the Dharma wheel.

"Then all the kings of the Brahma heavens prostrated themselves before the Buddha, circled around him a hundred thousand times, and then scattered the flowers from heaven over the Buddha. The flowers they scattered piled up like Mount Sumeru. Flowers were also offered to the Buddha's bodhi tree. When they had offered the flowers, each of them presented a palace to the Buddha, saying: 'Out of compassion for us and for our benefit, we beg you to accept and use the palaces we are offering!'

"Then all the kings of the Brahma heavens, before the Buddha, with one mind and voice praised him in verse, saying:

> World-Honored One, most difficult to meet,
> Destroyer of all afflictions,

After a hundred and thirty eons
At last we can see you.

Hungry and thirsty beings
Are filled by the rain of the Dharma.

One who has never been seen in the past,
One of immeasurable wisdom,
Rare as the udumbara flower,
We have met today.

All our palaces are made beautiful by your light.
World-Honored One,
Out of your great compassion,
We beg you to accept them.

"When the kings of the Brahma heavens had praised the Buddha in verse, each said: 'We beg the World-Honored One to turn the Dharma wheel, and lead all the gods, devils, Brahmas, mendicants, and brahmans of all the worlds to attain peace and comfort and be saved.'

"Then all the kings of the Brahma heavens with one mind and voice praised him in verse, saying:

Most honored of human and heavenly beings,
We beg you:

Turn the unexcelled Dharma wheel,
Beat the drum of the great Dharma,
Blow the conch of the great Dharma,
Rain down everywhere the rain of the great Dharma,
Saving innumerable beings!

We all direct our plea to you.
Let your profound voice be heard.

"Then the Tathagata Excellent in Great Penetrating Wisdom silently consented.

"Similarly, in the other directions from the southwest to the lower region similar things happened. Then, in the upper region, the great kings of the Brahma heavens of five million billion lands, each seeing his own palace radiant with light as never before, were amazed and ecstatic with joy. They all visited each other to discuss this matter together, asking 'What is the reason for this radiant light in our palaces?'

"In that assembly there was a great king of a Brahma heaven named Shikhin, who spoke for all the Brahma kings in verse:

> What is the reason
> That all our palaces
> Shine with such radiance,
> Made beautiful as never before?
>
> Such a wonderful sign
> We have never before seen or heard.
> Is it because a great and virtuous god has been born?
> Or is it that a buddha has appeared in the world?

"Then the five million billion kings of the Brahma heavens, together with their palaces, each taking a robe filled with heavenly flowers, went together toward the lower region to investigate. There they saw the Tathagata Excellent in Great Penetrating Wisdom at the place of the Way, seated on a lion seat under a bodhi tree, surrounded and revered by heavenly beings, dragon kings, centaurs, chimeras, pythons, and other human and nonhuman beings. And they saw the sixteen princes begging the Buddha to turn the Dharma wheel.

"Then all the kings of the Brahma heavens prostrated themselves before the Buddha, circled around him a hundred thousand times, and then scattered the flowers from heaven over the Buddha. The flowers they scattered piled up like Mount Sumeru. Flowers were also offered to the Buddha's bodhi tree. When they had offered the flowers, each of them presented a palace to the Buddha, saying: 'Out of compassion for us and for our benefit, we beg you to accept and use the palaces we are offering!'

"Then all the kings of the Brahma heavens, before the Buddha, with one mind and voice praised him in verse, saying:

How good it is to see the buddhas,
Holy honored ones who save the world,
Who can release the living
From the purgatories of the threefold world.

Universally wise,
Honored by human and heavenly beings,
Out of compassion for the many varieties of buds,
They can open wide the gates of nectar
For the salvation of all.

Innumerable eons
Have passed without buddhas.
When world-honored ones were not yet,
Darkness was everywhere all the time.

Those in the three evil paths increased,
And the asuras also flourished,
While the number of heavenly beings decreased,
And the dying often fell into evil paths.

Not hearing the Dharma from a buddha,
Most usually followed ways that were not good.
Their physical strength and wisdom
Just dwindled away.

Because of the evil actions
Done in the past
They lost joy and joyful thoughts.
And lived with wrong views.

Not knowing rules for good conduct,
Not receiving
The transforming teachings of buddhas,
They constantly fell into evil ways.

You, the Buddha, the eyes of the world,
Have appeared after many ages.
Out of compassion for the living
You have appeared in the world.

Transcending it, you gained true awakening.
We are very glad,
And all other beings rejoice
In what we have never had before.

All our palaces, receiving this light,
Are made beautiful.
Now we offer them to the World-Honored One.
Out of compassion for us, we beg you to accept them.

May these blessings
Extend to all,
That we with all the living
Together attain the Buddha way.

"When the five hundred billion kings of the Brahma heavens had praised the Buddha in verse, each said to him: 'We beg the World-Honored One to turn the Dharma wheel, bringing peace and comfort to many, saving many.'

"Then all the kings of the Brahma heavens spoke in verse, saying:

World-Honored One,
Turn the Dharma wheel,
Beat the drum of the Dharma,
Sweet as nectar,

Save the living beings
Who are suffering and in agony,
Open and show us
The way to nirvana.

We beg you to accept our pleas,
And with a great, wonderful voice,
Have mercy on us by laying out the Dharma
That you have practiced for innumerable eons.

"At that time the Tathagata Excellent in Great Penetrating Wisdom, receiving the pleas of the kings of the Brahma heavens of the ten directions and of the sixteen princes, immediately turned the Dharma wheel of twelve spokes three times. Neither mendicants, brahmans, heavenly beings, devils, Brahmas, nor any other beings in the world are able to do such a turning. He said: 'This is suffering; this is the cause of suffering; this is the elimination of suffering; this is the way to the elimination of suffering.'

"Then he taught the twelve causes and conditions, namely ignorance causes actions, actions cause consciousness, consciousness causes name and form, name and form cause the six kinds of sense, the six kinds of sense cause contact, contact causes sensations, sensations cause desires, desires cause attachments, attachments cause existence, existence causes birth, birth causes old age and death, anxiety and sorrow, suffering and anguish. If ignorance is extinguished, then action is extinguished. If action is extinguished, then consciousness is extinguished. If consciousness is extinguished, then name and form are extinguished. If name and form are extinguished, then the six kinds of senses are extinguished. If the six senses are extinguished, then contact is extinguished. If contact is extinguished, then sensation is extinguished. If sensation is extinguished, then desire is extinguished. If desire is extinguished, then attachments are extinguished. If attachments are extinguished, then existence is extinguished. If existence is extinguished, then birth is extinguished. If birth is extinguished then old age and death, anxiety and sorrow, suffering and anguish are extinguished.

"When the Buddha taught this Dharma in the midst of the great assembly of human and heavenly beings, six million billion myriads of people, because they refused to become attached to anything and freed themselves from fault, obtained profound and wonderful meditation, the three kinds of knowledge, the six divine powers, and the eight kinds of liberation. Likewise, when the Buddha preached the Dharma for a second, a third, and a fourth time, tens of millions of billions of myriads of living beings, as numerous as the sands of the Ganges, because they also refused to become attached to anything, were able to free themselves from faults. From this time on, the number of shravakas was innumerable and unlimited, beyond calculation.

"Meanwhile the sixteen princes left their home while still young and became novices. Their senses were sharp and their wisdom bright. They had already made offerings to hundreds of thousands of billions of buddhas, had observed noble practices in purity, and sought supreme awakening. Together they said to the Buddha: 'World-Honored One, all of these innumerable tens of millions of billions of great virtuous shravakas are already accomplished. World-Honored One, now you should preach the Dharma of supreme awakening for our sake. Once we have heard it, we will study and practice it together. World-Honored One, we are determined to gain the insight of a tathagata. What is deep in our hearts the Buddha must already know.'

"Then the eight trillion people in the assembly led by the wheel-turning saintly king, seeing that the sixteen princes had left their home to become novices, wanted to do the same. Hearing this, the king permitted them to do so.

"Then that buddha, responding to the pleas of the novices after twenty thousand eons had passed, in the presence of the four groups preached this Great Vehicle sutra named the Lotus Flower of the Wonderful Dharma, the Dharma by which bodhisattvas are taught and which buddhas watch over and keep in mind. When he had preached this sutra, the sixteen novices, for the sake of supreme awakening, all received and embraced it, learned and recited it, and deeply understood it.

"While this sutra was preached, the sixteen bodhisattva-novices all accepted it in faith. Among the many shravakas there were also those who believed in and understood it. But all the other thousands of billions of kinds of living beings had doubts.

"The Buddha preached this sutra for eight thousand eons without resting. When he had finished preaching it, he entered a quiet room and meditated for eighty-four thousand eons.

"Then the sixteen bodhisattva-novices, knowing that the Buddha had entered the room and was meditating quietly, each got on a Dharma seat and for eighty-four thousand eons taught and explained the Wonderful Dharma Flower Sutra everywhere to the four groups. In this way each of them saved six million billion myriads of living beings, as many as the sands of the Ganges, demonstrating and teaching it to them, enriching them and giving them joy, and leading them to aspire to supreme awakening.

"After eighty-four thousand eons had passed, Excellent in Great Penetrating Wisdom Buddha arose from his meditation, went up to the Dharma seat, and quietly sat down.

"Addressing the whole great assembly, he said: 'Such bodhisattva-novices as these sixteen are very rare. Their faculties are keen and their wisdom bright. They have made offerings to innumerable tens of millions of billions of buddhas. Under those buddhas they have always observed noble practices, received and embraced Buddha-wisdom, and opened it up for living beings, leading them to enter into it. All of you should go and make offerings to them again and again. Why? Because if any shravakas, pratyekabuddhas, or bodhisattvas are able to believe in the Dharma of the sutra preached by these sixteen bodhisattvas, and accept and embrace it without maligning it, all of them will attain supreme awakening, the wisdom of a tathagata.'"

Then the Buddha, addressing all the monks, said: "These sixteen bodhisattvas always want to teach this Sutra of the Lotus Flower of the Wonderful Dharma. The number of living beings each of them has transformed is like six million billion myriads times the number of sands of the Ganges. In life after life, all who followed these bodhisattvas heard the Dharma from them, believed in it, and understood it. For this reason they have been able to meet four trillion buddhas, world-honored ones, and even in the present have not ceased doing so.

"Monks, I tell you now, that these disciples of the Buddha, the sixteen novices, have all attained supreme awakening. In all the lands in every direction at the present time they preach the Dharma and have innumerable hundreds of thousands of billions of bodhisattvas and shravakas as their followers. Two of those novices became buddhas in the eastern region. One is named Akshobhya and lives in the Land of Joy. The other is named Sumeru Peak. Two are buddhas in the southeastern region, one named Lion's Voice, the other Lion's Character. Two buddhas are in the southern region, one named Space Dweller, the other Ever Extinguished. One of the two buddhas in the southwestern region is named Imperial Character, the other Brahma Character. Of the two buddhas in the western region, one is named Amida, the other Saving All Worlds from Suffering. Of the two buddhas in the northwestern region, one is named Tamalapatra Spiritually Powerful Sandal Fragrance, the other Sumeru Form. Of the two buddhas in the northern region, one is named Cloud Freedom, the other Cloud Freedom King. The buddha in the northeastern region is named Destroyer of All the World's Fear. And the sixteenth is I, Shakyamuni Buddha, having attained supreme awakening in this world.

"Monks, when we were novices, each of us taught and transformed living beings equal in number to innumerable hundreds of thousands of billions times the number of sands of the Ganges, and those who heard the Dharma from us attained supreme awakening. Among these living beings, even now there are some who remain at the stage of shravakas. We have always taught them about supreme awakening, so that through this Dharma all of them will be able gradually to enter the Buddha way. Why? Because the wisdom of the Tathagata is hard to believe and hard to understand. All those living beings, innumerable as the sands of the Ganges, who were transformed at that time are yourselves, monks, and those who will be my shravaka-disciples in ages to come after my extinction.

"Following my extinction there will also be disciples of mine who, neither hearing this sutra nor knowing or understanding the ways that bodhisattvas pursue, will by their own merits conceive an idea of extinction and enter what they think is nirvana. At that time I will be a buddha in another land under a different name. These disciples, though they conceive the idea of extinction and enter what they think is nirvana, will seek the wisdom of the Buddha in that other land and succeed in hearing this sutra. For only by the Buddha-Vehicle will they attain real extinction. There is no other vehicle except the teachings used as skillful means by the tathagatas.

"Monks, if a tathagata knows that his time of nirvana has arrived and that the assembly is pure, firm in faith and understanding, deeply understands the emptiness of things, and enters deeply into meditation, then he will gather together all the bodhisattvas and shravakas and preach this sutra to them. In the whole world there is no second vehicle for attaining extinction; there is only the One Buddha–Vehicle for attaining extinction.

"You should know, monks, that with skillful means the Tathagata reaches deeply into the nature of living beings. He knows that they delight in lesser teachings and are deeply attached to the five desires. For their sake he preaches nirvana so that if they hear it they will receive it in faith.

"Suppose there was a bad road five hundred leagues long, which was steep, wild, difficult, deserted, and far from where anyone lived, a truly frightening place. And a large group of people wanted to go along that road to a place where there were rare treasures. There was a leader and teacher, a guide, who was knowing and wise, knew the difficult road well, where it was open and where closed, and was experienced in leading groups that wanted to pass over it.

"The group he was leading became tired along the way and said to the guide: 'We are utterly exhausted and afraid as well. We can't go any further. Since the road before us goes on and on, now we want to turn back.'

"The guide, a person of many skillful means, thought: 'What a shame that these people want to give up on the great and rare treasures and turn back.' Having thought about it in this way, he used his powers of skillful means to conjure up a castle-city, which appeared about three hundred leagues down the difficult road. Then he said to the group: 'Don't be afraid! You must not turn back! Look! See that great city ahead. There you can stop and rest and do whatever you want. Enter this city and you will soon be completely at ease. Later, when you are able to go toward the place of treasures, you should leave this castle-city.'

"Then the hearts of the exhausted group were filled with great joy, and they exclaimed about such an unprecedented thing: 'Now we can surely escape from this dreadful road and find some peace and comfort.' So the group went into the fantastic castle-city. Thinking they had been rescued from their difficulties, they were soon calm and comfortable.

"Then the guide, seeing that the group was rested and no longer weary, made the fantastic city disappear. He said to the group: 'We have to go now. The place of the treasures is close. I created this large fantastic city a little while ago just for you to rest in.'

"Monks, so is it with the Tathagata. At present he is functioning as your great guide. He knows that the bad road of birth and death and afflictions is steep, difficult, long, and never ending, but that it must be taken and traveled over. If living beings only hear of the One Buddha–Vehicle, they will not want to see the Buddha or to approach him, but think that the Buddha way is long and never ending, and success something that can be attained only after long suffering from arduous work.

"The Buddha, knowing that this frame of mind is timid and weak, uses the power of skillful means, preaching the two kinds of nirvana in order to provide a resting place along the way. If living beings remain at these two stages, then the Tathagata will say to them: 'You have not yet understood what you have to do. The place where you remain is only close to Buddha-wisdom. Take note and think some more. The nirvana that you have attained is not the real one! The Tathagata, through skillful means, has only taken the One Buddha–Vehicle, made distinctions within it, and spoken of the three.'

"The Buddha is just like that guide who, in order to provide a place for the travelers to rest, conjured up a great castle-city and, after they had rested, told them: 'The place of treasures is close. This city is not real, but only something I conjured up.'"

At that time the World-Honored One, wanting to say what he meant once again, spoke in verse:

> Excellent in Great Penetrating Wisdom Buddha
> Sat at the place of the Way for ten eons,
> Yet the Buddha-dharma did not come to him,
> And he could not attain the Buddha way.

> Gods of heaven and dragon kings,
> Asuras, and other beings
> Constantly rained down heavenly flowers
> As offerings to that buddha.

> Gods beat their heavenly drums
> And made all kinds of music.
> Fragrant breezes swept away withered flowers,
> While fresh and beautiful ones rained down.

> When ten small eons had passed,
> He could finally attain the Buddha way.
> Both gods and people of the world
> Were ecstatic with joy.

The sixteen sons of the Buddha,
All with their followers,
Tens of millions of billions surrounding them,
All went to where the Buddha was.

Bowing low at the Buddha's feet,
They begged him to turn the Dharma wheel,
Saying: "Holy Lion, let the rain of Dharma fall,
Satisfying us and all others!"

A World-Honored One is hard to meet,
Appearing only once in a very long time.
And then to prepare the living for awakening
He shakes everything up.

In five million billion lands
Of the worlds to the east,
Palaces of Brahmas were illuminated
As never before.

Seeing this sign, the Brahmas
Searched until they reached the Buddha.
They honored him by scattering flowers
And offering him their palaces.

Begging him to turn the Dharma wheel,
They praised him in verse.
The Buddha, knowing the time was not yet ripe,
Received their pleas, but sat in silence.

In the three other directions
And the four in between,
And in the up and down directions,
The same thing occurred.

Scattering flowers
And offering their palaces,

The Brahma kings begged the Buddha
To turn the Dharma wheel.

"It is hard to meet a World-Honored One.
Out of your great compassion, we beg you—
Open wide the gates of nectar
And turn the unexcelled Dharma wheel!"

The World-Honored One of infinite wisdom,
Receiving the pleas of that crowd,
Proclaimed for them various teachings—
The four truths and the twelve causes.

Everything from ignorance to old age and death
Exists because of birth.
All such faults and pains as this,
All of you should know about.

When this Dharma was proclaimed,
Six million billion myriads of beings
Could bring every possible kind of suffering to an end
And become arhats.

The second time he preached the Dharma
A multitude of tens of millions,
As many as the sands of the Ganges,
Rejecting attachment to things, also became arhats.

After them, the number who attained the Way
Could not be calculated.
One could count them for a trillion eons
And never reach the end.

Then the sixteen princes
Who had left home and become novices
Together begged the Buddha
To proclaim the Dharma of the Great Vehicle.

"May we and our followers
Attain the Buddha way.
We want to be like the World-Honored One,
In having the purest eyes of wisdom."

The Buddha,
Knowing the minds of his children
And the things
They had done in previous lives,

With countless causal explanations
And various parables
Taught them six transcendental practices
And many other divine things.

Distinguishing the real Dharma,
The way of action of bodhisattvas,
He taught this Dharma Flower Sutra
In verses as numerous as the sands of the Ganges.

When the Buddha had finished teaching the sutra,
He went to a quiet room and entered meditation,
Single-mindedly sitting in a single place
For eighty-four thousand eons.

All the novices,
Seeing that he would not yet emerge from meditation,
Taught the Buddha's unexcelled wisdom for the assembly
Of innumerable hundreds of millions of beings.

Each sitting on a Dharma seat,
They taught this Great Vehicle sutra.
And even after the Buddha's peaceful nirvana
They taught and helped others turn to the Dharma.

The number of living beings saved
By each of those novices was

Six million billion,
As many as the sands of the Ganges.

After that buddha had passed into extinction
Those who heard the Dharma,
In whatever buddha-land,
Were reborn along with their teachers.

These sixteen novices,
Completely following the Buddha way,
Now dwell in the ten directions,
Each having attained true awakening.

Those who heard the Dharma at that time
Are all living with one of those buddhas.
Those who remain shravakas
Are gradually taught the Buddha way.

I was among the sixteen
And taught you in the past.
Therefore, by skillful means
I lead you in the quest for Buddha-wisdom.

Because of this connection in the past,
I now teach the Dharma Flower Sutra
To lead you to enter the Buddha way.
Pay attention and have no fear!

Suppose there was a steep, bad road,
Remote and teeming with dangerous beasts,
With neither water nor grass,
And terrifying to people.

An innumerable multitude of tens of millions of people
Wanted to go over this steep road,
A road reaching far into the distance,
Stretching over five hundred leagues.

There was a leader and teacher,
A guide who was knowledgeable and wise,
Clearheaded and determined,
One who could save people in danger from many troubles.

The people became tired and discouraged
And said to the guide:
"Now we are exhausted
And want to turn back."

The guide thought:
"These people are to be pitied.
How can they want to turn back
And give up such great, rare treasures ahead?"

Then he thought of a skillful means.
Using divine powers,
He conjured up a great walled castle-city
With splendidly adorned houses.

Surrounded with gardens and groves,
Brooks and ponds,
With double gates and tall pavilions,
It was filled with both men and women.

Having created this illusion,
He comforted the group, saying:
"Don't be afraid! You can enter this city
And enjoy yourselves as you like."

When they had entered the city,
All their hearts were filled with great joy.
They felt calm and comfortable,
Thinking they had been saved.

When the guide knew they were rested,
He assembled them and said,

"Now we should go forward!
This city is only a fantasy.

"Seeing that you were exhausted
And wanted to turn back midway,
I used my power of skillful means
To conjure up this castle-city for the time being.

"Now you must try very hard
So that together
You can reach the place
Where the treasure is."

I, too, in the same way,
Am the guide for all.

I see the seekers of the Way
Becoming discouraged midway through
And unable to cross the steep road
Of birth and death and afflictions.

So by power of skillful means
I taught nirvana so they could rest, saying:
"Your suffering is ended;
You have finished your work."

When I know they have reached nirvana
And all have become arhats,
Then I gather everyone together
And teach the real Dharma.

Through their powers of skillful means,
Buddhas make distinctions and teach three vehicles.
But there is really only One Buddha–Vehicle.
It is for a resting-place that the other two are taught.

Now I teach the truth for you:
What you have reached is not extinction.
To gain a buddha's comprehensive wisdom,
You have to make a great effort.

When you have gained comprehensive wisdom
And the ten powers of the Buddha-dharma,
And acquired the thirty-two characteristics,
Then that is real extinction.

The buddhas, as guides,
Teach nirvana to provide rest.
But seeing that you are rested,
They lead you on to Buddha-wisdom.

8. Assurance for the Five Hundred Disciples

AT THAT TIME Purna, son of Maitrayani—having heard the Buddha preach the Dharma in accord with wisdom, skillful means, and what was appropriate, hearing as well the assurance of supreme awakening for the great disciples, hearing explanations by stories of previous lives, and hearing of the great, unrestricted divine powers of the buddhas—received what he had never had before and became pure in heart and ecstatic with joy. He immediately got up from his seat, went before the Buddha, and prostrated himself at the Buddha's feet.

Then he withdrew to one side, gazed up at the face of the Honored One. Without turning his eyes away even for a moment, he thought: "The World-Honored One is very unusual. What he does is very exceptional. According to the natures of the various kinds of beings in this world, with insight and by skillful means, he teaches the Dharma for them and draws them away from their greed and attachments to various things. No words can express the Buddha's blessings. Only the Buddha, the World-Honored One, is able to know the natural inclination of our innermost hearts."

Then the Buddha said to the monks: "Do you see this Purna, son of Maitrayani? I have always declared him to be first among all those who preach the Dharma. And I have always praised his many blessings. He has diligently defended, upheld, and helped to proclaim my Dharma. In the midst of the assembly of the four groups he has demonstrated and taught it, enriching them and giving them joy. Thoroughly understanding and explaining the true Dharma of the Buddha, he has greatly and abundantly benefited fellow followers of noble practices. Except for the

208 THE SUTRA OF THE LOTUS FLOWER OF THE WONDERFUL DHARMA

Tathagata himself, there is no one who is so eloquent at explaining its theories.

"Do not think that what Purna is able to defend, uphold, and help to proclaim is only my Dharma. Under nine billion buddhas in the past he has defended, upheld, and helped to proclaim the true Dharma of the buddhas. Among those who preached the Dharma in those times, he was also the best. He had a clear and thorough understanding of the emptiness of things preached by the buddhas. He attained the four kinds of unobstructed wisdom and has always been able to preach the Dharma clearly, without doubt or perplexity. Though complete in divine bodhisattva powers, he observed noble practices all his life. All the people of those Buddha-eras spoke of him as a true shravaka.

"Thus, by use of this skillful means, Purna has abundantly benefited innumerable hundreds of thousands of living beings and transformed innumerable countless numbers of people, leading them toward supreme awakening. In order to purify buddha-lands, he has always done the Buddha's work, teaching and transforming the living.

"Monks, this Purna was first among those who preached the Dharma under the seven buddhas.[10] Now he is first among those who preach the Dharma under me. Likewise, among those who preach the Dharma under future buddhas in this present Eon of Sages, he will be first, and he will defend, uphold, and help to proclaim the Buddha-dharma. Also in the future he will defend, uphold, and help to proclaim the Dharma of an innumerable, unlimited number of buddhas, teaching, transforming, and abundantly benefiting innumerable living beings and leading them toward supreme awakening. In order to purify buddha-lands he will always diligently persevere in teaching the living.

"Gradually taking up the bodhisattva way, after innumerable, countless eons, he will attain supreme awakening in this land. He will be called Dharma Radiance Tathagata, one worthy of offerings, truly awakened, fully clear in conduct, well gone, understanding the world, unexcelled leader, trainer of men, teacher of heavenly beings and people, buddha, world-honored one.

"That Buddha will have a single buddha-land made up of as many three-thousand great thousandfold worlds as there are sands of the Ganges. Its ground will consist of the seven precious materials and will be as level as the palm of the hand, free from hills and valleys, ravines and ditches. The land will be filled with terraces and towers made of the seven precious materials. The palaces of its gods will be nearby in the sky, so that people and gods can meet and be in sight of each other. There will be no evil ways there, and no women. All living beings will be born through transformation and have no sexual passion. Having gained the great divine faculties, their bodies will emit rays of light; they will fly anywhere at will, and their intentions and resolutions will be firm. They will be diligent and wise, all of them golden-colored and adorned with the thirty-two characteristics. All the living in this land will regularly have two foods—one the food of joy in the Dharma, the other the food of delight in meditation. There will be multitudes of innumerable, countless bodhisattvas, that is, tens of millions of billions of myriads of bodhisattvas, who have attained the great divine faculties and the four kinds of unobstructed wisdom, and who have great skill in teaching all kinds of living beings. The number of shravakas will be beyond counting and calculation, and all will have the six divine powers, the three kinds of knowledge, and the eight kinds of liberation. That buddha-land will be adorned and completed with innumerable blessings of this kind.

"The Buddha's eon will be named Treasure Radiance, and his land named Well Purified. The lifetime of the Buddha will be innumerable, countless eons, and his Dharma will live for a very long time. And after the extinction of that buddha, stupas of the seven precious materials will be built throughout the land."

At that time the World-Honored One, wanting to say what he meant once again, spoke in verse:

> Monks, listen carefully!
> Because they have learned skillful means well,
> The way followed by children of the Buddha
> Is unthinkably wonderful.
>
> Knowing that most delight in lesser teachings
> And are overawed by great wisdom,
> Bodhisattvas become
> Shravakas or pratyekabuddhas.

Using innumerable skillful means,
They transform all kinds of beings
By proclaiming themselves to be shravakas,
Far removed from the Buddha way.

They save innumerable beings,
Enabling them to succeed.
Though most people are complacent and lazy,
In this way they are finally led to become buddhas.

Keeping their bodhisattva actions
As inward secrets,
Outwardly
They appear as shravakas.

They appear to have little desire
And to be tired of birth and death,
But in truth
They are purifying buddha-lands.

They show themselves having the three poisons
And seem to hold wrong views.
In this way, my disciples use skillful means
To save living beings.

If I explained
All their varied transformations,
Those who heard me
Would be doubtful and perplexed.

Now, this Purna
Under hundreds of billions of previous buddhas
Diligently practiced the Way,
Proclaiming and defending their teachings.

Seeking unexcelled wisdom,
He went to the buddhas

And became a leader among disciples
In listening and wisdom.

In preaching, he was without fear,
Able to lead everyone to rejoice.
He never became weary or tired
From helping the buddhas in their work.

Already having the great divine faculties,
He acquired the four kinds of unobstructed wisdom.
Knowing whether the minds of others were keen or dull,
He has always preached the pure Dharma.

Fluently explaining what these kinds of things mean,
He taught hundreds of billions of beings,
Leading them to dwell in the Great Vehicle Dharma,
And himself purifying buddha-lands.

In the future as well, he will make offerings
To unquantifiable, innumerable buddhas,
Defend and help in proclaiming the true Dharma,
And himself purify buddha-lands.

Always using skillful means,
He will preach the Dharma without fear,
Saving an incalculable number of beings and
Enabling them to attain comprehensive wisdom.

Making offerings to the tathagatas
And protecting and embracing the storehouse of the Dharma,
He will later become a buddha
Whose name will be Dharma Radiance.

His land, named Well Purified,
Will be made of the seven precious materials,
And his eon will be called
Treasure Radiance.

His bodhisattvas,
A great multitude,
Innumerable hundreds of millions in number,
Will fill that land,

All having crossed over
To the great divine faculties
And being endowed
With powers of dignity and virtue.

Numberless also will be his shravakas
With the three kinds of knowledge, the eight kinds of liberation,
Having attained the four kinds of unobstructed wisdom.
Such will be his community of monks.

All the living of that land
Will be free from sexual passion,
Born pure through transformation,
And adorned with all the features.

Joy in the Dharma and delight in meditation
Will be their food,
With no thought of anything else.
No women will be there, nor any evil ways.

The monk Purna,
Fully developed in all blessings,
Will have this pure land
Where the wise and the sages abound.

Such are the immeasurable things
Of which I have now only spoken briefly.

Then the twelve hundred arhats who were mentally free reflected: "We rejoice at having what we never had before. If the World-Honored One would assure each of us of becoming buddhas in the future as he has the other great disciples, how glad we would be!"

The Buddha, knowing what was in their minds, said to Maha-Kashyapa: "One by one I will assure each of these twelve hundred arhats now before me of their supreme awakening. In this assembly is my great disciple, the monk Kaundinya. After making offerings to sixty-two thousands of millions of buddhas, he will become a buddha named Universal Light Tathagata, one worthy of offerings, truly awakened, fully clear in conduct, well gone, understanding the world, unexcelled leader, trainer of men, teacher of heavenly beings and people, buddha, world-honored one. Five hundred arhats—Uruvilva-Kashyapa, Gaya-Kashyapa, Nadi-Kashyapa, Kalodayin, Udayin, Aniruddha, Revata, Kapphina, Bakkula, Chunda, Svagata, and others—will all attain supreme awakening, and all alike will be called Universal Light."

At that time the World-Honored One, wanting to say what he meant once again, spoke in verse:

> The monk Kaundinya
> Will see innumerable buddhas,
> And after countless eons have passed,
> Attain impartial, proper awakening.
>
> Always radiating great light,
> And having attained divine powers,
> His fame will spread in all directions,
> And he will be respected by all.
>
> Because he always teaches the unexcelled way,
> He will be called Universal Light.
> His land will be clean and pure.
> And all its bodhisattvas will be daring.
>
> Riding on wonderful towers,
> All will travel to the lands in the ten directions,
> With unexcelled offerings
> To give to the buddhas of those lands.
>
> Having made these offerings,
> Their hearts filled with joy,

They will soon return to their own land.
Such will be their divine powers.

That Buddha's life
Will be sixty thousand eons.
His true Dharma will remain for twice his lifetime.
The merely formal Dharma twice that.

And when his Dharma comes to an end,
Human and heavenly beings will mourn.

Five hundred monks
One by one will become buddhas,
With the same name of Universal Light.
Each will assure his successor, saying:

"After my extinction
So-and-so will become a buddha.
The world that he transforms
Will be like mine of today.

"The splendid purity of his land and his divine powers,
His bodhisattvas and shravakas,
His true and merely formal Dharma,
And the number of eons of his life,
Will all be as described above."

Kashyapa, you now know the future
Of these five hundred who are mentally free.
The rest of the shravakas
Will also be like them.

As for those who are not in this assembly,
You have to explain it to them.

Then the five hundred arhats before the Buddha, having received this assurance, were ecstatic with joy. Immediately they got up from their seats, went before the Buddha, prostrated themselves at the Buddha's feet, repented of their errors, and rebuked themselves, saying: "World-Honored One, we always thought we had attained final extinction already. Now we know we were foolish. Why? Because, while we were capable of reaching the wisdom of the Tathagata, we were content with lesser wisdom.

"World-Honored One, it is as if some man went to a good friend's house, got drunk on wine and fell asleep. Meanwhile his friend, having to go away on official business, took a priceless jewel, sewed it into the lining of the man's robe as a gift, and left. The man, being drunk and asleep, knew nothing of this. After getting up, he went on his way until he reached some other land. There he had to use much energy and effort finding food and clothing, undergoing exceedingly great hardship, and making do with whatever he could find.

"Later, his friend happened to meet him and said: 'How sad, old friend! Why do you have to do this for the sake of food and clothing? Wanting you to be in comfort and able to satisfy the five desires, a long time ago in such and such a year, month, and day, I sewed a price-less jewel into the lining of your robe. It should still be there. In your ignorance you are slaving and worrying to keep yourself alive. How dumb! Go and exchange that jewel for whatever you need. Then you can be free to have whatever you wish, and be free from all poverty and want.'

"The Buddha is like this friend. When he was a bodhisattva, he taught us to seek comprehensive wisdom, but we soon forgot, neither knowing nor perceiving. Having obtained the way of the arhat, we sup-posed we had reached the way to extinction. Finding it hard to make a living, we contented ourselves with whatever we could find. Yet our aspi-ration for comprehensive wisdom was never lost. And now the World-Honored One awakens us and says: 'Monks, what you have obtained is not final extinction. For a long time I had you plant good roots for becoming a buddha, and using skillful means showed you the character of nirvana. But you believed it to be the real way to extinction that you had obtained.'

"World-Honored One, now we understand that we are really bodhi-sattvas, assured of attaining supreme awakening. For this reason we are filled with joy, having gained something we never had before."

Then Ajnata-Kaundinya and the others, wanting to restate what they meant, spoke in verse:

Having heard the voice of assurance
Of unexcelled peace and comfort,
We rejoice in what we never had before
And pay our respect to the Buddha of incalculable wisdom.

Now before the World-Honored One
We repent our faults and errors.

Of all the Buddha's immeasurable treasure,
We have won only a bit of nirvana.
Like ignorant and foolish people,
We imagined that was enough.

It's like a poor man
Who arrived at the house of a good friend.
Being very rich, the friend
Served him a great variety of fine foods.

Taking a priceless jewel,
He sewed it into
The lining of the man's robe,
Making a present to him.

And he went away
Without saying a word,
While the man, sleeping,
Knew nothing about it.

When the man woke up
He traveled to other lands
To look for food and clothing to stay alive,
Having a very difficult time just making a living.

Getting by with what little he could get,
And not even hoping for something better,
He never realized that in the lining of his robe
There was a priceless jewel.

Later the friend who gave him the jewel
Happened to meet this poor man.
Sternly rebuking him,
He showed him the jewel sewed into the robe.

Seeing this jewel,
The poor man was filled with a great joy.
Being rich in valuables and other goods,
He could satisfy the five desires.

This is how we were too.
For long, the World-Honored One
Constantly took pity on us and taught us
To cultivate the highest aspiration.

But because of our ignorance
We neither perceived nor knew this.
Having gained just a little bit of nirvana,
We were satisfied and sought no more.

Now the Buddha has awakened us,
Saying: "This is not the real way to extinction.
Only with the attainment of unexcelled Buddha-wisdom
Is there real extinction."

Having heard from the Buddha
This assurance of becoming a buddha and its glories,
And how each will give this assurance to his successor,
Our bodies and minds are now full of joy.

9. Assurance for Arhats, Trained and in Training

AT THAT TIME Ananda and Rahula thought: "We have often thought, how happy we would be if we could receive assurance of supreme awakening!" Then they rose from their seats, went before the Buddha, prostrated themselves at the Buddha's feet, and together said to the Buddha: "World-Honored One, we too should have a share of this. We have put our trust only in the Tathagata. We are known and acknowledged by human and heavenly beings and asuras all over the world. Ananda always attends the Buddha, protecting and keeping the storehouse of the Dharma, and Rahula is the Buddha's son. If the Buddha assured us of supreme awakening, not only would our hopes be fulfilled but also the dreams of many."

Then the two thousand shravaka disciples who were in training and no longer in training all got up from their seats, bared their right shoulders, went before the Buddha, put their palms together with complete devotion, looked up at the World-Honored One reverently, repeated the wish of Ananda and Rahula, and stood off to one side.

Then the Buddha spoke to Ananda: "In the future you will become a buddha named King of the Wisdom of Mountains and Seas Who Is Unlimited in Power Tathagata, one worthy of offerings, truly awakened, fully clear in conduct, well gone, understanding the world, unexcelled leader, trainer of men, teacher of heavenly beings and people, buddha, world-honored one. You will make offerings to over six billion buddhas, protect and keep the storehouse of the Dharma, and afterward attain supreme awakening. Teaching and transforming two hundred million billion bodhisattvas, as numerous as the sands of the Ganges, you will enable

them to attain supreme awakening. Your land will be named Never Low-
ered Victory Banner. Its ground will be pure, with lapis lazuli for earth.

"The eon will be named World-Filling Wonderful Sound. That Bud-
dha's lifetime will be innumerable tens of millions of billions of count-
less eons, so that even if a man counts and calculates for tens of millions
of billions of innumerable, countless eons, it will be impossible to know
the full number. His true Dharma will remain in the world for twice his
lifetime and the merely formal Dharma for twice as long as the true
Dharma. Ananda, this buddha, King of the Wisdom of Mountains and
Seas Who Is Unlimited in Power, and his blessings will be praised by all
the buddha-tathagatas of the ten directions, unlimited tens of millions
of billions of them, like the sands of the Ganges."

Then the World-Honored One, wanting to say what he meant once
again, spoke in verse:

> I now say to you, monks,
> Ananda, upholder of the Dharma,
> Will make offerings to buddhas
> Afterward attaining true awakening.
>
> His name will be King of the Wisdom of Mountains and Seas
> Who Is Unlimited in Power.
> His land will be pure,
> Named Never Lowered Victory Banner.
>
> He will teach and transform bodhisattvas,
> As many as the sands of the Ganges.
> That Buddha will have great dignity and virtue,
> His fame going everywhere.
>
> Because of his sympathy for the living,
> The length of his life will be beyond calculation.
> His true Dharma will be twice his lifetime
> And the merely formal Dharma twice that.
>
> Countless living beings,
> As many as the sands of the Ganges,

In that buddha's Dharma
Will plant seeds that lead to the Buddha way.

Then the eight thousand bodhisattvas in the assembly who had recently started on the Way all thought to themselves: "We have not yet heard even of great bodhisattvas receiving such assurances as this. What can be the reason that these shravakas have obtained such assurance?"

The World-Honored One, knowing what was on the minds of the bodhisattvas, then said to them: "Good sons, together under the Buddha Emptiness King, Ananda and I started pursuing supreme awakening at the same time. Ananda always wanted to listen and learn, while I was devoted to active practice. This is why I have already managed to attain supreme awakening, while Ananda has been taking care of my teachings. He will take care of the Dharma storehouses of future buddhas, and teach, transform, and develop multitudes of bodhisattvas. Such was his original vow. So now he receives this assurance."

When Ananda heard his own assurance and the adornments of his land in the presence of the Buddha, his vow was fulfilled, and he was filled with joy at hearing something he had never heard before. Instantly he remembered the Dharma storehouses of unlimited tens of millions of billions of past buddhas, and understood them without difficulty, as if he were hearing them in the present. He also recalled his original vow.

Then Ananda spoke in verse:

> The rarely met World-Honored One
> Reminds me of the teachings
> Of innumerable buddhas in the past
> As if I were hearing them today.

> Now, having no more doubts,
> I dwell at peace in the Buddha way.
> As a skillful means, I will be a servant
> To protect and embrace the buddhas' teachings.

Then the Buddha spoke to Rahula: "In the future you will become a buddha named One Who Walks on Flowers of the Seven Treasures Tathagata, one worthy of offerings, truly awakened, fully clear in conduct, well gone, understanding the world, unexcelled leader, trainer of men, teacher of heavenly beings and people, buddha, world-honored one. You will make offerings to buddha-tathagatas equal in number to the specks of dust of ten worlds, always becoming the eldest son of those buddhas, just as you are at present. The adornments of the land of this buddha, One Who Walks on Flowers of the Seven Treasures, the length of his life, the disciples transformed by him, his true Dharma, and the merely formal Dharma will be just the same as those of King of the Wisdom of Mountains and Seas Who Is Unlimited in Power. And you will also become the eldest son of that buddha. Afterward you will attain supreme awakening."

Then the World-Honored One, wanting to proclaim this teaching once again, spoke in verse:

When I was a crown prince,
Rahula was my eldest son.
Now that I have attained the Buddha way,
He receives the Dharma and is my Dharma son.

In future lives,
He will see innumerable hundreds of millions of buddhas.
As the eldest son of each of them,
He will single-mindedly seek the Buddha way.

The hidden acts of Rahula
Only I am able to know.
As my eldest son
He is revealed to all.

Innumerable tens of thousands of millions
Are his blessings, beyond calculation.
Dwelling at peace in the Buddha-dharma,
He seeks the unexcelled way.

At that time the World-Honored One observed the two thousand people in training and no longer in training. They were gentle, quiet, and purehearted, giving their full attention to watching the Buddha.

The Buddha said to Ananda: "Do you see these two thousand people in training and no longer in training?"

"Yes, I see them."

"Ananda, these people will make offerings to as many buddha-tathagatas as there are specks of dust in fifty worlds. They will revere and honor them, and protect and keep their Dharma storehouses. Finally, at the same time, in all the lands of the ten directions, they will become buddhas. All will have the same name, Jewel Sign, and be tathagatas, worthy of offerings, truly awakened, fully clear in conduct, well gone, understanding the world, unexcelled leaders, trainers of men, teachers of heavenly beings and people, buddhas, world-honored ones. Their life-times will be one eon, and the splendor of their lands, and the number of their shravakas and bodhisattvas, their true Dharma and merely formal Dharma, will all be equal."

Then the World-Honored One, wanting to say what he meant once again, spoke in verse:

> To these two thousand shravakas
> Now in my presence,
> I give assurance that
> In the future all will become buddhas.
>
> The buddhas to whom they make offerings will be
> Numerous as the specks of dust mentioned above.
> After protecting and keeping their Dharma storehouses,
> They will reach true awakening.
>
> Each will have a land in one of the ten directions,
> And all will have the same name.
> At the same time sitting on the place of the Way,
> All will bear witness to the unexcelled wisdom.
>
> All will be named Jewel Sign.
> Their lands and disciples,
> Their true Dharma and merely formal Dharma
> Will all be equal and without difference.

With the same divine powers
They will everywhere liberate the living.
Their fame will spread everywhere.
And in time they will enter nirvana.

Then the two thousand people in training and no longer in training, hearing the Buddha's assurance, were ecstatic with joy and spoke in verse:

World-Honored One! Bright Lamp of Wisdom!
Hearing this voice of assurance,
We are filled with joy,
As though sprinkled with sweet nectar!

10. Teachers of the Dharma

AT THAT TIME the World-Honored One addressed the eighty thousand great leaders through the Bodhisattva Medicine King, saying: "Medicine King, do you see in this assembly the innumerable gods, dragon kings, satyrs, centaurs, asuras, griffins, chimeras, pythons, humans and nonhumans, as well as the monks, nuns, laymen and laywomen, those who seek to become shravakas, those who seek to become pratyekabuddhas, and those who seek the Buddha way? I assure all such beings who are before the Buddha that if they hear a single verse or a single phrase of the Wonderful Dharma Flower Sutra and respond in joy even for a single moment, they will attain supreme awakening."

Again addressing Medicine King, the Buddha said: "What's more, after the extinction of the Tathagata, if there is anyone who hears even a single verse or a single phrase of the Wonderful Dharma Flower Sutra, and responds in joy for even a single moment, I assure that one also of supreme awakening. Again, if there are any who receive and embrace, read, recite, explain, or copy even a single verse of the Wonderful Dharma Flower Sutra, or look upon this sutra with reverence as if it were the Buddha himself, or make offerings to it in various ways with flowers, incense, necklaces, powdered incense, paste incense, incense for burning, silk canopies, flags, banners, robes, or music, as well as revering it with palms together, you should understand, Medicine King, that these people have already made offerings to ten trillion buddhas and under those buddhas have worked to fulfill their great vow, and because they have sympathy for the living they have been born here among people.

"Medicine King, if anyone asks you what sort of living beings will become buddhas in ages to come, you should show them that these are the people who will certainly become buddhas in ages to come. Why? Because if any good sons or good daughters embrace, read, recite, explain, or copy even a single phrase of the Dharma Flower Sutra, or make offerings to it in various ways with flowers, incense, necklaces, powdered incense, paste incense, incense for burning, silk canopies, flags, banners, robes, or music, as well as revering it with palms together, these people will be looked up to and honored by the whole world. Offerings should be made to them as if they were tathagatas. You should understand that these people are great bodhisattvas who, having attained supreme awakening and out of compassion for living beings, are willing to be born in this world, where they can explain the Wonderful Dharma Flower Sutra and proclaim it everywhere. How much more true this is of those who are able to receive and embrace this whole sutra, and in various ways make offerings to it!

"You should understand, Medicine King, that these people have relinquished the rewards for their pure deeds by themselves, and that after my extinction, out of sympathy for living beings, they will be born in an evil age and proclaim this sutra everywhere. After my extinction, if any of these good sons or good daughters are able, even in secret, to teach to one person even one phrase of the Dharma Flower Sutra, then you should understand that they are emissaries of the Tathagata, sent by the Tathagata to do the work of the Tathagata. How much more true this is of those who teach this sutra for others everywhere before great crowds of people!

"Medicine King, even if some wicked person out of evil intent appears before the Buddha and unceasingly curses and reviles the Buddha for a whole eon, that person's offense will be rather light. But if anyone, even with a single ill word, curses or denigrates laypeople or monks or nuns who read and recite the Dharma Flower Sutra, the offense will be very heavy.

"Medicine King, you should understand that those who read and recite the Dharma Flower Sutra have put on the adornments of the Buddha and are carried on the shoulders of the Tathagata. Wherever they go, they should be greeted wholeheartedly with palms together. They should be revered, given offerings, honored, and praised. Flowers,

incense, necklaces, powdered incense, paste incense, incense for burn-
ing, silk canopies, flags and banners, robes, edibles and dainties, and
music, the finest things available among the people, should be given to
them as offerings. Treasures from heaven should be scattered over them
and offerings of piles of treasures from heaven should be given to them.
Why? Because such people enjoy teaching the Dharma. And if anyone
hears it, even for a moment, they attain supreme awakening."

Then the World-Honored One, wanting to explain what he meant
once again, spoke in verse:

> If you want to dwell in the Buddha way
> And gain natural wisdom,
> You should always be diligent about making offerings
> To those who receive and embrace the Dharma Flower.

> If you want to attain
> All-inclusive wisdom quickly,
> You should receive and embrace this sutra
> And make offerings to others who receive and embrace it.

> If anyone is able to receive and embrace
> The Wonderful Dharma Flower Sutra,
> You should know that that one was sent by the Buddha,
> Who has compassion for living beings.

> Those who are able to receive and embrace
> The Wonderful Dharma Flower Sutra,
> Having given up the pure land,
> Have been born here out of sympathy for the living.

> Know that such people,
> Free to be born where they want,
> Chose to be in this evil age
> To teach the unexcelled Dharma everywhere.

> With flowers and incense from heaven,
> Robes of heavenly jewels,

And heaps of wonderful treasures from heaven,
You should make offerings to such Dharma preachers.

In the evil age after my extinction,
Those who are able to embrace this sutra
Should be greeted and revered with palms together,
As if making offerings to the World-Honored One.

With the best of delicacies and abundant sweets,
And every kind of clothing,
You should make offerings to such followers of the Buddha,
In hope of hearing even a moment of their preaching.

In future ages,
If anyone is able to receive and embrace this sutra
I will send them to be among people
To do the work of the Tathagata.

If anyone in the course of an eon
Always harbors evil intentions
And with angry looks maligns the Buddha,
That person will be committing an extremely grave sin.

But if anyone directs evil words
Toward those who read, recite, and uphold
This Dharma Flower Sutra,
That one's sin is still greater.

Anyone who seeks the Buddha way,
And with palms together in my presence
Praises me with innumerable verses for an eon,
Will acquire innumerable blessings.

This is because they praise the Buddha.
But for anyone who praises
Those who uphold this sutra,
Good fortune will be even greater.

For eight billion eons,
With the most wonderful colors and sounds,
And what is most pleasing to smell, taste, and touch,
Make offerings to those who embrace this sutra!

If you make such offerings
And hear the Dharma even for a moment,
You will rejoice and say,
"I have gained great benefit."

Medicine King, I tell you now,
Of the sutras I have preached,
Among all of them
The Dharma Flower is the greatest.

Then the Buddha spoke once again to Medicine King Bodhisattva, the great one, saying: "My sutras are innumerable tens of millions of billions. Whether already taught, now being taught, or to be taught in the future, among all of them this Dharma Flower Sutra is the most difficult to believe and the most difficult to understand. Medicine King, this sutra is the storehouse of the hidden core of the buddhas. It must not be distributed or carelessly given to people. It has been protected by buddhas, world-honored ones. From ancient times until now it has never been openly preached. And since this sutra has aroused much resentment and envy while the Tathagata is still alive; how much more it will arouse after his passing!

"Medicine King, you should know that after the Tathagata's extinction, those who are able to copy, embrace, read, recite, make offerings to, and teach this sutra for the sake of others will be covered by the Tathagata with his robe, and will be protected and kept in mind by the buddhas now in other worlds. They will have great power of faith, the power of aspiration, and the power of good character. You should know that they will live with the Tathagata, and the Tathagata will touch their heads with his hand.

"Medicine King, in every place where this sutra is taught, or where it is read, or where it is recited, or where it is copied, or even where a roll of it is kept, one should put up a stupa of the seven precious materials, making it very high, spacious, and well adorned. But there is no need to put remains in it. The reason is that the whole body of the Tathagata will already be in it. Such a stupa should be revered, honored, and praised with offerings of all kinds of flowers, incense, garlands, silk canopies, banners, flags, music, and hymns. If anyone seeing such a stupa worships and makes an offering to it, you should know that they will come nearer to supreme awakening.

"Medicine King, though there are many people, both laypeople and monks, who walk in the bodhisattva way, if they are not able to see, hear, read, recite, copy, embrace, and make offerings to this Dharma Flower Sutra, you should know that they are not yet walking well in the bodhisattva way. But if any of them hear this sutra, then they will be able to walk well in the bodhisattva way. If any living beings who seek after the Buddha way either see or hear this Dharma Flower Sutra, and after hearing it believe, understand, and embrace it, then you should know that they are nearer to supreme awakening.

"Medicine King, it is like a man who is extremely thirsty and in need of water, and searches for it by digging on a high plain. So long as he sees only dry earth, he knows that water is still far away. But he does not cease digging, and in time sees damp earth, and then gradually reaches mud. Then he is determined to go on, knowing that water must be near.

"Bodhisattvas are also like this. If they have not heard, not understood, or not been able to study and put into practice this Dharma Flower Sutra, you should know that such people are still far from supreme awakening. But if they hear, understand, ponder, and study it and put it into practice, you may be sure that they are nearer supreme awakening. The reason for this is that the supreme awakening of every bodhisattva belongs to this sutra. This sutra opens the gateway of skillful means and reveals the principle of the true nature of things. The treasure-house of this Dharma Flower Sutra is deep and hidden, and so far away that no human being can reach it. But now, in order to teach, transform, and develop bodhisattvas, the Buddha has opened it up.

"Medicine King, if any bodhisattva responds with surprise, doubt, or fear from hearing this Dharma Flower Sutra, you should know that this is a bodhisattva who has only recently started out on this Way. If any shravaka responds with surprise, doubt, or fear from hearing this

Dharma Flower Sutra, you should know that this is an extremely arrogant person.

"Medicine King, after the extinction of the Tathagata, if there are good sons or good daughters who want to teach this Dharma Flower Sutra for the four groups, how should they teach it? Such good sons or good daughters should enter the room of the Tathagata, put on the robe of the Tathagata, sit on the seat of the Tathagata, and then teach this sutra everywhere for the four groups.

"To enter the room of the Tathagata is to have great compassion for all living beings. To wear the robe of the Tathagata is to be gentle and patient. To sit on the seat of the Tathagata is to contemplate the emptiness of all things. One should dwell in peace with all three and then, never becoming lazy or careless, teach this Dharma Flower Sutra everywhere to bodhisattvas and the four groups.

"Medicine King, I will send magically conjured messengers to other realms to gather people together to hear the Dharma. I will also send conjured monks, nuns, and male and female laypeople to hear the Dharma preached. All these conjured people, hearing the Dharma, will receive it in faith and obey it completely. If a preacher of the Dharma is in an empty, secluded place, I will send many gods, dragons, demons, spirits, centaurs, asuras, and others to hear the preaching of the Dharma. Though I will be in a different land, from time to time I will make it possible for preachers of the Dharma to see my body. If they forget any detail of this sutra, I will tell it to them so they can recite the sutra correctly and fully."

At that time the World-Honored One, wanting to proclaim this teaching once again, spoke in verse:

If you want to be rid of laziness and carelessness,
You should listen to this sutra!
Getting to hear it is difficult
And receiving it in faith is difficult as well.

A thirsty person needing water,
Who digs on a high plain
And sees only dry earth,
Knows water is still far away.

But with moist earth
And mud gradually appearing,
He is assured
That water is near.

Medicine King, you should know
That this is the way people are.
Those who do not hear the Dharma Flower Sutra
Are far from Buddha-wisdom.

But if they hear
This profound sutra,
Which determines the Dharma for shravakas
And is the king of all sutras,

And hearing it
Truly ponder over it,
You should know that those people
Are near the wisdom of a buddha.

If people are to teach this sutra,
Let them enter the Tathagata's room,
Put on the Tathagata's robe,
And sit on the Tathagata's seat.

Facing the multitude without fear,
Let them teach it clearly everywhere,

With great compassion as their room,
Gentleness and patience as their robe,
And the emptiness of all things as their seat.
Doing this, they should teach the Dharma.

When they teach this sutra,
If anyone speaks ill of them or abuses them,
Or attacks them with swords, sticks, tiles, or stones,
They should think of the Buddha and be patient.

In tens of millions of billions of lands,
I appear with a pure lasting body,
And in innumerable hundreds of millions of eons
Teach the Dharma for all the living.

After my extinction,
If anyone is able to teach this sutra,
I will send
The four magically conjured groups—

Monks and nuns, and pure men and women,
To make offerings to the Dharma teacher,
To lead living beings
And assemble them to hear the Dharma.

If people seek to attack the teachers
With swords and sticks or tiles and stones,
I will send conjured people
To guard and protect them.

If anyone preaches the Dharma
In an empty, secluded place,
Or in a quiet place
Where no human voice is heard,

And reads and recites
This sutra there,
Then I will appear to them
With a pure and radiant body.

If they forget sentences or words,
I will tell them
So that they can be
Thoroughly effective.

Whenever people with such virtues
Either teach the four groups

Or read and recite the sutra in seclusion,
They will always see me.

When such a person is in an empty place,
I will send gods, dragon kings,
Satyrs, demons, spirits, and others
To come together to hear the Dharma.

Such people will delight in teaching the Dharma
And analyze it without hindrance.
Because buddhas protect and keep them in mind,
They will be able to lead the many to rejoice.

Whoever is close to a Dharma teacher
Will quickly gain the bodhisattva way.
And one who becomes a follower of such a teacher
Will see as many buddhas as the sands of the Ganges.

11. The Sight of the Treasure Stupa

A T THAT TIME a stupa of the seven precious materials, five hundred leagues high and two hundred and fifty leagues wide and deep, sprang up from the earth in front of the Buddha and stood in the air. It was decorated with all kinds of valuable things. It had five thousand railings, tens of millions of niche-like spaces open to the outside, and was decorated with countless banners and flags. Garlands of jewels hung from it and tens of thousands of millions of jeweled bells were suspended from it. From its four sides came the fragrance of tamalapatra sandalwood, filling the whole world. All its banners and canopies were composed of the seven precious materials: gold, silver, lapis lazuli, seashell, agate, pearl, and carnelian. It was so tall it reached up to the palaces of the four kings of heaven.

The thirty-three gods rained down mandarava flowers from heaven as offerings to the treasure stupa. Other gods, dragons, satyrs, centaurs, asuras, griffins, chimeras, pythons, humans and nonhumans, all these tens of millions of billions of beings, made offerings to the stupa with all kinds of flowers, incense, garlands, streamers, canopies, and music, revering, honoring, and praising it.

Then from the midst of the treasure stupa came a loud voice of praise saying: "Well done, well done, World-Honored Shakyamuni! For the sake of the great assembly you are able to teach the Wonderful Dharma Flower Sutra of great impartial wisdom, the Dharma by which bodhisattvas are taught and which buddhas protect and keep in mind. It is just as you say, World-Honored Shakyamuni! All that you say is true."

Then the four groups, seeing the great treasure stupa in the air and hearing the voice that came from the stupa, were filled with joy in the Dharma and with wonder at these unprecedented things. They got up from their seats and, reverently putting their palms together, withdrew to one side.

Meanwhile, a bodhisattva great one named Great Delight in Preaching, perceiving uncertainty in the minds of the human and heavenly beings, asuras, and others of all the worlds, spoke to the Buddha, saying: "World-Honored One, for what reason has this treasure stupa sprung out of the earth and this voice come from within it?"

Then the Buddha told Great Delight in Preaching Bodhisattva: "In this treasure stupa there is the whole body of a tathagata. Once in the past, innumerable tens of millions of billions of countless worlds to the east, in a land named Treasure Purity, there was a buddha named Abundant Treasures. When that buddha was originally practicing the bodhisattva way, he made a great vow, saying: 'After I become a buddha and then extinct, if there is a place in any land in the universe where the Dharma Flower Sutra is taught, in order that I may listen to it, my stupa will appear there, bearing testimony to the sutra and praising it, saying, "Well done!"'

"When that buddha had finished the Buddha way, his extinction approaching, in the midst of a great assembly of human and heavenly beings, he said to the monks: 'After my extinction, if anyone wants to make offerings to my whole body, they should put up a great stupa.' Thus, throughout all the worlds of the universe, in any place at all where someone teaches the Dharma Flower Sutra, by his divine powers and the power of his vow, that Buddha has his treasure stupa, containing his whole body, appear before them and praises the sutra, saying: 'Well done, well done!'

"Great Delight in Preaching, it is because just now the Tathagata Abundant Treasures heard the Dharma Flower Sutra being taught that his stupa sprang up from the earth, bearing praise and saying: 'Well done, well done!'"

Then Great Delight in Preaching Bodhisattva, because of the divine powers of the Tathagata, said to the Buddha: "World-Honored One, we want to see this buddha's body."

The Buddha said to Great Delight in Preaching Bodhisattva, the great one: "This Buddha Abundant Treasures has taken a profound vow, saying: 'When my treasure stupa appears in the presence of one of the buddhas so that I can hear the Dharma Flower Sutra, if someone wants me to show my body to the four groups, let the buddhas who are embodiments of that buddha and are preaching the Dharma in the worlds of the ten directions return together and assemble in one place. Then my body will appear.' Thus, Great Delight in Preaching, I must now assemble the buddhas who are my embodiments and are preaching the Dharma in all the worlds."

Great Delight in Preaching replied to the Buddha: "World-Honored One, we would also like to see the buddhas who embody you, and worship and make offerings to them."

Then the Buddha emitted a beam of light from his tuft of white hair, immediately making visible all the buddhas in five million billion myriads of lands to the east, as many as the sands of the Ganges. All those lands had crystal for their ground and were adorned with jeweled trees and jeweled robes. They were filled with countless tens of millions of billions of bodhisattvas. Jeweled awnings were hung there and nets of jewels were overhead. All the buddhas in those lands preached various teachings with great, wonderful voices. And innumerable tens of millions of billions of bodhisattvas were also seen there, filling those lands and teaching the Dharma for the multitude. It was the same in the southern, western, and northern regions, in the four intermediate directions, and up and down—wherever the beam of light shone from the tuft of white hair.

Then each of the buddhas in the ten directions spoke to his multitudes of bodhisattvas, saying: "Good sons, now we have to go to Shakyamuni Buddha's world and make offerings to the treasure stupa of the Tathagata Abundant Treasures."

Then this world instantly became pure, with lapis lazuli for earth, jeweled trees adorning it, and cords of gold marking the boundaries of its eight divisions. There were no villages, towns, cities, great seas, great rivers, mountains, streams, forests, or thickets. Most precious incense was burning there, mandarava flowers were scattered over the ground, and jeweled nets and awnings were hanging there, with all kinds of jeweled bells. All other human and heavenly beings having been removed to other lands, there remained only the assembled congregation.

Then those buddhas, each bringing a great bodhisattva as his attendant, arrived at this world and went to the foot of a jeweled tree. Each of the jeweled trees was five hundred leagues high, adorned with branches, leaves, flowers, and fruit in proper order. Under each of those jeweled trees was a lion seat five leagues high, also decorated with large jewels. Then the buddhas went to those seats and sat cross-legged on them. Thus the three-thousand great thousandfold world was being filled, though those embodying Shakyamuni Buddha had not yet finished arriving from even one direction.

Then Shakyamuni Buddha, wanting to make room for all the buddhas who embodied him, transformed two million billion myriads of lands in each of the eight directions, making them pure, without purgatories, hungry spirits, animals, or asuras. What's more, he removed their human and heavenly beings to other lands. The lands thus transformed also had lapis lazuli for earth and were adorned with jeweled trees five hundred leagues high, and with branches, leaves, flowers, and fruit in proper order. Under every tree was a jeweled lion seat five leagues high, decorated with all kinds of jewels. There were no large seas or rivers, or any mountain kings such as Mount Mucilinda, Mount Great Mucilinda, Iron Circle Mountains, Great Iron Circle Mountains, Mount Sumeru, and so on. The whole area made up a single buddha-land. Its jeweled ground was even and smooth. Jewel-decked awnings were spread and streamers and canopies were hung everywhere, while most precious incense burned, and precious flowers from heaven everywhere covered the ground.

In order that the buddhas who were arriving might be seated, Shakyamuni Buddha once again transformed two million billion myriads of lands in each of the eight directions, making them pure, without purgatories, hungry spirits, animals, or asuras. What's more, he removed their human and heavenly beings to other lands. The lands thus transformed also had lapis lazuli for ground and were adorned with jeweled trees five hundred leagues high, and with branches, leaves, flowers, and fruit in proper order. Under every tree was a jeweled lion seat five leagues high, decorated with great jewels. There were no large seas or rivers, or any Mount Mucilinda, Mount Great Mucilinda, Iron Circle Mountains, Great Iron Circle Mountains, Mount Sumeru, and so on. The whole area made up a single buddha-land. Its jeweled ground was even and smooth. Everywhere jewel-decked awnings were spread and streamers and canopies were hung, while most precious incense burned, and precious flowers from heaven everywhere covered the ground.

At that moment, those embodying Shakyamuni to the east, buddhas who preached the Dharma in hundreds of thousands of billions of myriads of lands, lands as numerous as the sands of the Ganges, arrived and assembled. In the same way, all the buddhas from the ten directions gradually arrived and assembled and took their seats in the eight directions. Then each direction was filled with buddha-tathagatas from four million billion myriads of lands.

Then all the buddhas, each seated on a lion seat under a jeweled tree, sent their attendants, each with a handful of precious flowers, to make inquiries of Shakyamuni Buddha, telling them: "Good sons, go to Holy Eagle Peak, where Shakyamuni Buddha is, and say to him, as I am instructing you: 'Are your illnesses and troubles few? In spirit and energy are you well? And are your bodhisattvas and shravakas at peace?' Then make offerings to the Buddha by sprinkling these precious flowers before him, and say this: 'Such and such a buddha would like to have this treasure stupa opened.'" All the buddhas sent their attendants in this way.

Then Shakyamuni Buddha, seeing the buddhas who embodied him assembled together, each seated on a lion seat, and hearing that those buddhas all wanted the treasure stupa to be opened, immediately got up from his seat and went up into the air. All four groups stood up, put their palms together, and gazed at the Buddha in rapt attention. Then Shakyamuni Buddha opened the door of the stupa of the seven precious materials with the fingers of his right hand. From the stupa there came a great sound, like the withdrawing of the bar when the gate to a great city is opened. Suddenly the whole congregation saw the Tathagata Abundant Treasures on a lion seat in the treasure stupa, with his whole body in one piece, sitting as though he were in meditation. And they heard him say: "Well done, well done, Shakyamuni Buddha! You have preached this Dharma Flower Sutra gladly, which is what I have come to this place to hear."

Then the four groups—seeing the buddha who had passed away, and had been extinct for innumerable tens of millions of billions of eons, speak such words as these, praising such an unprecedented event— scattered heaps of precious flowers from heaven on Abundant Treasures

Buddha and on Shakyamuni Buddha. Abundant Treasures Buddha offered half his seat within the treasure stupa to Shakyamuni Buddha, saying: Shakyamuni Buddha, take this seat." Then Shakyamuni Buddha entered the stupa, took half the seat, and sat with folded legs.

Seeing the two tathagatas sitting with folded legs on the lion seat in the stupa of the seven precious materials, those in the great assembly then thought: "The buddhas are sitting high and far away. It would be good if the tathagatas would use their divine powers to enable all of us to be up in the air."

Immediately Shakyamuni Buddha used his divine powers to bring all of the great assembly to where he was up in the air. In a loud voice he addressed all four groups, saying: "Who is able to teach the Wonderful Dharma Flower Sutra everywhere throughout this world? Now indeed is the time. Before long the Tathagata will enter nirvana. So that it will last forever, the Buddha wants to entrust this Wonderful Dharma Flower Sutra to someone."

Then the World-Honored One, wanting to say what he meant once again, spoke in verse:

> This holy lord, World-Honored One,
> Though long extinct,
> Sits in his treasure stupa
> And comes here for the sake of the Dharma.
>
> How then can anyone not be dutiful
> For the sake of the Dharma?
>
> This Buddha passed away
> Countless eons ago,
> Yet in place after place he listens to the Dharma
> Because such chances are rare.
>
> This Buddha's original vow was:
> "After my extinction,
> Wherever I go, wherever I am,
> It will always be to hear the Dharma."

And my embodiments,
Buddhas as innumerable as the sands of the Ganges,
Have come to hear the Dharma
And to see the extinct Abundant Treasures Tathagata.

Leaving his wonderful land
And a multitude of disciples,
Human and heavenly beings and dragon-gods,
And all their offerings to him,

Each has come to this place
So that the Dharma may live for a long time.

In order to seat these buddhas,
With divine powers
I have moved innumerable beings
And purified the land.

One by one, the buddhas
Have gone under the jeweled trees.
They are like lotus flowers
Decorating a clear and cool pond.

Under those jeweled trees,
Seated on the lion seats,
The buddhas are
Brilliant and resplendent.

Just as in the darkness of night
Great torches burn brightly,
From them comes a wonderful fragrance
Spreading over all the lands.

Living beings showered in this fragrance
Are beside themselves with joy,

Like little tree branches
Quivering in a great wind.

They use this skillful means
So that the Dharma will live for a long time.

To this great assembly I ask:
"After my extinction,
Who can receive and embrace,
Read and recite this sutra?

"Let them come before the Buddha now
And declare their vow!"

This Abundant Treasures Buddha,
Though he passed away long ago,
In accord with his great vow,
Roars like a lion.

The Tathagata Abundant Treasures
And I myself,
And the assembled buddhas embodying me,
Certainly know this intention.

Among all my Buddha children,
If anyone is able to keep the Dharma,
They should make a great vow
So that it may live for a long time!

One who is able to keep
This sutra-dharma
Has already made offerings
To me and to Abundant Treasures.

This Abundant Treasures Buddha,
Living in the treasure stupa

Is always willing to go anywhere
For the sake of this sutra.

One who keeps this sutra has also made offerings
To all the buddhas embodying me assembled here,
Who adorn and make resplendent
All the worlds.

Anyone who teaches this sutra
Will be able to see me
And the Tathagata Abundant Treasures,
And also the buddhas embodying me.

All my good sons
Should carefully consider this!
This is a difficult task,
Requiring the making of a great vow.

If one taught
All the other sutras,
Numerous as the sands of the Ganges,
That would not be really difficult.

If one picked up Mount Sumeru
And hurled it far away
To innumerable buddha-lands,
That too would not be difficult.

If someone used their toe
To move a great thousandfold world
And hurl it far away to other lands,
That too would not be difficult.

If one stood on the highest heaven
And for the sake of others
Preached countless other sutras,
That too would not be difficult.

But after the Buddha's extinction,
In the midst of an evil age,
If someone teaches this sutra,
That indeed will be difficult!

If someone
Took the sky in his hand
And wandered around with it,
That would not be difficult.

But after my extinction,
If someone copies and keeps this sutra
Or causes another to copy it,
This indeed will be difficult!

If someone took the whole earth,
Put it on his or her toenail,
And ascended to the Brahma heaven,
That would not be difficult.

But after the Buddha's extinction,
In the midst of an evil age,
If someone reads this sutra aloud for even a moment,
This indeed will be difficult!

In the fire at the eon's end,
If someone carried a load of dry hay
Into the fire without getting burned,
That would not be difficult.

But after my extinction,
If anyone embraces this sutra
And teaches it even to one person,
This indeed will be difficult!

If one embraced the storehouse
Of eighty-four thousand teachings

And the twelve divisions of the sutras,
And preached them to others,

Leading those who hear
To gain the six divine powers;
Even if one could do all this,
That would not be difficult.

But after my extinction,
If anyone hears and accepts this sutra
And inquires about its meaning,
This indeed will be difficult!

If one taught the Dharma
And led tens of millions of billions
Of countless, innumerable beings,
As many as the sands of the Ganges,

To become arhats
With the six divine powers;
Even if one conferred such benefits,
That would not be difficult.

But after my extinction,
If anyone is able to honor and embrace
Such a sutra as this,
That indeed will be difficult!

For the sake of the Buddha way,
In innumerable lands
From the beginning until now,
I have taught many sutras everywhere.

Among them all
This sutra is the most excellent.
Anyone who is able to embrace it
Embraces the body of the Buddha.

Good sons,
After my extinction
Who will be able to receive and embrace,
Read and recite this sutra?

Let them come before the Buddha now
And declare their vow!

This sutra is so difficult to embrace,
If anyone embraces it even for a short time,
I will be pleased,
And so will all the buddhas.

Someone who can do this
Will be praised by all the buddhas.

Such a one is courageous,
Such a one is diligent,
Such a one is an observer of precepts
And follower of ascetic practices.

Such a one will attain quickly
The unexcelled Buddha way.

In the future,
Someone who can read and embrace this sutra
Will truly be a child of the Buddha,
Living in a land that is pure and good.

After the Buddha's extinction,
One who can understand its meaning
Will be the eyes of the world
For both human and heavenly beings.

In that frightening age,
One who can teach this sutra even for a moment
Should receive offerings
From all human and heavenly beings.

12. Devadatta

AT THAT TIME the Buddha addressed the bodhisattvas, the human and heavenly beings, and the four groups, saying: "Through innumerable eons in the past, I tirelessly sought the Dharma Flower Sutra. Throughout those many eons I was a king who vowed to seek unexcelled awakening. Never faltering, and wanting to become fully developed in the six transcendental practices, the king diligently and unstintingly gave alms—elephants, horses, the seven rare things, countries, cities, wives, children, male and female servants, attendants, and even his own head, eyes, marrow, brain, flesh, hands, and feet—not sparing his body or life.

"At that time a person's lifetime was beyond measure. For the sake of the Dharma, he gave up his kingdom and throne, left the government to the crown prince, sounded drums and sent proclamations in all directions, seeking the Dharma, and saying: 'For the rest of my life, I will be the provider and servant for anyone who can teach me the Great Vehicle.'

"Then a seer came to the king and said: 'I have a Great Vehicle sutra named the Lotus Flower of the Wonderful Dharma. If you will obey me, I will explain it for you.' Hearing what the seer said, the king became ecstatic with joy and immediately went with him, providing for his needs, gathering fruit, drawing water, collecting firewood, laying out his food, even offering his body as a seat and bed, yet never feeling tired physically or emotionally. During this period of service, all for the sake of the Dharma, a thousand years passed in which he diligently provided for the seer so he would lack nothing."

Then the World-Honored One, wanting to restate what he meant, spoke in verse:

> I remember past eons.
> Though I was a king of a land in this world,
> Seeking the great Dharma,
> I did not crave gratification of the five desires.

> By striking a bell,
> I announced in the four directions:
> If anyone possesses the great Dharma and explains it to me,
> I will become his servant.

> At the time there was a seer named Asita,
> Who came and said to the great king:

> "I have a fine and wonderful Dharma,
> Rarely heard in this world.
> If you are able to practice it well,
> I will teach it to you."

> Then the king,
> Hearing the words of the seer,
> With a heart full of great joy
> Went with the seer.

> Providing for his needs,
> He gathered firewood, fruit, and gourds
> And reverently offered them
> At appropriate times.

> By keeping the wonderful Dharma
> In his heart,
> He never tired
> Physically or emotionally.

For the sake of all living beings everywhere
He diligently sought the great Dharma,
But not for his own sake
And not for gratification of the five desires.

Thus the king of a great land
By diligently seeking, obtained this Dharma
And finally became a buddha.
Therefore, I now teach it to you.

The Buddha said to all the monks: "The king at that time was me and the seer was the present Devadatta. Because Devadatta was a good friend to me I was able to become fully developed in the six transcendental practices, in kindness, compassion, joy, and impartiality, in the thirty-two characteristics, the eighty different attractive features, the deep gold color, the ten powers, the four kinds of freedom from fear, the four social teachings, the eighteen kinds of uniqueness, and the powers of the divine way. That I have attained impartial, proper awakening and saved many of the living is due to my good friend Devadatta."

"I declare to all four groups that after innumerable eons have passed Devadatta will become a buddha whose name will be Heavenly King Tathagata, one worthy of offerings, truly awakened, fully clear in conduct, well gone, understanding the world, unexcelled leader, trainer of men, teacher of heavenly beings and people, buddha, world-honored one. His world will be named Heaven's Way. At that time Heavenly King Buddha will live in the world for twenty intermediate eons, teaching the wonderful Dharma everywhere for the sake of all the living. Living beings as numerous as the sands of the Ganges will enjoy being arhats; innumerable beings will aspire to be pratyekabuddhas; and living beings as numerous as the sands of the Ganges, aspiring to the unexcelled way, will attain assurance of not being reborn and the stage of never backsliding. After the complete nirvana of Heavenly King Buddha, the true Dharma will dwell in his world for twenty intermediate eons. The remains of his entire body will be put in a stupa of the seven precious materials sixty leagues high and forty leagues in length and width. All the human and heavenly beings, with various flowers, powdered incense, incense for burning, paste incense, robes, garlands, banners, flags, jeweled canopies, and music and song, will respectfully greet and make offerings to the wonderful stupa of the seven precious materials. Innumerable living beings will enjoy being arhats; incalculable numbers of living beings will become awakened as pratyekabuddhas; and inconceivable numbers of the living will aspire to become awakened and reach the stage of never backsliding."

The Buddha then said to the monks: "In the future, if there are any good sons or good daughters who, hearing this Devadatta chapter of the Wonderful Dharma Flower Sutra, faithfully respect it with pure hearts and are free from doubt, they will not fall into a purgatory or become a hungry spirit or a beast, but will be born into the presence of the buddhas of the ten directions. Wherever they are born they will always hear this sutra. If they are born among human or heavenly beings, they will enjoy marvelous delights. And if they are reborn in the presence of a buddha, they will be born by transformation from lotus flowers."

Then a bodhisattva from a lower region, named Accumulated Wisdom, an attendant of Abundant Treasures, the World-Honored One, said to Abundant Treasures Buddha: "Let us return to our homeland."

But Shakyamuni Buddha said to Accumulated Wisdom: "Good man, wait a while. There is a bodhisattva here named Manjushri. You should meet him and discuss the wonderful Dharma with him, and then return to your homeland."

Then Manjushri, sitting on a thousand-petaled lotus flower as large as a carriage wheel, accompanied by bodhisattvas who had come with him also sitting on treasured lotus flowers, emerged naturally from the palace of Sagara Dragon King in the great ocean. Suspended in the air, he went to Holy Eagle Peak, got down from his lotus flower, went before the Buddha, and reverently prostrated himself at the feet of the two world-honored ones. When he had expressed his respect he went over to Accumulated Wisdom, and after they had exchanged greetings, they withdrew and sat to one side. Accumulated Wisdom Bodhisattva asked Manjushri: "When you were at the dragon palace, how many beings did you convert?"

Manjushri responded: "The number of them is innumerable, incalculable. It cannot be expressed in words or fathomed by the mind. Just wait a moment and there will be proof." And before he had finished speaking innumerable bodhisattvas sitting on treasured lotus flowers emerged from the ocean and went to Holy Eagle Peak, where they were suspended in the air. All these bodhisattvas had been transformed and delivered by Manjushri. They had done bodhisattva practice and together discussed the six transcendental practices. Those in the air, originally shravakas, taught shravaka practices, even though they were now all practicing the Great Vehicle principle of emptiness. Then Manjushri said to Accumulated Wisdom: "This is the result of my teaching and converting in the ocean."

Accumulated Wisdom Bodhisattva then praised him in verse:

> With great wisdom, virtue, courage, and strength
> You have transformed and delivered innumerable beings.
> Now those in this great assembly
> And I myself have seen them.
>
> You have fluently explained
> The principle of the true nature of things
> And opened and made clear the one-vehicle Dharma,
> Leading living beings everywhere to attain awakening quickly.

Manjushri replied: "What I always proclaimed when I was in the ocean was only the Wonderful Dharma Flower Sutra."

Accumulated Wisdom Bodhisattva asked Manjushri: "This sutra is very profound, fine and wonderful, the jewel of all the sutras, a rare thing in the world. Is there any living being who, diligently and devotedly practicing this sutra, can quickly become a buddha?"

Manjushri replied: "There is the daughter of the dragon king Sagara. Just eight years old, she is wise and has sharp faculties, and is well acquainted with the faculties and actions of living beings. She has mastered incantations. She has been able to receive and embrace all the profound inner core treasures preached by the buddhas. She has entered deeply into meditation and gained an understanding of all things. Within a moment, she aspired to become awakened and reached the stage of never backsliding. Her eloquence knows no bounds, and she has compassion for all the living as if they were her own children. She is full of blessings, and the thoughts in her mind and the explanations from her mouth are both subtle and great. Compassionate and respectful of others, kind and gentle, she is able to attain awakening."

Accumulated Wisdom Bodhisattva said: "I have seen how Shakya-muni Tathagata carried out arduous and difficult practices for innumerable eons, accumulating blessings and piling up virtue by following the way of the bodhisattva without resting. I have observed that in the three-thousand great thousandfold world there is not even a spot as small as a mustard seed where he has not laid down body and life as a bodhisattva for the sake of the living. Only after that did he attain the path of the awakened. It is unbelievable that this girl, in an instant, can become truly awakened."

But before he had finished talking, the daughter of the dragon king suddenly appeared and, after reverently prostrating herself at the Buddha's feet, withdrew to one side, praising him in verse:

> Profound in insight into the nature of good and evil,
> He illuminates the universe.
> His fine and wonderful pure Dharma body
> Has the thirty-two characteristics.

> The eighty different attractive features adorn his Dharma body.
> Human and heavenly beings look up to him,
> Dragons and gods revere him,
> And all kinds of living beings hold him in reverence.

> Having heard him, I can become awakened
> Only the Buddha can bear witness to this.
> I will reveal the teaching of the Great Vehicle
> To save living beings from suffering.

Then Shariputra said to the dragon girl: "You think that in no time at all you will attain the unexcelled way. This is hard to believe. Why? Because the body of a woman is filthy and impure, not a vessel for the Dharma. How could you attain unexcelled awakening? The Buddha way is long and extensive. Only after innumerable eons of enduring hardship, accumulating good works, and thoroughly carrying out all the practices can it be reached. Moreover, a woman's body has five hindrances: first, she cannot become a king of a Brahma heaven; second she cannot become king Indra; third, she cannot become a devil king;

fourth she cannot become a wheel-turning saintly king; and fifth she cannot have the body of a buddha. How then could you, in a woman's body, so quickly become a buddha?"

Then the dragon girl took a precious jewel that she had with her, worth as much as a three-thousand great thousandfold world, and presented it to the Buddha. The Buddha immediately accepted it. The dragon girl then said to Accumulated Wisdom Bodhisattva and the Venerable Shariputra: "I presented my precious jewel and the World-Honored One accepted it—was that not done quickly?" "Most quickly," they answered. The daughter told them: "Use your holy powers to watch me become a buddha even more quickly than that!"

Then the entire congregation saw the dragon girl instantly transformed into a male, take up bodhisattva practice, and immediately go to the world named Spotless, in the southern region, where, sitting on a precious lotus blossom, she attained impartial, proper awakening. With the thirty-two characteristics and eighty different attractive features she proclaimed the wonderful Dharma to all living beings everywhere in the universe.

Then from afar the bodhisattvas, shravakas, gods, dragons, the eight-fold assembly, humans, and nonhumans in this world watched the dragon girl become a buddha and teach the Dharma to all the gods and people in the assembly. Their hearts filled with great joy, they paid their respects from afar. Hearing the Dharma, countless living beings were able to understand it and reach the stage of never backsliding. The countless multitude also received assurance of attaining the Way. The world Spotless trembled and shook in six ways. Three thousand living beings in this world reached the stage of never backsliding, while three thousand living beings aspired to become awakened and obtained assurance of doing so.

Accumulated Wisdom Bodhisattva and Shariputra and the whole congregation silently believed and accepted this.

13. Encouragement to Uphold the Sutra

AT THAT TIME the Bodhisattva Medicine King, the great one, and the Bodhisattva Great Delight in Preaching, the great one, with their following of twenty thousand bodhisattvas, all in the presence of the Buddha, made a vow, saying: "We beg you, World-Honored One, do not worry! After the extinction of the Buddha we will honor and embrace, read and recite, and teach this sutra. In the evil age to come, living beings will have fewer and fewer good roots, while their utter arrogance will increase. Their desire for profitable offerings will grow, increasing their roots that are not good, taking them further from liberation. Though it may be difficult to teach and transform them, we will have the strength of great patience and will read and recite this sutra, embrace, teach, and copy it, and make all kinds of offerings to it, without sparing our bodies or lives."

Then the five hundred arhats in the assembly who had been assured of becoming buddhas said to the Buddha: "World-Honored One, we also vow to teach this sutra everywhere in different lands."

There were also eight thousand people, both in training and trained, who already had been assured. Rising from their seats and putting their palms together facing the Buddha, they made a vow, saying: "World-Honored One, we also will teach this sutra everywhere throughout other lands. Why? Because in this world people are corrupt and evil, full of utter arrogance, of shallow virtues, angry, fawning, devious, and insincere."

Then the sister of the Buddha's mother, the nun Mahaprajapati, with six thousand nuns, in training and trained, rose from their seats and, putting their palms together in complete attention, gazed up at the face of the honored-one without taking their eyes away for even a moment.

The World-Honored One then said to Gautami: "Why do you gaze at the Tathagata in such a troubled way? Are you wondering why I have not mentioned your name to assure you of supreme awakening? Gautami, I have already announced that all shravakas generally are assured. Now, if you want to have your assurance, I will tell you that in future lives, in the midst of the teachings of sixty-eight thousand millions of buddhas, you will become a great Dharma teacher and these six thousand nuns, in training and trained, will all become Dharma teachers. Thus you will gradually fulfill the bodhisattva way and become a buddha named Seen with Joy by All the Living Tathagata, one worthy of offerings, truly awakened, fully clear in conduct, well gone, understanding the world, unexcelled leader, trainer of men, teacher of heavenly beings and people, buddha, world-honored one. Gautami, this Seen with Joy by All the Living Buddha will in turn assure six thousand bodhisattvas of supreme awakening."[11]

Then the mother of Rahula, the nun Yashodhara, thought: "In his assurances, the World-Honored One has left only my name unmentioned."

The Buddha said to Yashodhara: "In future lives, in the midst of the Dharma of hundreds of thousands of billions of buddhas, by doing bodhisattva practice you will become a great Dharma teacher, gradually fulfilling the Buddha way, and in a good land become a buddha named Having Ten Million Shining Characteristics Tathagata, one worthy of offerings, truly awakened, fully clear in conduct, well gone, understanding the world, unexcelled leader, trainer of men, teacher of heavenly beings and people, buddha, world-honored one. The lifetime of that buddha will last innumerable, countless eons."

Then the nuns Mahaprajapati and Yashodhara, together with all their following, were full of joy, having gained something they had never had before. In the presence of the Buddha they immediately spoke in verse:

World-honored leader and teacher,
Comforter of human and heavenly beings,
Hearing your assurance was just what we needed.
We are at peace.

After reciting this verse, the nuns said to the Buddha: "World-Honored One, we too are able to proclaim this sutra everywhere throughout the lands in other regions."

Then the World-Honored One looked at the eighty trillion myriads of bodhisattva great ones. All these bodhisattvas were at the stage of never backsliding, had turned the never-retreating Dharma wheel, and mastered incantations. They got up from their seats, went before the Buddha, and putting their palms together in complete devotion, thought to themselves: "If the World-Honored One orders us to embrace and teach this sutra, we will proclaim this Dharma everywhere as the Buddha has taught it." And then they thought: "The Buddha is now silent and gives us no orders. What should we do?"

Respectfully obeying the Buddha's will and themselves wanting to fulfill their original vows, these bodhisattvas raised a lion's roar and vowed before the Buddha, saying: "World-Honored One, after the extinction of the Tathagata, we will travel around throughout the worlds in all directions in order to lead all the living to copy this sutra, receive and embrace it, read and recite it, explain its meaning, practice it as their Dharma, and keep it in mind correctly. All this will be done through the Buddha's majestic power. Please, World-Honored One, though in another region, see us and protect us from afar!"

Then the bodhisattvas all raised their voices together and spoke in verse:

> Please do not worry.
> After the Buddha's extinction,
> In a frightful and evil age
> We will teach everywhere.

> Though many ignorant people
> Will curse and abuse us
> Or attack us with swords and sticks,
> We will endure it all.

> In that evil age there will be monks
> With twisted minds and fawning, crooked hearts,

Boasting and full of pride,
Claiming to have attained what they have not.

There will be forest dwellers
Wearing patched robes and living in seclusion,
Pretending that they practice the true way
While disrespecting and putting other people down.

Greedily attached to lucrative offerings,
They will teach the Dharma to white-robed laypeople,
And be respected and revered by the world
As if they were arhats with the six divine powers.

Cherishing evil in their hearts,
Always thinking of earthly things,
And assuming the name of forest dwellers,
They will love to find fault with us,

Saying such things as
"These monks,
Greedy for lucrative offerings,
Teach non-Buddhist doctrine.

"They fabricate their own sutras
To delude the people of the world.
Just to become famous,
They make distinctions and teach this sutra."

They will continually try to ruin us
In the midst of the great assembly
By slandering and speaking ill of us
Before kings and ministers,

Before brahmans and ordinary citizens,
And other groups of monks,
Saying: "These are people of wrong views
Who teach non-Buddhist doctrines."

But out of reverence for the Buddha,
We will endure all these evils.
Even when spoken to contemptuously
With phrases such as:

"All of you, no doubt, are buddhas."
Even such scorn and arrogance
We will patiently endure—
All such arrogant and contemptuous words.

In an evil age of a muddied eon,
Full of dreadful things,
Evil spirits will take possession of others
To curse, abuse, and insult us.

But, revering and trusting in the Buddha,
We will wear an armor of patient endurance.
In order to teach this sutra
We will endure all such difficult things.

We will cherish neither our bodies nor our lives,
But care only for the unexcelled way.
In ages to come, we will protect and uphold
What the Buddha has entrusted to us.

World-Honored One,
You must know that in the muddied age
Evil monks who do not understand
The Buddha's skillful means—

How the Dharma is taught
In accord with
What is appropriate—
Will frown upon and abuse us.

Repeatedly we will be driven out
And exiled far from stupas and monasteries.

Remembering the Buddha's orders,
We will endure all such evils.

Wherever in villages and towns
There are those who seek the Dharma,
We will go there and teach the Dharma
Entrusted to us by the Buddha.

We are emissaries of the World-Honored One.
Facing multitudes without fear,
We will teach the Dharma well.
May the Buddha live in peace and comfort.

In the presence of the World-Honored One
And the buddhas who have come from all directions,
We make this vow.
The Buddha knows what is in our hearts.

14. Safe and Easy Practices

A T THAT TIME Manjushri Bodhisattva, the great one, Prince of the Dharma, said to the Buddha: "World-Honored One, rare indeed are such bodhisattvas. Respectfully obeying the Buddha, they have made great vows that in the evil age to come they will defend, embrace, read, recite, and teach this Dharma Flower Sutra. World-Honored One, how will these bodhisattvas, the great ones, be able to teach this sutra in the evil age to come?"

The Buddha responded to Manjushri: "If any bodhisattva great ones want to teach this sutra in the evil age to come, they should dwell at peace in four teachings.

"First, they should dwell at peace in bodhisattva practices and associations, so that they will be able to preach this sutra to living beings.

"Manjushri, what do I mean by the practices of bodhisattva great ones? If a bodhisattva great one is always patient, is gentle and agreeable, is never violent, and never gets alarmed, and if, moreover, such a bodhisattva does not act in such a way as to become attached to anything, but perceives the nature of the reality of all things, not acting, not discriminating—this is what I call the practices of bodhisattva great ones.

"What do I mean by the associations of bodhisattva great ones? Bodhisattva great ones should not be closely associated with kings, princes, ministers, or office heads. They should not associate closely with non-Buddhists, brahmans, Jains, and so on, or with writers of worldly literature or books praising non-Buddhist teachings. They should not associate closely with materialists or anti-materialists. They should not be closely associated with dangerous sports such as boxing or wrestling, or with dancers or actors or others who create illusions. Neither should they associate closely with people of the candala caste, or with those who raise pigs, sheep, poultry, or dogs, or with hunters or fishermen, or with others engaged in such evil pursuits. When such people occasionally come to them, a bodhisattva should teach the Dharma for them, expecting nothing in return.

"Further, they should not associate closely with monks or nuns or with laymen or laywomen who seek to become shravakas, nor should they talk with them or visit them, and they should not stay with them, whether in the same room, recreation area, or lecture hall. They should not join in their activities. If at times such people come to one, a bodhisattva should teach the Dharma appropriately, expecting nothing in return.

"Manjushri, a bodhisattva great one should not teach the Dharma to women in a way that might arouse passionate thoughts, nor should he take pleasure in seeing women. If he enters someone else's home, he should not talk with girls, unmarried women, or widows. Nor should he become friendly with any of the five kinds of unmanly men. He should not enter someone else's home alone; and if for some reason he has to enter someone's house alone, he should concentrate on thinking only of the Buddha. If he teaches the Dharma to women, he should not display his teeth by smiling or allow his chest to be seen. Not even for the sake of the Dharma should he ever become intimate, much less for any other reason.

"He takes no pleasure in having young pupils, novices, or children, nor in sharing the same teacher with them. Always preferring meditation and seclusion, he should learn to quiet his mind. Manjushri, this is the first kind of association he should have.

"Further, a bodhisattva great one views all things as empty, as they really are. Things by themselves should not be regarded as upside-down or moving, or receding or revolving. They are like empty space, insubstantial, beyond words, unborn, non-emerging, non-arising, nameless, formless, truly without substance, innumerable, unlimited, boundless, without hindrances. It is only through causes and conditions that they exist; only through perversity that they are born. This is why I teach that one should always delight in seeing the character of things. This is what I call the second kind of association that bodhisattva great ones should have."

Then the World-Honored One, wanting to say what he meant once again, spoke in verse:

> If there are any bodhisattvas in the evil age to come
> Who with fearless hearts want to teach this sutra,
> These are the practices and associations
> They should enter.
>
> Kings and princes, ministers and office heads,
> Those involved in dangerous sports,
> Candala people, non-Buddhists, and brahmans
> Should always be avoided.
>
> Also extremely arrogant people
> Who are attached to a small vehicle,
> And like to study its three collections,
> Should not be associated with.
>
> Nor should one associate with monks
> Who fail to observe precepts, arhats in name only,
> With nuns who like to laugh and play,
> Or with laywomen deeply attached to the five desires
> Or seeking a way to extinction in the present.
>
> One should not associate with any of them.
> But if such people do come to a bodhisattva
> With sincere intentions
> To hear about the Buddha way,
>
> Then a bodhisattva,
> Without fear
> And expecting nothing in return,
> Can teach the Dharma for them.

With widows and unmarried women
And any kind of unmanly men
They should never associate
Or become close friends.

Nor should they associate with
Butchers, meat cutters,
Hunters, or fishermen,
Who hurt and kill for profit,

Or with those who sell meat to make a living
Or those who display and sell women.
With such people as these
They should not associate.

And with those in dangerous sports,
Wrestling, and other games,
Or with lewd women and the like,
They should never associate.

One should never be alone in a room,
To teach the Dharma to a woman.
If one does teach the Dharma to a woman,
There should be no flirting or laughing.

When one enters a village to beg for food,
He should take along another monk.
And if there is no other monk,
He should concentrate on thinking of the Buddha.

These, then, are what are called
Practices and associations.
By maintaining these two
One can teach safely and easily.

Moreover, one should not hold to things as
Higher, middle, or lower,

Constituted or unconstituted,
Real or unreal.

Also one should not make distinctions,
Saying, "This is a man, this is a woman."
One should not seek to grasp things,
Know them, or see them.

These, then, are what are called
Bodhisattva practices.

All things are empty
And without being,
Without permanence,
Neither arising nor ending.

This is called that with which
Wise people associate.

By perverse distinctions,
All things are or are not,
Are real or unreal,
Are born or unborn.

In a quiet place
One can master one's mind and heart,
Dwelling as peacefully and unmoved
As Mount Sumeru,

Regarding all things
As non-substantial,
Like empty space,
Without solidity,

Not born, not emerging,
Not moving, not regressing,

Always having the same character.
This is what is called proper association.

If any monk takes up these practices
Or this kind of association after my extinction,
When he teaches this sutra
He will not be afraid or weak.

When a bodhisattva
At times enters a quiet room
And with correct ideas
Views things in accord with their meaning,

And, arising from meditation—
For the sake of the king,
Princes, ministers and people,
Brahmans and others—

Opens up, explains,
And teaches this sutra,
He will become tranquil
And not be afraid or weak.

Manjushri, this is called the first teaching
In which bodhisattvas should dwell at peace,
Enabling them, in future generations,
To teach the Dharma Flower Sutra.

"Further, Manjushri, after the extinction of the Tathagata, during the time of the decline of the Dharma, those who want to teach this sutra should make these safe and easy practices part of their lives. When they preach or read a sutra orally, they should take no pleasure in telling of the errors of other people or sutras. Nor should they have contempt for other Dharma teachers, or speak of the likes and dislikes or strong and weak points of other people. They should not refer to shravakas by name and discuss their faults, or by name praise their good points. They should not allow themselves to become resentful or hateful. If they keep such a peaceful and happy disposition, listeners will not oppose them. To difficult questions, they should not respond with the Dharma of a small vehicle but only explain things with the Great Vehicle, so that all-inclusive wisdom will be obtained."

Then the World-Honored One, wanting to say what he meant once again, spoke in verse:

> Bodhisattvas always delight
> In teaching the Dharma
> In a peaceful,
> Comforting way.
>
> In a clean and pure place,
> They spread a mat,
> Anoint themselves with oil,
> And wash away the dust and dirt.
>
> They put on a new, clean robe,
> And, clean within and without,
> Sit calmly on a Dharma seat
> And teach in accord with questions.
>
> If monks or nuns are present,
> Laymen or laywomen,
> Kings or princes, officials,
> Gentlemen or ordinary people,
>
> They teach the fine
> And wonderful meaning
> Of the Dharma
> With a peaceful face.
>
> If there are difficult questions, they should
> Answer according to the meaning of the Dharma.
> With causes and conditions and with parables
> They should lay them out and analyze them.

By these skillful means
They will cause all to aspire to awakening,
To advance steadily
And enter the Buddha way.

They rid themselves of laziness and lazy thinking.
Free from all kinds of worry,
Teaching the Dharma with compassion day and night,
They constantly advance teachings of the unexcelled way.

With various causal explanations
And innumerable parables,
They reveal them to the living,
Causing all to rejoice.

Clothing and bedding,
Food, drink, and medicine—
For all such things
They have no anticipation.

They concentrate only on reasons
For preaching the Dharma.
Their desire is to achieve the Buddha way
And cause others to do the same,
Bringing them great gain and trouble-free offerings.

After my extinction,
If there are monks who are able to preach
This Wonderful Dharma Flower Sutra,
They will be free from jealousy and anger,
From distress and obstacles.

People will not abuse them.
They will be free from fear,
Neither attacked with swords or sticks
Nor driven away.

Because they are always patient,
Wise people will be
Good at developing themselves in this way,
And be peaceful and happy, as described previously.

The blessings of such people
Are so beyond calculation,
Tens of millions of billions of eons
Would not be enough to describe them.

"Again, Manjushri, at the end of the age, when the Dharma is about to die, bodhisattva great ones who receive and embrace, read and recite this sutra should not be envious or deceitful and should not slight or abuse others who study the Buddha way, or seek out their strong and weak points.

"If there are monks or nuns, laymen or laywomen, who seek to become shravakas or seek to become pratyekabuddhas, or seek the bodhisattva way, one should not make trouble for them, causing them to have doubts or regrets, by saying such things to them as: 'You are far from the Way and will never be able to have all-inclusive wisdom. Why? Because you are undisciplined people and lazy about the Way.'

"Moreover, one should not indulge in small talk about the teachings or argue over them. One should think of all the living with great compassion. One should think of tathagatas as loving fathers. One should think of bodhisattvas as great teachers. With the deepest sincerity, one should always revere and worship the great bodhisattvas of the ten directions. And one should teach the Dharma equally to all living beings. Just because some follow the Dharma, one should not teach more to some and less to others. Even for those who deeply cherish the Dharma, one should not teach more of the Dharma.

"Manjushri, if among the bodhisattva great ones at the end of the age when the Dharma is about to die, there are some who have fulfilled this third kind of safe and easy practice, when they teach this sutra nothing will upset them. They will find good fellow students to read and recite this sutra with them. And a large number of people will come to hear and receive it from them. After hearing it, the people will embrace it; after embracing it, will recite it; after reciting it, will teach it; and after teaching it, will copy or lead others to copy it. They will make offerings to the sutra rolls, revering, respecting, and praising them."

Then the World-Honored One, wanting to proclaim this teaching once again, spoke in verse:

> If you would teach this sutra,
> You should get rid of jealousy and anger,
> Arrogance, deceit, and dishonesty
> And always do what is honest and right.
>
> You should have contempt for no one,
> Nor quibble about the teachings,
> Nor cause others to have doubt or regret
> By saying, "You will never become a buddha!"
>
> A child of the Buddha teaching the Dharma
> Will always be gentle and patient,
> And compassionate toward all,
> Never become negligent.
>
> Toward the great bodhisattvas in all directions
> Who practice the Way out of sympathy for all,
> One should have reverence and respect,
> Saying, "These are my great teachers."
>
> One should think of world-honored buddhas
> As unexcelled fathers.
> Ridding oneself of arrogance,
> One should teach the Dharma without obstacle.
>
> Such is the third teaching.
> The wise should keep and observe it.
> Such a wholehearted, safe, and easy practice
> Will be honored by countless multitudes of people.

"Manjushri, at the end of the age, when the Dharma is about to die, bodhisattva great ones who receive and embrace this Dharma Flower

Sutra should have a spirit of great kindness toward laypeople and monastics, and a spirit of great compassion toward those who are not yet bodhisattvas. They should think: 'Such people have missed the Tathagata's preaching of the Dharma by skillful means according to what is appropriate. They have not heard, or known, or realized, or inquired, or believed, or understood. Yet, though they have not inquired about, believed in, or understood this sutra, when I have attained supreme awakening, wherever I am, using divine powers and the powers of wisdom, I will lead them to take this Dharma into their lives.'

"Manjushri, after the extinction of the Tathagata, bodhisattva great ones who have fulfilled this fourth teaching will be free from error when they teach this Dharma. They will always be given offerings and be revered, honored, and praised by monks and nuns, laymen and laywomen, kings and princes, ministers and people, brahmans and ordinary citizens, and by others. Heavenly beings in the sky also, in order to hear the Dharma, will always follow them. Whether they are in a village or town or in a secluded forest, when someone comes wanting to put difficult questions to them, day or night, for the sake of the Dharma, heavenly beings will always guard and protect them, making all their hearers rejoice. Why? Because this sutra is protected by the divine powers of all the past, future, and present buddhas.

"Manjushri, in countless lands not even the name of this Dharma Flower Sutra can be heard. How much less can it be seen, received and embraced, read and recited!

"Manjushri, it is like a powerful wheel-turning saintly king who wants to conquer other countries by force, but the petty kings will not obey his orders. The wheel-turning king calls up his various armies and goes to suppress them. Seeing his soldiers distinguish themselves in the war, the king is greatly pleased and rewards them according to their merit, giving them fields, houses, villages, and towns; or robes and personal ornaments; or various kinds of treasures such as gold, silver, lapis lazuli, seashell, agate, coral, and amber; or elephants, horses, carriages, servants, and subjects. The only thing he does not give is the bright jewel in his topknot. Why? Because this jewel can only be on the head of a king. If he gave it away, all the king's followers would certainly be astonished and suspicious.

"Manjushri, the Tathagata is also like this. He uses powers of meditation and wisdom to win lands for the Dharma and is king of the threefold world. But the devil kings are unwilling to submit. The Tathagata's wise and holy generals fight against them. With those who distinguish themselves he is pleased, and in the midst of the four groups he teaches sutras, causing them to rejoice. He gives them the meditations, the liberation, the flawless roots and powers and other treasures of the teachings. In addition, he gives them the city of nirvana, telling them that they have attained extinction, and guiding them so that they all rejoice. Yet for them he does not teach this Dharma Flower Sutra.

"Manjushri, when the wheel-turning king sees that some soldier has distinguished himself, he is so extremely pleased that now at last he gives to him the incredible jewel so long worn on his head and never carelessly given to anyone.

"So it is also with the Tathagata. As the great Dharma king of the threefold world, he is teaching and transforming all the living with the Dharma. When he sees his wise and holy army fighting the devils of the five constituent aggregates, the devils of afflictions, and the devils of death, and winning great distinction and merit, eliminating the three poisons, emerging from the threefold world, and breaking the nets of the devils, then the Tathagata also is greatly pleased. Though it will meet hostility and be difficult to believe, this Dharma Flower Sutra can lead all the living to comprehensive wisdom. Though it has never before been taught, I now teach it.

"Manjushri, this Dharma Flower Sutra is the greatest teaching of the tathagatas and the most profound of them all. I give it to you last, just as that powerful king in the end gave the bright jewel he had guarded for so long.

"Manjushri, this Dharma Flower Sutra is the secret treasury of the buddhas, supreme above all sutras. Guarded and protected for a long time, it has not been recklessly taught. Today for the first time I lay it out for all of you."

Then the World-Honored One, wanting to say what he meant once again, spoke in verse:

One should always endure patiently,
With compassion for all,

And preach the sutra
Praised by the Buddha.

At the end of the age,
Those who embrace this sutra
Must have compassion toward laypeople and monastics
And those not yet bodhisattvas.

They should think:
"Those who do not hear
Or believe this sutra
Suffer a great loss.

"When I attain the Buddha way,
I will teach this Dharma to them
By skillful means,
That they may dwell within it."

This is like a powerful wheel-turning king
Who rewards his soldiers
Who have distinguished themselves in war
With many things—

Elephants, horses, carriages,
Personal ornaments,
Fields and houses,
Villages and towns,

Or gives them robes,
Various kinds of treasures,
Servants, and other valuable things,
Giving all such things gladly.

But only for the brave and strong
Who have done difficult things,
Does the king take from his topknot
The bright jewel and present it to him.

The Tathagata is also like this.
He is the king of all things.
He has great strength for enduring patiently
And a treasury of wisdom.

With great compassion
He transforms the world
According to the Dharma.

He sees all human beings
In suffering and agony,
Seeking liberation
And fighting against the devils.

For all these living beings
He has taught various things,
And as a great skillful means
Has taught these sutras.

And when he knows that the living
Have gained strength through them,
At last, for their sake,
He teaches this Dharma Flower,

Just as the king
Took from his topknot
The bright jewel
And gave it away.

Among all the sutras
This sutra is highest.
I have always guarded and protected it,
And never recklessly revealed it.

This is the right time
To teach it for all of you.

After my extinction,
All those who seek the Buddha way
And want to preach this sutra in peace and comfort
Should tie themselves tightly to these four teachings.

Everyone who reads this sutra
Will always be free from anxiety and stress
And from illness and pain.
Their faces will be fresh and bright.
They will not be born poor, servile, or ugly.

Living beings will delight in seeing them
And respect them as sages or saints.
Children from heaven
Will be their servants.

They will not be struck by swords or sticks.
Poison will not harm them.
If anyone speaks ill of them or curses them,
That person's mouth will be closed.

They will be able to go anywhere
Without fear, like lion kings.
The radiance of their wisdom
Will shine like the sun.

Even in their dreams
They will see only wonderful things:

Various tathagatas
Sitting on lion seats,
Preaching the Dharma
To groups of monks around them,

And dragons, spirits,
Asuras, and others,

Numerous as the sands of the Ganges,
Their palms together in reverence.

And they will see themselves there
Teaching the Dharma for others.

They will see buddhas
With their characteristic golden bodies
Radiating immeasurable light, illuminating all things,
Their Brahma-voices preaching what had been taught.

For the four groups,
The Buddha will be teaching the unexcelled Dharma
And they will find themselves among them,
Praising the Buddha with palms together.

They will hear the Dharma with joy,
Make offerings,
Master incantations,
And witness to the wisdom of never backsliding.

When the Buddha knows
They have entered deeply into the Buddha way,
Then he will assure them
Of reaching the highest true awakening.

"You, my good son,
In a future life
Will obtain immeasurable wisdom,
The great way of the Buddha.

"Your land will be decorated and pure,
And incomparably huge.
The four groups will be there
With palms together, listening to the Dharma."

They will also see themselves
In mountains and forests,
Studying and putting into practice the good Dharma
And witnessing to the reality of things.

Deep in meditation,
They will see the buddhas in all directions—
Golden-colored buddhas
Adorned with a hundred signs of blessings.

Those who hear and teach for others
Will always have good dreams like this.

They will dream they are kings
Who forsake palaces and servants
And the exquisite wonders of the five desires
To go to the place of the Way.

They will sit on lion seats
Under bodhi trees
And after seeking the Way for seven days
Attain the wisdom of buddhas.

Having attained the unexcelled way,
They will get up and turn the Dharma wheel,
And for the four groups they will teach the Dharma
For tens of millions of billions of eons.

After teaching the flawless, wonderful Dharma
And saving innumerable living beings,
They will enter nirvana,
As the smoke stops when a lamp goes out.

If anyone in an evil age to come
Teaches this preeminent Dharma,
They will gain great benefits
Such as the blessings above.

15. Springing Up from the Earth

AT THAT TIME the bodhisattvas, the great ones, who had come from other lands and were more numerous than the sands of eight Ganges, arose in the great assembly and with palms together greeted and spoke to the Buddha, saying: "World-Honored One, if the Buddha will allow us diligently and devotedly to protect and embrace this sutra, read and recite it, copy it, and make offerings to it in this world after your extinction, we would teach it everywhere throughout this land."

Then the Buddha said to the whole group of bodhisattva great ones: "Enough, my good sons, there is no need for you to protect and embrace this sutra. Why? Because in my world itself there are as many bodhisattva great ones as there are sands in sixty thousand Ganges. And each one of these bodhisattvas has as many followers as there are sands in sixty thousand Ganges. After my extinction, they will be able to protect and embrace, read and recite, and teach this sutra everywhere."

When the Buddha had said this, the earth of this three-thousand great thousandfold world trembled and split open, and from it innumerable tens of millions of billions of bodhisattva great ones sprang up together. These bodhisattvas all had golden-hued bodies, the thirty-two characteristics, and immeasurable radiance. Previously they had all been living in the world of empty space below this world, and when these bodhisattvas heard the sound of the voice of Shakyamuni Buddha preaching, they appeared from below.

Each of these bodhisattvas was the leader of a huge group, a following as numerous as the sands of sixty thousand Ganges. And this is not to mention those who led followings as numerous as the sands of fifty thousand, forty thousand, thirty thousand, twenty thousand, or ten thousand Ganges; or those who had followings as small as the sands of one Ganges, the sands of half a Ganges, a quarter of a Ganges, or as few as one part in ten million billion myriads of Ganges ; or those with as few as ten million billion myriads of followers, or a billion followers, or ten million, a million, or just ten thousand, a thousand, a hundred, or even ten; or those who led five, four, three, or two disciples, or only one; or those who were alone, preferring solitary practice. Such were they, then, as to be innumerable, unlimited, beyond comprehension by powers of calculation or parable and simile.

When these bodhisattvas had emerged from the earth, each went up in the air to the wonderful stupa of the seven precious materials, where Tathagata Abundant Treasures and Shakyamuni Buddha were. When they reached it they bowed and prostrated themselves to both world-honored ones. Then they went to the buddhas seated on the lion seats under the jeweled trees and greeted them, circled around them to the right three times with palms together in respect, and praised them with all kinds of bodhisattva praise. Then they stood to one side, gazing with joy at the two world-honored ones.

While these bodhisattva great ones who had sprung up from the earth praised the buddhas with all kinds of bodhisattva praises, fifty small eons went by. During this time Shakyamuni Buddha sat in silence, and silent also for the fifty eons were the four groups. But the divine powers of the Buddha made it seem to the great multitude like only half a day.

At that time the four groups, also by the divine powers of the Buddha, saw the bodhisattvas filling the skies of innumerable hundreds of thousands of billions of lands. Among all these bodhisattvas were the four leaders: the first named Superior Practice, the second Unlimited Practice, the third Pure Practice, and the fourth Firm Practice. These four bodhisattvas were the foremost leaders and teachers of the entire group. Before the great assembly, with palms together, each of them looked toward Shakyamuni Buddha and inquired: "World-Honored One, are your ailments and troubles few, and is your practice going smoothly? Are those you want to save readily receiving your teachings? Doesn't the effort they require make the World-Honored One tired?"

Then the four great bodhisattvas said in verse:

Is the World-Honored One at ease,
With few ailments and troubles?
In teaching all the living,
Are you free from weariness?

And are all the living
Readily accepting your teaching?
Don't they make
The World-Honored One tired?

Then the World-Honored One, in the great assembly of bodhisattvas, said: "Yes, yes, my good sons, the Tathagata is at ease, with few ailments and few troubles. The living beings here are easy to transform and save, and they do not make me tired. Why? Because all these beings, for generation after generation, have been transformed by me. And they have made offerings to previous buddhas and honored them, planting good roots. When all these beings saw me for the first time and heard my preaching, they received it in faith and entered the wisdom of a tathagata. The exception was those who had previously studied and practiced the small vehicle, but now I have made it possible even for such people to hear this sutra and enter Buddha-wisdom."

Then these great bodhisattvas spoke in verse:

Good, good, Great Hero,
World-Honored One!
All these living beings
Are easily transformed and saved.

They are well able to inquire
About the profound wisdom of buddhas,
And, upon hearing, have faith and understanding.
We rejoice!

Then the World-Honored One praised these leaders, the great bodhisattvas, saying: "Good, good, my good sons. You express joy in your hearts for the Tathagata."

Then Maitreya Bodhisattva and the multitude of other bodhisattvas, as numerous as the sands of eight thousand Ganges, all thought: "Never in the past have we seen or heard of such a multitude of great bodhisattva great ones emerging from the earth, standing now in the presence of the world-honored ones, with palms together, making offerings and inquiring about the Tathagata!"

Then Maitreya Bodhisattva, the great one, aware of thoughts in the minds of all the bodhisattvas as numerous as the sands of eight thousand Ganges, and wanting also to resolve his own doubt, put his palms together facing the Buddha and asked him in verse:

> Innumerable tens of millions of billions,
> A great multitude of bodhisattvas
> Such as we have never seen before—
>
> Please, most honored of people,
> Explain where they have come from
> And why they have come.
>
> Huge in body, with the great divine faculties,
> With incomprehensible wisdom,
> Strength in mind and will
>
> And great powers of patience,
> Whom all the living rejoice to see—
> Where have they come from?
>
> Each of these bodhisattvas
> Leads a following with numbers beyond counting,
> Like the sands of the Ganges.
>
> Some of these great bodhisattvas
> Lead followers as numerous as
> The sands of sixty thousand Ganges.
>
> Such great multitudes,
> With complete devotion,
> Seek the Buddha way.

These great leaders,
As many as the sands of sixty thousand Ganges,
All come to make offerings to the Buddha
And to protect and embrace this sutra.

Some, still more numerous,
Lead followers as numerous as the sands of fifty thousand Ganges,
Or forty thousand, or thirty thousand,
Or twenty thousand, or ten thousand,

Or a thousand, or a hundred,
Or the sands of one Ganges,
One-half, one-third, one-forth,
Or just one part in a billion.

Those who lead billions of myriads,
Or trillions of disciples,
Or even half a billion,
Are still more numerous.

Those with a million,
Ten thousand or a thousand,
Or a hundred followers,
Fifty or ten, three, two, or one,

And those who enjoy solitude alone
With no following,
All have come to the Buddha
In numbers even greater than those above.

These great multitudes are such
That if someone tried to tally them on an abacus
For as many eons as the sands of the Ganges,
They still could not know how many they were.

These multitudes of bodhisattvas,
With their great dignity, virtue, and diligence—

Who taught the Dharma for them,
Educated, transformed, and developed them?

Under whom did they begin to seek awakening?
What Buddha-dharma do they praise?
What sutras have they received, embraced, and practiced?
What Buddha way have they studied and put into practice?

In all four regions the earth trembled and split,
And these bodhisattvas
With divine powers and the power of great wisdom
Emerged from within it.

World-Honored One,
In the past we have never seen such things.
Please tell us where they come from
And the name of that land.

I have traveled around
In many lands,
But have never seen
Such a thing as this.

In all of this multitude
There is not one that I know.
Suddenly they have come from the earth.
Please tell us why!

The innumerable millions and millions
Of bodhisattvas and others
Now here in this great congregation
Want to know these things.

What are the reasons for the beginning and end
Of this multitude of bodhisattvas?
World-Honored One of immeasurable virtue,
Please dispel the doubts of this congregation!

Meanwhile, the buddhas embodying Shakyamuni Buddha, who had come from innumerable tens of millions of billions of lands in other directions, were sitting cross-legged on the lion seats under the jeweled trees spread out in the eight directions. The attendants of these buddhas all saw the great multitude of bodhisattvas who emerged from the earth in all four regions of the three-thousand great thousandfold world and were now suspended in the air. Each spoke to his own buddha, saying: "World-Honored One, this great, innumerable, unlimited, countless multitude of bodhisattvas—where have they come from?"

Then each of those buddhas told his own attendants: "Good sons, wait a while. There is a bodhisattva great one named Maitreya, who has been assured by Shakyamuni Buddha that he is to be the next buddha. He has already asked about this matter and the Buddha is about to answer him. You should listen for yourselves to what he has to say."

Then Shakyamuni Buddha said to Maitreya Bodhisattva: "Good, good, Ajita, that you have asked the Buddha about so great a matter. All of you, with complete devotion, should put on the armor of perseverance and exhibit a firm will. The Tathagata now intends to reveal and proclaim the wisdom of buddhas, the unhindered divine powers of buddhas, the fierce, lionlike powers of buddhas, and the brave and mighty powers of buddhas."

Then the World-Honored One, wanting to state his meaning once again, spoke in verse:

> Persevere and pay attention.
> I am about to explain this matter.
> Have no doubts or regrets.
> Buddha wisdom is difficult to understand.

> Now show your faith.
> Be patient and good,
> For you are all about to hear
> The Dharma never heard before.

> I will now put your minds at ease.
> Have neither doubt nor fear.

The Buddha has only true words.
His wisdom is beyond measure.

The supreme Dharma he attained
Is profound and beyond analysis.
I will now teach it.
Give me your complete attention and listen.

Then the World-Honored One, having spoken these verses, said to Maitreya Bodhisattva: "I now declare to all of you in this great assembly, Ajita, that all these great bodhisattva great ones, in unquantifiable, innumerable, countless numbers, who have emerged from the earth and whom you have never seen before—after attaining supreme awakening in this world, I taught, transformed, and led these bodhisattvas, trained them, and caused them to aspire to the Way. All these bodhisattvas live in the empty space beneath this world, where they read, recite, gain insight into, ponder over, and analyze various sutras, and remember them correctly.

"Ajita, these good sons find no pleasure in talking among the crowd, but enjoy being in quiet places, diligently and persistently practicing without rest. They do not rely only on human or heavenly beings, but always delight in profound wisdom, being free from obstacles. They always delight in the Dharma of buddhas, with complete devotion persistently seeking unexcelled wisdom."

Then the World-Honored One, wanting to proclaim this teaching once again, spoke in verse:

Ajita, you should know:
All these great bodhisattvas,
For innumerable eons,
Have studied and practiced the wisdom of the Buddha.

All of them are my converts.
I made them aspire to the great way.
They are my children,
Living in this world, and following ascetic practices.

Liking quiet places, rejecting the noise of crowds,
Finding no pleasure in much talk,
Such sons as these
Study and practice my Dharma and Way.

Persevering day and night
In order to seek the Buddha way,
They live in the space
Beneath this world.

Firm in the power of their intentions,
Always diligently seeking wisdom,
They teach all kinds of wonderful things
And are without fear.

In the city of Gaya,
Sitting under the bodhi tree,
I attained the truest awakening,
And turned the unexcelled Dharma wheel.

Then I taught and transformed them,
Causing them to aspire to the Way for the first time.
Now they all live in the state of never backsliding.
All will become buddhas.

What I say now is true.
Believe me wholeheartedly.
From the long distant past
I have been teaching and transforming this multitude.

Then Maitreya Bodhisattva, the great one, as well as the innumerable bodhisattvas, had some doubt in their minds. Wondering about this strange and unprecedented thing, they thought: "How has the World-Honored One in so short a time taught and transformed such an innumerable, unlimited, countless number of great bodhisattvas, enabling them to dwell in supreme awakening?"

Then, addressing the Buddha, he said: "World-Honored One, when the Tathagata was a crown prince, you left the Shakya palace, sat at the place of the Way not far from the city of Gaya, and attained supreme awakening. Since then only a little over forty years have passed. World-Honored One, in so short a time how could you have done so much work of a buddha? By what powers of a buddha or blessings of a buddha have you taught and transformed such an innumerable multitude of great bodhisattvas, enabling them to attain supreme awakening? World-Honored One, even if someone counted such a multitude of great bodhisattvas through tens of millions of billions of eons, one would never come to an end or reach their limit. From the remote past, under innumerable and countless buddhas, they would have planted roots of goodness, fulfilled the bodhisattva way, and always observed noble practices. World-Honored One, the world will find it hard to believe a thing such as this.

"It is as if a twenty-five-year-old man of fine complexion and black hair pointed to a hundred-year-old person and said: 'This is my child!' Or it is as if a hundred-year-old pointed to a young person and said: 'This is the man who fathered and raised me!' This would be hard to believe. So also is what the Buddha has said.

"Actually, it has not been long since you attained the Way. Yet this great multitude of bodhisattvas, for innumerable tens of millions of billions of eons, have already diligently devoted themselves for the sake of the Buddha way. They have entered into, come out of, and dwelt in innumerable hundreds of thousands of billions of concentrations, have attained the great divine faculties, and for a long time observed noble practices. Step by step they have been able to learn all kinds of good teachings, and they are skillful in questions and answers. They are treasures among people and extremely rare in all the worlds. And now, today, the World-Honored One has told us that in the time since you attained the Buddha way you have caused them to aspire to awakening, have taught and transformed them, led them, and enabled them to turn toward supreme awakening!

"It is not long ago that the World-Honored One became a buddha. Yet you have been able to carry out this great, meritorious activity. We still believe that the Buddha's preaching is appropriate, that you never say anything empty or false, and that the Buddha's knowledge has all thoroughly penetrated and been mastered. But if, after the Buddha's extinction, newly aspiring bodhisattvas hear this, they may not be able to receive and believe it, causing the crime of violating the Dharma. Therefore, World-Honored One, please explain it, to put our doubts to rest, so that, in the future, when good sons hear of this matter, they too will have no doubts."

Then Maitreya Bodhisattva, wanting to restate what he meant, spoke in verse:

> In the past the Buddha
> Left his home with the Shakya clan
> And sat under the bodhi tree near Gaya.
> That was not long ago.

> Yet these children of the Buddha,
> Uncountable in number,
> Have already practiced the Buddha way for a long time,
> With divine powers and the power of wisdom.

> They have learned the bodhisattva way well,
> And are untainted by worldly things,
> Just as the lotus flower in the water
> Emerges from the earth.

> All of them show reverence
> As they stand before the World-Honored One.

> This matter is difficult to understand or discuss.
> How can it be believed?
> It is only recently that the Buddha attained the Way,
> Yet the number of your accomplishments is huge!

> Please remove the doubts of the assembly.
> Explain it clearly and tell us the truth.

> It is as if a young man, just twenty-five years old,
> Pointed at a hundred-year-old man
> With white hair and wrinkled face
> And said, "I fathered him."

And the old man also said, "This is my father."
A young father with an old child—
The whole world would not believe it.
So is it with the World-Honored One.

You attained the Way only recently.
Yet all these bodhisattvas,
Strong willed, neither timid nor weak,
Have practiced the bodhisattva way for innumerable eons.

Skilled in answering difficult questions,
They know no fear,
Are patient and resolute,
Decent, virtuous, and dignified.

Praised by the buddhas in the ten directions,
They are able to explain clearly.
They don't like being with the crowd,
But always prefer to be in meditation.

In order to pursue the Buddha way
They have lived in the space below.
Hearing this from the Buddha,
We have no doubts in this matter.

But, so that it can be understood in the future,
We beg the Buddha to preach.
If any should have doubts about or fail to believe this sutra,
They will fall into evil ways.

Please explain it for them now:
How have these innumerable bodhisattvas
In such a short time
Been taught, transformed, and led to have aspiration,
And reached the stage of never backsliding?

16. The Lifetime of the Tathagata

A T T H A T T I M E the Buddha said to the bodhisattvas and to all the great assembly: "Have faith in and understand, all you good sons, the truthful words of the Tathagata." Again he said to the great assembly: "Have faith in and understand the truthful words of the Tathagata." And yet again he said to the great assembly: "Have faith in and understand the truthful words of the Tathagata."

Then the great multitude of bodhisattvas, Maitreya at their head, put their palms together and said to the Buddha: "World-Honored One, we beg you to explain this matter. We will believe and accept the Buddha's words." They said this three times, repeating the words: "We beg you to explain this matter. We will believe and accept the Buddha's words."

Then the World-Honored One, knowing that the bodhisattvas' request, now repeated three times, would not be stopped, said to them: "You should all listen carefully to hear about the Tathagata's secret and divine powers. In all the worlds, the humans, heavenly beings, and asuras think that the present Shakyamuni Buddha left the palace of the Shakya clan, sat at the place of the Way not far from the city of Gaya, and attained supreme awakening. But, my good sons, in fact there have been innumerable, unlimited hundreds of thousands of billions of myriads of eons since I became a buddha.

"Suppose someone were to take five hundred thousand billions of myriads of countless three-thousand great thousandfold worlds and grind them into dust. Then, after going east through five hundred thousand billions of myriads of innumerable lands, one of those specks of dust was deposited. And suppose he continued eastward until he had used up all those specks. What do you think, my good sons? Is it possible to imagine or calculate the number of all those worlds?"

Maitreya Bodhisattva and the others said to the Buddha: "World-Honored One, those worlds are innumerable, unlimited, beyond the reach of calculation and beyond the reach of thought. Not even all the shravakas and pratyekabuddhas, with their flawless wisdom, would be able to imagine or understand such numbers. And we too, though we are at the stage of non-regression, cannot comprehend these matters. World-Honored One, such worlds would be innumerable and unlimited."

Then the Buddha said to all those bodhisattva great ones: "Good sons, now I will speak to you clearly. Suppose you took all those worlds, where a speck of dust has been deposited and where none has been deposited, and reduced them to dust. Let one speck be equal to an eon. The time that has passed since I became a buddha exceeds these by hundreds of thousands of billions of myriads of countless eons. Since that time I have constantly been in this world—preaching, teaching, and transforming. And in other places, in hundreds of thousands of billions of myriads of countless other lands, I have led and enriched living beings.

"Good sons, during this time I have talked about the Buddha Burning Light and others, and have told of their entering nirvana. In all of this I used skillful means to analyze things.

"Good sons, whenever living beings come to me, I use my Buddha's eyes to observe whether the faculties of their faith and so on are keen or dull. Accordingly, I appear in various places under different names and speak of the length of time during which my teachings will be effective. Sometimes I tell them I will enter nirvana. In various skillful ways, I teach the profound and wonderful Dharma, leading the living to rejoice.

"Good sons, the Tathagata sees that among the living there are those who prefer lesser teachings, and are of little virtue and heavy with filth. For these people I teach about how as a young man I left home and attained supreme awakening. But in reality the time since I became a buddha is very long, as I have said. It is just that I use skillful means to teach and transform living beings, so that they may enter the way of the Buddha.

"Good sons, all the sutras preached by the Tathagata are for the purpose of saving all the living. Sometimes I speak of myself, sometimes of others; sometimes I appear as myself, sometimes as someone else; sometimes I appear in my own actions, sometimes in the actions of others; but all that I say is true and not empty.

"Why is this? The Tathagata has insight into the character of the threefold world as it really is. For him there is no birth or death, neither retreat from nor emergence into the world. Nor is there any existing in the world and entering extinction following that. Nothing is simply real, nothing simply empty, nothing as it seems, nothing the opposite. The threefold world is not as we experience it. The Tathagata sees all such things clearly, without mistake.

"Because living beings have different natures, different desires, different activities, and different assumptions and ways of analyzing things, and because I wanted to lead them to put down roots of goodness, I have used a variety of causal explanations, parables, and other kinds of expression to share various teachings. I have never for a moment neglected the Buddha's work.

"Thus, since I became Buddha a very long time has passed, a lifetime of innumerable countless eons of constantly living here and never entering extinction. Good sons, from the beginning I have practiced the bodhisattva way, and that life is not yet finished, but will be twice as long as what has already passed. Even now, though I will not actually enter extinction, I announce that I will adopt the way of extinction. By using such skillful means, the Tathagata teaches and transforms living beings.

"Why is this? If the Buddha lives for a long time in this world, people of little virtue will not plant roots of goodness, and those who are poor and of humble origins will become attached to the five desires and be caught in a net of assumptions and false views. If they see that the Tathagata is always alive and never extinct, they will become arrogant and selfish or discouraged and neglectful. Unable to realize how difficult it is to meet him, they will not have a respectful attitude toward him.

"Therefore the Tathagata teaches by using skillful means, saying: 'Monks, you should know that it is difficult to meet a buddha who has come into the world.' Why is this? In the course of countless hundreds of thousands of billions of eons, some people of little virtue may see a buddha while others may never see one. For this reason I say this: 'Monks, it is difficult to see a tathagata.' Living beings, hearing such words, surely will realize that it is difficult to meet a buddha. They will yearn for one. Then they will cultivate roots of goodness. This is why the Tathagata announces his extinction even though he does not in reality become extinct.

"Good sons, the teachings of all the buddha-tathagatas are all like this. They are for the sake of liberating all the living. They are true and not empty.

"Suppose, for instance, there is a fine physician who is wise and clever and knows how to make medicines for curing all sorts of disease. He has many sons—say, ten, twenty, even a hundred. To take care of some business he goes off to a distant land. After he leaves, his children drink some poisonous drugs, which drives them into deliriums of agony and leaves them writhing on the ground.

"At this point their father comes back home to find the sons have drunk the poison. Some have lost their minds, others have not. Seeing their father in the distance, they are all very happy. Kneeling to greet him, they say: 'How good it is that you have returned safely! Foolishly we have taken some poison by mistake. Please heal us and give us back our lives.'

"The father sees his children in such suffering and agony and, following various formulas, looks for good medicinal herbs, perfect in color, fragrance, and flavor. Then he pounds, sifts, and mixes them and gives them to his children, telling them: 'This excellent medicine is perfect in color, fragrance, and flavor. Take it and you will quickly be rid of your suffering and agony, and be free from the illness.'

"Those children who have not lost their minds, seeing this excellent medicine of good color and fragrance, take it immediately and are completely cured of their illness. The others, who have lost their minds, are also happy to see their father return and ask him to heal their illness. Yet when the medicine is given to them, they refuse to take it. Why? Because the poison has penetrated deeply into them and they have lost their minds. Even though this medicine has good color and fragrance, they think it is no good.

"The father thinks to himself: 'These poor children. Because of the poison in them, their minds are completely unbalanced. Though they are glad to see me and ask to be healed, they refuse to take this good medicine. Now I have to use some skillful means to get them to take this medicine.' Then he says to them: 'You should know that I am now worn out with old age, and the time for me to die has now arrived. I will leave this excellent medicine here. You should take it and not worry that it will not make you better.' After instructing them in this way, he leaves again for another land, from which he sends back a messenger to inform them: 'Your father is dead.'

"Now, when those children hear that their father has died and left them behind, they become very distressed and think to themselves: 'If our father were alive he would have been kind to us, and would have saved us. But now he has abandoned us and died in a distant land. We think of ourselves as orphans, with no one to rely on.'

"This continuous grief brings them to their senses. They recognize that the medicine is excellent in color, fragrance, and flavor, and they take it and are fully healed of the poison. The father, hearing that the children have all recovered, returns home immediately, so that they all see him again.

"Good sons, what do you think? Can anyone say that this fine physician is lying?"

"No, World-Honored One."

The Buddha said: "I too am like this. Since I became Buddha, innumerable, unlimited hundreds of thousands of billions of myriads of countless eons have passed. For the sake of living beings, I use the power of skillful means and say that I will take the way of extinction. Yet, taking the circumstances into account, no one can accuse me of being guilty of lying."

At that time the World-Honored One, wanting to restate what he meant, spoke in verse:

> Since I became a buddha,
> Innumerable hundreds of thousands
> Of billions of countless
> Numbers of eons have passed.
>
> For countless eons I have taught the Dharma ceaselessly,
> Teaching and transforming
> Innumerable hundreds of millions of living beings,
> Enabling them to enter the Buddha way.

In order to liberate the living,
As a skillful means I appear to enter nirvana.
Yet truly I am not extinct.
I am always here teaching the Dharma.

I am always here.
But due to my divine powers
Perverse living beings fail to see me
Even though I am close.

When the many see me as extinct
They make offerings to my remains everywhere.
All long for me,
Adore and yearn for me.

And when the living have become faithful,
Honest and upright and gentle,
And wholeheartedly want to see the Buddha,
Even at the cost of their own lives,

Then, together with the assembly of monks
I appear on Holy Eagle Peak.

Then I tell all the living
That I am always here, not extinct.
Yet by the power of skillful means
I reveal both extinction and non-extinction.

If there are living beings in other lands
Who are reverent and sincere in their faith,
Then among them as well
I will teach the unexcelled Dharma.

Not hearing about this,
You think only that I am extinct.

When I look at living beings,
I see them drowning in a sea of suffering.

So I do not show myself,
Making them adore and yearn for me
Until they are full of longing.
Then I appear to teach the Dharma for them.

Such are my divine powers.
Throughout countless eons,
I have always lived on Holy Eagle Peak
And in various other places.

When the living witness the end of an eon,
When everything is consumed in a great fire,
This land of mine remains safe and tranquil,
Always filled with human and heavenly beings.

Its gardens and groves, halls and pavilions,
Are adorned with all kinds of gems.
Jeweled trees are full of flowers and fruit,
And living beings freely enjoy themselves.

Gods beat on heavenly drums,
Always making various kinds of music.
Mandarava blossoms rain down
And are scattered over the Buddha and the great assembly.

My Pure Land will never be destroyed,
Yet the multitude see it as being consumed in fire,
Everywhere filled with grief and fear
And all kinds of suffering.

Sinful living beings,
Because of the evil they have done in the past
Throughout countless eons,
Fail to hear the names of the three treasures.

But those who do good,
Who are gentle and honest,
Will all see me here
Teaching the Dharma.

At times for this multitude
I teach that the Buddha's life is immeasurable,
And to those who see the Buddha only after a long time
I teach that it is difficult to meet a buddha.

The power of my wisdom is such
That its light shines immeasurably.
I gained this life of countless eons
From long-cultivated practice.

You who are wise
Should have no doubt about this.
You should reject doubt forever,
For the Buddha's words are true, not false.

Like the physician who uses skillful means
To cure his deranged children,
Though actually alive, he announces his death,
Yet cannot be charged with lying.

I am the father of this world,
Healing all who suffer or are sick.
For the sake of ordinary, perverse people,
Though truly alive, I say I am extinct.

If people see me all the time,
They become arrogant and selfish,
Indulge in the five desires without restraint,
And fall into evil paths.

I always know which living beings
Practice the Way and which do not.

In accord with what they need to be saved,
I share various teachings for them.

I am always thinking:
"How can I lead all the living
To enter the unexcelled way
And quickly perfect their Buddha-bodies?"

17. The Variety of Blessings

AT THAT TIME, when the great congregation heard the Buddha teach that the length of his life was such a large number of eons, innumerable, countless living beings received great, abundant benefits.

Then the World-Honored One said to Maitreya Bodhisattva, the great one: "Ajita, when I taught that the length of the Tathagata's life is very long, living beings as numerous as the sands of six hundred and eighty billion myriads of Ganges accepted the teaching of the non-arising of all things. And a thousand times more bodhisattva great ones attained mastery of the incantation that enables them to hear and to retain what they hear. And bodhisattva great ones as numerous as the specks of dust in an entire world delighted in being eloquent and unhindered in speech. And bodhisattva great ones as numerous as the specks of dust in an entire world attained the power of incantation which enables them to make hundreds of thousands of billions of repetitions. And bodhisattva great ones as numerous as the specks of dust in a three-thousand great thousandfold world turned the irreversible Dharma wheel. And bodhisattva great ones as numerous as the specks of dust in two thousand middle-sized lands turned the pure Dharma wheel. And bodhisattva great ones as numerous as the specks of dust in a thousand small lands were assured of attaining supreme awakening after eight rebirths. And bodhisattva great ones as numerous as the specks of dust in four four-continent worlds were assured of attaining supreme awakening after four rebirths. And bodhisattva great ones as numerous as the specks of dust in three four-continent worlds were assured of attaining supreme awakening after three rebirths. And bodhi-sattva great ones as numerous as the specks of dust in two four-continent worlds were assured of attaining supreme awakening after two rebirths. And bodhisattva great ones as numerous as the specks of dust in a single four-continent world were assured of attaining supreme awakening after one rebirth. And living beings as numerous as the specks of dust in eight worlds all aspired to supreme awakening."

When the Buddha had told about those bodhisattva great ones obtaining such great benefits of the Dharma, mandarava and great man-darava flowers rained down from the sky and were scattered over the innumerable hundreds of thousands of billions of buddhas seated on lion seats under the jeweled trees. They were also scattered over Shakya-muni Buddha and the long-extinct Abundant Treasures Tathagata on the lion seat in the stupa of the seven precious materials. And they were scattered over all the great bodhisattvas and the four groups. Fine san-dalwood and aloe powders and so forth also rained down. And in the sky heavenly drums resounded by themselves with a wonderful deep reso-nance. A thousand kinds of robes from heaven also rained down, and various kinds of necklaces—pearl necklaces, mani-jewel necklaces, and wish-granting jewel necklaces—were everywhere in the nine directions. Censers of many jewels burned priceless incense, which moved all around of its own accord, making an offering to the great congregation. Bodhisattvas held canopies over each buddha, one above another, right up to the Brahma heaven. All these bodhisattvas sang countless hymns with exquisite voices, praising the buddhas.

Then Maitreya Bodhisattva rose from his seat, bared his right shoul-der, put his palms together facing the Buddha, and spoke in verse:

The Buddha has taught a rare Dharma
Never heard before.
The powers of the World-Honored One are great.
His lifetime is beyond estimation.

Countless children of the Buddha,
Hearing the World-Honored One analyze
And tell of the enrichment they will obtain from the Dharma,
Have been filled with joy.

Some are at the stage of never backsliding,
Some have mastered incantations,
Some take delight in unhindered speech,
Some have the ability to retain trillions of repetitions.

Bodhisattvas as numerous as the specks of dust
In a thousand major worlds
Are all able to turn
The irreversible Dharma wheel.

Bodhisattvas as numerous as the specks of dust
In a thousand middle-sized worlds
Are all able to turn
The pure Dharma wheel.

Bodhisattvas as numerous as the specks of dust
In a thousand minor worlds
After eight more rebirths
Will attain the Buddha way.

Bodhisattvas as numerous as the specks of dust
In four, three, or two times
A world of four continents
After the same number of rebirths will become buddhas.

And bodhisattvas as numerous as the specks of dust
In one four-continent world
After one more rebirth
Will attain comprehensive wisdom.

Thus, when living beings
Hear about the long life of the Buddha,
They gain countless
Flawless and pure fruits.

Also, living beings as numerous
As the specks of dust in eight worlds,

Hearing the Buddha speak of his lifetime,
Have all aspired for the unexcelled.

The World-Honored One,
By teaching the immeasurable, inconceivable Dharma,
Brings abundant benefits to many,
As unlimited as space.

Mandarava flowers from heaven
And great mandaravas rain down.
Indras and Brahmas as numerous as the sands of the Ganges
Come from countless buddha-lands.

Sandalwood and aloes
Rain down, jumbled together.
Like birds coming down from the sky,
They are scattered over the buddhas as an offering.

Heavenly drums in the sky
Resound by themselves with wonderful resonance.
Tens of millions of billions of kinds of robes from heaven
Come whirling down.

Wonderful censers of many jewels
Burn priceless incense,
Which moves all around of its own accord,
As an offering to the world-honored ones.

The multitude of great bodhisattvas
Hold canopies with the seven precious materials,
Tall and wonderful, and in trillions of varieties,
One above the other, up to the Brahma heaven.

Before each of the buddhas,
Jeweled streamers hang and flutter.
And tens of millions of billions of verses of praise
Are sung to the tathagatas.

Such things as these
We have never known before.
Hearing that the Buddha's lifetime is immeasurable,
All beings are filled with joy.

The Buddha's name is heard throughout the universe,
Bringing abundant benefit to the living everywhere.
All their roots of goodness
Help them aspire for the unexcelled.

Then the Buddha said to Maitreya Bodhisattva, the great one: "Ajita, those living beings who have heard that the lifetime of the Buddha is of such long duration, and have been able to believe and understand it even for a moment, will obtain blessings beyond limit or measure. Suppose there are good sons or good daughters who, for the sake of supreme awakening, over eighty trillion myriads of eons follow the five transcendental practices—generosity, morality, patience, perseverance, and meditation, leaving out wisdom. Compared with those mentioned above, the blessings they attain will not equal even a hundredth, a thousandth, or one part of a hundred thousand billion. Indeed, such a comparison cannot be made either with numbers or with parables and similes. If any good sons have such a blessing as this, they cannot fail to obtain supreme awakening."

Then the World-Honored One, wanting to say what he meant once again, spoke in verse:

Suppose someone seeking Buddha-wisdom
Were to follow
The five transcendental practices
For eighty trillion myriads of eons.

And during those eons,
As alms and offerings to buddhas,
Pratyekabuddhas and disciples,
And the multitude of bodhisattvas,

Were to give rare and varied foods and drinks,
Fine clothing and bedding,
Or monasteries built of sandalwood and
Adorned with gardens and woods.

If such people were to continue to give
Such a wonderful variety of alms
Through all those eons
And transfer the merit to the Buddha way,

And if they were to observe the precepts
Purely and without flaw or fault,
And seek the unexcelled way
That all buddhas praise,

And were they to patiently endure insult
And live in a state of gentle harmony,
Not letting their mind be disturbed
Even though various evils were to come upon them,

And when people who think they have the Dharma
And are filled with utmost arrogance
Make light of them and make them suffer,
They would patiently bear even this.

Or were they diligent and persevering,
Always strong in mind and will,
For innumerable hundreds of millions of eons,
Single-mindedly never neglectful,

For innumerable eons
Dwelling in secluded places,
And, whether sitting or walking,
Avoiding sleepiness and always concentrating,

Were they able by this means
To produce states of meditation,

And to remain undisturbed, dwelling at peace
For eight hundred thousand millions of eons,

And, maintaining this blessing of single-mindedness,
Were to seek the unexcelled way, saying,
"I will attain comprehensive wisdom
And attain all the states of meditation,"

If such a person, for hundreds of thousands
Of billions of eons,
Were to do such meritorious practices
As those described here,

Their reward would still be surpassed by
Any good man or woman
Who hears me teach about the length of my life,
And believes it for even a single moment.

If anyone is entirely free
From doubts and misgivings
And deeply believes, even for a moment,
Their blessings will be like this.

Such bodhisattvas
Who have followed the Way for innumerable eons,
Hearing me teach about the length of my life,
Will be able to believe and accept it.

Such people will
Gratefully accept this sutra and say:
"In the future we too hope to have
Long lives for liberating the living.

"Just as the present World-Honored One,
King of the Shakyas,
At the place of the Way, with a lion's roar
Teaches the Dharma without fear,

"So may we in ages to come,
Honored and revered by all,
When sitting on the place of the Way,
In like manner tell of the duration of our lives."

If there are any who are profound in spirit,
Who are purehearted
And do what is right,
Who, hearing much, retain it all,

Who understand the Buddha's words
According to their meaning,
Such people
Will have no doubt.

"What's more, Ajita, if anyone hears of the long duration of the Buddha's life and understands its meaning, the blessings they obtain will be unlimited, awakening them to the unexcelled wisdom of tathagatas. How much more so if someone is devoted to hearing this sutra, or causes others to hear it, or embraces it themselves, or causes others to embrace it, or copies it themselves, or causes others to copy it, or with flowers, incense, garlands, banners, flags, silk canopies, and lamps of fragrant oil and clarified butter makes offerings to the sutra. Such a person's blessings will be innumerable and unlimited, and will give rise to all-inclusive wisdom.

"Ajita, if any good sons or good daughters hear me teach about the long duration of my life, and believe and understand it deeply, they will see the Buddha always on Holy Eagle Peak, surrounded by a multitude of great bodhisattvas and shravakas, preaching the Dharma. And they will see this world—with its land of lapis lazuli smooth and level, its eight roads marked off with Jambunada gold and lined with jeweled trees, its tall buildings, all made of precious materials, in which multitudes of bodhisattvas live together. If anyone is able to see such things, you should know that this is a sign of their profound faith and understanding.

"Further, after the extinction of the Tathagata, if people hear this sutra and do not speak ill of it, but rejoice in it, you should know that this is a sign of their already having deep faith and understanding. How much greater is that of those who read and recite, receive and embrace it. Such people wear the Tathagata like a crown.

"Ajita, such good sons or good daughters do not need to put up stupas, temples, or monasteries for me, or make the four types of offerings to the monks. Why? Because such good sons and daughters, by receiving and embracing, reading and reciting this sutra, have already put up stupas, built monasteries, and made offerings to the monks. That is, they have already put up stupas of the seven precious materials for the Buddha's remains, tall stupas wide at the base, tapering up to the Brahma heaven, hung with flags and canopies and jeweled bells, and with flowers, incense for burning, garlands, powdered incense, paste incense, various drums, musical instruments, pipes, flutes, harps, all kinds of dances and plays and wonderful songs and praises. They have already made these offerings for innumerable tens of millions of billions of eons.

"Ajita, after my extinction, if anyone hears this sutra and is able to embrace it and copy it themselves or lead others to copy it, then they have already built monasteries with thirty-two halls of red sandalwood, and as tall as eight tala trees, lofty, spacious, and beautifully decorated, in which hundreds of thousands of monks live. They have gardens, groves, bathing pools, walking paths and meditation cells, clothing, food and drink, bedding, medicine and all kinds of things for comfort. Such monasteries and halls, hundreds of thousands of billions, countless numbers of them, have been given here in my presence as an offering to me and to the monks.

"Therefore I say that after the extinction of the Tathagata, if anyone receives and embraces, reads and recites this sutra, teaches it for the sake of others, either copies it himself or causes others to copy it, and makes offerings to it, they no longer need to put up stupas and temples or build monasteries and make offerings to the monks. How much more true this is of those who are able to embrace this sutra and also practice generosity, morality, patience, perseverance, single-mindedness, and wisdom. Their virtue will be the greatest, immeasurable and unlimited, just as space, which in the east, west, south, and north, the four intermediate directions, and up and down, is immeasurable and unlimited. So too the blessings of such people will be immeasurable and unlimited, and they will quickly reach all-inclusive wisdom.

"If anyone reads and recites, receives and embraces this sutra, teaches it for the sake of others, copies it himself, or causes others to copy it, they have already put up stupas or built monasteries, served and praised the community of shravakas, and also, in hundreds of thousands of billions of ways, praised the merits of the bodhisattvas.

"If, for the sake of others, with various causes and conditions they explain this Dharma Flower Sutra in accord with its meaning; if they are already able to observe the precepts in purity and able to live with those who are gentle, patient, without anger, and firm in will and thought; if, always valuing sitting meditation, they have attained profound concentration, have patiently and zealously understood good teachings, and are clever and wise in responding to difficult questions—Ajita, if after my extinction there are good sons and good daughters who receive and embrace, read and recite this sutra, who have such excellent merits as these, you should know that they have already proceeded to the place of the Way, sat under the tree of awakening, and are nearing supreme awakening. Ajita, wherever those good sons or good daughters sit or stand or walk, in that place a stupa should be erected, and all human and heavenly beings should make offerings to it as though it were a stupa of the Buddha."

Then the World-Honored One, wanting to say what he meant once again, spoke in verse:

> If people, after my extinction,
> are able to honor and embrace this sutra,
> Their blessings will be immeasurable,
> As explained above.
>
> It is as though they had made
> All kinds of offerings,
> And for the Buddha's remains had put up stupas
> Adorned with the seven precious materials,
>
> Stupas tall and wide,
> Tapering up to the Brahma heaven,
> With banners and tens of millions of billions of jeweled bells,
> Stirred by the wind to make wonderful music.

For innumerable eons
They make offerings to these stupas
With flowers, incense, and various kinds of garlands,
With robes from heaven

And a variety of musical instruments,
And by burning perfumed oil
And clarified butter lamps,
Which constantly illuminate the whole area.

In the evil age of the decline of the Dharma,
One who can embrace this sutra
Will have done the equivalent of making
All the offerings described above.

If people can embrace this sutra,
It will be as if in the presence of the Buddha
They had built monasteries of ox-head sandalwood
As offerings to him—

Monasteries of thirty-two halls,
Eight tala trees high,
Complete with superior food,
Fine robes, and bedding,

With quarters for hundreds of thousands,
With gardens, groves, and bathing pools,
With walking paths and meditation cells,
All variously and beautifully adorned.

If anyone with faith and understanding
Receives, embraces, reads, recites, and copies this sutra,
Or even causes others to copy it,
And makes offerings to the sutra,

Scattering flowers,
Incense, and powdered incense,

And constantly burning perfumed oil made from
Sumana, gardenia, or atimuktaka flowers—

Anyone who makes such offerings
Will obtain innumerable blessings.

Just as space is unlimited,
So too are that person's blessings.
How much more so anyone who embraces this sutra
And at the same time is generous, moral, and patient,

Who enjoys meditation,
Does not get angry or speak ill of others,
Is reverent toward stupas and mausoleums,
And humble toward monks,

Who is never even close to getting arrogant,
Always pondering about wisdom,
And does not get angry when asked difficult questions,
Explaining to questioners appropriately.

If anyone is able to do all this,
That person's blessings will be immeasurable.

If anyone meets
Such a Dharma teacher,
One who has attained such virtues,
They should scatter flowers from heaven over him,

Cover him with robes from heaven,
And greet him
By prostrating themselves at his feet,
As though they were thinking of the Buddha.

What's more, they should think:
Soon he will be going to the place of the Way

To become faultless and unconditioned,
Greatly enriching human and heavenly beings.

Wherever such a teacher lives or stays,
Walks, sits, or lies down,
Or teaches even a verse,
There a stupa should be erected.

It should be wonderfully
And beautifully adorned.
And offerings of many kinds
Should be made to it.

When children of the Buddha live in such a place,
It means that the Buddha accepts them
And always lives among them,
Whether walking, sitting, or lying down.

18. Blessings of Responding with Joy

AT THAT TIME Maitreya Bodhisattva, the great one, said to the Buddha: "World-Honored One, if there are good sons or good daughters who, hearing this Dharma Flower Sutra, respond with joy, how many blessings will they gain?"

And he also asked this in verse:

> After the extinction of the World-Honored One,
> If anyone, hearing this sutra,
> Is able to respond with joy,
> How much happiness will they gain?

Then the Buddha said to Maitreya Bodhisattva, the great one: "Ajita, after the extinction of the Tathagata, if any monks, nuns, laymen, laywomen, or other wise people, young or old, respond with joy to hearing this sutra, and leave this Dharma assembly to go somewhere else, whether to a monk's quarters or to a solitary place, or to a city, settlement, town, or village, and make a great effort to preach what they have heard according to their ability for their fathers and mothers, relatives, or good friends and acquaintances, then all these people, having heard it, will respond with joy as well, and go on to share the teaching with others, and these others, having heard it, will also respond with joy, and they will share the teaching, and so on in turn to the fiftieth person. Ajita, now I will tell you about the blessings of that fiftieth good son or good daughter who joyfully receives it. Listen carefully!

316 THE SUTRA OF THE LOTUS FLOWER OF THE WONDERFUL DHARMA

"Think of all the living beings in the six states, in four million billion countless worlds born in the four ways, from an egg, from a womb, from moisture, or by metamorphosis, whether with form or formless, whether thinking or unthinking, whether not thinking or not unthinking, whether footless, two-footed, four-footed, or many-footed.

"Suppose that among all those living beings there was someone seeking the happiness of these living beings who, according to their desires, provides all of them with all kinds of playthings and amusements, giving each one a whole world full of gold, silver, lapis lazuli, seashell, agate, coral, and amber and other wonderful and rare treasures of all sorts, including elephants, horses, carriages, and palaces and towers built of the seven precious materials and so forth.

"This great gift giver, having given such gifts for a full eighty years, then thinks: 'I have already given all kinds of playthings and amusements to all these beings according to their desires. But now they have all grown old and decrepit. They are over eighty years old, with white hair and wrinkled faces. It will not be long before they die. I should teach and guide them with the Buddha-dharma now.'

"Then, gathering those beings together, he proclaims transformation through the Dharma, demonstrating and teaching it, enriching them and giving them joy. In a moment they all achieve the way of the stream-enterer, the way of the once-returner, the way of the non-returner, and the way of the arhat, exhausting their faults and enabling them to enter profound meditation and become free, equipped with the eight kinds of liberation. What do you think? Are the blessings of this great gift giver many or not?"

Maitreya said to the Buddha: "World-Honored One, the blessings of this man are very many, innumerable and unlimited. Even if this gift giver had only given all sorts of playthings to those beings, his blessings would be innumerable. How much more so when he enables them to receive the fruits of being an arhat!"

Then the Buddha said to Maitreya: "I will now speak clearly to you. This man gave all kinds of playthings to living beings in the six states in four million billion countless worlds, enabling them to attain the fruits of being an arhat. But the blessings he gains do not compare with the blessings of that fiftieth person who, hearing just a single verse of the Dharma Flower Sutra, responds to it with joy. They are not equal to one hundredth, or one thousandth, or one part in a hundred thousand billion. Neither calculation nor parables and similes can express this.

"Ajita, the blessings of such a fiftieth person who hears the Dharma Flower Sutra in turn and responds to it with joy are indeed innumerable, unlimited, and countless. How much more are those of someone who is the first in the assembly to hear and respond to it with joy. That person's happiness is still more immeasurable, unlimited, and beyond numbers. There is no comparison!

"What's more, Ajita, suppose anyone, for the sake of this sutra, goes to a monastery and, sitting or standing, hears and receives it even for a moment. Because of that blessing, when they are reborn they will have fine, superior, and wonderful elephants, horses and carriages, and jeweled palanquins and litters, and ride up to palaces in heaven. Or if someone is sitting in a place where a lecture on the Dharma is being given and, when others come, persuades them to sit down and listen, or shares a seat with them so that they can sit, their blessings will be such that when they are reborn it will be where Indra is sitting, or Brahma the king of heaven is sitting, or where a wheel-turning saintly king is sitting.

"Moreover, Ajita, if anyone says to another: 'There is a sutra named the Dharma Flower. Let's go and listen to it together.' And if those who are so persuaded go and hear it, even for a moment, the blessings of those who have done the persuading will be such that when they are reborn they will be born in the same place as bodhisattvas who have attained powers of incantation. They will be sharp and wise, and for hundreds of billions of ages will never be dumb. They will not have foul breath. Neither their tongues nor their mouths will ever become diseased. Their teeth will never be stained or black, nor will they get yellow or have big gaps, or fall out or be irregular or crooked. Their lips will not hang down or get twisted or wizened, or become coarse and rough, or have sores or scabs, or be cracked or broken or awry or out of shape, or be too thick or too big, or discolored or black or ugly in any other way. Their noses will not be too flat or too thin. Their faces will not be dark, nor will they be long and narrow or sunken and distorted. There will be nothing unpleasing about them. Their lips, tongues, and teeth will all be beautiful, their noses long, high, and straight, their faces round and full, their eyebrows high and long, their foreheads broad and smooth. They will have all the features proper to a human being. Whenever they are born, they will see the Buddha, hear the Dharma, and accept and believe the teachings.

"Ajita, just notice, if the blessings obtained from persuading one person to go and hear the Dharma are like this, how much greater they will be if someone wholeheartedly hears, teaches, reads, and recites the Dharma, analyzes it for the people in the great assembly, and practices what it teaches!"

Then the World-Honored One, wanting to say what he meant once again, spoke in verse:

> Suppose anyone in a Dharma assembly
> Hears even one verse of this sutra,
> And, responding with joy,
> Teaches it for others.
>
> And in this way the teaching rolls on
> Until it reaches the fiftieth person.
> The blessings of this last person
> I will now analyze for you.
>
> Suppose a great gift giver
> For a full eighty years
> Makes offerings to countless multitudes
> According to their desires.
>
> Then he sees signs of their getting old and decrepit,
> With white hair and wrinkled faces,
> Missing teeth and withered bodies,
> And he sees that they are close to death.
>
> "Now," he thinks, "I should teach them
> To gain the fruits of the Way."
> And by skillful means he then
> Teaches them the real Dharma of nirvana:
>
> "Nothing in the world is stable,
> Like bubbles or spray or flames.

You should quickly cultivate
Detachment from things."

When people hear this Dharma
They will become arhats
Endowed with the six divine powers,
The three kinds of knowledge,
And eight kinds of liberation.

But the last and fiftieth person
Who hears even one verse and responds with joy
Will gain far greater happiness,
Beyond comparison by parable or simile.

If someone whose turn to hear is so distant
Has such immeasurable blessings,
How much greater is that one in the Dharma assembly
Who first hears it and responds with joy!

Suppose someone encourages only one person
And brings that person to listen to the Dharma Flower,
Saying: "This sutra is profound and wonderful,
Hard to meet in ten million eons."

And suppose that person is persuaded and goes to listen
And hears it only for a moment.
The blessings such a person gets in reward
I will now explain clearly to you.

For ages their mouths will never be diseased.
Their teeth will not be missing, or get yellow or black.
Their lips will not be too thick, twisted, or cracked,
Or have any ugly features.

Their tongues will not be dry, black, or short.
Their noses will be high, long, and straight,
Their foreheads broad and smooth,

Their faces and eyes completely right and beautiful,
The kind that people enjoy seeing.

They will not have bad breath,
The fragrance of blue lotus flowers
Always coming from their mouths.

Suppose someone goes to visit a monastery
In order to hear the Dharma Flower Sutra,
And, hearing it only for a moment, rejoices.
I will now tell of their happiness.

From now on
They will be born among human and heavenly beings
And have fine elephants, horses, and carriages,
Jeweled palanquins and litters,
And ride up to palaces in heaven.

Where the Dharma is preached,
If someone encourages people
To sit and hear the sutra,
The happiness they receive will enable them
To have the seat of an Indra, a Brahma, a wheel-turning king.

How much more so for those
Who listen with complete attention,
Explain the sutra's meaning,
And practice according to its teaching—
Their happiness will be unlimited!

19. The Blessings of the Dharma Teacher

THEN THE BUDDHA said to the Bodhisattva Constant Effort, the great one: "If any good sons or good daughters receive and embrace this Dharma Flower Sutra, or read it, or recite it, or explain it, or copy it, they will obtain eight hundred blessings of the eyes, twelve hundred blessings of the ears, eight hundred blessings of the nose, twelve hundred blessings of the tongue, eight hundred blessings of the body, and twelve hundred blessings of the mind. With these blessings they will adorn the six faculties, making all of them pure.

"Such good sons or good daughters, with the pure physical eyes received from their parents at birth, will see whatever exists, whether exposed or hidden, in the three-thousand great thousandfold world— the mountains, forests, rivers, and seas down to the deepest purgatory and up to the highest heaven. They will see all the living beings in it and recognize both all of the causes and conditions and all of the effects and consequences resulting from their past actions."

Then the World-Honored One, wanting to say what he meant once again, spoke in verse:

> If anyone in the great assembly
> Fearlessly teaches
> This Dharma Flower Sutra,
> Here are the blessings they will receive:
>
> They will gain eight hundred
> Blessings of superior vision.

Because of these adornments
Their eyes will be completely pure.

With the eyes received from their parents at birth
They will see the whole three-thousandfold world,
The exposed and the hidden Mount Meru,
Mount Sumeru, the Iron Circle Mountains,

And all the other mountains and forests,
As well as the waters of the great seas, rivers, and streams
Down to the deepest purgatory
And up to the highest heaven.

They will see all the living beings
Within that world.
Though not yet having divine vision,
Their physical eyes will have this kind of power.

"What's more, Constant Effort, if any good sons or good daughters receive and embrace this sutra, read or recite it, or explain or copy it, they will obtain twelve hundred blessings of the ears. With pure ears they will hear all the various words and sounds in the three-thousand great thousandfold world, whether exposed or hidden, down to the deepest purgatory and up to the highest heaven—elephant sounds, horse sounds, cattle sounds, sounds of carriages, sounds of weeping, sounds of lamentation, conch sounds, drum sounds, gong sounds, bell sounds, sounds of laughter, sounds of conversation, sounds of men and women, sounds of boys and girls, sounds of the righteous and the unrighteous, sounds of suffering and of delight, sounds of common people and of holy people, happy and unhappy sounds, sounds of gods, sounds of dragons, of satyrs and centaurs, of asuras and griffins, of chimeras and pythons, sounds of fire, sounds of water, sounds of wind, sounds from those in purgatories, sounds of animals, of hungry spirits, of monks and nuns, of shravakas and pratyekabuddhas, of bodhisattvas and of buddhas. In sum, though they have not yet obtained divine ears, whatever sounds there are in the three-thousand great thousandfold world, whether exposed or hidden, they will hear and understand them with the normal pure ears they received at birth from their parents. And while they will be able to distinguish all these various sounds, their ability to hear will not be harmed."

Then the World-Honored One, wanting to say what he meant once again, spoke in verse:

The ears received at birth from one's parents
Are pure and unpolluted.
With these ordinary ears you can hear
The sounds of the three-thousandfold world—

Sounds of elephants, horses, carriages, and oxen,
Sounds of gongs, bells, conches, and drums,
Sounds of lutes and harps, of pipes and flutes,
Sounds of pure and lovely songs.

You can hear all these
Without becoming attached to them.
You can hear the sounds of countless kinds of people,
And understand all of them.

You can hear the sounds of heavenly beings,
The singing of fine and wonderful voices.
You can hear the voices of men and women
And the voices of boys and girls as well.

In mountains, streams, and gorges,
The sounds of kalavinkas,
Jivakajivakas, and other birds—
All such sounds can be heard.

The pains of the multitudes in purgatory
And the sounds of their suffering,
The sounds of hungry spirits driven by hunger and thirst,
Searching for something to eat and drink,

And asuras and others
Living by ocean shores,

When talking together or emitting loud cries—
Can all be heard.

Dharma preachers such as this,
Dwelling at peace with them,
Hear all these sounds from the distance
Without doing harm to their ability to hear.

In the worlds in all directions,
Birds and beasts cry and call to one another,
And a Dharma preacher
Hears them all from here.

From all the Brahma heavens and above,
The Light Sound or the Universal Purity Heaven,
Or from the highest heaven,
Sounds of conversations can all be heard
By a Dharma teacher living here.

All the many monks and all the nuns,
Reading or reciting sutras,
Or teaching them for others,
Can all be heard by the Dharma teacher living here.

What's more, voices of bodhisattvas can be heard
Reading or reciting the teachings of sutras,
Or teaching them for others,
Selecting passages and explaining their meaning.

The buddhas, the great saints and honored ones,
The teachers and transformers of living beings,
Preaching the wonderful Dharma in their great assemblies,
Can all be heard by one who embraces this Dharma Flower.

In the three-thousand great thousandfold world,
Sounds exposed or hidden,

Down to the deepest purgatory and up to the highest heaven,
Can all be heard without doing harm to one's ability to hear.

And because their hearing is sharp,
They can analyze and know everything.

One who embraces this Dharma Flower,
Though not yet having divine ears,
With the ears with which they were born
Already has such blessings as these.

"Moreover, Constant Effort, if any good sons or good daughters receive and embrace this sutra, read, recite, explain, or copy it, they will attain eight hundred blessings of the nose. Their ability to smell will be purified, so that they will be able to smell all kinds of fragrances in the upper and lower, inner and outer parts of the three-thousand great thousandfold world, the fragrances of sumana flowers, jatika flowers, mallika flowers, gardenia flowers, patala flowers, red lotus flowers, blue lotus flowers, white lotus flowers, flowering trees, fruit trees, sandalwood, aloes, tamalapatras and tagaras, and incense blended from tens of millions of materials, powdered incense, incense pellets, and paste incense. Anyone who embraces this sutra, while living here, will be able to distinguish all of these. What's more, he or she will be able to distinguish the odors of living beings, of elephants, horses, cattle, sheep, of men, women, boys, and girls, and of plants, trees, bushes, and woods. Whether near or far, whatever odor there is, they will smell them all and distinguish among them without mistake.

"One who embraces this sutra, though living here, will also detect the odors of the gods in the heavens, of parijata and kovidara trees, of mandarava flowers and great mandarava flowers, manjushaka and great manjushaka flowers, of sandalwoods and aloes, and of many kinds of powdered incense made of a mixture of flowers—all such heavenly fragrances, and those from which they are mixed, such a person will never fail to smell and recognize.

"And he or she will smell the scents of the bodies of gods, the scent of Indra Devendra in his great palace, indulging the five desires and amusing himself, or the scent of when he is in his Hall of the Wonderful

Dharma preaching the Dharma to the gods of the Trayastrimsha heaven, or when he walks around in his gardens for pleasure. Also from a distance such a person will detect the scents of the bodies of the other male and female gods. Up to the Brahma heaven and up to the highest heaven, such a person will smell all the scents of the bodies of the gods. What's more, he or she will smell the incense burned by the gods and the scents of shravakas, of pratyekabuddhas, of bodhisattvas, and of the bodies of buddhas—he or she will smell all of them from afar and know where they live. Though they smell all these scents, their ability to smell will not be harmed or impaired. And if they wish to describe such scents to others, they will be able to remember them without making mistakes."

Then the World-Honored One, wanting to proclaim this teaching once again, spoke in verse:

> The noses of such people will be so pure
> They will be able to smell and identify
> All kinds of odors, fragrant or bad,
> Throughout this world:
>
> Sumana and jatika,
> Tamalapatra and sandalwood,
> Aloes and cassia,
> And aromas of various flowers and fruit.
>
> They will know aromas of living beings,
> Aromas of men and women.
> Though living far away, a preacher
> Knows well where they are by scent.
>
> Powerful wheel-turning kings,
> Minor wheel-turners and their children,
> Their ministers and attendants—
> Where they are can be well known by scent.
>
> The jewels they wear on their bodies,
> Their treasures stored in the ground,

The jeweled queens of wheel-turning kings—
Where they are can be well known by scent.

From the jewelry adorning people,
Their clothes and necklaces,
And the perfumes they use—
Who they are can be well known by scent.

Whether the gods walk or sit,
Play or use their magical powers,
Those who uphold this Dharma Flower
Can know all of this by scent.

From the scents of flowering trees and fruit
And the fragrance of butter oil,
Those who embrace this Dharma Flower,
Living here, know well where they are.

In deep and steep mountain gorges,
Where sandalwood trees blossom,
And living beings live among them—
One can know all by scent.

On the Iron Circle Mountains, in the great seas,
And in the ground are living beings.
One who embraces this sutra
Knows well where they are by scent.

When male and female asuras
And all their tribes of followers
Quarrel or play together,
One is able to know it by scent.

On the prairies and in narrow places
Are lions, elephants, tigers, wolves,
Buffalo, and water buffalo.
One can know where they are by scent.

If a woman is pregnant
And cannot tell whether the child is male or female,
Defective or less than human,
One can know by scent.

By the power of smell
One can know when a woman has just become pregnant,
Whether her pregnancy will be successful or not,
And whether she will have a safe and healthy delivery.

By the power of smell
The thoughts of men and women can be known,
Their greedy desires, stupidity, and anger,
And whether they are doing good can also be known.

The treasures stored in the earth,
Gold, silver, and rare treasures
Heaped in copper vessels,
Can all be known by scent.

All sorts of necklaces,
Of value beyond knowing what they are worth,
Where they came from, and where they are now,
Can all be known by scent.

The flowers in the heavens,
Mandaravas, manjushakas,
And parijata trees,
Can all be known by scent.

The palaces in the heavens,
Upper, middle, or lower,
Decorated with precious flowers,
Can all be known by scent.

The heavenly gardens, groves, and superb palaces,
The studies and wonderful Dharma halls,

And those who enjoy them
Can all be known by scent.

Whether the gods listen to the Dharma
Or indulge in the five desires,
Coming, going, walking, sitting, or lying down,
Can all be known by scent.

The robes worn by goddesses,
Adorned with beautiful flowers and perfumes,
And when they dance about for enjoyment,
Can all be known by scent.

Extending one's sense of smell
Up to the Brahma heavens,
Those entering or emerging from meditation
Can all be known by scent.

Who is in the Light Sound Heaven
Or Universally Pure Heaven or the highest heaven,
From birth to death,
Can all be known by scent.

The whole group of monks
Always persevering for the Dharma,
Whether sitting or walking around,
Reading or reciting a sutra,

Or devoting their energies to meditation
Beneath trees in the forest—
One who embraces this sutra
Knows where they all are by scent.

Whether firm-willed bodhisattvas
Are in meditation, reading a sutra,
Or preaching the Dharma to others
Can all be known by scent.

The world-honored ones in all directions,
Revered and respected by all,
Who preach the Dharma out of sympathy for all,
Can all be known by scent.

The living who in a buddha's presence
Hear the sutra and rejoice together,
And act in accord with the Dharma,
Can all be known by scent.

Though not yet having the nose of a bodhisattva
Who has attained the flawless Dharma,
Those who uphold the sutra
Will first have the kind of nose described here.

"Further, Constant Effort, if any good sons or good daughters receive and embrace this sutra and either read, recite, explain, or copy it, they will gain twelve hundred blessings of the tongue. Whether something is pleasant or unpleasant, tasty or not, bitter or astringent, whenever it is on their tongues it will change into something delicious, like nectar from heaven, and there will be nothing that is unpleasant about it.

"If one's tongue is used to preach in the assembly, it will produce a deep and wonderful voice that can enter into hearts, giving people pleasure and joy. And when sons and daughters of heaven, Indra, Brahma, and the other gods hear this deep and wonderful voice speaking so clearly, they will all come and listen. Male and female dragons, male and female satyrs, male and female centaurs, male and female asuras, male and female griffins, male and female chimeras, and male and female pythons will all come to hear the Dharma and to associate with, revere, and make offerings to such a person. Monks and nuns, laymen and laywomen, kings and princes with their ministers and followers, and minor and great wheel-turning kings with their seven treasures, their thousand princes, and with their inner and outer followings, all will come riding in their palaces to listen to the Dharma.

"Because such bodhisattvas preach the Dharma so well, brahmans, citizens, and people from all over the land will follow, wait on, and make offerings to them for the rest of their lives. And shravakas, pratyekabuddhas, bodhisattvas, and buddhas will always be delighted to see them. Wherever such people live, the buddhas will all face in that direction when preaching, and such bodhisattvas will be able to receive and embrace all of the Buddha-dharma. They will also make the deep and wonderful sounds of the Dharma."

Then the World-Honored One, wanting to proclaim this teaching once again, spoke in verse:

Because the tongues of such people are pure,
They will never experience bad tastes.
Whatever they eat,
It will become like nectar.

With pure, deep, wonderful voices
They will teach the Dharma in the assembly.
With various causal explanations and parables
They will lead the living.

All who hear them will rejoice
And make the best of offerings.
Gods, dragons, satyrs, asuras, and others
Will approach them together in reverence to hear the Dharma.

If people who preach the Dharma like this
Want to make their wonderful voices
Fill three thousand worlds,
They will be able to do so at will.

Great and minor wheel-turning kings
With their thousands of children and servants,
Palms together in reverence,
Will always come to hear and receive the Dharma.

Gods, dragons, and satyrs,
And ogres and man-eating goblins,
Also with joyful hearts,
Will always enjoy bringing offerings.

332 THE SUTRA OF THE LOTUS FLOWER OF THE WONDERFUL DHARMA

Brahma, king of heaven, the king of devils,
Freedom, Great Freedom,
And all such heavenly beings
Will always come to where they are.

Buddhas and their disciples,
Hearing the sound of such preaching of the Dharma,
Will always keep them in mind and protect them,
At times revealing themselves for their sake.

"What's more, Constant Effort, if any good sons or good daughters receive and embrace this sutra, or if they read it, or if they recite it, or if they teach it, or if they copy it, they will obtain eight hundred blessings of the body, including a pure body, pure as lapis lazuli, which all the living delight to see. Because of the purity of their bodies, the living beings of the three-thousand great thousandfold world, as they are born or die, whether as superior or inferior, fine or ugly, or in good or bad places—all will be reflected in these bodies. The Iron Circle Mountains, Great Iron Circle Mountains, Mount Meru, Mount Great Meru, and other kings among mountains, and the living beings on them, will all be reflected in these bodies. Down to the deepest purgatory and up to the highest heaven, all things and living beings will be reflected in these bodies. Shravakas, pratyekabuddhas, bodhisattvas, and buddhas preaching the Dharma will all have their forms and images reflected in these bodies."

Then the World-Honored One, wanting to express this teaching once again, spoke in verse:

If someone embraces the Dharma Flower Sutra,
Their body will become completely pure,
Like one of lapis lazuli.
All the living will delight to see it.

As in a pure, bright mirror,
Every image will be reflected.
Bodhisattvas, in their pure bodies,
Will see everything in the world.

They alone will see clearly
What others do not see.
The whole multitude of beings
In the three-thousandfold world,

Human and heavenly beings, asuras,
Beings in purgatories, spirits, animals—
All such forms and images
Will be reflected in their bodies.

The palaces of the gods up to the highest heaven,
Iron Circle and Meru mountains, Mount Great Meru,
And great oceans and bodies of water
Will be reflected in their bodies.

Buddhas and shravakas,
And children of the Buddha, the bodhisattvas,
Whether alone or preaching for multitudes,
All will be reflected.

Though not yet having
A flawless, wonderful, Dharma-nature body,
In their pure ordinary bodies
Everything will be reflected.

"Furthermore, Constant Effort, if any good sons or good daughters, after the extinction of the Tathagata, receive and embrace this sutra, or read it, recite it, preach it, or copy it, they will obtain twelve hundred blessings of the mind. When they hear even a single verse or phrase with their pure minds, they will deeply understand its innumerable and unlimited meanings. Having understood those meanings, they will be able to preach on that single phrase or verse for a month, four months, even a year. And their many teachings will be in accord with the meanings, and never contrary to the true nature of reality.

"If they teach about some secular text, or speak about the political world or about matters related to livelihood, in every case they will do so in accord with the true Dharma. They will know all the workings of the minds, the movements of the minds, and the foolishness in the minds of the beings in the six states of the three-thousand great thousandfold world.

"Though not yet having attained flawless wisdom, their minds will have the kind of purity that whatever they think, plan, or speak will all be in accord with the truth of the Buddha-dharma and with what previous buddhas have taught in the sutras."

Then the World-Honored One, wanting to say what he meant once again, spoke in verse:

> The minds of these people will be pure,
> Lucid, keen, and unsullied.
> With such wonderful minds
> They will know all things—high, low, and in between.
>
> Hearing even a single verse,
> They will understand deeply its innumerable meanings
> And teach them in proper order and in accord with the Dharma
> For a month, four months, or a year.
>
> Whatever all the living beings of
> The inner and outer parts of this world—
> Gods, dragons, human beings,
> Satyrs, demons, spirits, and others,
>
> Those in the six states—
> Are thinking
> Will be known instantly as a reward
> By those who embrace the Dharma Flower.
>
> They will hear, receive, and embrace
> The Dharma preached for all the living,
> Preached by the innumerable buddhas of the universe,
> With a hundred signs of good fortune.
>
> They will ponder the innumerable meanings,
> Preach the Dharma innumerable times,

And never forget or make a mistake
Because they embrace the Dharma Flower.

Knowing the characteristics of all things,
Knowing their proper order according to their meaning,
Comprehending names and words,
They will preach about them as they know them.

Whatever they preach,
It will always be the Dharma of previous buddhas.
And because they proclaim this Dharma,
They will have no fear in the assembly.

Anyone who embraces the Dharma Flower Sutra
Has this kind of pure mind.
Though not yet flawless,
They will first have these characteristics.

Those embracing this sutra,
Dwelling at peace on rare ground,
Are cherished, respected, and enjoyed
By all living beings.

With tens of millions
Of good, skillful words
They are able to analyze and preach
Because they embrace the Dharma Flower Sutra.

20. Never Disrespectful Bodhisattva

AT THAT TIME the Buddha spoke to the Bodhisattva Great Strength, the great one: "You should know now that when monks, nuns, laymen, or laywomen embrace the Dharma Flower Sutra, if anyone curses, abuses, or slanders them, that person will receive great punishment, as taught earlier. But those who attain blessings as taught before will have their eyes, ears, noses, tongues, bodies, and thoughts purified.

"Great Strength, long ago, innumerable, unlimited, inconceivable, and countless eons ago, there was a buddha named Majestic Voice King Tathagata, one worthy of offerings, truly awakened, fully clear in conduct, well gone, understanding the world, unexcelled leader, trainer of men, teacher of heavenly beings and people, buddha, world-honored one. His eon was named Free from Decline, and his land Great Achievement.

"In that world, Majestic Voice King Buddha taught the Dharma for the sake of human and heavenly beings and asuras. For those seeking to be shravakas, he taught the Dharma according to the four truths, to free them from birth, old age, disease, and death, leading them finally to nirvana. For those seeking to be pratyekabuddhas, he taught the Dharma according to the twelve causes and conditions. For bodhisattvas, to lead them to supreme awakening he taught the Dharma according to the six transcendental practices, enabling them to gain Buddha-wisdom.

"Great Strength, the lifetime of Majestic Voice King Buddha lasted for eons equal in number to the sands of forty trillion myriads of Ganges. The number of eons during which his true Dharma remained in the world was equal to the specks of dust in Jambudvipa. And the number of eons during which his merely formal Dharma remained was equal to the specks of dust in four continents. After this buddha had abundantly benefited living beings, he passed into extinction.

"After the true Dharma and merely formal Dharma had entirely disappeared, another buddha appeared in that land. He was also named Majestic Voice King Tathagata, and was worthy of offerings, truly awakened, fully clear in conduct, well gone, understanding the world, unexcelled leader, trainer of men, teacher of heavenly beings and people, buddha, world-honored one. In this way there were two trillion buddhas in succession, all with the same name.

"After the extinction of the first Majestic Voice King Tathagata, and after the end of the true Dharma, during the period of the merely formal Dharma, extremely arrogant monks had great power. At that time there was a bodhisattva-monk named Never Disrespectful. Great Strength, why do you think he was named Never Disrespectful? That monk bowed in obeisance before everyone he met, whether monk, nun, layman, or laywoman, and praised them, saying: 'I deeply respect you. I would never dare to be disrespectful or arrogant toward you. Why? Because all of you are practicing the bodhisattva way and surely will become buddhas.'

"This monk did not devote himself to reading and reciting sutras, but simply went around bowing to people. If he saw the four groups off in the distance he would make a point of going up to them, bowing in obeisance, and praising them, saying: 'I would never dare to disrespect you, because surely you are all to become buddhas.'

"Among the four groups were those who became angry, enraged, and mean-spirited, and reviled and cursed him, saying: 'This ignorant monk, who takes it on himself to announce that he does not disrespect us and assures us of becoming buddhas, where did he come from? We have no use for such empty, false assurances.'

"Thus he passed many years, constantly being cursed but never becoming angry or enraged, and always saying: 'Surely you are to become buddhas.' When he spoke this way, some would hit him with sticks, tiles, or stones. But even if he ran off and stood at a distance, he would continue to cry out loudly: 'I would not dare to disrespect you. Surely all of you are to become buddhas.' And because he always spoke in this way, the extremely arrogant monks, nuns, laymen, and laywomen called him Never Disrespectful.

"When this monk was nearing death, from the sky he heard two hundred million billion verses of the Dharma Flower Sutra, which Majestic Voice King Buddha had previously taught, and he was able to receive and embrace them all. Immediately he obtained the purity of vision and of the faculties of the ears, nose, tongue, body, and mind described earlier. Having obtained the purity of these six faculties, his life was extended for two million billion myriads of years, and he taught this Dharma Flower Sutra everywhere for the people.

"Then the extremely arrogant monks, nuns, laymen, and laywomen who had slighted and shown contempt for this man and given him the name Never Disrespectful, seeing him with the power of great divine faculties, powers of joyful and eloquent speech, and powers of great goodness and tranquility, and having heard him preach, all believed in him and followed him.

"This bodhisattva transformed a multitude of tens of millions of billions, enabling them to dwell in a state of supreme awakening. After his lifetime, he met two hundred billion buddhas, all of whom were named Sun and Moon Light, and under their Dharma he taught this Dharma Flower Sutra. Through the causes and conditions created by this, he also met two hundred billion buddhas, all with the same name, King of Light and Master of Clouds. Under the Dharma of those buddhas he received, embraced, read, recited, and taught this sutra for all four groups. Thus his ordinary vision became pure, as did the faculties of his ears, nose, tongue, body, and mind. Among the four groups he taught the Dharma fearlessly.

"Great Strength, in this way Never Disrespectful Bodhisattva, the great one, made offerings to numerous buddhas, revering, honoring, and praising them. After planting such roots of goodness, he met tens of millions of billions of buddhas once again, and under the Dharma of those buddhas taught this sutra, gaining blessings that enabled him to become a buddha.

"Great Strength, what do you think? Can Never Disrespectful Bodhisattva, who lived at that time, be unknown to you? He was really me! If I had not received and embraced, read and recited this sutra and taught it to others in previous lives, I would not have been able to attain supreme awakening so quickly. Because I received and embraced, read and recited this sutra and taught it for others under previous buddhas, I attained supreme awakening quickly.

"Great Strength, at that time the four groups—monks, nuns, laymen, and laywomen—angrily treated me with contempt and scorn. Thus for twenty billion eons they never met a buddha, never heard the Dharma, never saw a monastic community, and for a thousand eons they experienced great suffering in the deepest purgatory. After they had finished paying for their sin, once again they met and were taught and transformed by the supreme awakening of Never Disrespectful Bodhisattva.

"Great Strength, what do you think? Can those four groups of that time, who always slighted that bodhisattva, be unknown to you? They are now in this assembly—Bhadrapala and his group of five hundred bodhisattvas, Lion Moon and her group of five hundred nuns, Thinking of Buddha and his group of five hundred laymen, all of whom will never regress in their pursuit of supreme awakening.

"You should know, Great Strength, that this Dharma Flower Sutra abundantly benefits the bodhisattvas, the great ones, and enables them to reach supreme awakening. This is why the bodhisattvas, the great ones, after the extinction of the Tathagata, should always embrace, read and recite, and explain and copy this sutra."

Then the World-Honored One, wanting to restate this teaching, spoke in verse:

In the past there was a buddha
Called Majestic Voice King,
Immeasurable in divine wisdom,
Commander and leader of all.

Gods and people and dragon-gods
Joined in making offerings to him.

After this buddha's extinction,
When his Dharma was near its end,
There was a bodhisattva
Whose name was Never Disrespectful.

At that time the four groups
Were attached to the Dharma superficially.

Never Disrespectful Bodhisattva would go to them
And say: "I would never disrespect you,
For you are following the Way
And surely will all become buddhas."

When people heard this
They made light of him or cursed him.
Never Disrespectful Bodhisattva
Withstood it all patiently.

When he had been cleansed of his sins
And his life was coming to an end,
He heard this sutra
And his six faculties were purified.

Because of his divine powers
His life was prolonged,
And for the sake of all the people
He taught this sutra everywhere.

All those who adhered to the Dharma
Were taught, transformed, and developed
By this bodhisattva
And led to dwell in the Buddha way.

At the end of his life
Never Disrespectful met countless buddhas,
And through teaching this sutra
Gained immeasurable happiness.

Gradually developing his blessings,
He quickly attained the Buddha way.

The Never Disrespectful of that time
Was really me.
The four groups of that time,
Who were attached to the Dharma,

And heard Never Disrespectful say,
"You are to become buddhas,"
And for this reason met countless buddhas,
Are now here in this assembly.

They are the group of five hundred bodhisattvas
And the four groups,
Men and women of pure faith,
Who are now before me listening to the Dharma.

In my previous lives,
I encouraged these people
To hear and receive this sutra,
The unsurpassed Dharma.

I revealed and taught it to people,
Enabling them to dwell in nirvana.
Through age after age
They have received and embraced sutras.

During billions and billions of eons
Of inconceivable time,
Rare are the times that one can hear
This Dharma Flower Sutra.

During billions and billions of eons
Of inconceivable time,
Buddhas, world-honored ones,
Rarely taught this sutra.

Therefore its followers,
After the Buddha's extinction,

On hearing such a sutra as this,
Should have no doubt or perplexity.

They should wholeheartedly
Teach this sutra everywhere.
Meeting buddhas in age after age,
They will quickly achieve the Buddha way.

21. Divine Powers of the Tathagata

AT THAT TIME all the bodhisattvas, the great ones, who had sprung up from the earth, equal in number to the specks of dust of a thousand worlds, put their palms together in complete attention before the Buddha, reverently looked up at his face, and said to him: "World-Honored One, after the extinction of the Buddha, in whatever lands the World-Honored One is embodied, wherever he has become extinct, we will teach this sutra everywhere. Why? Because we too want to gain this true and pure, great Dharma, to embrace, read and recite, explain, copy, and make offerings to it."

Then the World-Honored One revealed his great divine powers before Manjushri and the other innumerable hundreds of thousands of billions of bodhisattvas, the great ones, who had lived in this world for a long time, as well as monks, nuns, laymen and laywomen, gods, dragons, satyrs, centaurs, asuras, griffins, chimeras, pythons, humans and nonhumans, and so on. Before all these beings, he extended his long and broad tongue until it reached up to the Brahma world, while light of immeasurable and innumerable colors radiated from every pore, illuminating everything everywhere throughout the worlds in all directions. Under all the jeweled trees, the buddhas, seated on lion seats, did the same thing, extending their long, broad tongues and radiating immeasurable light.

While Shakyamuni Buddha and all the other buddhas under the jeweled trees were displaying their divine powers, hundreds of thousands of years went by. After that they drew back their tongues, coughed simultaneously, and snapped their fingers in unison. These two sounds went through all the buddha worlds in all directions, and all these lands trembled and shook in the six ways.

Thanks to the divine powers of the Buddha, all the living beings in these worlds, the gods, dragons, satyrs, centaurs, asuras, griffins, chimeras, pythons, humans and nonhumans, and others, saw in this world the innumerable, unlimited hundreds of thousands of billions of buddhas seated on the lion seats under all the jeweled trees, and they saw Shakyamuni Buddha together with Abundant Treasures Tathagata sitting on a lion seat in the treasure stupa. And they also saw the innumerable, unlimited hundreds of thousands of billions of bodhisattvas, the great ones, and the four groups reverently surrounding Shakyamuni Buddha. Having seen this, they were all filled with great joy, having obtained something they had never had before.

At the same time, heavenly beings in the sky sang with loud voices: "Beyond these innumerable, unlimited hundreds of thousands of billions of countless worlds, there is a land named Saha, and in it there is a buddha named Shakyamuni. For the sake of all bodhisattvas, the great ones, he now teaches the Great Vehicle sutra called the Lotus Flower of the Wonderful Dharma, the Dharma by which bodhisattvas are taught and which buddhas watch over and keep in mind. You should rejoice from the depths of your hearts. Worship him and make offerings to Shakyamuni Buddha!"

All those living beings, having heard the voices in the sky, put their palms together facing this world and exclaimed: "Praise to Shakyamuni Buddha! Praise to Shakyamuni Buddha!"

Then they took various flowers, incense, garlands, banners, and canopies, as well as personal ornaments, gems, and other wonderful things, and together from afar scattered them in the direction of this world. The things scattered from every direction came like gathering clouds, which changed into a jeweled canopy covering the whole area above the buddhas. Then passage between all the worlds in all directions became unobstructed, uniting them as one buddha-land.

At that time the Buddha spoke to Superior Practice and the multitude of other bodhisattvas: "The divine powers of buddhas, as you have seen, are innumerable, unlimited, inconceivable. Even if for the sake of entrusting this sutra to others I were to use these divine powers to declare its blessings for innumerable, unlimited hundreds of thousands of billions of countless eons, I would be unable to exhaust them. In brief, all the teachings of the Tathagata, all the unhindered, divine powers of the Tathagata, the hidden core of the whole storehouse of the Tathagata, and all the profound matters of the Tathagata are proclaimed, demonstrated, revealed, and preached in this sutra.

"Therefore, after the extinction of the Tathagata, you should all wholeheartedly embrace, read and recite, explain and copy, and practice it as you have been taught. In any land, wherever anyone accepts and embraces, reads and recites, explains and copies, and practices it as taught, or wherever a volume of the sutra is kept, whether in a garden, or in a woods, or under a tree, or in a monk's cell or a layman's house, or in a palace, or in a mountain valley or an open field, in all these places you should put up a stupa and make offerings. Why? You should understand that all such places are places of the Way. They are where the buddhas attain supreme awakening; they are where the buddhas turn the Dharma wheel; they are where the buddhas reach complete nirvana."

At that time the World-Honored One, wanting to proclaim this teaching once again, spoke in verse:

> The buddhas, the saviors of the world,
> Having great divine faculties,
> Reveal their innumerable divine powers
> In order to bring joy to living beings.
>
> Their tongues reach to the Brahma heaven.
> Their bodies emit countless rays of light.
> For those who seek the Buddha way
> They reveal such rare things.
>
> The sounds of the buddhas coughing
> And the snapping of their fingers
> Are heard throughout the lands in all directions,
> And those lands shake in six ways.
>
> Because there will be some who embrace this sutra
> After the Buddha's extinction,

The buddhas rejoice
And display innumerable divine powers.

Because the buddhas want to entrust this sutra,
Those who embrace it are praised.
Even if it is for innumerable eons,
Such praise cannot be exhausted.

The blessings received by such a person
Will be unlimited and without end,
Like the empty space in every direction,
For which no one can find a limit.

One who can embrace this sutra
Is one who has already seen me,
As well as Abundant Treasures Buddha
And all the buddhas embodying me.

Such a one also sees me today
Teaching and transforming bodhisattvas.

Anyone who can embrace this sutra
Will cause me and my embodiments,
And the already extinct Abundant Treasures Buddha,
All to rejoice.

The buddhas present in all directions,
And those of the past and the future,
Will also be seen, and be given offerings,
And led to rejoice by such a person.

Anyone who embraces this sutra
Before long will surely gain as well
The hidden core of the Dharma
Attained by the buddhas in their places of the Way.

One who embraces this sutra
Will delight in endlessly teaching
Meanings of what has been taught,
With their names and expressions,
Like a wind in the sky, which never meets obstacles.

After the extinction of the Tathagata,
Anyone who knows the sutras preached by the Buddha,
Their causes and conditions and proper order,
Will teach them truthfully in accord with their true meaning.

Just as the light of the sun and the moon
Can dispel darkness,
Such a person, working in the world,
Can dispel the gloom of living beings,

Leading innumerable bodhisattvas
Finally to dwell in the one vehicle.

Therefore, one who has wisdom,
Hearing of the blessings to be gained,
After my extinction
Should embrace this sutra.

Such a person will be determined to follow,
Without doubts, the Buddha way.

22. Entrustment

AT THAT TIME Shakyamuni Buddha rose from his Dharma seat and displayed great divine powers. Laying his right hand on the heads of the innumerable bodhisattvas, the great ones, he said: "For incalculable hundreds of thousands of billions of eons, I have studied and practiced this rare Dharma of supreme awakening. Now I entrust it to you. You should wholeheartedly disseminate this Dharma, making its benefits spread everywhere."

In this way, he touched the heads of the bodhisattvas, the great ones, three times with his hand, saying: "For incalculable hundreds of thousands of billions of eons, I have studied and practiced this rare Dharma of supreme awakening. Now I entrust it to you. You should receive and embrace, read and recite, and proclaim it, so that all living beings everywhere may hear and understand it. Why? Because the Tathagata has great compassion, is not stingy or begrudging, has no fear, and gives to living beings Buddha-wisdom, Tathagata-wisdom, natural wisdom. The Tathagata is the great gift giver for all living beings. You too should follow the teachings of the Tathagata and not be stingy or begrudging.

"In the future, if good sons or good daughters have faith in the wisdom of the Tathagata, you should preach this Dharma Flower Sutra for them, so that they can hear and understand it. In this way they can be led to Buddha-wisdom. If there are living beings who do not have faith in it or accept it, you should use other profound teachings of the Tathagata to demonstrate and teach it, enriching them and giving them joy. If you do this, then you will have repaid the grace of the buddhas."

When all the bodhisattvas, the great ones, heard the Buddha say this, they were filled with great joy and paid him even greater reverence, facing the Buddha and bending over, bowing their heads, putting their palms together, and crying with one voice: "We will respectfully do all that the World-Honored One has commanded. Please, World-Honored One, do not worry about that." The whole group of bodhisattvas, the great ones, repeated this three times, crying with one voice: "We will respectfully do all that the World-Honored One has commanded. Please, World-Honored One, do not worry about that."

Then Shakyamuni Buddha had all the buddhas embodying him, who had come from all directions, return to their own lands, saying: "Buddhas, go in peace. Let the stupa of Abundant Treasures Buddha be as it was."

When these words were spoken, the innumerable embodiment buddhas from all directions, who were seated on lion seats under the jeweled trees, as well as Abundant Treasures Buddha, Superior Practice, and the multitude of innumerable, countless bodhisattvas, Shariputra and the other shravakas, the four groups and others, and all the human and heavenly beings, asuras, and so on in all the worlds, hearing the Buddha preach, were filled with great joy.

23. Previous Lives of Medicine King Bodhisattva

A T THAT TIME the Bodhisattva Constellation-King Flower said to the Buddha: "World-Honored One, why does Medicine King Bodhisattva travel around in this world? World-Honored One, Medicine King Bodhisattva has done hundreds of thousands of billions of difficult and painful practices! World-Honored One, I beg you! Please explain it a little. The gods, dragon-gods, satyrs, centaurs, asuras, griffins, chimeras, pythons, humans and nonhumans, and the bodhisattvas who have come from other lands, as well as these shravakas, will all be very glad to hear you."

Then the Buddha said to Constellation-King Flower Bodhisattva: "Many eons ago, as incalculable as the sands of the Ganges, there was a buddha named Pure and Bright Excellence of Sun and Moon Tathagata, one worthy of offerings, truly awakened, fully clear in conduct, well gone, understanding the world, unexcelled leader, trainer of men, teacher of heavenly beings and people, buddha, world-honored one. That Buddha had eight billion great bodhisattva great ones, and a great assembly of shravakas, as many as the sands of seventy-two Ganges. The lifetime of that buddha was forty-two thousand eons, and the lifetimes of his bodhisattvas were the same.

"In his land there were no women, no one living in purgatories, no hungry spirits, no animals, no asuras, and no difficulties of any kind. The land was as level as the palm of one's hand and made of lapis lazuli. It was adorned with jeweled trees, covered with jeweled curtains, and hung with banners of treasured flowers. Jeweled vases and incense burners were everywhere. There were platforms made of the seven precious materials, with trees for each platform, the trees being arrows shot from the platforms. Under all these jeweled trees bodhisattvas and shravakas were seated. And above each of the platforms tens of billions of gods were making heavenly music and singing praises to the Buddha as an offering.

"Then that buddha taught the Dharma Flower Sutra for the sake of the Bodhisattva Seen with Joy by All the Living, all the bodhisattvas, and the multitude of shravakas. This Seen with Joy by All the Living Bodhisattva enjoyed severe practices following the teachings of Pure and Bright Excellence of Sun and Moon Buddha. He had made progress through perseverance, going about single-mindedly seeking to become a buddha for a full twelve thousand years. After that he attained the concentration in which one can take on any form. Having attained this concentration, he was full of joy and thought to himself: 'Gaining the concentration in which one can take on any form is entirely due to the power that comes from hearing the Dharma Flower Sutra. I should now make offerings to Pure and Bright Excellence of Sun and Moon Buddha and to the Dharma Flower Sutra.'

"As soon as he had entered into this concentration, he had mandarava flowers, great mandarava flowers, and a fine dust of hard black sandalwood rain down from the sky, filling it and descending like clouds. He also caused incense of sandalwood from the closer seashore to come down, six grains of this incense being worth as much as this whole world. All this he did as an offering to the Buddha.

"Having made this offering, he arose from concentration and thought to himself: 'Though I have made offerings to the Buddha with my divine powers, that is not as good as offering my body.'

"Then he put on many kinds of incense—sandalwood, kunduruka, turushka, prikka, aloes, and resin incense—and drank the fragrant oil of gardenia and other kinds of flowers for fully twelve hundred years. With his body anointed with fragrant oil and wrapped in jeweled heavenly robes, he went before Pure and Bright Excellence of Sun and Moon Buddha, anointed himself again with fragrant oil, and, making a vow by his divine powers, set fire to his own body.

"The light illuminated worlds as numerous as the sands of eight billion Ganges. The buddhas in those lands all praised him at the same time, saying: 'Well done, well done, good son; this is true devotion. It is what is called a true Dharma offering to the Tathagata. Offerings of flowers, scents, necklaces, incense for burning, powdered incense, paste incense, flags and canopies of heavenly silk, and incense made from sandalwood from the closer seashore, all kinds of offerings cannot match this! Even offerings of towns, countries, and wives and children cannot match this! Good son, this is what is called the greatest gift, the most highly regarded and supreme of gifts, because it is an offering of the Dharma to the tathagatas.'

"After saying this, they all became silent.

"The bodhisattva's body continued to burn for twelve hundred years, after which it burned itself out.

"After Seen with Joy by All the Living Bodhisattva had made this Dharma offering and his life had come to an end, he was born in the land of Pure and Bright Excellence of Sun and Moon Buddha, in the house of King Pure Virtue. He was born suddenly by transformation, sitting cross-legged. At once he spoke in verse for the benefit of his father:

> Now you should know, great king,
> Having walked around in this world,
> I suddenly attained the concentration
> By which one can take on any form,
> And I practiced with great devotion
> By sacrificing the body I cherished.

"After reciting this verse, he said to his father: 'Pure and Bright Excellence of Sun and Moon Buddha is still alive in the present. Having first made offerings to that buddha, I obtained the power of incantation of interpreting the words of all the living. What's more, I heard this Dharma Flower Sutra in eight hundred thousand billions of myriads of millions, billions, trillions of verses. Great king, now I should return to that buddha and make offerings to him.'

"Having said this, he took his seat on a platform of the seven precious materials, rose in the air as high as seven tala trees, and went to where that buddha was, prostrated himself at his feet, and, putting his ten fingers together, praised the Buddha in verse:

Most rare and wonderful countenance,
Your radiance illuminates the universe.
I made offerings to you in the past,
And now I have returned to see you again.

"Having recited this verse, Seen with Joy by All the Living Bodhisattva said to that buddha: 'World-Honored One, is the World-Honored One still alive in the world?'

"Then Pure and Bright Excellence of Sun and Moon Buddha said to Seen with Joy by All the Living Bodhisattva: 'My good son, the time has come for my nirvana. The time has come for my extinction. You may arrange a comfortable bed for me. Tonight I will enter complete nirvana.'

"Again he ordered Seen with Joy by All the Living Bodhisattva: 'My good son, I entrust the Buddha-dharma to you. And I give to you all my bodhisattvas and great disciples, along with the Dharma of supreme awakening, the three-thousand great thousandfold world made of the seven precious materials, with its jeweled trees and platforms, and their divine attendants. I also entrust to you whatever remains there are after my extinction. Let them be distributed and let offerings be made to them everywhere. Let thousands of stupas be put up.'

"Having given these orders to Seen with Joy by All the Living Bodhisattva, in the last watch of the night the Buddha Pure and Bright Excellence of Sun and Moon entered nirvana.

"Then Seen with Joy by All the Living Bodhisattva, seeing that the Buddha was extinct, was sad and distressed, and lovingly longed for him. Then he made a pyre of sandalwood from the closer seashore, and, making an offering, cremated the body of the Buddha. After the fire had died out, he gathered the remains, made eighty-four thousand jeweled urns, and built eighty-four thousand stupas as high as three worlds. These stupas were adorned with central poles hung with streamers and canopies and many jeweled bells.

"Then Seen with Joy by All the Living Bodhisattva once again thought to himself: 'Though I have made this offering, I am still not satisfied. I should make another offering to the Buddha's remains.'

"Then he spoke to the bodhisattvas and chief disciples, and to the gods, dragons, satyrs, and the whole group, saying: 'Pay complete attention, for I am now about to make an offering to the remains of Pure and Bright Excellence of Sun and Moon Buddha.'

"Having said this, before the eighty-four thousand stupas he burned his arms, which had a hundred marks of good fortune, for seventy-two thousand years. This led an innumerable multitude of those seeking to be shravakas and innumerable, countless numbers of other people to seek supreme awakening, enabling all of them to dwell in the concentration in which one can take on any form.

"Then all those bodhisattvas, human and heavenly beings, asuras, and others, seeing him without arms, were troubled and sorrowful, and they said: 'This Seen with Joy by All the Living Bodhisattva is indeed our teacher. He has taught and transformed us. But now he has burned off his arms; his body is incomplete.'

"Then Seen with Joy by All the Living Bodhisattva made a vow in the great assembly, saying: 'Having thrown away both my arms, I certainly will obtain a buddha's golden body. If this be true and not false, let both my arms be restored to what they were before.'

"As soon as he had made this vow, as a consequence of the purity and weight of this bodhisattva's merit, virtue, and wisdom, his arms were spontaneously restored. At that moment the entire world trembled and shook in the six ways, treasured flowers rained down from heaven, and human and heavenly beings all attained something they had never had before."

The Buddha said to Constellation-King Flower Bodhisattva: "What do you think? Is Seen with Joy by All the Living Bodhisattva some unknown foreigner? He is the present Medicine King Bodhisattva! He has thrown away his body as an offering in this way innumerable hundreds of thousands of billions of myriads of times.

"Constellation-King Flower, if anyone aspiring for and seeking supreme awakening burns the fingers of his hand or even a toe of his foot as an offering to a buddha's stupa, he will surpass someone who makes offerings with lands, towns, wives, children, mountains, forests, rivers, ponds, and other precious things of the three-thousand great thousand-fold world.

"Even if someone were to give a three-thousand great thousandfold world full of the seven precious materials as an offering to the Buddha, great bodhisattvas, pratyekabuddhas, and arhats, the blessings such a person would gain would not equal those of someone who receives and embraces even a single four-line verse of this Dharma Flower Sutra. Happiness greater than this won't be found.

"For example, Constellation-King Flower, just as among all the bodies of water—brooks, streams, rivers, and others—the ocean is supreme, so too this Dharma Flower Sutra is the most profound and the greatest among all the sutras preached by tathagatas.

"Just as among all the mountains—Earth Mountain, Black Mountain, the Lesser Iron Circle Mountains, the Great Iron Circle Mountains, the Ten Jewels Mountains, and others—Mount Sumeru is supreme, so too this Dharma Flower Sutra is the highest.

"Just as among all the stars and such, the moon, a son of heaven, is supreme, so too this Dharma Flower Sutra is the most illuminating among the tens of millions of billions of kinds of sutra teachings.

"Just as the sun, a son of heaven, can dispel the darkness, so too this sutra can destroy the darkness of all that is not good.

"Just as among all the minor kings a wheel-turning saint-king is first, so too this sutra is the most honored among all the sutras.

"Just as Indra is king among the thirty-three gods, so too this sutra is the king of all sutras.

"Just as great Brahma, king of heaven, is the father of all living beings, so too this sutra is the father of all sages and saints, of those trained and in training, and those who aspire to be bodhisattvas.

"Just as shravakas who have entered the Way, shravakas who will return to the world only once, shravakas who do not have to return to the world, shravakas who are arhats, and pratyekabuddhas are first among all the common people, so too this sutra is first and foremost among all the various sutras preached by the tathagatas, preached by bodhisattvas, or preached by shravakas.

"So, too, those who receive and embrace this sutra are first among all the living.

"Among all the shravakas and pratyekabuddhas, bodhisattvas are first. So, too, with this sutra—among all the sutra teachings, it is first.

"As the Buddha is king of the Dharma, so too this sutra is king of all the sutras.

"Constellation-King Flower, this sutra can liberate all the living. This sutra can enable all the living to be free from pain and suffering.

This sutra can bring great and abundant benefit to all the living and fulfill their hopes.

"Just like a clear, cool pool, it can satisfy all who are thirsty. Like fire to someone who is cold, like clothing to someone naked, like a leader found by a group of merchants, like a mother found by her children, like a ferry found by passengers, like a doctor found by the sick, like a lamp found by people in the dark, like riches found by the poor, like a ruler found by the people, like a sea lane found by traders, and like a torch dispelling the darkness, this Dharma Flower Sutra can enable all the living to liberate themselves from all suffering, disease, and pain, loosening all the bonds of mortal life.

"If anyone hearing this Dharma Flower Sutra either copies it themselves or causes others to copy it, the number of blessings from doing that will be so great that they could not be calculated even with the wisdom of a buddha. If anyone copies the rolls of this sutra and makes offerings to them with flowers, fragrances, garlands, incense for burning, powdered incense, paste incense, banners, canopies, robes, or various kinds of lamps such as clarified butter lamps, oil lamps, lamps of various fragrant oils—lamps of gardenia oil, lamps of sumana oil, lamps of begonia oil, lamps of varshika oil, or lamps of jasmine oil—the blessings obtained will also be innumerable.

"Constellation-King Flower, if there is anyone who hears this chapter of the previous lives of Medicine King Bodhisattva, that person too will obtain innumerable, unlimited blessings. If there is any woman who hears this chapter of the previous lives of Medicine King Bodhisattva and is able to embrace it, after using up her woman's body, she will not receive another.

"After the extinction of the Tathagata, in the last five hundred years, if there is a woman who hears this sutra and acts according to its teaching, at the end of this life she will be born on a jeweled seat in the middle of a lotus flower in the world of peace and happiness where Amida Buddha lives, surrounded by a multitude of great bodhisattvas. Never again will she be troubled by greed, or by anger or folly, nor ever again will she be troubled by pride and arrogance, envy, or by other filth. She will attain the divine powers of a bodhisattva and accept the non-arising of all things. Having accepted this, her vision will be clear and pure, and with this clear and pure vision she will see buddha-tathagatas as numerous as the sands of seven million, two hundred billion myriads of Ganges.

"Then buddhas will unite in praising her from afar, saying: 'Well done, well done, good son. In the midst of the Dharma of Shakyamuni Buddha you have been able to embrace, read and recite, and ponder over this sutra and teach it for others. The merit and virtue you have obtained is immeasurable and unlimited. This is something fire cannot burn and water cannot wash away. Your blessings are beyond the powers of a thousand buddhas to explain. You have now been able to destroy the devilish thieves, to smash the forces of mortality, and to wipe out all other enemies.

"'Good son, hundreds of thousands of buddhas together protect you with their divine powers. Among the human and heavenly beings of all the worlds, none is equal to you except the Tathagata. The wisdom and ability in meditation of shravakas, pratyekabuddhas, or even bodhisattvas is not equal to yours.'

"Constellation-King Flower, such are the blessings and powers of wisdom attained by this bodhisattva.

"If there is anyone who, hearing this chapter of the previous lives of Medicine King Bodhisattva, is able joyfully to receive and praise it, during their present lives they will always breathe out the fragrance of the blue lotus flower, and the pores of their bodies will always emit the fragrance of ox-head sandalwood. Their blessings will be as stated above.

"Therefore, Constellation-King Flower, I entrust this chapter of the previous lives of Medicine King to you. After my extinction, in the last five hundred years, proclaim and spread it widely throughout Jambudvipa. Never let it die, or the evil devil, the devil's people, gods, dragons, satyrs, and kumbhandas will gain the upper hand.

"Constellation-King Flower, use your divine powers to guard and protect this sutra. Why? Because this sutra is good medicine for the ills of the people of Jambudvipa. If anyone is sick, when they hear this sutra their sickness will quickly disappear and they will neither grow old nor die.

"Constellation-King Flower, if you see anyone who receives and embraces this sutra, you should scatter blue lotus flowers with powdered incense heaped up on them. After scattering them, you should think to yourself: 'Before long, surely this person will take a grass mat and sit at the place of the Way, defeat the armies of the devil, and, blowing the conch of the Dharma and beating the drum of the great Dharma, save all living beings from the sea of old age, sickness, and death.'

"This is why whenever anyone who seeks the Buddha way sees someone who accepts and embraces this sutra, they should give them this kind of respect and reverence."

While this chapter of the previous lives of Medicine King Bodhisattva was being taught, eighty-four thousand bodhisattvas attained the power of incantation which enables them to interpret the words of all the living. The Tathagata Abundant Treasures in the treasure stupa praised Constellation-King Flower Bodhisattva, saying: "Well done, well done, Constellation-King Flower. You have attained inconceivable blessings, for you have been able to ask Shakyamuni Buddha about such things, enriching innumerable living beings."

24. Wonderful Voice Bodhisattva

A T THAT TIME Shakyamuni Buddha emitted a beam of light from the knob on the top of his head, a mark of a great man, and emitted as well a beam of light from the tuft of white hair between his eyebrows, illuminating Buddha-worlds in the eastern direction equivalent in number to the sands of a hundred and eight trillion myriads of Ganges.

Beyond those many worlds there was a world named Adorned with Pure Light, and in that land there was a buddha named Wisdom King of the Pure Flower Constellation Tathagata, one worthy of offerings, truly awakened, fully clear in conduct, well gone, understanding the world, unexcelled leader, trainer of men, teacher of heavenly beings and people, buddha, world-honored one. Surrounded and revered by a great multitude of incalculable, countless bodhisattvas, he taught the Dharma to them. The beam of light from the tuft of white hair of Shakyamuni Buddha shone throughout their land.

In the land Adorned with Pure Light at that time there was a bodhisattva named Wonderful Voice, who from long ago had planted many roots of virtue and had made offerings to, and been associated with, innumerable hundreds of thousands of billions of buddhas. He had gained every kind of profound wisdom. And he had attained the concentration of the wonderful banner sign, the concentration of the Dharma Flower, the concentration of pure virtue, the concentration of the Constellation King's sport, the concentration of being without conditions, the concentration of the seal of wisdom, the concentration that enables one to understand the words of all beings, the concentration that collects all blessings, the concentration of purity, the concentration of the play of divine powers, the concentration of the wisdom torch, the concentration of the adorned king, the concentration of pure light, the concentration of the pure storehouse, the concentration that is not shared, and the concentration of the revolving sun. He had attained such great concentrations equal in number to the sands of hundreds of thousands of billions of Ganges.

When the beam of light from Shakyamuni Buddha shone on his body, he immediately said to Wisdom King of the Pure Flower Constellation Buddha: "World-Honored One, I should go to visit that world to worship, associate with, and make offerings to Shakyamuni Buddha, and to see the Dharma Prince Manjushri Bodhisattva, and bodhisattvas Medicine King, Courageous Giver, Constellation-King Flower, Intent on Superior Practice, Adornment King, and Lord of Medicine."

Then Wisdom King of the Pure Flower Constellation Buddha said to Wonderful Voice Bodhisattva: "Do not make light of that land or think it is inferior. Good son, that world is uneven, with high and low places. It is full of earth, stones, mountains, and filth. The body of its Buddha is small and short, and its many bodhisattvas are also small. Your body, in contrast, is forty-two thousand leagues tall, and mine is six million eight hundred thousand leagues tall. Your body is the most perfect, with hundreds of billions of merits and an especially wonderful radiance. Therefore, when you go there do not make light of that world, nor have a low opinion of its Buddha, its bodhisattvas, or the land there."

Wonderful Voice Bodhisattva replied to that buddha: "World-Honored One, my going to that world is all due to the Tathagata's power and the Tathagata's comfort with divine powers, and it is an adornment to the Tathagata's blessings and wisdom."

Then Wonderful Voice Bodhisattva, without rising from his seat and without stirring his body, entered into a concentration. By the power of his concentration, eighty-four thousand clusters of treasured lotus flowers with stems of Jambunada gold, leaves of white silver, stamens of diamond, and calyxes of kimshuka gems magically appeared on Holy Eagle Peak, not far from the Dharma seat.

Then Manjushri, son of the Dharma king, seeing those lotus flowers, said to the Buddha: "World-Honored One, for what reason does this auspicious sign appear here? There are tens of millions of billions of lotus flowers with stems of Jambunada gold, leaves of white silver, stamens of diamond, and calyxes of kimshuka gems."

Shakyamuni Buddha then said to Manjushri: "In order to make offerings to me, associate with, and worship me, Wonderful Voice Bodhisattva, the great one, wants to come to this world with a company of eighty-four thousand bodhisattvas from the land of the Buddha Wisdom King of the Pure Flower Constellation. He also wants to make offerings to and hear the Dharma Flower Sutra."

Manjushri asked the Buddha: "World-Honored One, what roots of virtue has that bodhisattva planted, what blessings has he cultivated, that he is able to have such power of great divine faculties? What concentration does he practice? I beg you to teach us the name of this concentration. We too want to practice it diligently, for by practicing this concentration we may be able to see that bodhisattva—his physical characteristics and size, his bearing and behavior. We beg you, World-Honored One, to use your divine faculties and powers and have this bodhisattva come here so that we can see him."

Then Shakyamuni Buddha said to Manjushri: "The Tathagata Abundant Treasures, so long extinct, should have him appear for you."

Immediately, Abundant Treasures Buddha said to that bodhisattva: "Come, good son. Manjushri, son of the Dharma king, wants to see you."

Then Wonderful Voice Bodhisattva disappeared from his land, setting out together with eighty-four thousand bodhisattvas. The lands through which they passed shook in the six different ways. Lotus flowers of the seven precious materials rained down in all the lands. And hundreds of thousands of heavenly instruments sounded spontaneously.

That bodhisattva's eyes were like the big broad leaves of the blue lotus. A combination of hundreds of billions of moons together would not surpass the beauty of his face. His body was pure gold in color and adorned with innumerable hundreds of thousands of signs of blessings. The flourishing of his dignity and virtue was radiant and brilliant. He was marked with signs of perfection and had a body as strong as Narayana's.

Taking his place on a platform made of the seven precious materials, he rose up in the air to a height of seven tala trees above the ground. Surrounded by a multitude of revering bodhisattvas, he came to Holy Eagle Peak in this world. When he arrived, he came down from the platform of seven precious materials. Taking a necklace worth hundreds of thousands, he went to where Shakyamuni Buddha was, prostrated himself at the Buddha's feet, and presented the necklace, saying: "World-Honored One, Wisdom King of the Pure Flower Constellation Buddha wants to inquire about the World-Honored One: 'Are your ailments and troubles few? Is your daily life and practice going smoothly? Are the four elements in you in harmony? Are the affairs of the world tolerable? Are living beings easy to save? Are they not excessively greedy, angry, foolish, jealous, and arrogant? Are they not lacking in proper regard for their parents? Are they not disrespectful to novice monks? Do they not have wrong views and inadequate goodness? Are their five emotions not out of control? World-Honored One, are living beings able to overcome their enemies, the devils? Has the long-extinct Tathagata Abundant Treasures living in the stupa of the seven precious materials come to listen to the Dharma?' Pure Flower Constellation Buddha also wants to inquire about Tathagata Abundant Treasures: 'Is he comfortable and of few worries? Will he be content to stay long?' World-Honored One, I would now like to see the body of Abundant Treasures Buddha. I beg you, World-Honored One, to let me see him."

Then Shakyamuni Buddha said to Abundant Treasures Buddha: "This Bodhisattva Wonderful Voice wants to see you."

Abundant Treasures Buddha said to Wonderful Voice: "Well done, well done; you have been able to come here to make offerings to Shakyamuni Buddha, to hear the Dharma Flower Sutra and see Manjushri and the others."

Then Flower Virtue Bodhisattva said to the Buddha: "World-Honored One, this Wonderful Voice Bodhisattva—what roots of goodness has he planted, what merits did he earn, to give him such divine powers?"

The Buddha answered Flower Virtue Bodhisattva: "In the past there was a buddha named King of the Sound of Thunder in the Clouds Tathagata, an arhat, fully a buddha, whose land was named Displaying All Worlds and whose eon was called Seen with Joy. For twelve thousand years Wonderful Voice Bodhisattva made offerings to King of the Sound of Thunder in the Clouds Buddha with a hundred thousand kinds of music and presented him eighty-four thousand alms bowls made of the seven precious materials. Being rewarded for this, he has now been born in the land of Wisdom King of the Pure Flower Constellation Buddha and has such divine powers.

"Flower Virtue, what do you think? Wonderful Voice Bodhisattva, who at that time made offerings to King of the Sound of Thunder in the Clouds Buddha with music and offerings of jeweled vessels—is he unknown to you? It was the present Wonderful Voice Bodhisattva, the great one.

"Flower Virtue, this Wonderful Voice Bodhisattva has already made offerings to and been close to innumerable buddhas. Long ago he planted roots of virtue and met hundreds of billions of myriads of buddhas, as numerous as the sands of the Ganges.

"Flower Virtue, you see merely the one body of Wonderful Voice Bodhisattva which is here. But this Bodhisattva appears in many different bodies, everywhere teaching this sutra for the sake of the living. Sometimes he appears as King Brahma, sometimes he appears as Indra. Sometimes he appears as Ishvara or as Maha-Ishvara, or as a great general of heaven. Sometimes he appears as the king of heaven Vaishravana, as a wheel-turning saintly king, or as a lesser king; or he appears as an elder, as an ordinary citizen, as a high official, as a brahman, or as a monk, nun, layman, or laywoman; or he appears as the wife of an elder or householder, the wife of a high official, or the wife of a brahman, or as a boy or girl; or he appears as a god, a dragon, satyr, centaur, asura, griffin, chimera, python, human or nonhuman being, and so on, and teaches this sutra. Those who are in a purgatory, or are hungry spirits or animals, and all who are in difficult circumstances can be saved. And for the sake of those in the king's harem he transforms himself into a woman and teaches this sutra.

"Flower Virtue, this Wonderful Voice Bodhisattva is able to save and protect all the living in this world. By transforming himself and appearing in these various ways in this world, he teaches this sutra to all the living. But his divine faculties, his transformative powers, and his wisdom are never diminished by this. This Bodhisattva uses many kinds of wisdom to illuminate this world, so that every one of the living gains appropriate knowledge; and he does this in all the worlds in every direction, numerous as the sands of the Ganges.

"For those who need the form of a shravaka to be liberated, he appears in the form of a shravaka and teaches the Dharma. For those who need the form of a pratyekabuddha to be liberated, he appears in the form of a pratyekabuddha and teaches the Dharma. For those who need the form of a bodhisattva to be liberated, he appears in the form of a bodhisattva and teaches the Dharma. For those who need the form of a buddha to be liberated, he appears in the form of a buddha and teaches the Dharma. In these various ways, according to what is needed for liberation, he appears in various forms. Even if it is appropriate to enter extinction for the sake of liberation, he shows himself as one who enters extinction.

"Flower Virtue, such is the power of great divine faculties and wisdom attained by Wonderful Voice Bodhisattva, the great one."

Then Flower Virtue Bodhisattva said to the Buddha: "World-Honored One, this Wonderful Voice Bodhisattva has indeed planted roots of goodness deeply. World-Honored One, in what concentration does this bodhisattva live, that he is able in this way to transform and manifest himself according to what is needed to save the living?"

The Buddha answered Flower Virtue Bodhisattva: "Good son, it is called the concentration in which one can take on any form. Wonderful Voice Bodhisattva, living in this concentration, is able to bring abundant benefits to countless living beings."

While this chapter about Wonderful Voice Bodhisattva was being taught, the eighty-four thousand who had come with Wonderful Voice Bodhisattva all attained the concentration in which one can take on any form, and countless bodhisattvas in this world also attained this concentration and incantation.

Then Wonderful Voice Bodhisattva, the great one, having made offerings to Shakyamuni Buddha and to the stupa of Abundant Treasures Buddha, returned to his own land. The lands through which he passed shook in the six different ways, precious lotus flowers rained down, and hundreds of thousands of billions of pieces of music played.

Having arrived at his own land, with the eighty-four thousand bodhisattvas around him, he went to Wisdom King of the Pure Flower Constellation Buddha and said to him: "World-Honored One, I reached this world, brought abundant benefits to its living beings, saw both Shakyamuni Buddha and the stupa of Abundant Treasures Buddha, and worshiped and made offerings to them. I have also seen Manjushri Bodhisattva, Prince of the Dharma, as well as Medicine King

Bodhisattva, Attainer of Power to Persevere Bodhisattva, Courageous Giver Bodhisattva, and others, and I enabled eighty-four thousand bodhisattvas to attain the concentration in which one can take on any form."

While this chapter on the comings and goings of Wonderful Voice Bodhisattva was being taught, the forty-two thousand children of heaven accepted the non-arising of all things, and Flower Virtue Bodhisattva attained the concentration termed Dharma Flower.

25. The Universal Gateway of the Bodhisattva Regarder of the Cries of the World

AT THAT TIME the Bodhisattva Inexhaustible Mind got up from his seat, bared his right shoulder, put his palms together facing the Buddha, and said: "World-Honored One, for what reason does the Bodhisattva Regarder of the Cries of the World have the name Regarder of the Cries of the World?"

The Buddha answered Inexhaustible Mind Bodhisattva: "Good son! If there were countless hundreds of thousands of billions of living beings experiencing suffering and agony who heard of this Regarder of the Cries of the World Bodhisattva, and wholeheartedly called his name, Regarder of the Cries of the World Bodhisattva would immediately hear their cries, and all of them would be freed.

"If anyone who embraces the name of Regarder of the Cries of the World Bodhisattva falls into a great fire, the fire will not burn that person, due to the divine authority and power of that bodhisattva. If anyone, carried away by a flood, calls his name, that person will immediately reach some shallows. If there are hundreds of thousands of billions of beings who, in search of gold, silver, lapis lazuli, seashell, agate, coral, amber, pearls, and other treasures, go out to sea and have their ships blown off course by a fierce wind to the land of the ogre demons, and if among them there is even a single person who calls the name of Regarder of the Cries of the World Bodhisattva, all those people will be saved from difficulties caused by the ogres. This is why the bodhisattva is named Regarder of the Cries of the World.

"Or if someone faced with immediate attack calls the name of Regarder of the Cries of the World Bodhisattva, the swords and clubs of the attackers will instantly break into pieces and they will be freed from the danger.

"Even if the three-thousand great thousandfold world were full of satyrs and ogres seeking to torment people, these evil spirits, hearing the people call the name of Regarder of the Cries of the World Bodhisattva, with their wicked eyes they would not even be able to see them, much less hurt them.

"If, moreover, someone, guilty or not guilty, is captured and put in stocks or manacles and chains, and they call the name of Regarder of the Cries of the World Bodhisattva, their bonds will be broken and they will be freed.

"Suppose a three-thousand great thousandfold world were full of vengeful thieves, and a caravan leader was guiding a group of merchants carrying costly treasures over a dangerous road. If just one among the merchants speaks out, saying: 'Good sons, do not be afraid. Wholeheartedly call the name of Regarder of the Cries of the World Bodhisattva, for this bodhisattva is able to give courage to all the living. If you invoke this bodhisattva's name, you will be freed from these vengeful thieves.' Hearing this, if all the traders together with one voice cry out, 'Praise to Regarder of the Cries of the World Bodhisattva,' by calling that name they will be freed from the danger.

"Inexhaustible Mind, such are the awesome divine powers of the great one, Regarder of the Cries of the World Bodhisattva.

"If any living beings are afflicted with a great deal of lust, let them keep in mind and revere Regarder of the Cries of the World Bodhisattva and they will be freed from their desire. If they have a great deal of anger and rage, let them keep in mind and revere Regarder of the Cries of the World Bodhisattva and they will be freed from their anger. If they are deluded by great folly, let them keep in mind and revere Regarder of the Cries of the World Bodhisattva and they will be freed from their stupidity.

"Inexhaustible Mind, Regarder of the Cries of the World Bodhisattva has such great divine powers and can abundantly benefit the living. Therefore all the living should constantly keep this bodhisattva in mind.

"Even if a woman wants to have a son and worships and makes offerings to Regarder of the Cries of the World Bodhisattva, she will bear a son blessed with merit, virtue, and wisdom. If she wants a daughter, she will bear one marked with beauty, one who had long before planted roots of virtue and will come to be cherished and respected by all.

"Inexhaustible Mind, such is the power of Regarder of the Cries of the World Bodhisattva. If anyone reveres and worships this bodhisattva, their happiness will not be neglected. Therefore, let all the living cherish the name of Regarder of the Cries of the World Bodhisattva.

"Inexhaustible Mind, suppose someone receives and embraces the names of as many bodhisattvas as there are sands in over six billion Ganges, and throughout their lives makes offerings to them of food, drink, clothing, bedding, and medicines. What do you think? Would such a good son or good daughter have abundant blessings or not?"

Inexhaustible Mind replied: "Extremely abundant, World-Honored One."

The Buddha said: "Suppose someone receives and embraces the name of Regarder of the Cries of the World Bodhisattva and just once worships and makes offerings to him. The blessings of these two people will be exactly the same, without any difference. They could never be exhausted in hundreds of thousands of billions of eons. Inexhaustible Mind, such is the immeasurable, unlimited merit and virtue one will obtain who receives and embraces the name of Regarder of the Cries of the World Bodhisattva."

Inexhaustible Mind Bodhisattva said to the Buddha: "World-Honored One, why does Regarder of the Cries of the World Bodhisattva travel around in this world? How does he teach the Dharma for the sake of the living? What sort of power of skillful means does he have?"

The Buddha replied to Inexhaustible Mind Bodhisattva: "Good son, if living beings in any land need someone in the body of a buddha in order to be saved, Regarder of the Cries of the World Bodhisattva appears as a buddha and teaches the Dharma for them.

"For those who need someone in the body of a pratyekabuddha in order to be saved, he appears as a pratyekabuddha and teaches the Dharma for them.

"For those who need someone in the body of a shravaka in order to be saved, he appears as a shravaka and teaches the Dharma for them.

"For those who need someone in the body of a Brahma king in order to be saved, he appears as a Brahma king and teaches the Dharma for them.

"For those who need someone in the body of Indra in order to be saved, he appears as Indra and teaches the Dharma for them.

"For those who need someone in the body of Ishvara in order to be saved, he appears as Ishvara and teaches the Dharma for them.

"For those who need someone in the body of Maha-Ishvara in order to be saved, he appears as Maha-Ishvara and teaches the Dharma for them.

"For those who need someone in the body of a great general of heaven in order to be saved, he appears as a great general of heaven and teaches the Dharma for them.

"For those who need someone in the body of Vaishravana in order to be saved, he appears as Vaishravana and teaches the Dharma for them.

"For those who need someone in the body of a lesser king in order to be saved, he appears as a lesser king and teaches the Dharma for them.

"For those who need someone in the body of an elder in order to be saved, he appears as an elder and teaches the Dharma for them.

"For those who need someone in the body of an ordinary citizen in order to be saved, he appears as an ordinary citizen and teaches the Dharma for them.

"For those who need someone in the body of a high official in order to be saved, he appears as a high official and teaches the Dharma for them.

"For those who need someone in the body of a brahman in order to be saved, he appears as a brahman and teaches the Dharma for them.

"For those who need someone in the body of a monk, nun, layman, or laywoman in order to be saved, he appears as a monk, nun, layman, or laywoman and teaches the Dharma for them.

"For those who need someone in the body of the wife of an elder, ordinary citizen, high official, or brahman in order to be saved, he appears as a wife and teaches the Dharma for them.

"For those who need someone in the body of a boy or girl in order to be saved, he appears as a boy or girl and teaches the Dharma for them.

"For those who need someone in the body of a heavenly being, dragon, satyr, centaur, asura, griffin, chimera, python, human, or non-human in order to be saved, he appears in such a body and teaches the Dharma for them.

"For those who need someone such as the god Diamond-Holder in order to be saved, he appears as the god Diamond-Holder and teaches the Dharma for them.

"Inexhaustible Mind, such are the blessings attained by this Regarder of the Cries of the World Bodhisattva and the various forms in which he travels around in many lands to save the living. This is why all of you should wholeheartedly make offerings to Regarder of the Cries of the World Bodhisattva. This Regarder of the Cries of the World Bodhisattva, this great one, is able to bestow freedom from fear on those who are faced with a frightening, urgent, or difficult situation. This is why in this world everyone gives him the name Bestower of Freedom from Fear."

Inexhaustible Mind Bodhisattva said to the Buddha: "World-Honored One, now I should make an offering to Regarder of the Cries of the World Bodhisattva." Then he took from his neck a necklace of many valuable gems worth a hundred thousand pieces of gold and presented it to him, saying: "Benevolent One, accept this necklace of valuable gems as a Dharma gift." But Regarder of the Cries of the World Bodhisattva would not accept it then. Again Inexhaustible Mind Bodhisattva said to Regarder of the Cries of the World Bodhisattva: "Benevolent One, out of sympathy for us, accept this necklace."

Then the Buddha said to Regarder of the Cries of the World Bodhisattva: "Out of sympathy for this Inexhaustible Mind Bodhisattva, for the four groups, and for the gods, dragons, satyrs, centaurs, asuras, griffins, chimeras, pythons, humans, nonhumans, and others, you should accept this necklace."

Then Regarder of the Cries of the World Bodhisattva, out of sympathy for the four groups, and for the gods, dragons, humans, nonhumans, and others, accepted the necklace, and dividing it into two parts, offered one part to Shakyamuni Buddha and the other to the stupa of Abundant Treasures Buddha.

"Inexhaustible Mind, freely using such sovereign divine powers, Regarder of the Cries of the World Bodhisattva travels about in this world."

Then Inexhaustible Mind Bodhisattva asked his question in verse:

> World-Honored One of wonderful features,
> Let me now ask you again,
> Why is this buddha-son named
> Regarder of the Cries of the World?

The Honored One with wonderful features answered Inexhaustible Mind in verse:

Listen to the actions of the Cry Regarder.
How well he responds in every region.
His great vow is as deep as the sea,
Unfathomable even after eons.

Serving many hundreds
Of billions of buddhas,
He has made a great pure vow.
Let me tell you briefly about it.

Those who listen to his name,
See his body, and keep him in mind,
Not wasting time,
Will be able to put an end to all their suffering.

If someone intending to harm you
Throws you into a burning pit,
Keep in mind the Cry Regarder's powers
And the pit of fire will become a pond!

Or if you are drifting around in a great ocean,
Threatened by dragons, fish, and various demons,
Keep in mind the Cry Regarder's powers
And you will not drown in the waves!

If you are on the peak of Sumeru
And someone pushes you off,
Keep in mind the Cry Regarder's powers
And you will stay in the sky like the sun!

Or if you are pursued by bad people
And thrown down from Diamond Mountain,
Keep in mind the Cry Regarder's powers
And not a hair will be injured!

If you are surrounded by robbers,
Each with a knife ready to use on you,
Keep in mind the Cry Regarder's powers
And their hearts will become compassionate!

Or if you get into trouble with the king
And are threatened with execution,
Keep in mind the Cry Regarder's powers
And the executioner's sword will break into pieces!

If you are imprisoned, shackled, and chained,
Your arms and legs in stocks,
Keep in mind the Cry Regarder's powers
And you will be freed from your bonds!

Or if someone tries to hurt you
With curses or poisons,
Keep in mind the Cry Regarder's powers
And the harm will revert to its originator.

Or if you meet evil ogres,
Poisonous dragons or various spirits,
Keep in mind the Cry Regarder's powers
And none of them will dare to harm you.

If you are surrounded by evil beasts,
With sharp tusks and frightening claws,
Keep in mind the Cry Regarder's powers
And they will flee in every direction.

If there are lizards, snakes, vipers, or scorpions
With poisonous breath that burns like fire,
Keep in mind the Cry Regarder's powers
And at the sound of your voice they will flee.

Or if clouds bring thunder and lightning flashes,
Hail pelts you, or rain pours down,

Keep in mind the Cry Regarder's powers
And all will instantly disappear.

If living beings suffer adversity
And are oppressed by countless pains,
The power of the wonderful wisdom of the Cry Regarder
Will liberate them from the world's suffering.

Perfect in divine powers,
Practicing wisdom of skillful means everywhere,
Throughout the universe there is no place
Where he does not appear.

All evil circumstances
In the realms of purgatories, hungry spirits, and animals,
In suffering birth, old age, sickness, and death—
Gradually he brings all of them to an end.

Hearing this from the Buddha, Inexhaustible Mind Bodhisattva joyfully said to the Buddha in verse:[12]

True regarder, pure regarder,
Vast wisdom regarder,
Compassionate and kind regarder—
Always called upon, always looked up to!

His pure and spotless radiance
Is a wisdom-sun, destroying all kinds of darkness.
He subdues the storms and fires of disaster.
He illumines the whole world!

Precepts from his compassionate body shake like thunder.
His compassion is like a great cloud
Pouring Dharma rain like nectar,
Quenching the flames of affliction!

If you are brought before a judge in a dispute,
Or terrified in the midst of a battle,
Keep in mind the Cry Regarder's powers
And all vengeance will be driven away.

Wonderful voice, regarder of the cries of the world,
Brahma-voice, voice of the rolling tide,
World-surpassing voice—
He should always be kept in mind.

Never have a moment of doubt about him,
The pure and holy Regarder of the Cries of the World.
By those in suffering and agony, or facing death,
He can be relied on for protection.

Equipped with all blessings,
Viewing all with compassionate eyes,
His ocean of accumulated blessings is immeasurable.
Heads should be bowed to him.

Then the Bodhisattva Earth Holder rose from his seat, went before the Buddha, and said to him: "World-Honored One, if any living being hears this Bodhisattva Regarder of the Cries of the World chapter, hears of the freedom of his actions and the divine power of the revelation of the universal gateway, it should be known that this person's blessings are not few."

While the Buddha taught this chapter on the universal gateway, all eighty-four thousand living beings in the assembly became determined to reach the incomparable state of supreme awakening.

26. Incantations

A T THAT TIME Medicine King Bodhisattva rose from his seat, bared his right shoulder, put his palms together facing the Buddha, and said to him: "World-Honored One, if there are good sons or good daughters who can embrace the Dharma Flower Sutra, read and recite it, gain insight into it, or copy it onto a scroll, how many blessings will they obtain?"

The Buddha responded to Medicine King: "Suppose good sons or good daughters make offerings to buddhas equal in number to the sands of eight million billion myriads of Ganges. In your opinion will their blessings be great or not?"

"Very great, World-Honored One."

The Buddha continued: "If any good sons or good daughters are able to embrace even a single four-line verse of this sutra, read and recite it, understand the meaning of it, and do as it says, their blessings will be very great."

Then Medicine King Bodhisattva said to the Buddha: "World-Honored One, I will now make an incantation for the preachers of the Dharma. It will protect them." Then he made the following incantation.[13]

   *A ni,[1] ma ni,[2] ma ne,[3] ma-ma ne,[4]
   shi re,[5] sha ri-te,[6] sha mya,[7] sha bi-tai,[8]

---

sen te,[9] moku te,[10] moku-ta bi,[11]

sha bi,[12] ai-sha bi,[13] so bi,[14] sha bi,[15] sha e,[16] a sha e,[17]

a gi ni,[18] sen te,[19] sha bi,[20] da ra ni,[21]

a ro kya ba-sai-ha-sha bi-sha ni,[22] nei bi te,[23]

a ben ta ra-ne bi te,[24] a tan da-ha re-shu dai,[25]

u ku re,[26] mu ku re,[27] a ra re,[28] ha ra re,[29]

shu gya shi,[30] a sam ma-sam bi,[31] bodda-bi ki ri-jit te,[32]

da ru ma-ha ri-shi te,[33] so gya ne-ku sha ne,[34]

ba sha-ba sha-shu dai,[35] man ta ra,[36] man ta ra-sha ya ta,[37]

u ro ta,[38] u ro ta-kyo-sha rya,[39] a sha ra,[40] a sha ya-ta ya,[41]

a ba ro,[42] a ma nya-na ta ya.[43]

The Sanskrit reads:
anye manye mane mamane
citte carite same samitā
viśānte mukte muktatame
same aviṣame samasame jaye kṣaye akṣaye
akṣiṇe śānte samite
dhāraṇī āloka-bhāṣe pratyavekṣaṇi
nidhiru abhyantara-niviṣṭe abhyantara-pāriśuddhi
utkule mutkule araḍe paraḍe
sukānkṣi asamasame buddhavilokite
dharma-parikṣite saṃgha-nirghoṣaṇi nirghoṇi bhayābhaya-viśodhani
mantre mantrākṣayate rute ruta-kauśalye akṣaye
akṣaya-vanatāye vakkule baloḍra amanyanatāye svāhā

A Pinyin reading would be:
ān ěr[1] màn ěr[2] mó mí[3] mó mó mí[4]
zhǐ lì[5] zhē lí dì[6] shē miè[7] shē lǚ duō wěi[8]
shàn dì[9] mù dì[10] mù duō lǚ[11]
suō lǚ[12] ē wěi suō lǚ[13] sāng lǚ[14] suō lǚ[15] chà yì[16] ē chà yì[17]
ē qí nì[18] shān dì[19] shē lǚ[20] tuó luó ní[21]
ē lú qié pó suō bò zhè pí chā nì[22] mí pí tì[23]
ē biàn duō luó mí lǚ tì[24] ē dǎn duō bō lì shū dì[25]
ōu jiū lì[26] móu jiū lì[27] ē luó lì[28] bō luó lì[29]
shǒu jiā cī[30] ē sān mó sān lǚ[31] fó tuó pí jí lì zhì dì[32]
dá mó bō lì cī dì[33] sēng qié niè qú shā mí[34]
pó shě pó shě shū dì[35] màn duō luó[36] màn duō luó chā yè duō[37]
yóu lóu duǒ[38] yóu lóu duō jiāo shě luè[39] è chā luó[40] è chā yě duō yě[41]
ē pó lú[42] ē mó ruò nà duō yè[43]

"World-Honored One, these sacred incantations have been made by buddhas as numerous as the sands of over six billion Ganges rivers. If anyone does violence to these Dharma teachers, they will have done violence to those buddhas."

Then Shakyamuni Buddha praised Medicine King Bodhisattva, saying: "Good, good, Medicine King! Because you are compassionate and protect these Dharma teachers, you have made these incantations. They will bring abundant benefits to the living."

Then Courageous Giver Bodhisattva said to the Buddha: "World-Honored One, for the protection of those who read, recite, and embrace the Dharma Flower Sutra, I too will make incantations. If these Dharma teachers have these incantations, neither satyrs, nor ogres, nor incubi, nor succubi, nor kumbhandas, nor hungry spirits, nor others spying out their shortcomings will have a chance." Then, in the presence of the Buddha, he made the following incantation:

Za re,[1] ma ka-za re,[2] uk ki,[3] mok ki,[4]
a re,[5] a ra-ha te,[6] ne re te,[7] ne re ta-ha te,[8]
i chi ni,[9] i chi ni,[10] shi chi ni,[11]
ne re-chi ni,[12] ne ri chi-ha chi.[13]

"World-Honored One, these sacred incantations have been made by buddhas as numerous as the sands of the Ganges, and all of them responded with joy. If anyone does violence to these Dharma teachers, they will have done violence to those buddhas."

Then the king of heaven Vaishravana, protector of the world, said to

---

The Sanskrit reads:
jvale mahā-jvale ukke tukke mukke
aḍe aḍāvati nṛtye nṛtyāvati
iṭṭini viṭṭini ciṭṭini
nṛtyani nṛtyāvati svāhā

A Pinyin reading would be:
cuó lì[1] mó hé cuó lì[2] yù zhī[3] mù zhī[4]
ē lì[5] ē luó pó dì[6] niè lì dì[7] niè lì duō pó dì[8]
yī zhì nǐ[9] wéi zhì nǐ[10] zhǐ zhì nǐ[11]
niè lì chí nǐ[12] niè lí chí pó dì[13]

the Buddha: "World-Honored One, I, too, out of compassion for the living and for the protection of these Dharma teachers, will make these incantations." Then he made the following incantation:

A ri,[1] na ri,[2] to na ri,[3]
a na ro,[4] na bi,[5] ku na bi.[6]

"World-Honored One, with these sacred incantations I will protect the Dharma teachers. What's more, I myself will protect those who embrace this sutra, so that within a hundred leagues no weakness or illness will come upon them."

Then the king of heaven Realm Upholder, who was in this congregation, with a multitude of tens of millions of billions of myriads of centaurs surrounding him reverently, went before the Buddha and, putting his palms together, said to him: "World-Honored One, I too, with sacred incantations, will protect those who embrace the Dharma Flower Sutra." Then he made the following incantation:

A kya ne,[1] kya ne,[2] ku ri,[3] ken da ri,[4] sen da ri,[5]
ma to gi,[6] jo gu ri,[7] bu ro-sha ni,[8] acchi.[9]

The Sanskrit reads:
aṭṭe taṭṭe naṭṭe vanaṭṭe
anaḍe nāḍi kunaḍi svāhā

A Pinyin reading would be:
ē lí[1] nà lí[2] nòu nà lí[3]
ē nà lú[4] nà lǔ[5] jū nā lǔ[6]

The Sanskrit reads:
agaṇe gaṇe gauri gandhāri caṇḍāli
mātaṅgi pukkasi saṅkule vrūsali sisi svāhā

A Pinyin reading would be:
ē qié mí[1] qié mí[2] qú lì[3] qián tuó lì[4] zhān tuó lì[5]
mó dēng qí[6] cháng qiú lì[7] fú lóu shā nǐ[8] è dǐ[9]

"World-Honored One, these sacred incantations have been made by over four billion buddhas. Anyone who does violence to these Dharma teachers will have done violence to those buddhas."

At this time some ogresses were there, the first named Lamba, the second named Vilamba, the third named Crooked Teeth, the fourth named Flowery Teeth, the fifth named Black Teeth, the sixth named Much Hair, the seventh named Insatiable, the eighth named Necklace Holder, the ninth named Kunti, and the tenth named Snatcher of the Spirits of all the Living. These ten ogresses, together with Mother of Demon Children with her children and followers, all went to the Buddha and with one voice said to him: "World-Honored One, we too would protect those who read and recite, receive, and embrace the Dharma Flower Sutra, so that no weakness or illness will come upon them. If anyone attempts to spy out the shortcomings of these Dharma teachers, we will prevent them from having any chance." Then in the presence of the Buddha they made the following incantation:

I de bi,[1] i de bin,[2] i de bi,[3] a de bi,[4] i de bi,[5]
de bi,[6] de bi,[7] de bi,[8] de bi,[9] de bi,[10]
ro ke,[11] ro ke,[12] ro ke,[13] ro ke,[14]
ta ke,[15] ta ke,[16] ta ke,[17] to ke,[18] to ke.[19]

"Let troubles fall on our heads rather than on the Dharma teachers. Neither satyrs, nor ogres, nor hungry spirits, nor incubi, nor succubi, nor vampires, nor ghouls, nor lamias, nor convulsives, nor satyr-succubi, nor human-succubi; nor fevers, whether the fever is for a single day, or two,

The Sanskrit reads:
itime, itime, itime, itime, itime,
nime, nime, nime, nime, nime,
ruhe, ruhe, ruhe, ruhe, ruhe,
stuhe, stuhe, stuhe, stuhe, stuhe svāhā

A Pinyin reading would be:
Yī tí lǚ[1] yī tí mǐn[2] yī tí lǚ[3] ē tí lǚ[4] yī tí lǚ[5]
ní lǚ[6] ní lǚ[7] ní lǚ[8] ní lǚ[9] ní lǚ[10]
lóu xī[11] lóu xī[12] lóu xī[13] lóu xī[14]
duō xī[15] duō xī[16] duō xī[17] dōu xī[18] nòu xī[19]

three, four, or seven days, or unremitting; whether they are in the form of a male or a female, or of a boy or a girl, even in dreams, they will never cause them any trouble." Then before the Buddha they spoke in verse:

> If anyone resists our incantations
> And makes trouble for a Dharma preacher,
> Their heads will split into seven pieces,
> Like the branches of a basil tree.
>
> Their crime will be like that of someone
> Who kills their father and mother,
> Or someone who commits the offense of pressing oil,
> Or someone who cheats with measures and scales,
>
> Or someone who, like Devadatta,
> Tries to divide the monks.
> Anyone who offends these Dharma teachers,
> Will have committed this kind of offense.

After the ogresses had spoken these verses, they said to the Buddha: "World-Honored One, with our own bodies we ourselves will protect those who receive and embrace, read and recite, and practice this sutra. We will give them peace and comfort, free them from weakness or illness, and quell the effects of poisonous plants."

The Buddha said to the ogresses: "Good, good, if you can protect those who receive and keep even the name of the Dharma Flower Sutra, your blessings will be immeasurable. How much more so if you protect those who receive and embrace the whole sutra, and make offerings to the sutra rolls with flowers, incense, garlands, powdered incense, paste incense, incense for burning, banners, canopies and music, burning various kinds of lamps—clarified butter lamps, oil lamps, lamps of various fragrant oils: lamps of sumana flower oil, lamps of gardenia oil, lamps of varshika flower oil, and lamps of udumbara flower oil—with hundreds of thousands of kinds of offerings like these. Kunti, you and your followers should protect such Dharma teachers as these."

When this chapter of incantations was taught, sixty-eight thousand people accepted the non-arising of all things.

27. The Previous Life
of King Wonderfully Adorned

AT THAT TIME the Buddha addressed the great assembly: "Long ago, in a previous age, innumerable, unlimited, and inconceivably countless eons ago, there was a buddha named Wisdom Blessed by the King of Constellations Called the Sound of Thunder in the Clouds Tathagata, an arhat, full buddha, whose land was named Adorned with Light and whose eon was named Seen with Joy. Under the Dharma of that buddha there was a king named Wonderfully Adorned. The wife of that king was called Pure Virtue, and there were two sons, one named Pure Treasury, the other named Pure Eyes.

"Those two sons had great divine powers, merit, virtue, and wisdom. For a long time they had followed the way of bodhisattva practice—that is, the practice of generosity, the practice of morality, the practice of patience, the practice of perseverance, the practice of meditation, the practice of wisdom, the practice of skillful means, kindness, compassion, joy, impartiality, and the thirty-seven kinds of aids to the Way. All of these they thoroughly mastered. They had also attained the bodhisattva concentrations—the pure concentration, the sun, stars, and constellations concentration, the pure light concentration, the pure color concentration, the pure illumination concentration, the long adornment concentration, and the concentration of the treasury of great dignity and virtue. They had thoroughly mastered these concentrations.

"Then that buddha, wanting to guide King Wonderfully Adorned and having compassion for the living, taught this Dharma Flower Sutra.

"Meanwhile the two sons, Pure Treasury and Pure Eyes, went to their mother and, putting their ten fingers and palms together, said to her: 'We beg you, mother, to go and visit Wisdom Blessed by the King of Constellations Called the Sound of Thunder in the Clouds Buddha. We also would wait on, associate with, make offerings to, and worship him. Why? Because this buddha is teaching the Dharma Flower Sutra among the multitudes of human and heavenly beings, and we ought to hear and receive it.'

"The mother replied to her sons: 'Your father has faith in a non-Buddhist way, deeply attached to brahman teachings. You should go and talk to your father so that he may participate and go with you.'

"Pure Treasury and Pure Eyes, putting their ten fingers and palms together, said to their mother: 'We are sons of the Dharma king, yet we were born in this home of wrong views!'

"The mother said to her sons: 'You should be concerned about your father and show him some divine marvels, so that when he sees them his mind will become clear and he will permit us to go to the Buddha.'

"Because they were concerned about their father, the two sons leapt up into the air to the height of seven tala trees and performed many kinds of divine marvels—walking, standing, sitting, and lying down in the air; emitting water from the upper part of their bodies and fire from the lower, or emitting water from the lower and fire from the upper; enlarging themselves until they filled the sky and then becoming small again, or making themselves small and then appearing large again; vanishing from the air and suddenly appearing on the ground; going into the ground as though it were water; walking on water as though it were the ground. By showing various divine marvels like this, they led their father, the king, to cleanse his mind for faith and understanding.

"When their father saw his sons with such divine powers, which he had never experienced before, he was overjoyed and with palms together greeted his sons, saying: 'Who is your teacher? Whose disciples are you?'

"The two sons replied: 'Great king, Wisdom Blessed by the King of Constellations Called the Sound of Thunder in the Clouds Buddha, who is now under the bodhi tree of seven precious materials seated on the Dharma seat among the human and heavenly beings of all the worlds, is teaching the Dharma Flower Sutra everywhere. He is our teacher. We are his disciples.'

"The father then said to his sons: 'Now I too would like to go to see your teacher. Let us go together.'

"With this, the two sons descended from the air, went to their mother, and with palms together said to her: 'Our father, the king, has now come to believe and understand, and has been able to set his mind on supreme awakening. We have done the Buddha's work for our father's sake. Please mother, allow us to leave home and pursue the Way under the Buddha.'

"Then the two sons, wanting to restate their intention, spoke to their mother in verse:

> Please mother, permit us
> To leave home and become mendicants.
> Meeting a buddha is very difficult,
> And we would be followers of this buddha.
>
> Rare as the blossoms of the udumbara are,
> Even harder is it to meet a buddha.
> And it is hard to get rid of difficulties.
> Please allow us to leave home.

"Then the mother said: 'I will allow you to leave home. Why? Because it is difficult to meet a buddha.'

"With this, the two sons said to their parents: 'Good, father and mother! We beg you in time to go to Wisdom Blessed by the King of Constellations Called the Sound of Thunder in the Clouds Buddha, approach him, and make offerings to him! Why? Because a buddha is as difficult to meet as an udumbara flower, or as a one-eyed tortoise meeting the hole in a floating log. But we, being richly blessed from the past, have been born at a time when we could encounter the Buddha-dharma. Therefore, father and mother, you should listen to us and allow us to leave home. Why? Because buddhas are difficult to meet and it is difficult to find the right time as well.

"At that time all the eighty-four thousand women in the rear palace of King Wonderfully Adorned became capable of receiving and embracing this Dharma Flower Sutra. Pure Eyes Bodhisattva had long ago mastered the Dharma Flower concentration and Pure Treasury Bodhisattva had mastered the concentration of freedom from evil levels of existence innumerable hundreds of thousands of billions of eons ago. This was because he wanted to lead all the living away from the evil levels of existence. The wife of that king had attained the buddhas' assembly concentration and knew the secret resources of buddhas. Her two sons, using their powers of skillful means, skillfully transformed their father, enabling him to have faith in, to understand, and to love and delight in the Buddha-dharma.

"Then King Wonderfully Adorned, accompanied by his ministers and followers; Queen Pure Virtue, accompanied by the ladies and followers from the rear palace; and the king's two sons, accompanied by forty-two thousand people, set out together to visit the Buddha. Arriving, they prostrated themselves at his feet, circled around the Buddha three times, and then withdrew to one side.

"Then that buddha taught the Dharma for the sake of the king, demonstrating and teaching it to him, enriching him and bringing him joy. The king was joyous with delight.

"Then King Wonderfully Adorned and his queen removed necklaces of pearls worth hundreds of thousands from their necks and tossed them above the Buddha. In the sky they were transformed into a four-columned jeweled platform. On the platform was a large jeweled couch with hundreds of billions of heavenly coverings. Sitting cross-legged on them was the Buddha, emitting a great light.

"Then King Wonderfully Adorned thought to himself: 'The Buddha's body is rare, dignified, and extraordinary, in form most subtle and wonderful!'

"Then Wisdom Blessed by the King of Constellations Called the Sound of Thunder in the Clouds Buddha said to the four groups: 'Do you see this King Wonderfully Adorned standing before me with his palms together? This king, having been a monk under my Dharma, and diligently studying and putting into practice the Dharma that helps one along the Buddha way, will become a buddha named Sal-Tree King. His land will be named Great Light, and his eon named Great High King. This Buddha Sal-Tree King will have countless bodhisattvas and countless shravakas. His land will be level and smooth. Such will be his blessings.'

"The king immediately turned over his land to his younger brother and, together with his queen and two sons and all their followings, gave up his home and practiced the Way under the Dharma of that buddha.

"Having left his home, for eighty-four thousand years the king was always dutiful and diligent in practicing the Wonderful Dharma Flower Sutra. And after these years had passed he attained the concentration of being adorned with all the pure blessings.

"Then he rose in the air to a height of seven tala trees and said to the Buddha: 'World-Honored One, these two sons of mine have already done the work of the Buddha by their divine transformations, changing my wrong views, enabling me to dwell at peace in the Buddha-dharma, and allowing me to see the World-Honored One. These two sons are my good friends. They wanted to awaken the roots of goodness from my previous lives, bringing abundant benefits to me. That is why they were born into my family.'

"Then Wisdom Blessed by the King of Constellations Called the Sound of Thunder in the Clouds Buddha said to King Wonderfully Adorned: 'That's right, that's right; it is just as you say. By planting roots of goodness, any good son or good daughter will have good friends in life after life, and these good friends will be able to do the Buddha's work, demonstrating and teaching the Dharma, enriching and bringing joy to others, enabling them to enter supreme awakening. Great king, you should understand that a good friend is the great cause and condition by which one is transformed, led to see the Buddha and aroused to seek supreme awakening. Great king, do you see these two sons? These two sons have already made offerings to as many buddhas as sixty-five hundreds of billions of myriads of sands of the Ganges, associating with and revering them. In the presence of those buddhas they have received and embraced the Dharma Flower Sutra, having compassion for living beings with wrong views and enabling them to live with right views.'

"King Wonderfully Adorned then came down from the air and said to the Buddha: 'World-Honored One, a tathagata is extremely rare. Because of his blessings and wisdom the knob on the top of his head shines brilliantly. His eyes are long, wide, and deep blue. The tuft of hair between his eyebrows is as white as a bright moon. His teeth are white, even, close together, and always shining. His lips are red and as beautiful as bimba fruit.'

"When King Wonderfully Adorned had praised that buddha's count-less hundreds of thousands of billions of blessings in this way, putting his palms together before the Tathagata in complete devotion, he spoke to that buddha once again, saying: 'World-Honored One, this is unprece-dented. The Dharma of the Tathagata is completely full of inconceiv-able and wonderful blessings. The practice of his teachings and precepts will bring peace and comfort and good feelings. From this day forward I will no longer follow my own whims, nor will I allow myself wrong views, pride or arrogance, anger, or any other evil states.'

"Having spoken these words, he bowed to the Buddha and left."

The Buddha said to the great assembly: "What do you think? Is this King Wonderfully Adorned unknown to you? He is the present Bodhi-sattva Flower Virtue. The Queen Pure Virtue is the Bodhisattva Marks of Shining Adornment who is now in the presence of the Buddha. Out of mercy for King Wonderfully Adorned and his people, she was born among them. The two sons are the present Medicine King Bodhisattva and Superior Medicine Bodhisattva.

"These bodhisattvas, Medicine King and Superior Medicine, have already attained great blessings, and under countless hundreds of thou-sands of billions of buddhas, have planted roots of virtue and attained good blessings beyond conception. If there is anyone who is acquainted with the names of these two bodhisattvas, human and heavenly beings in all the worlds should worship them."

When the Buddha taught this chapter, "The Previous Life of King Wonderfully Adorned," eighty-four thousand people separated them-selves from uncleanliness and acquired pure Dharma eyes for seeing all things.

28. Encouragement of
Universal Sage Bodhisattva

A T THAT TIME the Bodhisattva Universal Sage, with his freedom
in divine powers, his dignity, virtue, and fame, and accompanied
by unlimited, innumerable, incalculable numbers of great
bodhisattvas, came from the east. All of the lands through which he
passed shook, treasured lotus flowers rained down, and countless hun-
dreds of thousands of billions of kinds of music played. In addition he
was surrounded by a great assembly of uncountable numbers of various
gods, dragons, satyrs, centaurs, asuras, griffins, chimeras, pythons, peo-
ple, nonhuman beings, and others, all displaying dignity, virtue, and
divine powers.

Arriving at Holy Eagle Peak in this world, he prostrated himself before
Shakyamuni Buddha, circled around him to the right seven times, and
said to the Buddha: "World-Honored One, in the land of the Buddha
Jeweled King of Superior Dignity and Virtue, from a distance I heard the
Dharma Flower Sutra being taught in this world. I have come with this
multitude of countless, innumerable hundreds of thousands of billions of
bodhisattvas to hear and receive it. Please, World-Honored One, teach it
to us, and tell us how good sons and good daughters will be able to obtain
this Dharma Flower Sutra after the extinction of the Tathagata."

The Buddha replied to Universal Sage Bodhisattva: "If any good sons
or good daughters meet four conditions, after the extinction of the
Tathagata they will obtain this Dharma Flower Sutra. The first is to be
protected and kept in mind by the buddhas; the second is to plant roots
of virtue; the third is to join those who are headed for awakening; and

the fourth is to be determined to save all the living. After the extinction of the Tathagata, any good sons or good daughters who meet these four conditions will be certain to acquire this sutra."

Then Universal Sage Bodhisattva said to the Buddha: "World-Honored One, in the last five hundred years of the corrupt and evil age, I will protect whoever receives and embraces this sutra, free them from weakness and disease, give them peace and comfort, and make sure no one takes advantage of them—neither the devil, the devil's sons, the devil's daughters, the devil's followers, nor anyone controlled by the devil, and neither satyrs, ogres, kumbhandas, man-eating goblins, succubi, incubi, vampires, nor any other beings who torment people, will be able to take advantage of them.

"Whenever such people, whether walking or standing, read and recite this sutra, I will mount the white six-tusked king of elephants and with a multitude of great bodhisattvas go to where they are. Showing myself, I will make offerings to them and protect them, putting their minds at ease. This is because I want to serve the Dharma Flower Sutra.

"Wherever any such person sits, pondering this sutra, I will also mount the white king of elephants and show myself to them. If any such person forgets even a single phrase or verse of the Dharma Flower Sutra, I will teach it to them, and read and recite it with them so that they can learn it once again. At that time anyone who receives, embraces, reads and recites the Dharma Flower Sutra will be able to see me, and will be filled with joy and have their devotion renewed. Through seeing me, they will acquire the concentrations or incantations called the revolving incantation, the hundreds of thousands of billions of revolutions incantation, and the skill in Dharma-sounds incantation. They will acquire all these kinds of incantations.

"World-Honored One, later in the five-hundred-year corrupt and evil age, if there are monks, nuns, laymen, or laywomen who seek, accept, embrace, read, recite, or copy this Dharma Flower Sutra, who want to study it and put it into practice, they should single-mindedly devote themselves to it for twenty-one days. After the twenty-one days are completed, I will mount the white elephant with six tusks and, with countless bodhisattvas surrounding me, appear before those people in a form that all the living delight to see, and teach the Dharma for them, demonstrating and teaching it, enriching them, and giving them joy.

Moreover, I will give them incantations. And because they have these incantations, no nonhuman will be able to injure them, nor any woman beguile them. Also, I myself will always protect them. Please, World-Honored One, permit me to make these incantations." Then in the presence of the Buddha he made an incantation:[18]

A tan-dai,[1] tan da ha-dai,[2] tan da-ha te,[3] tan da-ku sha re,[4]
tan da-shu da re,[5] shu da re,[6] shu da ra-ha chi,[7] bod dha ha-sen ne,[8]
saru ba-da ra ni-a ba ta ni,[9] saru ba-ba sha-a ba ta ni[10]
shuu-a ba ta ni,[11] so gya ha-bi sha ni,[12] so gya ne-kya da ni,[13]
a so-gi,[14] so-gya ha-gya dai,[15]
te re-a da-so gya-to rya-a ra te-ha ra te,[16]
saru ba-so-gya-sam ma ji-kya ran dai,[17]
saru ba-da ru ma-shu-ha ri-set te,[18]
saru ba-satta-ru da kyo-sha rya-a to-gya-dai,[19]
shin-na bi ki ri-dai te.[20]

"World-Honored One, if any bodhisattvas hear these incantations, they should know the divine powers of Universal Sage. When the Dharma Flower Sutra moves through Jambudvipa, if there be some who

---

The Sanskrit reads:
adaṇḍe daṇḍapati daṇḍāvartani daṇḍakuśale daṇḍasudhāri
sudhārapati buddhapaśyane sarvadhāraṇi āvartani saṃvartani
saṃghaparīkṣite saṃghanirghātani dharmaparīkṣite
sarvasattvarutakauśalyānugate siṃhavikrīḍite anuvarte vartani vartāli svāhā

A Pinyin reading would be:
ē tán dì[1] tán tuó pó dì[2] tán tuó pó dì[3] tán tuó jiū shě lì[4]
tán tuó xiū tuó lì[5] xiū tuó lì[6] xiū tuó luó pó dǐ[7] fó tuó bō shān mí[8]
sà pó tuó luó ní ē pó duō ní[9] sà pó pó shā ē pó duō ní[10]
xiū ē pó duō ní[11] sēng qié pō lǔ chā ní[12] sēng qié niè qié tuó ní[13]
ē sēng qí[14] sēng qié pō qié dì[15]
dì lì ē duò sēng qié dōu luè ē luó dì bō luó dì[16]
sà pó sēng qié dì sān mó dì qié lán dì[17]
sà pó dá mó xiū bō lì chà dì[18]
sà pó sà duō lóu tuó jiāo shě luè ē nòu qié dì[19]
xīn ē pí jí lì dì dì[20]

receive and embrace it, let them think to themselves: 'This is all due to the mighty divine powers of Universal Sage.' If any receive and embrace it, read and recite it, remember it correctly, understand its meaning, and practice it as taught, they should know that they are doing the work of Universal Sage. They have planted good roots deeply under innumerable, countless buddhas, and their heads will be touched by the hands of tathagatas.

"If they do no more than copy it, when their lives come to an end they will be born in the heaven of the thirty-three gods. On that occasion eighty-four thousand goddesses, performing all kinds of music, will come to welcome them. Wearing crowns of the seven precious materials, they will amuse and enjoy themselves among those goddesses. How much more so those who receive and embrace it, read and recite it, remember it correctly, understand its meaning, and practice it as taught.

"If there are any who receive and embrace it, read and recite it, remember it correctly, and understand its meaning, when their lives come to an end the hands of a thousand buddhas will be extended to them, freeing them from fear and preventing them from falling into evil realms. They will go straight to the Tushita Heaven where Maitreya Bodhisattva is. Maitreya Bodhisattva has the thirty-two characteristics, is surrounded by a multitude of great bodhisattvas, and has hundreds of thousands of billions of goddesses who have been born into his family. Such will be their blessings and enrichments.

"Therefore the wise should wholeheartedly copy the sutra themselves, or lead others to copy it, receive and embrace it, read and recite it, remember it correctly, and practice it as taught. World-Honored One, by my divine powers I will now protect this sutra so that after the extinction of the Tathagata it will spread widely throughout Jambudvipa and never come to an end."

Then Shakyamuni Buddha praised him, saying: "Well done, well done, Universal Sage. You are able to protect and help this sutra well, bringing peace, happiness, and enrichment to the living in many places. You have already gained inconceivable blessings and profound compassion. From long ago you have aspired to supreme awakening, and by divine powers have made a vow to protect this sutra. By my divine powers I will protect those who receive and embrace the name of Universal Sage Bodhisattva.

"Universal Sage, if there are any who receive and embrace, read and recite, remember correctly, study, practice, and copy this Dharma Flower Sutra, it should be known that they have seen Shakyamuni Buddha. It is as though they heard this sutra from the Buddha's mouth. It should be known that they have made offerings to Shakyamuni Buddha. It should be known that the Buddha has praised them for doing good. It should be known that Shakyamuni Buddha has touched the heads of such people with his hand. It should be known that such people are covered by the robes of Shakyamuni Buddha.

"Such people will never again be greedy for or attached to worldly pleasures. They will have no liking for scriptures of non-Buddhists or other jottings, nor ever again take pleasure in associating with such people or with other evil people, be they butchers or those who raise pigs, sheep, chickens, and dogs, or hunters, or pimps. But such people will be upright in mind. They will have good recall. They will have powers of merit and virtue. They will not be troubled by the three poisons, or by envy, pride, conceit, or extreme arrogance. With few desires, they will be easily satisfied, and will do the work of Universal Sage Bodhisattva.

"Universal Sage, after the extinction of the Tathagata, in the last five hundred years, if anyone sees someone who receives and embraces, reads and recites the Dharma Flower Sutra, they should think: 'This person will soon go to the place of the Way, destroy the devil's multitudes, attain supreme awakening, turn the Dharma wheel, beat the Dharma drum, blow the Dharma conch, and pour down the rain of the Dharma. Such a person should sit on the lion seat of the Dharma in the midst of a great assembly of human and heavenly beings.'

"Universal Sage, whoever in future ages receives and embraces, reads and recites this sutra will no longer be greedy for or attached to clothes, bedding, food and drink, or other necessities of life. Their wishes will not be in vain. In the present life, happiness will be their reward. Suppose someone disparages them, saying: 'You are only crazy. Pursuing this Way in vain will never get you anything.' The consequence of such an offense is blindness for generation after generation. But if anyone makes offerings to and praises them, they should obtain visible rewards in the present world.

"Again, if anyone sees someone who receives and embraces this sutra and exposes their faults, whether true or false, such a person will be afflicted with leprosy in their present life. If they disparagingly smirk at them, for generation after generation their teeth will be sparse or completely missing, their lips will be ugly, their nose flat, their hands and feet deformed, their eyes squinty. Their body will stink and be filthy with evil sores and bloody pus, and they will suffer from water in the belly, shortness of breath, and other severe illnesses. Therefore, Universal Sage, if anyone sees someone who receives and embraces this sutra, they should get up and greet them from afar, as if they were paying reverence to the Buddha."

When this chapter on the encouragement of Universal Sage Bodhisattva was taught, innumerable, incalculable bodhisattvas equal in number to the sands of the Ganges mastered the incantation, which has hundreds of thousands of billions of uses, and bodhisattvas equal in number to the particles of dust of a three-thousand great thousandfold world became perfect in the way of Universal Sage.

When the Buddha taught this sutra, everyone in the whole of the great assembly—Universal Sage and the other bodhisattvas, Shariputra and the other shravakas, and the gods, dragons, humans, and nonhumans—was filled with great joy. Receiving and embracing the Buddha's words, they paid their respects to him and left.

The Sutra of
Contemplation of the Dharma Practice
of Universal Sage Bodhisattva

This is what I heard.

AT ONE TIME the Buddha was staying in the kingdom of Vaisali, in the multi-storied assembly hall of the Great Forest Monastery. He said to all the monks: "After three months, surely I will enter complete nirvana."

Then the Venerable Ananda rose from his seat, straightened his robe, put his palms together, and circled around the Buddha three times. Kneeling with his palms together, he paid his respects, gazing at the Tathagata attentively without turning away for even a moment. Maha-Kashyapa, the elder, and Maitreya Bodhisattva, the great one, also rose from their seats and, with palms together and gazing up at his honored face, paid respects to the Buddha.

Then the three great leaders spoke to the Buddha in one voice: "World-Honored One, after the extinction of the Tathagata, how can living beings aspire to be bodhisattvas, follow the Great Vehicle sutras, the Expansive Teaching, and think about the world of one truth correctly? How can they keep from losing their aspiration for unexcelled awakening? Without cutting off their afflictions and renouncing the five desires, how can they purify their sense organs and completely rid themselves of their sins? With the natural pure eyes received at birth from their parents, and without leaving the world of the five desires, how can they see past their hindrances?"

The Buddha said to Ananda: "Listen carefully! Listen carefully! Consider what I am about to say, and remember it well! Long ago, on

Holy Eagle Peak and in other places, the Tathagata has already thoroughly explained the way of one truth. But now in this place, for all living beings and others in the future who want to practice the unsurpassable Dharma of the Great Vehicle, and for those who want to learn the practice of Universal Sage and to follow the practice of Universal Sage, I will now teach this method of contemplation. For all those who are able to see Universal Sage, as well as for those who do not see him, I will now explain in detail how to eliminate evils.

"Ananda, Universal Sage Bodhisattva was born in the east, in the Land of Pure Wonder. I have already described the nature of his land at length in the Flower Garland Sutra. Now I will briefly explain it again in this sutra.

"Ananda, if any monks, nuns, laymen, laywomen, the eight kinds of guardians, gods, dragons and others, or any other living beings, recite the Great Vehicle, study the Great Vehicle, aspire to the Great Vehicle, want to see the material body of Universal Sage Bodhisattva, want to see the stupa of Abundant Treasures Buddha, want to see Shakyamuni Buddha and the buddhas who embody him, or want to gain purity of the six senses, they should learn this contemplation.

"The blessings of this contemplation will eliminate their hindrances and allow them to see the excellent and wonderful form of the Buddha. Even though they have not yet entered into concentration, just because they recite and embrace the Great Vehicle they will devote themselves to studying it and putting it into practice, and after keeping their attention continuously on the Great Vehicle for one day, or for three weeks, they will be able to see Universal Sage.

"Those who have heavy hindrances will see him after seven weeks. Those who have heavier hindrances will see him after one lifetime. Those who have still heavier hindrances will see him after two lifetimes. And those who have yet heavier hindrances will see him after three lifetimes. Thus past actions have a variety of consequences. They are not always the same. This is why I teach in a variety of ways."

The body of Universal Sage Bodhisattva is unlimited, the range of his voice is unlimited, and the forms of his image are unlimited. When he wants to come to this world he uses his own divine powers to shrink his body to a smaller size. Because the three hindrances of the people in Jambudvipa are heavy, through the power of his wisdom he transforms himself and rides a white elephant.

The elephant has six tusks and is supported by seven legs. Under its seven legs are seven live lotus flowers. The elephant is as white as snow, the most brilliant of whites. Even crystal or the Himalayas cannot be compared with it. The body of the elephant is four hundred and fifty leagues long and four hundred leagues tall.

At the tips of its six tusks are six bathing pools, and in each bathing pool grow fourteen lotus flowers, filling them all equally. The flowers bloom majestically, like the king of heavenly foliage. On each of these flowers sits a jade maiden, with a crimson face surpassing even that of a goddess. In the hands of each of the maidens five harps appear spontaneously, each accompanied by five hundred other musical instruments. Five hundred birds, as colorful as precious gems, including wild ducks, wild geese, and mandarin ducks, are among the leaves and flowers. On the elephant's trunk there is a flower with a stalk the color of red pearl. The flower itself is gold in color and looks like a bud that has not yet blossomed.

After witnessing this, if anyone continues to repent and contemplates the Great Vehicle sincerely, unceasingly pondering over it with clear vision, they will be able to see the flower bloom and radiate a golden color.

The calyx of the lotus flower is made of kimshuka jewels and wonderful and pure mani jewels. Its stamens are made of diamonds. A transformed buddha can be seen sitting on the calyx of the lotus flower with a host of bodhisattvas sitting on the stamens. From between the eyebrows of the transformed buddha comes a golden light, which goes into the elephant's trunk with the color of a red lotus flower. This light comes out of the elephant's trunk and enters its eyes. Then it shines from the elephant's eyes and enters its ears. It then comes out of the elephant's ears, illuminates the top of its head, and changes into a golden platform.

On the elephant's head are three transformed attendants. One has a golden wheel in its hands, another holds a mani jewel, and another grasps a diamond pounder. When the attendant raises the pounder and points it at him, the elephant immediately takes a few steps. The elephant does not step on the ground but hovers in the air, seven feet above the earth, yet it leaves its footprints on the ground. The footprints have in them a Dharma wheel with a hub and a thousand spokes, all of them perfect. In each Dharma wheel is a great lotus flower, on which there is a transformed elephant. These elephants also have seven legs and walk behind the great elephant. Every time one of these elephants raises and brings down a foot, seven thousand elephants appear, all following behind the great elephant.

On the elephant's trunk, the color of a red lotus flower, sits a transformed buddha, who emits light from between his eyebrows. This golden light, as before, enters the elephant's trunk, which is the color of a red lotus flower. This light comes out of the elephant's trunk and enters its eyes. Then it shines from the elephant's eyes and enters its ears. It then comes out of the elephant's ears and reaches the top of its head.

Gradually going up the elephant's back, the light is transformed into a golden saddle adorned with the seven precious materials. On all four sides of the saddle are pillars made of the seven precious materials and decorated with sets of jewels, making a jeweled pedestal. On this pedestal there is a lotus flower stamen of the seven precious materials, and that stamen also has on it a hundred jewels. The blossom of that lotus flower is made of a great mani jewel.

The bodhisattva named Universal Sage sits there cross-legged. On his body, pure as a white jewel, are fifty lights of fifty different colors, forming a halo over his head. Golden light radiates from the pores of his body, and innumerable transformed buddhas are at the ends of the golden rays, accompanied by transformed bodhisattvas to serve them.

The elephant walks deliberately and carefully. Going slowly, he pours large jeweled lotus flowers before a follower. When this elephant opens its mouth, the jade maidens in the bathing pools on the elephant's tusks play fine and wonderful music that praises the one true way of the Great Vehicle. Having seen this, the follower rejoices and shows respect, again reading and reciting the profound sutras, showing respect to the innumerable buddhas in all directions wherever they may be, to the stupa of Abundant Treasures Buddha, to Shakyamuni Buddha, and to Universal Sage and other great bodhisattvas.

Then a follower makes this wish: "If I have any blessings stored up, surely I should see Universal Sage soon. Honorable Universal Fortune, please show me your physical body!"

Having made this wish, followers should show respect to the buddhas in all directions six times day and night, and practice the teaching of repentance. Followers should read the Great Vehicle sutras and recite them, think about the meaning of the Great Vehicle, and reflect on its practice. Reverence should be given and offerings made to those who embrace it. All people should be regarded as though they were the Buddha, and all living beings as though they were one's father and mother.

While a follower is reflecting in this way, Universal Sage Bodhisattva will immediately send forth a ray of light from the tuft of white hair between his eyebrows, which is the sign of a great man. With the appearance of this light, the body of Universal Sage Bodhisattva will become as dignified as a mountain of purple gold, so well ordered and refined that it has all the thirty-two characteristics. From the pores of his body he will emit great rays of light, illuminating the great elephant and turning it into the color of gold. All transformed elephants will be gold colored as well, and all transformed bodhisattvas also. When these rays of light shine on the innumerable worlds to the east, all of them will turn to the color of gold. The same thing will happen in the southern, western, and northern directions, in the four intermediate directions, and in the up and down directions.

Then in each of the directions one will find a bodhisattva mounted on a six-tusked, white king elephant, like Universal Sage, with no difference at all. In this way, by his divine powers Universal Sage Bodhisattva will enable all those who embrace the sutras to see transformed elephants filling the innumerable and unlimited worlds in every direction. Then, seeing all the bodhisattvas, a follower will rejoice in body and mind, and, showing respect for them, will say to them: "Great kind ones, great compassionate ones, out of pity for me, please teach the Dharma for me!" When anyone speaks in this way, with one voice all the bodhisattvas will teach the pure Great Vehicle Dharma sutras and will praise them in verse. This is called the first stage in which a follower first contemplates Universal Sage Bodhisattva.

Having seen this, when followers keep the Great Vehicle in mind without forsaking it day and night, even while sleeping, they will be able to see Universal Sage teach the Dharma for them in a dream. Just as if followers were awake, the Bodhisattva will put their minds at ease, saying: "In what you have recited and embraced, you have forgotten this phrase or that verse." Then a follower, hearing Universal Sage teach the profound Dharma, will understand its meaning and keep it in mind without forgetting it. As this is done day by day, the follower's mind will gradually benefit. Universal Sage Bodhisattva will enable a follower to keep the buddhas in all directions in mind. According to the teaching of Universal Sage, the follower will think and remember correctly. With mental eyes the follower will gradually see the buddhas in the eastern direction, with bodies gold in color, majestic and wonderful. Having seen one buddha, a follower will see another buddha, in this manner gradually seeing all the buddhas everywhere in the eastern direction. And as a benefit of this valuable reflection, a follower will see all the buddhas everywhere in all directions. Having seen the buddhas and feeling joyous, a follower will say these words:

"Thanks to the Great Vehicle, I have been able to see great leaders. Because of the powers of great leaders, I have also been able to see buddhas. Though I have seen these buddhas, still I have not seen them completely. When I close my eyes I see the buddhas, but when I open my eyes I lose sight of them."

After saying this, followers should everywhere show respect to the buddhas in all directions, prostrating themselves on the ground. Having paid respect to the buddhas, followers should kneel with palms together and say: "The buddhas, the world-honored ones, have the ten powers, courage, the eighteen unique qualities, great compassion, great kindness, and the three kinds of mental stability. These buddhas, always living embodied in this world, have the finest form. What is the sin that makes me fail to see them?"

Having said this, a follower should repent still more. When followers have been purified through repentance, Universal Sage Bodhisattva will appear before such persons once again and will not leave them, whether they are walking, standing, sitting, or lying down. Even in their dreams, he will always teach the Dharma for them. After waking up they will be comforted by delight in the Dharma. In this manner, after twenty-one days and nights have passed, a follower will acquire the revolving incantation. Having acquired this incantation, one will be able to keep in mind the wonderful Dharma, which the buddhas and bodhisattvas have preached without forgetting any of it.

Also, though only Shakyamuni Buddha will teach the Dharma for them, in their dreams, followers will always see the seven buddhas of the past. Each of these world-honored ones will praise the Great Vehicle sutras. Then a follower, feeling joyous, once again will kneel and show respect to the buddhas everywhere in all directions. After respect has been shown to the buddhas, Universal Sage Bodhisattva, present before such people, will explain for them all the bonds from actions in their previous lives, and have them confess all of their dark, evil, sinful acts. Turning to the world-honored ones, followers should confess in their own words.

After confessing, a follower will attain the concentration by which buddhas appear. Having attained this concentration, in the eastern direction one will see with complete clarity Akshobhya Buddha and the Kingdom of Wonderful Joy. In like manner, one will see with complete clarity the exceptionally wonderful lands of the buddhas in all directions. After seeing the buddhas in all directions, one will have a dream in which on an elephant's head there is a man who handles diamond pounders who points a diamond pounder at the six sense organs. After the six organs have been pointed at, Universal Sage Bodhisattva will teach the Dharma for this follower, to purify the six organs through repentance. In this way the follower will repent for a day or for twenty-one days.

Then, by the power of the concentration by which the buddhas appear and by the beauty of the preaching of Universal Sage Bodhisattva, with their ears followers will gradually hear sounds without hindrance, their eyes will gradually see things without hindrance, and their noses will gradually smell odors without hindrance. This is as taught extensively in the Wonderful Dharma Flower Sutra.

Having purified the six organs, a follower will be joyous in body and mind and free of evil ideas. Devoting oneself to this Dharma so that it can be complied with, a follower will acquire again a hundred thousand myriad millions of the revolving incantation and will again see hundreds of thousands of myriads of millions of innumerable buddhas everywhere.

These world-honored ones will reach out with their right hands, laying them on the heads of followers, and will say: "Good, good. You are a follower of the Great Vehicle. You aspire to great adornment. You keep the Great Vehicle in mind. Long ago, when we aspired to become awakened, we also were like that. You should firmly keep this aspiration, without losing anything. Because we practiced the Great Vehicle in previous lives, we now have the pure bodies of the truly awakened.

"Now you should practice diligently and never be lazy. These Great Vehicle sutras are the buddhas' storehouse of the Dharma; they are the eyes of the buddhas in all directions and in the past, present, and future; and they are the seeds that give birth to tathagatas in the past, present, and future. One who embraces these sutras embraces the body of the Buddha and does the work of the Buddha. Such a person should understand that he or she has been sent by the buddhas and are covered by robes of buddhas, the world-honored ones. This is a child of the true Dharma of the buddhas, the tathagatas. Practice the Great Vehicle and do not cut off the seeds of Dharma! Now carefully contemplate the buddhas in the eastern direction."

When this has been said, a follower will see all the innumerable worlds in the eastern direction, their lands as level as the palm of one's hand, with no hills, burial mounds, or brambles. They will have earth of lapis lazuli, with golden cords to mark divisions. So too with the worlds in all directions. Having seen this, a follower will see jewel trees that are tall and wonderful, five thousand leagues high. These trees will always produce decorations of deep gold, white silver, and the seven precious materials. Under each of these tall and wonderful trees a lion seat of jewels will appear spontaneously, itself two thousand leagues high. From this seat will radiate the light of a hundred jewels. In the same way the light of a hundred jewels will radiate from each of the trees and seats of jewels. From each of the trees and seats of jewels will emerge spontaneously five hundred white elephants with Universal Sage Bodhisattvas on each of them.

Then a follower, showing respect to all these Universal Sages, should say: "Due to what sin have I only seen earth of jewels, seats of jewels, and jewel trees, but have not seen the buddhas?"

When a follower finishes saying this, sitting on each of the seats of jewels will be a world-honored one, majestic and wonderful. Having seen the buddhas, a follower's heart will be full of joy, and he will recite and learn the Great Vehicle sutras once again. By the power of the Great Vehicle, a voice in the sky will praise him, saying: "Good, good, good son! Due to your blessings from practicing the Great Vehicle, you have seen buddhas. Though you have now been able to see buddhas, world-honored ones, you cannot see Shakyamuni Buddha yet, the buddhas who embody him, or the stupa of Abundant Treasures Buddha."

After hearing the voice in the sky, a follower will again vigorously recite and learn the Great Vehicle sutras. Because followers recite and learn the sutras of the Great Vehicle, the Expansive Teaching, even in dreams they will see Shakyamuni Buddha with the great assembly on Holy Eagle Peak, teaching the Dharma Flower Sutra and demonstrating the principle of one truth. After hearing this teaching, and repenting and yearning, one will want to see the Buddha. Then a follower should put his palms together and, kneeling in the direction of Holy Eagle Peak, should say: "The Tathagata, the World's Hero, is always in this world. Out of pity for me, please reveal yourself to me."

After saying this, a follower will see Holy Eagle Peak, adorned with the seven precious materials and with countless monks, shravakas, and a great assembly. Lined with jewel trees, its ground of jewels level and even, it will even have a wonderful lion seat of jewels with Shakyamuni Buddha on it sending out a ray of light from between his eyebrows, illuminating all the worlds in the ten directions and passing through all the innumerable worlds in all ten directions.

The buddhas embodying Shakyamuni Buddha in all directions where this ray reaches will assemble like a cloud, and teach the wonderful Dharma everywhere in accord with the Wonderful Dharma Flower Sutra. Each of these embodiment buddhas, having a body of purple gold, has an unlimited body, sits on a lion seat and has countless hundreds of millions of great bodhisattvas in his retinue. The practice of each of these bodhisattvas is the same as that of Universal Sage. Accordingly, in the ten directions it is the same in the retinues of countless buddhas and bodhisattvas.

When the great assembly has gathered together like a cloud, they will see Shakyamuni Buddha emitting rays of golden light from the pores of his whole body, in each of which are hundreds of millions of transformed buddhas. From the tufts of white hair between their eyebrows, the sign of a great man, the embodiment buddhas will emit rays of light that stream into the head of Shakyamuni Buddha. Seeing this, from all the pores of their bodies the embodiment buddhas will also emit rays of golden light, in each of which are transformed buddhas, numerous as the grains of sands in the Ganges.

Then Universal Sage Bodhisattva will emit another ray of light from between his eyebrows, the sign of a great man, and he will send it into the hearts of followers. After this ray has entered their hearts, followers themselves will remember that under countless hundreds and thousands of buddhas in the past they had received and embraced, read and recited the Great Vehicle sutras. Having the ability to penetrate clearly to previous states of existence, they will see their own former bodies with complete clarity, exactly as if they had the ability to see into the past.

Attaining a sudden and great awakening, followers will acquire the revolving incantation and teachings about billions and billions of other incantations. Rising from concentration, they will see before them all the embodied buddhas sitting on lion seats under jewel trees. They will also see a ground of lapis lazuli, with bunches of lotus flowers springing up from the sky below the earth. In the spaces between the flowers, bodhisattvas as numerous as the grains of sand in the Ganges will be sitting cross-legged. They will also see the bodhisattvas who embody Universal Sage in their assemblies praising the Great Vehicle. Then, with one voice from different mouths, the bodhisattvas will have followers purify their six sense organs.

> One will say, "You should reflect on the Buddha."
> Another will say, "You should reflect on the Dharma."
> Another will say, "You should reflect on the monastic community."
> Another will say, "You should reflect on morality."
> Another will say, "You should reflect on generosity."
> Another will say, "You should reflect on the heavens."

"These six methods express an aspiration to become a buddha. They give birth to bodhisattvas. Before the buddhas, you should now confess your past sins and sincerely repent.

"In innumerable previous lives, because of your eyes you have been greedily attached to material forms. Because of your attachment to such forms, you greedily desire the dust of the passions. Because of your desire for the dust of the passions, you receive a woman's body. Living in age after age, you are deluded by and attached to forms. Forms harm your eyes and you become a slave to desire. This is why forms cause you to wander in the threefold world. This makes you so blind you can see nothing at all.

"You have now recited the sutras of the Great Vehicle, the Expansive Teaching. In these sutras the buddhas of all directions teach that their forms and bodies do not become extinct. You have now seen them, and you can judge whether this is true or not. Your no-good eyes do a lot of damage to you. Following what we say, you should faithfully return to the buddhas and to Shakyamuni Buddha, tell them of your sins and errors due to your eyes, and say: 'May I be cleansed and purified by the Dharma water of the buddhas and bodhisattvas of the wisdom-eyes!'"

Having spoken in this way, a follower should show respect to the buddhas in all directions. Turning to Shakyamuni Buddha and the Great Vehicle sutras, again one should say: "I now repent for the heavy sins of my eyes. My eyes are such an obstacle and are so tainted that I am blind and can see nothing at all. With your great kindness, may the Buddha have mercy on me and protect me!

"Universal Sage Bodhisattva, accompanied by countless bodhisattvas from all of the directions, rides the ship of the great Dharma, the ship that carries all beings to the other side. My one wish is that out of pity for me he will enable me to hear about the method of repentance by which my no-good eyes will be purified of the hindrances that come from the bad and evil things they have done in the past."

Saying this three times, followers should prostrate themselves on the ground and reflect correctly about the Great Vehicle without forgetting anything. This is called the teaching of repenting for the sins of the eyes.

If anyone invokes the name of a buddha, burns incense, strews flowers, displays the spirit of the Great Vehicle, hangs paintings, flags, or canopies, speaks of the errors and afflictions of their eyes, and repents of their sins, such a person will see Shakyamuni Buddha in the present world, the buddhas embodying him or countless other buddhas, and not fall into the evil paths for countless eons. Thanks to the power of the Great Vehicle and to the Great Vehicle vow, such a person, together with all the incantation-bodhisattvas, will become a follower. Anyone who reflects in this way thinks correctly. Anyone who reflects otherwise is said to have wrong thoughts. This is called the mark of the first stage of purification of the eyes.

Having finished purifying their eyes, followers should continue to read and recite the Great Vehicle sutras. Kneeling on the right knee and repenting six times day and night, they should say: "Why can I only see Shakyamuni Buddha and the buddhas who embody him, but not the stupa or remaining whole body of Abundant Treasures Buddha? The stupa of Abundant Treasures Buddha is always living, never extinct. My eyes are polluted by evil. This is why I cannot see the stupa."

Having said this, followers should continue repenting, and after seven days the stupa of Abundant Treasures Buddha will spring out of the earth. With his right hand, Shakyamuni Buddha will open the door of the stupa, where Abundant Treasures Buddha will be seen deep in the concentration of universal manifestation of bodily forms. From all the pores of his body he will emit rays of light as numerous as the grains of sands of the Ganges. In each of the rays will be hundreds of thousands of billions of transformed buddhas. When such a sign appears, followers will make a procession around the stupa, rejoicing and uttering verses of praise. When they have finished processing around the stupa seven times, Abundant Treasures Tathagata will praise them with a great voice, saying: "Child of the Dharma, you have truly practiced the Great Vehicle and, obediently following Universal Sage, have repented for your eyes. For this reason, I will go to you and give testimony for you."

Having said this, in praise of the Buddha he will say: "Well done, well done, Shakyamuni Buddha! You could teach the great Dharma, pour down the rain of the great Dharma, and save living beings who are polluted with evil."

Having seen the stupa of Abundant Treasures Buddha, a follower will then go to Universal Sage Bodhisattva once again and, putting palms together, rejoice and show respect for him, saying: "Great Teacher, teach me to repent of my faults."

Universal Sage will respond: "Because of your ears, you have sought external sounds for many eons. Hearing wonderful sounds gives rise to deluded attachment to them. Hearing evil sounds brings about the damage of a hundred and eight kinds of affliction. This kind of retribution from evil ears results in evil things. Incessantly hearing evil sounds gives rise to various entanglements. Due to your perverted hearing, you will fall into truly evil paths, remote places, or wrong views where the Dharma cannot be heard.

"Today you have recited and embraced the oceanic storehouse of blessings which is the Great Vehicle. For this reason, you have seen the buddhas in all ten directions, and the stupa of Abundant Treasures Buddha has appeared to give testimony for you. You should confess your own errors and evils and repent for all of your sins."

Having heard this, followers should then put their palms together again and, prostrating themselves on the ground, should say: "Truly enlightened World-Honored One, reveal yourself and bear testimony for me. With the sutras of the Expansive Teaching you are the master of compassion. My one request is that you look upon me and hear what I say. For many eons, until I had this body, because of my ears I was deluded by sounds and attached to hearing them, just as lacquer sticks to grass. When I hear evil sounds, a pervasive poison of afflictions arises, deluding me and attaching me to everything, without resting even a little. Bad sounds wear on my nerves and make me fall into the three destinies. Now, understanding this for the first time, turning to the world-honored ones, I confess and repent of it."

Having finished repenting, a follower will see Abundant Treasures Buddha emitting a great ray of light, a ray that is gold in color and illuminates everything in the eastern direction, as well as in the worlds in all the other directions, where countless buddhas appear with their bodies of pure golden color. From the sky of the eastern direction will come a voice saying: "Here is a buddha, a world-honored one named Good Virtue, who also is embodied in innumerable buddhas who sit cross-legged on lion seats under jewel trees. All these world-honored ones, in the concentration of universal manifestation of bodily forms, speak to a follower, praising him and saying: 'Good, good, good son! You have now read and recited the Great Vehicle sutras. What you have recited is in the sphere of the buddhas.'"

After these words have been spoken, Universal Sage Bodhisattva will again teach the Dharma of repentance for followers, saying: "In the innumerable eons of your previous lives, because of your lust for odors, you developed sense discriminations and became constantly attached to them, and you fell into life after life. Now you should contemplate the cause of the Great Vehicle. This cause of the Great Vehicle is the true character of all things."

Having heard these words, prostrating themselves on the ground, followers should repent once again. Having repented, one should say:

"Praise to Shakyamuni Buddha! Praise to the stupa of Abundant Treasures Buddha! Praise to all the buddhas in the ten directions embodying Shakyamuni Buddha!" Having said this, one should show respect to the buddhas everywhere in all directions, saying: "Praise to the Buddha Good Virtue in the eastern direction and to the buddhas who embody him!" Followers should also show respect to each of these buddhas as wholeheartedly as if they had seen them with their naked eyes, and they should make offerings to them with incense and flowers. After making offerings to the buddhas, they should kneel with palms together and praise them with a variety of verses. After praising them, they should speak of the ten evil actions and repent of all of their sins. Having repented, they should say this: "During the innumerable eons of my previous lives, I craved aromas, tastes, and feelings from touch and did many evil things. For this reason, for innumerable lives I have always found myself born in various undesirable bodies, including those of beings in purgatories, hungry spirits, animals, beings in remote places, and people of wrong views. Today, confessing such evil deeds, and going to the buddhas, kings of true Dharma, I confess and repent of my sins."

Having repented in this way, a follower should again read and recite the Great Vehicle sutras without neglecting body or mind. Because of the power of the Great Vehicle, a voice in the sky will proclaim: "Child of the Dharma, turning to the buddhas in the ten directions, you should now praise the Dharma of the Great Vehicle and speak of your faults before the buddhas. Buddha-tathagatas are your kind fathers. You should speak about the bad and evil things done by your tongue, saying: 'This tongue, moved by thoughts of evil actions, makes me praise deluded speech, idle talk, harsh words, divisive talk, slander, lies, and wrong views, and it also makes me speak useless words. With such a multitude and variety of evil actions, which provoke fights and dissension, I teach what is not Dharma as if it were Dharma. I now repent for all such sins.'"

Having spoken in this way before the world's heroes, followers should revere the buddhas everywhere in all ten directions, prostrating themselves on the ground to show respect for them. Putting their palms together and kneeling, they should say: "The errors of this tongue are countless and without limit. Thorns of evil actions are rooted in the tongue. It is this tongue that stops the wheel of the true Dharma. Such an evil tongue cuts off the seeds of blessings. Meaningless things are frequently forced on others. Praising wrong views is like adding wood to a fire, bringing greater harm to beings already in raging flames. It is like someone who dies from drinking poison without getting any sores. Recompense for my sins, for the evil, wrong, and bad things I have done, should result in my falling into evil paths for hundreds or thousands of eons. Because of lying I will fall into a great purgatory. Now going to the buddhas of the southern direction, I confess my errors and sins."

When a follower thinks in this way, a voice in the sky will say: "In the southern direction there is a buddha named Sandalwood Virtue, who also is embodied in countless other buddhas. All these buddhas teach the Great Vehicle and cut off sins and evils. Turning to these innumerable buddhas, world-honored ones of great compassion in all directions, you should confess your sins and evils and sincerely repent of them." These words having been spoken, followers should show respect to the buddhas once again, prostrating themselves on the ground.

Then the buddhas will emit rays of light, illuminating the followers' bodies and making the followers naturally joyous in body and mind, giving them great compassion, and causing them to reflect on all things. Then, for the sake of followers, the buddhas will everywhere teach the Dharma of great compassion and generosity, leading followers to use kind words and practice the six ways of harmonious respect. Having heard these instructions, their hearts overflowing with joy, followers will recite and study again and again, never becoming tired.

Once again in the sky there will be a wonderful voice saying: "Now you should repent of body and mind. The sins of the body are killing, stealing, and fornication, while thinking bad thoughts is the sin of the mind. Committing the ten evil actions and the five irredeemable sins is just like being a monkey, or like birdlime glue. Attachment to all sorts of things leads to the passions of the six sense faculties. The actions of these six sense faculties fill every threefold world, the twenty-five states of existence, and all places where there is life, filling them with heavy branches, small branches, flowers, and leaves. Such actions also increase ignorance, old age, death, and the twelve kinds of suffering, and inevitably involve the eight evils and the eight difficulties. You should now repent of such evil and bad deeds."

Then a follower, having heard these words, asks the voice in the sky:

"Where can I practice the teaching of repentance?" The voice in the sky will then say: "Shakyamuni Buddha is called Vairocana, the Omnipresent. His dwelling place is called Always Tranquil Light, a place that is taken up by constant practice, a place that is made stable by self-practice, a place where the characteristics of existence are extinguished by pure practice, a place where body and mind cannot live in comfortable practice, a place where the character of existing or nonexisting cannot be seen in anything, and a place of tranquil liberation, which is the practice of wisdom. Because these forms are the ever present Dharma, you should now meditate on the buddhas in the ten directions."

Then the buddhas in all ten directions will reach out with their right hands to touch the head of a follower, saying: "Good, good, good son! Because you have now read and recited the Great Vehicle sutras, the buddhas in all directions will teach the Dharma of repentance for you. Bodhisattva practice is neither a matter of cutting off all bonds and services nor of living in the ocean of servitude. If you contemplate your mind, you will find no mind, except the mind that comes from perverse conceptions. The mind with such conceptions arises from delusion. Like the wind in the sky, it has no grounding. Such a character of things neither appears nor disappears.

"What is sin? What is virtue? As the thought of self is itself empty, neither sin nor virtue is our master. In this way, all things are neither permanent nor destroyed. If one repents like this, meditating on one's mind, one finds no mind. Things also do not dwell in things. All things are liberated, show the truth of extinction, and are calm and tranquil. Such a thing is called great repentance, sublime repentance, repentance without sin, the destruction of consciousness of mind. People who practice this repentance are pure in body and mind, like flowing water, not attached to things. Whenever they reflect they will be able to see Universal Sage Bodhisattva and the buddhas in all directions."

Then all the world-honored ones, emitting rays of light of great mercy, will teach for followers the Dharma of formlessness. The followers, hearing the first principle of emptiness being taught, are not surprised by hearing this. In due time they will gain the status of true bodhisattvas.

The Buddha said to Ananda: "Practicing in this way is called repentance. This is the method of repentance practiced by buddhas and great bodhisattvas in all ten directions."

The Buddha then said to Ananda: "After the extinction of the Buddha, if his disciples want to repent of their evil and bad actions, they only have to read and recite the Great Vehicle sutras. These sutras of the Expansive Teaching are the eyes of the buddhas. By means of these sutras the buddhas have been able to attain five kinds of eyes, and from them are born the three kinds of buddha bodies. This is the mark of the great Dharma, marking the ocean of nirvana. From such an ocean the three kinds of pure buddha bodies are born. These three kinds of bodies are a field of blessings for human and heavenly beings, and most worthy of offerings. If anyone recites and reads the sutras of the Great Vehicle, the Expansive Teaching, it should be known that they have the blessings of a buddha and, having extinguished their various evils long ago, are born of buddha-wisdom."

At that time the World-Honored One spoke in verse:

> If you have evil in your eyes,
> Impure with hindrances from actions in the past,
> You should recite the Great Vehicle
> And reflect on its first principle.
>
> This is called eye repentance.
> It exhausts past bad actions.
>
> When the ears hear noise,
> The principle of harmony is upset.
> This produces craziness,
> Like that of a foolish monkey.
>
> You should recite the Great Vehicle
> And meditate on the emptiness and formlessness of things,
> To exhaust all evils for a long time,
> And hear sounds from all directions with heavenly ears.
>
> The nose is attached to scents.
> In accord with its contamination, contacts occur.
> In this way the deluded nose, in accord with its contamination,
> Gives birth to all kinds of entanglements.

If you recite the Great Vehicle sutras
And meditate on the reality of things,
You will long be free from evil actions done in the past
And not do them in future lives.

The tongue causes five kinds of bad consequences
From harsh words spoken in the past.

If you want to control it yourself,
You should make an effort to practice compassion,
Think of the meaning of the true quiescence of things,
And not conceive by making distinctions.

The mind is like a monkey,
Never resting for a moment.

If you want to subdue it,
You should make an effort to recite the Great Vehicle,
Keeping in mind the Buddha's great awakened body,
His power, and his freedom from fear.

The body, master of its organs,
Dances freely among these six harmful faculties
Without obstacle,
Like dust swirling in the wind.

If you want to be rid of these evils,
Long separated from dirt and trouble,
Ever in the comfort of nirvana,
And at ease with a calm heart,

You should recite the Great Vehicle sutras
And keep in mind the mother of bodhisattvas.

Innumerable excellent skillful means will be obtained
By reflecting on the true nature of things.

These so-called six methods
Purify the six sense organs.

The whole ocean of hindrances from past actions
Arises from illusion.
If you want to repent, you should sit upright
And reflect on the true nature of things.

All sins are like frost and dew.
The sun of wisdom can dissipate them.
For this reason, with all your heart
You should repent of the six senses.

Having recited these verses, the Buddha said to Ananda: "Repent now of the six sense faculties, embrace the teaching of meditation on Universal Sage Bodhisattva, and explain it clearly everywhere for all the heavenly beings and people in all directions. After the extinction of the Buddha, if the disciples receive and embrace, read and recite, and explain the sutras of the Great Vehicle, the Expansive Teaching, in a quiet place, such as a graveyard or under the trees of a monastery, they should read and recite the sutras of the Expansive Teaching and should think about the meaning of the Great Vehicle. As a result of the strong power of reflecting, they will be able to see my body, the stupa of Abundant Treasures Buddha, the countless buddhas embodied in all directions, Universal Sage Bodhisattva, Manjushri Bodhisattva, Medicine King Bodhisattva, and Medicine Lord Bodhisattva. As a result of revering the Dharma, these buddhas and bodhisattvas, living in the sky with wonderful flowers, will praise and revere those who practice and embrace the Dharma. And as a result just of their reciting the sutras of the Great Vehicle, the Expansive Teaching, the buddhas and bodhisattvas will make offerings day and night to those who embrace the Dharma."

Then the Buddha said to Ananda: "Because the bodhisattvas, the buddhas in all directions, and I too have thought about the true meaning of the Great Vehicle in an age of wisdom, we have now rid ourselves of the sins of life and death that occurred over hundreds of myriads of thousands of billions of eons. By means of this excellent, wonderful teaching of repentance, each of us has become one of the buddhas in the ten directions. If anyone wants to reach supreme awakening rapidly and see the buddhas in the ten directions and Universal Sage Bodhisattva in this life, they should purify themselves by taking a bath, putting on clean clothes, burning rare incense, and living in a secluded place. They should recite and read the Great Vehicle sutras and think about the meaning of the Great Vehicle."

The Buddha then said to Ananda: "If you find living beings who want to meditate on Universal Sage Bodhisattva, they should meditate in this way. Anyone who meditates in this way is called one who meditates correctly. Anyone who meditates in a different way is called one whose meditation is wrong.

"After the extinction of the Buddha, if his disciples faithfully follow the Buddha's words and practice repentance, it should be known that they are doing the work of Universal Sage. Those who do the work of Universal Sage neither see evil characteristics nor experience retribution from evil actions. If there are living beings who show respect to the buddhas in all ten directions six times night and day, recite the Great Vehicle sutras, and think about the profound first principle of the teaching of emptiness, in the time it takes to snap one's fingers they will rid themselves of the sins of life and death committed during hundreds of myriads of thousands of billions of eons. Anyone doing this work is truly a child of the Buddha, born from the buddhas. The buddhas in all directions and the bodhisattvas will become their teachers. Such people will be said to be perfect in bodhisattva precepts. Without going through a special ceremony, they will become accomplished naturally, and be worthy of receiving offerings from all human and heavenly beings."

If followers then want to perfect themselves in bodhisattva precepts, they should live in an open, quiet place and, putting their palms together, show respect to the buddhas in all directions, repent of their sins, and confess their own errors. After this, in a calm place, they should speak to the buddhas in all directions in this way: "The buddhas, the world-honored ones, are always alive in this world. Because of hindrances due to my actions in the past, even though I have faith in the Expansive Teaching, I cannot clearly see buddhas.

"Now I take refuge in the buddhas. Shakyamuni Buddha, truly en-lightened, World-Honored One, I beg you just to be my teacher. Man-jushri, great compassionate one, I beg you to use your wisdom to instruct me in the pure teachings of bodhisattvas. Maitreya Bodhisattva, sun of superior and great kindness, out of sympathy for me, you should listen to my plea to receive the teachings of bodhisattvas. Buddhas in all direc-tions, reveal yourselves and testify for me. Great bodhisattvas, superior and great leaders, since we extol your names, protect all living beings. Help and protect us!

"Today I have received and embraced the sutras of the Expansive Teaching. Even if I should lose my life, fall into a purgatory, and suffer endlessly, I would never harm or slander the true Dharma of the bud-dhas. Therefore, Shakyamuni Buddha, for this reason and by the power of this blessing, be my teacher now! Manjushri, be my educator! Maitreya of the world to come, I beg you to instruct me in the Dharma! Buddhas in all directions, I beg you to teach me true wisdom! Bodhi-sattvas of great virtue, I beg you to be my companions! Due to the pro-found and mysterious meaning of the Great Vehicle sutras, I now take refuge in the Buddha, take refuge in the Dharma, and take refuge in the monastic community." This should be said three times.

Having taken refuge in the three treasures, one should next vow to receive the six kinds of teaching. Having received the six kinds of teach-ing, one should then diligently observe noble practices without obstruc-tion and, aspiring to save all living beings, receive the eight kinds of teaching. Having made such a vow, in an open, quiet place one should burn rare incense, spread flowers, make offerings to all the buddhas, bodhisattvas, and sutras of the Great Vehicle, the Expansive Teaching, and should say: "Today I have aspired to awakening. May the blessings from this save all the living!"

Having said this, followers should once again bow their heads before all the buddhas and bodhisattvas and think about the meaning of the Expansive Teaching. For a day or for three weeks, whether a monastic or a layperson, they will not need a teacher, nor need to resort to a master, nor need a special ritual. Due to the power of receiving and embracing, reading and reciting the Great Vehicle sutras, and because of Universal Sage Bodhisattva's work of helping others, one can become the eyes of the true Dharma of the buddhas in all directions, and with this Dharma naturally be able to take on the five-part Dharma body: precepts, concentration, wisdom, liberation, and insight into liberation. The buddha-tathagatas have been born of this Dharma and have received assurance of becoming buddhas from the Great Vehicle sutras.

For this reason, wise-ones, suppose a shravaka violates the threefold refuge; or breaks the five precepts, the eight precepts, or the precepts of monks, nuns, male novices, female novices, or advanced female novices; or fails to act in a dignified way; or, because one is ignorant, bad, and evil, fails to keep many precepts and rules of dignified behavior. If one wants to be rid of this disease and return to being a monk and fulfilling the Dharma of mendicants, one should diligently read the sutras of the Expansive Teaching, think about the profound first principle of the teaching of emptiness, and bring this wisdom about emptiness into one's heart and mind.

It should be known that with each of his thoughts such a person will gradually exhaust the defilements of all his long-standing sins, with none remaining. This is called being perfect in the teachings and precepts of mendicants and fulfilling their dignified behavior. Such a person should receive offerings from all people and heavenly beings.

Suppose a layman acts in an undignified way and does bad things. To do bad things means to point out the errors and faults in the so-called Buddha's teachings, to discuss criminal, evil things done by the four groups, and to feel no shame even from theft or debauchery. If one wants to repent and be rid of these sins, one should diligently read and recite the sutras of the Expansive Teaching and think about their first principle.

Suppose a king, a minister, a brahman, an ordinary citizen, an elder, a government official, any such kind of person, never tiring of indulgently seeking after things, commits the five wicked sins, slanders the sutras of the Expansive Teaching, or commits the ten evil actions. Retribution for these great evils will make them fall into evil paths faster than the sudden appearance of a rainstorm. Surely they will fall into the lowest purgatory. If they want to rid themselves of these hindrances due to actions in their past and destroy them, they should experience shame and repent for all of their sins.

The Buddha said: "What is the teaching of repentance for kshatriyas and citizens? The teaching of repentance for kshatriyas and citizens is that they should always have proper minds and hearts, not slander the

Three Treasures, not hinder monks, and not make trouble for those observing noble practices. They should practice concentrating on the teaching of six thoughts. They should also support, make offerings to, and definitely honor those who embrace the Great Vehicle. They should also remember the profound teachings of sutras and the first principle of emptiness. Anyone who thinks of this teaching practices the first repentance of kshatriyas and citizens.

"The second repentance is to fulfill one's filial duties to one's father and mother and to respect one's teachers and seniors. Anyone who does this is practicing the teaching of the second repentance.

"The third repentance is to govern one's country with the true Dharma and not oppress the people unjustly. Anyone who does this is practicing the third repentance.

"The fourth repentance is to issue an order within one's region to hold the six days of fasting and, to the extent of their powers, have non-killing practiced. Anyone who does this is practicing the fourth repentance.

"The fifth repentance is simply to believe deeply that events have causes and results, believe in the way of one truth, and know that the buddhas never disappear. Anyone who does this is practicing the fifth repentance."

Then the Buddha said to Ananda: "In the future, when anyone studies and puts into practice these teachings of repentance, you should know that such a person has put on robes of shame, is helped and protected by buddhas, and before long will attain supreme awakening."

As these words were spoken, ten thousand children of heaven acquired the purity of the eyes of the Dharma, and all the great bodhisattvas, Maitreya Bodhisattva and others, and Ananda too, hearing the Buddha preach, rejoiced and acted accordingly.

Notes

1. This phrase, "the true character of things" (諸法實相義) has been variously translated and interpreted. There are two major possibilities: One is that it is an affirmation of the reality of the everyday world of concrete realities, as opposed to views that understand this world to be a product of our minds, an illusion. The other is that it is a claim that the buddhas' teachings reveal the nature of things, namely, that all things are interrelated and interdependent.

2. Sometimes referred to as the "ten suchnesses" or "ten reality aspects" (十如是), this passage does not appear in any existing Sanskrit versions of the Lotus Sutra. Each of the first nine items are rendered in Chinese with three characters, beginning in each case with 如是. In Tiantai interpretation, this three-part structure is important, as it is assimilated to the understanding of conventional existence, emptiness, and the middle way. This has led some to believe that the term should be rendered in English as "such-like," a term that, so far as I can tell, makes no sense in English. The text itself, apart from Tiantai interpretation, seems to indicate only that any thing that exists has some kind of characteristics, some kind of nature, and so on. In this translation, "such a" has been used in deference to the common practice of referring to the "ten suchnesses."

3. The "twelve hundred" figure is apparently what was called twelve thousand in chapter 1.

4. This list of nine kinds of Buddhist scripture is unique to the Lotus Sutra in content. The common list of nine, found both in Pali sutras and in other Mahayana sutras, includes assurance of becoming a buddha (授記), self-initiated teaching (自説), and extended teaching (方廣), but not causal explanations, parables and similes, or passages of dialogue. All of these do occur, however, in many of the much more common lists of twelve types of scripture.

5. This "nine" is no doubt a reference to the earlier passage (see the preceding note): "He teaches [1] sutras, [2] poetry, / [3] Stories of disciples' previous lives, / [4] Stories of buddhas' previous lives / [5] And [stories] of unprecedented things, / As well as [6] causal explanations, / [7] Parables and similes, / [8] Verses which repeat them, / [9] And passages of dialogue."

6. A list of these thirty-two characteristic features or marks of a buddha can be found in the first chapter of the Sutra of Innumerable Meanings. In the Prajñāpāramitā Sūtra (The Large Sutra on Perfect Wisdom), a text older than the Lotus Sutra and from a different part of India, the thirty-two distinguishing characteristics of a buddha's body include: flat feet; Dharma wheels on the bottom of the feet; soft palms and soles; long fingers and toes; webbed fingers and toes; broad heels; high ankles; slender, tapered legs, like those of a deer; a tall, erect body; arms that extend past the knees; a penis concealed in a sheath; body hair that has one hair per pore and is soft and curls to the right; body hair that points upward, is black and soft, and curls to the right; skin that is smooth and delicate; a body that is golden in color and shines; seven protuberances, two on the bottom of the feet, two on the hands, two on the shoulder blades, and one on the back of the neck; a dignified body, like that of a lion; full, gently curved shoulders; a full, broad chest; a well-proportioned body, with an arm span equal to the height of the body; jaws like a lion's; forty teeth; no gaps between the teeth; teeth equal in size; very white teeth; a superior sense of taste; a long, slender tongue; a beautiful, clear and charming voice; pure black eyes; beautiful eyelashes, like those of a bull; a tuft of soft white hair between the eyebrows; a protrusion on the top of the head.

7. These characteristics of the great carriages have been interpreted as symbolizing characteristics of those who follow the great way. That the carriage is tall and spacious means that those who follow the Buddha way have high aspirations and are broad-minded. The many jewels symbolize the many good deeds of those who live the Buddha way. The railings symbolize the ability to ward off evil. The bells indicate the power or ability to teach well. The canopy over the great carriage is for the ability to protect living beings. The rare and precious jewels are the many skillful means used by those who follow the Buddha way. The strings of precious stones are the four universal vows of the bodhisattva, while the garlands of flowers are the many special vows of bodhisattvas. The beautiful mats are a symbol of comfort and, therefore, of meditation and the calm of those who follow the Way. The rose-colored pillows stand for true wisdom. The white of the ox represents purity, especially the pure hearts of those who follow the Way. The handsomeness and pure skin symbolize health, and therefore a rich and lively wisdom. The power of the ox is a symbol of the power of ridding beings of their delusions. Walking with smooth steps signifies walking in the middle way, while walking with the speed of the wind means that those who follow the Way can quickly become awakened.

8. How this chapter came by its title, in Chinese 信解 *hsin chieh* (*shinge* in Japanese reading), and thus "faith and understanding" or possibly "faithful understanding" in English, is an interesting question. It's generally assumed to be a translation. The trouble with this is that the Sanskrit title *adhimukti* does not mean faith and understanding, but something more like disposition or attitude. It's a reference to the son's attitude toward his own life. So it seems that Kumarajiva, rather than translating, may have devised a new chapter title. Though it is used in a scattering of places throughout the sutra, the term does not appear at all in chapter 4 itself.

9. In Kumarajiva's version, though the title is literally "Medicinal Herbs Parable," in the chapter itself there is no parable having to do with medicinal herbs. In the text we have, there is a simile about a cloud, likened to the Buddha; rain, likened to Buddha-dharma; and a great variety of plants, likened to the variety of living beings. Medicinal herbs are

mentioned as being among the plants, but they do not play a significant role in the simile. Since this simile has long been called a "parable," and the Chinese term is broad enough to refer to both similes and parables, I have titled the chapter "Parable of the Plants." Sanskrit versions do have a parable about medicinal herbs. Somehow it was completely left out of Kumarajiva's translation, whether by accident or by design we do not know. A translation directly from Sanskrit of this parable can be found in Hurvitz, trans., *Scripture of the Lotus Blossom of the Fine Dharma*, pp. 110–19.

10. The seven buddhas of the past are normally thought to be Vipaśyin, Śikhin, Viśvabhū, Krakucchanda, Kanakamuni, Kāśyapa, and Śākyamuni, but here the text seems to indicate that Śākyamuni is the eighth.

11. Here an obvious mistake in the Chinese translation has been corrected. It says that both the bodhisattvas and Seen with Joy by All the Living Buddha will be assured of supreme awakening. Sanskrit versions have the Buddha assuring the bodhisattvas of their ultimate awakening, making much more sense.

12. While it is found in extant Sanskrit versions, this sentence does not appear in Kumarajiva's translation or in contemporary Chinese and Japanese versions. It is inserted here because it is needed to make clear who is speaking.

13. The incantations (dhāraṇī 陀羅尼) here and in chapter 28 have not been translated. As Leon Hurvitz says (*Scripture of the Lotus Blossom of the Fine Dharma*, p. 20n), "the meanings are frequently obscure, and the results would be pure guesswork." Obviously most of the words are Indic, some pure Sanskrit, but some seem to make no sense at all. They are highly valued for their sound, whether that be in Chinese, Japanese, or even Sanskrit. Here the Japanese reading of the sounds is based on what is provided in *KYOTEN: Sutra Readings, Extracts from the Lotus Sutra*, published by Rissho Kosei-kai of North America, 2008. Japanese denominations recite these incantations with many slight variations in pronunciation. The Sanskrit versions in these notes follow Hurvitz's rendering.

Glossaries

TWO GLOSSARIES are included here. The first is a list of proper names—names of buddhas, bodhisattvas, shravakas, places, buddha-lands, and so on. The second is a list of important terms found in the text.

The list of proper names is arranged alphabetically by the name used in the translation (in most cases, the names have been translated into English). This is followed by an indication of whether the name refers to a buddha, a bodhisattva, a place, and so on. A third column shows in which of the three sutras the name occurs. This is followed by Sanskrit versions of these names in Roman letters. But in the cases of both the Innumerable Meanings and the Universal Sage Sutras, since there are no existing Sanskrit versions, Sanskrit versions of names that do not also occur in the Lotus Sutra are not provided. In most cases it would be possible to translate from Chinese to Sanskrit by guessing what might have been translated into Chinese, but since we really don't know what the Sanskrit of these texts was, or even for certain whether they were translated from Sanskrit, it could be misleading to "invent" Sanskrit versions of the Chinese names. Following the Sanskrit versions of the names are Chinese-character versions, followed by Pinyin and Japanese pronunciations. While I have not attempted to be exhaustive in including variant versions of Chinese characters, in cases where different versions are quite commonly found, both are given here. Entries are often followed by explanatory notes.

The second glossary is similar to the first, except that rather than proper names a large selection of terms found in these three texts is provided, along with Sanskrit and Chinese versions with Pinyin and Japanese pronunciations and quite often notes on the meaning of the term. Since almost none of these terms are unique to the Lotus Sutra but can be found in various Buddhist texts, I have not indicated in which of the three translated sutras they occur. Though some translations of common Buddhist terms into English have become standard, a great deal of variation remains. This glossary makes it possible to a reader to see readily what Chinese and Sanskrit terms lie behind the English found in this translation. In some cases, alternative translations have been provided in the notes. Generally, I have not included alternative translations that I consider unreasonable or inappropriate.

In the Lotus Sutra and in Buddhism in general there are many lists, which no doubt were originally provided to assist in memorization. Very often in the Lotus Sutra such lists are only referred to, assuming perhaps that the reader will already know what the items are. In fact, however, in a great many cases one can find alternative sets of such terms. Usually it is impossible to know exactly which version is behind the reference in the Lotus Sutra. What I have provided here is a likely reference, but we cannot be certain that this is what the translators into Sanskrit or Chinese actually had in mind.

The Pinyin pronunciations have generously been provided by Charles Muller, founder, developer, and chief editor of the on-line Digital Dictionary of Buddhism. The Japanese pronunciations can be found in several Japanese-English Buddhist dictionaries.

Glossary of Proper Names

Legend

(DF) Sutra of the Lotus Flower of the Wonderful Dharma

(IM) Sutra of Innumerable Meanings

(US) Sutra of Meditation on the Dharma Practice of Universal Sage Bodhisattva

Name	Category	Sutra	Sanskrit	Chinese	Pinyin	Japanese
Above the Threefold World	bodhisattva	IM DF	Trailokyavikrāmin	越三界	Yuè sānjiè	Otsusangai
Abundant Treasures Also translated as "Many Treasures."	buddha	DF US	Prabhūtaratna	多宝/多寶	Duōbǎo	Tahō
Accumulated Jewels	bodhisattva	IM DF	Ratnākara	宝積/寶積	Bǎojī	Hōshaku
Accumulated Wisdom	prince	DF	Jñānākara	智積	Zhìjī	Chishaku
Accumulated Wisdom	bodhisattva	DF	Prajñākūṭa	智積	Zhìjī	Chishaku
Acyuta May be the same person as Chunda in the DF.	shravaka, monk	IM		阿閦陀	Āzhōutuó	Ashuda
Adorned	bodhisattva	IM		莊嚴/庄嚴	Zhuāngyán	Shōgon
Adorned with Great Treasures	eon	DF	Mahāratnapratimaṇḍitā	大宝莊嚴/大寶莊嚴	Dà bǎo zhuāngyán	Daihōshōgon
Adorned with Pure Light	buddha land	DF	Vairocanaraśmipratimaṇḍitā	淨光莊嚴/淨光莊嚴	Jìngguāng zhuāngyán	Jōkōshōgon
Adorned with Light	buddha land	DF	Vairocanaraśmipratimaṇḍitā	光明莊嚴/光明莊嚴	Guāngmíng zhuāngyán	Kōmyōshōgon
Adornment King	bodhisattva	DF	Vyūharāja	莊嚴王/庄嚴王	Zhuāngyán wáng	Shōgon-nō
Ajatashatru The king of Magadha, the most powerful kingdom in the region during the Buddha's time.	king	DF	Ajātaśatru	子阿闍世	Ziadushi	Ajase

Name	Type	Abbr.	Sanskrit	Chinese	Pinyin	Japanese
Ajnata-Kaundinya	shravaka, monk	IM DF	Ājñāta-Kauṇḍinya	阿若憍陳如	Āruò qiáochénrú	Anya-kyōjinnyo
A servant of Shakyamuni before he left home, and one of the original disciples.						
Akanishtha	heaven	DF	Akaniṣṭha	阿迦尼吒	Ājiānízhà	Akanita
The highest heaven of the world of form.						
Akshobhya	buddha	DF US	Akṣobhya	阿閦	Āchù	Ashuku
Mentioned in chapter 7 of the Lotus Sutra and in the Universal Sage Sutra, he became important in esoteric Buddhism, where he is one of five buddhas of the Diamond World. His pure land is in the East.						
Always Tranquil Light	buddha land	US		常寂光	Chángjìguāng	Jōshakkō
The home of Vairocana Buddha.						
Amida	buddha	DF	Amitāyas / Amitāba	阿彌陀	Āmítuó	Amida
Mentioned in chapters 7 and 23 of the Lotus Sutra, this buddha became the highest object of devotion in Pure Land Buddhism.						
Ananda	shravaka, monk	IM DF US	Ānanda	阿難	Ānán	Anan
A cousin of Shakyamuni and, as the Buddha's personal attendant, one of the ten disciples. It is reported that at the First Council he recited all of the sutras from memory and that the words "This is what I heard" at the beginning of sutras refer to Ananda.						
Anavatapta	dragon king	DF	Anavatapta	阿那婆達多	Ānàpódáduō	Anabadatta
Aniruddha	shravaka, monk, arhat	IM DF	Aniruddha	阿耨樓馱	Ānòulóutuó	Anuruda
A cousin of Shakyamuni and one of the ten disciples.						
Asita	seer	DF	Asita	阿私仙	Āsī xiān	Ashi-sen
The seer in chapter 12 who later became Devadatta.						
Attainer of Power to Persevere	bodhisattva	DF	Vīryabalavegaprāpta	得勤精進力	Dé qínjìng jìnlì	Tokugonshō-jinriki

Name	Category	Sutra	Sanskrit	Chinese	Pinyin	Japanese
Bakkula	shravaka, monk, arhat	DF	Bakkula	薄拘羅	Bójūluó	Hakura
Balin	asura king	DF	Balin	婆稚	Pózhì	Baji
Beautiful	centaur king	DF	Madhura	美	Měi	Mi
Beautiful Sound	centaur king	DF	Madhurasvara	美音	Měiyīn	Mion
Bestower of Freedom from Fear	bodhisattva	DF	abhayaṃdada	施無畏者	Shī wúwèi zhě	Se mui sha
Bhadrapala	bodhisattva	DF	Bhadrapāla	跋陀婆羅	Bátuópóluó	Batsudabara
Bharadvaja	buddha	DF	Bharadvāja	頗羅墮	Pōluóduò	Harada
Birthplace of Jewels	buddha land	DF	Ratnasaṃbhava	宝生/寶生	Bǎoshēng	Hōshō
Black Mountain	mountain	DF		黑山	Hēishān	Kokusan
Black Teeth	ogre	DF	Makuṭadantī	黑齒	Hēichǐ	Kokushi
Bold Almsgiver	bodhisattva	DF	Pradānaśūra	勇施	Yǒngshī	Yūze
Brahma	god	IM DF	Brahmā	梵	Fàn	Bon

An important Indian god adopted by Buddhism as a protector of the Dharma. In this sutra he is often said to be a king of heaven or the King of the Brahma Heaven, the heaven which is closest to the level of human beings. Since there are many worlds, there are many Brahma heavens and many Brahma kings.

Name	Category	Sutra	Sanskrit	Chinese	Pinyin	Japanese
Brahma Character	buddha	DF	Brahmadhvaja	梵相	Fànxiàng	Bonsō
Burning Light	bodhisattva	DF	Dīpaṃkara	然燈	Rándēng	Nentō

English	Category		Sanskrit	Chinese	Pinyin	Japanese
Burning Light	buddha	DF	Dīpaṃkara	然燈	Rándēng	Nentō
Chunda	shravaka, monk	DF	Cunda	周陀	Zhōutuó	Shuda
Cloud Freedom	buddha	DF	Megheśvaradīpa	雲自在	Yún zìzài	Unjizai
Cloud Freedom King	buddha	DF	Megheśvararāja	雲自在王	Yún zìzài wáng	Unjizai-ō
Constant Effort	bodhisattva	DF	Nityodyukta	常精進	Chángjīngjìn	Jōshōjin
Constantly Persevering	bodhisattva	IM		常精進	Chángjīngjìn	Jōshōjin
Constellation-King Flower Literally, perhaps, "Blessed by the King of Constellations."	bodhisattva	DF	Nakṣatra-rāja-saṃkusumitābhijña	宿王華	Sùwánghuā	Shukuōke
Courageous Giver	bodhisattva	DF	Pradānaśūra	勇施	Yǒngshī	Yuze
Courageous Power	bodhisattva	IM			Yǒngruìlì	Yueiriki
Crooked Teeth	ogre	DF	Kūṭadantī	曲齒	Qūchǐ	Kokushi
Deer Park Where the Buddha delivered his first sermon.	place	IM			Lùyěyuàn	Rokuya-on
Destroyer of All the World's Fear	buddha	DF	Savalokabhayacchambhita-tvavidhvaṃsanakara	壞一切世間怖畏	Ràng yīqiē shìjiān bùwèi	E-issai-seken-fui
Devadatta A cousin and rival of the Buddha, known outside of the Lotus Sutra as the epitome of evil. Infamous for trying to kill the Buddha.	monk	DF	Devadatta	提婆達多	Dípódáduō	Daibadatta
Dharma	chimera king	DF	Dharma	法	Fǎ	Hō

Name	Category	Sutra	Sanskrit	Chinese	Pinyin	Japanese
Dharma Flower Sutra Usually referred to in English as the Lotus Sutra.	sutra	DF		法華經	Fǎhuá jīng	Hokekyō
Dharma Intention	prince	DF	Dharmamati	法意	Fǎyì	Hōi
Dharma Radiance	buddha	DF	Dharmaprabhāsa	法明	Fǎmíng	Hōmyō
Diamond-holder A god or spirit who holds a vajra.	god	DF	Vajra-pāṇi	執金剛神	Shí jīngāng shén	Shūkongōshin
Diamond Mountain	mountain or mountain range	DF		金剛山	Jīngāng shān	Kongōsen
Displaying All Worlds	buddha land	DF	Sarvarūpasaṃdarśanā	現一切世間	Xiàn yīqiè shìjiān	Gen-issai-seken
Earth Holder	bodhisattva	DF	Dharaṇiṃdhara	持地	Chídì	Jiji
Earth Mountain	mountain			土山	Tǔshān	Dosan
Emptiness King	buddha	DF	Dharmagaganābhyudgatarāja	空王	Kōngwáng	Kūō
Eon of Sages The present age.	eon	DF	Bhadra-kalpa	賢劫	Xiánjié	Gengō
Ever Extinguished	buddha	DF	Nityaparinirvṛta	常滅	Chángmiè	Jōmetsu
Excellent in Great Penetrating Wisdom	buddha	DF	Mahābhijñājñānābhibhū	大通知勝	Dà tōngzhī shèng	Daitsuchishō

	Type	US	Sanskrit		Fāng děng	Hōdō
Expansive Teaching In the Universal Sage Sutra this appears to be an alternative name or description of Mahayana teachings.				方等		Hōdō
Fame Seeker	bodhisattva	DF	Yaśaskāma	求名	Qiúmíng	Gumyō
Famous Features	buddha	DF	Śaśiketu	名相	Míngxiàng	Myōsō
Ferocious Lion	bodhisattva	IM		師子威猛	Shīzǐwēiměng	Shishiimi-yōbuku
Firm Practice	bodhisattva	DF	Supratiṣṭhitacārita	安立行	Ānlì xíng	Anryūgyō
Flower Banner	bodhisattva	IM		華幢	Huāchuáng	Kedō
Flower Garland	sutra	IM US	Avataṃsaka	華嚴	Huayan	Kegon
Flower Light	buddha	DF	Padmaprabha	華光	Huāguāng	Kekō
Flower Light Banner	bodhisattva	IM		華光幢	Huāguāngchuáng	Kekodō
Flower Virtue	bodhisattva	DF	Padmaśrī	華德	Huādé	Ketoku
Flowery Feet Calmly Walking	buddha	DF	Padmavṛṣa-bhavikrāmin	華足安行	Huāzú ānxíng	Kesokuangyō
Flowery Teeth	ogre	DF	Puṣpadantī	華齒	Huāchǐ	Keshi
Fragrant Elephant	bodhisattva	IM		香象	Xiāngxiàng	Kōzō
Freedom	god	DF	Īśvara	自在	Zì zài	Jizai
Free from Decline	eon	DF	Vinirbhoga	離衰	Lishuāi	Risui

Name	Category	Sutra	Sanskrit	Chinese	Pinyin	Japanese
Free of Dirt	buddha land	DF	Viraja	離垢	Lígòu	Riku
Full of Firmness	bodhisattva	DF	Dhṛtipaaripūrṇa	堅滿	Jiānmǎn	Kenman
Full of Joy	eon	DF	Ratipūrṇa	喜滿	Xǐmǎn	Kiman
Full Moon	bodhisattva	DF	Pūrṇacandra	滿月	Mǎnyuè	Mangatsu
Ganges	river	IM DF	Gaṅgā	恆河	Hénghé	Gōga
Located in the northeast and flowing into the Bay of Bengal, the Ganges is the most sacred river in India.						
Gautami	nun	DF		憍曇彌	Gyodammi	Kyōdonmi
Another name for Mahaprajapati, the younger sister of Shakyamuni's mother who raised him after his mother died.						
Gavampati	shravaka, monk	DF	Gavāṃpati	憍梵波提	Qiáofànbōtí	Kyōbon-hadai
Gaya	place	DF	Gayā	伽耶城	Jiāyé chéng	Gayajō
Now a city in the state of Bihar, in the Buddha's time it was in the state of Magadha. About ten miles south of the city of Gaya is the place where the Buddha became awakened. It is now a small city known as Bodhgaya. This place is sometimes referred to in Buddhist texts simply as Gayā.						
Gaya-Kashyapa	arhat	IM DF	Gayā-Kāśyapa	伽耶迦葉	Qiéyé jiāshě	Gaya-kashō
The younger brother of Uruvilva-Kashyapa and Nadi-Kashyapa.						
Good Intention	prince	DF	Sumati	善意	Shànyì	Zenni
Good Treasury	bodhisattva	DF	Śrīgarbha	德藏	Dézàng	Tokuzō
Good Virtue	buddha	US		善德	Shàndé	Zentoku
Great Achievement	buddha land	DF	Mahāsaṃbhavā	大成	Dàchéng	Daijō

English	Type	Source	Sanskrit	Chinese	Pinyin	Japanese
Great Body	griffin king	DF	Mahākāya	大身	Dàshēn	Daishin
Great Brahma Bright Radiance	god	DF	Mahā-Jyotiṣprabha	光明大梵	Guāngmíng dàfàn	Kōmyō daibon
Great Brahma Shikhin	god	DF	Mahā-Śikhin	尸棄大梵	Shīqì dàfàn	Shiki daibon
Great Compassion	brahma king	DF	Adhimātrakāruṇika	大悲	Dàbēi	Daihi
Great Dharma	chimera king	DF	Mahādharma	大法	Dàfǎ	Daihō
Great Delight in Preaching	bodhisattva	DF	Mahā-pratibhāna	大樂說	Dàlèshuō	Daigyōsetsu
Great Dignity and Virtue	griffin king	DF	Mahātejas	大威德	Dà wēidé	Daiitoku
Great Features	eon	DF	Mahārūpa	大相	Dàxiàng	Daisō
Great Forest Monastery		US		大林精舍	Dàlín jīngshè	Dairinshō
Great Fragrant Elephant	bodhisattva	IM		大香象	Dàxiāngxiàng	Daiōzō
Great Freedom A name of the Indian god Shiva.	god	DF	Maheśvara	大自在天	Dàzìzài-tiān	Daijizai-ten
Great Fullness	griffin king	DF	Mahāpūrṇa	大滿	Dàmǎn	Daiman
Great High King	eon	DF	Abhyudgatarāja	大高王	Dàgāowáng	Daikō-ō
Great Iron Circle Mountains	mountain range	DF	Mahācakravāḍa	大鐵圍山/大鐵圍山	Tiěwéishān	Daitetchisen
Great Light	buddha land	DF	Vistīrṇarvatī	大光	Dàguāng	Daikō
Great Meru	mountain	DF		摩訶彌樓山	Móhēmílúshān	Makamirosan

Name	Category	Sutra	Sanskrit	Chinese	Pinyin	Japanese
Great Power	bodhisattva	DF	Mahāvikrāmin	大力	Dàlì	Dairiki
Great Power Obtained	bodhisattva	IM		大勢至	Dàshìzhì	Daiseishi
Great Strength	bodhisattva	DF	Mahāsthāmaprāpta	得大勢	Dédàshì	Tokudaisei
Great Vehicle	division of Buddhism	IM DF US	Mahāyāna	大乘	Dàshéng	Daijō
The way that is capable of leading everyone to supreme awakening, to being a buddha, distinguished in the Lotus Sutra from the small or lesser vehicle.						
Great Wisdom Sutra	sutra	IM		摩訶般若	Móhēbōrě	Makahanya
Guidance	bodhisattva	DF	Susārthavāha	導師	Dǎoshī	Dōshi
Having Intention	prince	DF	Mati	有意	Yǒuyì	Ui
Having Ten Million Shining Characteristics	buddha	DF	Raśmiśatasahasra-paripūrṇadhvaja	具足千萬光相	Jùzú qiānwàn guāngxiàng	Gusoku-senmankōsō
Heaven's Way	buddha land	DF	Devasopāna	天道	Tiāndào	Tendō
Heavenly King	buddha	DF	Devarāja	天王	Tiānwáng	Temō
Heaven of the thirty-three	heaven	DF	Trāyastriṃśá	切利天	Dāolìtiān	Tōriten
The second of the heavens of this world, the world of desire and the home of Indra.						
Holy Eagle Peak	place	IM DF US	Gṛdhrakūṭa	耆闍崛	Qíshéjué	Gishakusen
Sometimes translated as "Vulture Peak" or "Divine Vulture Peak." Also translated into Chinese as 靈鷲山.						

Name / Description	Category	Source	Sanskrit	Chinese	Pinyin	Japanese
Honorable Universal Fortune — Another name for Universal Sage.	bodhisattva	US		尊者遍吉	Zūnzhěbiànjí	Sonjahenkitsu
Immeasurable Power	bodhisattva	DF	Anantavikrāmin	無量力	Wúliánglì	Muryōriki
Imperial Character	buddha	DF	Indradhvaja	帝相	Dìxiàng	Taisō
Increasing Intention	prince	DF	Viśeṣamati	增意	Zēngyì	Zōi
Indra / Indra Devendra — Sometimes called "Shakra," he is a very important god in the Vedas.	god	DF	Śakra Devānām Indra	釋提桓因	Shì tíhuányīn	Shakudaikannin
Inexhaustible Mind	bodhisattva	DF	Akṣayamati	無盡意	Wújìnyì	Mujinmi
Infinite Intention	prince	DF	Anantamati	無量意	Wúliáng yì	Muryōi
Insatiable	ogre	DF	Acalā	無厭足	Wúyànzú	Muenzoku
Intent on Superior Practice	bodhisattva	DF	Viśiṣṭacāritra	上行意	Shàngxíng yì	Jōgyōi
Iron Circle Mountains / Lesser Iron Circle Mountains	mountain range	DF	Cakravāḍa	鉄圍山/ 小鐵圍山	Tiěwéishān/ Xiǎotiěwéishān	Tecchi-sen/ Shōtecchi-sen
Jambudvipa — Literally "mango island," Jambudvipa is a mythical triangular shaped continent to the south of Mt. Sumeru. It is said to be populated with ordinary suffering people and is, therefore, the place in which Buddhism spreads. At times it appears to signify the Indian subcontinent, at other times this world in general.	place	DF US	Jambudvīpa	一閻浮提	Yīyánfútí	Ichimembudai
Jambunada gold — Apparently gold found in the river Jambu (mango) which flows through Jambudvipa.		DF	Jāmbūnada-kan	閻浮檀金	Yánfútán jīn	Embudan-gon
Jambunada Golden Light	buddha	DF	Jāmbūnada-kanaka	閻浮那提金光	Yánfúnàdì jīnguāng	Embunadai-konkō

Name	Category	Sutra	Sanskrit	Chinese	Pinyin	Japanese
Jeweled King of Superior Dignity and Virtue	buddha	DF	Jāmbūnada-prabhāsa	宝威德上王/寶威德上王	Bǎowēidéshàng wáng	Hō-itoku-jō-ō
Jeweled Moon	bodhisattva	DF	Ratnatejobhyudgatarāja	宝月/寶月	Bǎoyuè	Hōgatsu
Jeweled Palm	bodhisattva	DF	Ratnacandra	宝掌/寶掌	Bǎozhǎng	Hōshō
Jewel Light	god	DF	Ratnapāṇi	宝光/寶光	Bǎoguāng	Hōkō
Jewel Sign	buddha	DF	Ratnaprabha	宝相/寶相	Bǎoxiàng	Hōsō
Kalodayin	arhat	DF	Ratnaketu	迦留陀夷	Jiāliútuóyí	Karudai
Kapphina	shravaka, monk, arhat	IM DF	Kalodayin	劫賓那	Jiébīnnà	Kōhinna
Kaundinya	shravaka, monk	DF	Kapphiṇa	憍陳如	Qiáochénrú	Kyōjinnyo
Kharaskandha	asura king	DF	Kauṇḍinya	佉羅騫馱	Qūluóqiāntuó	Karakenda
King Incantation Freedom	bodhisattva	IM	Kharaskandha	陀羅尼自在王	Tuóluónízìzài wáng	Daranijizai-ō
Kingdom of Wonderful Joy — Home of Akshobhya Buddha	buddha land	US		妙喜國	Miàoxǐguó	Myōji koku
King Mara — See Mara.		DF	Māra-rāja	魔王	Mówáng	Ma-ō
King of Light and Master of Clouds	buddha	DF	Meghasvara-rāja	雲自在燈王	Yúnzìzàidēng wáng	Unjizaitō-ō

English	Category	DF/IM	Sanskrit	Chinese	Pinyin	Japanese
King of the Sound of Thunder in the Clouds	buddha	DF	Meghadundubhisvara-rāja	雲雷音王	Yúnléiyīn wáng	Unraion-nō
King of the Wisdom of Mountains and Seas Who Is Unlimited in Power	buddha	DF	Sāgaravaradharabuddhi-vikrīḍitābhijña	山海慧自在通王	Shānhǎihuì zìzài tōng wáng	Sengaie-jizaitsū-ō
Kunti	ogre	DF	Kuntī	皋諦	Gāodì	Kōtai
Lamba	ogre	DF	Lambā	藍婆	Lánpó	Ranba
Land of Joy	buddha land	DF	Abhiratir lokadhātuh	歡喜國	Huānxǐ guó	Kanjikoku
Leader	bodhisattva	IM		導首	Dǎoshǒu	Dōshu
Leader in Valuable Signs	bodhisattva	IM		宝印首/寶印首	Bǎoyìnshǒu	Hōinshu
Light Sound	heaven	DF	Ābhāsvara	光音	Guāngyīn	Kō-on
Lion at Play in the World	bodhisattva	IM		師子遊戲世	Shīzǐyóuxì sh	Shishiyukese
Lion Moon	nun	DF	Simhacandrā	師子月	Shīzǐyuè	Shishigatsu
Lion's Character	buddha	DF	Simhadhvaja	師子相	Shīzǐxiàng	Shishisō
Lion's Perseverance	bodhisattva	IM		師子精進	Shīzǐjīngjìn	Shishishōjin
Lion's Powerful Quickness	bodhisattva	DF	Simhavikrīḍita	師子奮迅	Shīzǐ fènxùn	Shishifunjin
Lion's Voice	buddha	DF	Simhaghoṣa	師子音	Shīzǐyīn	Shishion
Lion's Roar King	bodhisattva	IM		師子吼王	Shīzǐhǒuwáng	Shishiku-ō

Name	Category	Sutra	Sanskrit	Chinese	Pinyin	Japanese
Lord of Medicine	bodhisattva	IM DF	Bhaiṣajyarājasamudgat	藥上	Yàoshàng	Yakujō
Magnificently Adorned	bodhisattva	IM DF	Mahāvyūha	大莊嚴/大莊嚴	Dàzhuāngyán	Daishōgon
Magnificently Adorned	eon	DF	Mahāvyūha	大莊嚴/大莊嚴	Dàzhuāngyán	Daishōgon
Maha-Kashyapa	shravaka, monk	IM DF US	Mahā-Kāśyapa	摩訶迦葉	Móhē jiāyè	Maka-kashō
Maha-Katyayana	shravaka, monk	IM DF	Mahā-Kātyāyana	摩訶迦旃延	Móhē jiāzhānyán	Maka-kasennen
Maha-Kausthila	shravaka, monk	DF	Mahā-Kauṣṭhila	摩訶拘絺羅	Móhē jūchīluó	Maka-kuchira
Maha-Maudgalyayana	shravaka, monk	IM DF	Mahā-Maudgalyāyana	大目犍連	Dà Mùqiánlián	Daimokkenren

One of the ten great disciples of the Buddha. Often "maha" is not used.

Name	Category	Sutra	Sanskrit	Chinese	Pinyin	Japanese
Mahaprajapati	nun	DF	Mahāprajāpatī	摩訶波闍波提	Móhē bōshébōtí	Makahajahadai

Also known as "Gautami." The younger sister of Shakyamuni's mother, who died shortly after his birth. Mahaprajapati raised the Buddha from infancy.

Name	Category	Sutra	Sanskrit	Chinese	Pinyin	Japanese
Maitrayani		IM DF	Maitrāyaṇī	彌多羅尼	Míduōluóní	Mitrani

Mother of Purna.

Name	Category	Sutra	Sanskrit	Chinese	Pinyin	Japanese
Maitreya	bodhisattva	IM DF US	Maitreya	彌勒	Mílè	Miroku

The bodhisattva who, on most accounts, is now residing in his Tushita Heaven and is to become the next buddha. He is also called "Ajita."

Name	Category	Sutra	Sanskrit	Chinese	Pinyin	Japanese
Majestic Voice King	buddha	DF	Bhīṣmagarjitasvararāja	威音王	Wēiyīn wáng	Ionnō
Manasvin	dragon king	DF	Manasvin	摩那斯	Mónàsī	Manashi
Manjushri	bodhisattva	IM DF US	Mañjuśrī	文殊師利	Wénshūshīlì	Monjushiri

A bodhisattva known for great wisdom due to extensive experience, Manjushri plays a major role in the Lotus Sutra.

English	Category	Sources	Sanskrit	Chinese	Pinyin	Japanese
Marks of Shining Adornment	bodhisattva	DF	Vairocanaraśmiprati-maṇḍitadhvajarāja	光照莊嚴相/光照莊嚴相	Guāngzhào zhuāngyán xiàng	Kōshō-shōgonsō
Maudgalyayana						
See Maha-Maudgalyayana.						
Medicine King	bodhisattva	IM DF US	Bhaiṣajyarāja	藥王	Yàowáng	Yakuō
Medicine Lord	bodhisattva	US		藥上	Yàoshàng	Yakujō
Meru	mountain	DF		彌樓山	Mílóushān	Mirosan
Sometimes taken to be a short version of "Sumeru" but apparently understood in this text to be a different mountain.						
Mind Pleasing	buddha land	DF	Manobhirāma	意樂	Yìyào	Iraku
Moon Light	bodhisattva	DF	Ratnaprabha	月光	Yuèguāng	Gakkō
Mother of Demon Children	ogre	DF	Hāritī	訶利帝	Hēlìdì	Hariti
Also translated into Chinese as 鬼子母神 and 鬼子母.						
Much Hair	ogre	DF	Keśinī	多髮	Duōfà	Tahotsu
Nadi-Kashyapa	shravaka, monk, arhat	IM DF	Nadī-Kāśyapa	那堤迦葉	Nàdī Jiāyè	Nadai-kashō
Nanda	dragon king	DF	Nanda	難陀	Nántuó	Nanda
Nanda	shravaka, monk	DF	Nanda	難陀	Nántuó	Nanda
Narayana	god	DF	Nārāyaṇa	那羅延	Náluóyán	Naraen
One of the names of the Indian god Vishnu.						

NAME	CATEGORY	SUTRA	SANSKRIT	CHINESE	PINYIN	JAPANESE
Necklace Holder	ogre	DF	Mālādhārī	持瓔珞	Chíyīngluò	Jiyōraku
Never Disrespectful The Sanskrit term means "always despised."	bodhisattva	DF	Sadāparibhūta	常不輕/常不輕	Cháng Bùqīng	Jōfukyō
Never Lowered Victory Banner	buddha land	DF	Anavanāmitavaijayantī	常立勝幡	Chánglì Shèngfān	Jōrisshōban
Never Resting	bodhisattva	DF	Anikṣipadhura	不休息	Bùxiūxí	Fukusoku
One Who Walks on Flowers of the Seven Treasures	buddha	DF	Saptaratnapadma-vikrāntagāmin	蹈七宝華/蹈七寶華	Dàoqībǎohuā	Tōshippōke
Pilindavatsa	shravaka, monk	DF	Pilindavatsa	畢陵伽婆蹉	Bìlíngqié pócuō	Hitsuryōgabasha
Pleasant	centaur king	DF	Manojña	樂	Lè	Gaku
Pleasant Sound	centaur king	DF	Manojñasvara	樂音	Lèyīn	Gakuon
Possessing Jewels	eon	DF	Ratnāvabhāsa	有宝/有寶	Yǒubǎo	Uhō
Precious Intention	prince	DF	Ratnamati	宝意/寶意	Bǎoyì	Hōi
Pure and Bright Excellence of Sun and Moon	buddha	DF	Candrasūryavimalaprabhāśrī	日月淨明德	Rìyuè jìngmíng dé	Nichigatsu-jōmyōtoku
Pure Body	buddha	DF	Vimalanetra	淨身	Jìngshēn	Jōshin
Pure Eyes	prince	DF	Vimalanetra	淨眼	Jìngyǎn	Jōgen
Pure Practice	bodhisattva	DF	Viśuddhacāritra	淨行	Jìngxíng	Jōgyō

English	Category	Sanskrit	Code	Chinese	Pinyin	Japanese
Pure Treasury	prince	Vimalagarbha	DF	淨藏	Jìngzàng	Jōzō
Pure Virtue	queen	Vimaladattā	DF	淨德	Jìngdé	Jōtoku
Pure Virtue	king	Vimaladatta	DF	淨德王	Jìngdé Wáng	Jōtoku-ō
Pure Wonder	buddha land		US	淨妙國土	Jìngmiàoguótǔ	Jōmyō kokudo
Purna son of Maitrayani — One of the ten great disciples.	shravaka, monk	Pūrṇa Maitrāyaṇīputrah	IM DF	富樓那彌多羅尼子	Fùlóunà míduōluónízǐ	Furuna Mitranishi
Radiance	buddha	Raśmiprabhāsa	DF	光明	Guāngmíng	Kōmyō
Radiant Virtue	buddha land	Avaprabhāsaprāptā	DF	光德	Guāngdé	Kōtoku
Rahu	asura king	Rāhu	DF	羅睺	Luóhuó	Rago
Rahula — The son of Shakyamuni, who became one of the ten disciples.	shravaka, monk	Rāhula	IM DF	羅睺羅	Luóhuóluó	Ragora
Rajagriha — Literally King's House. The capital of the northeast Indian kingdom of Magadha during the Buddha's time.	place	Rājagṛha	IM DF	王舍	Wángshè	Ōsha
Rare Moon	god	Candra	DF	名月	Míngyuè	Myōgatsu
Realm Upholder — One of the four kings of heaven.	king of heaven	Dhṛtarāṣṭra	DF	持國	Chíguó	Jikoku
Regarder of the Cries of the World	bodhisattva	Avalokiteśvara	IM DF	觀世音	Guānshìyīn	Kanzeon

In Chinese pronunciation often shortened to Guanyin or Kuanyin and in Japanese to Kannon. Literally, the Chinese/Japanese name means "perceiver of the world's sounds." Also translated as World-Voice-Perceiver, Perceiver of the World's Sounds, He Who Observes the Sounds of the World, and so on.

Name	Category	Sutra	Sanskrit	Chinese	Pinyin	Japanese
Resounding Intention	prince	DF	Ghoṣamati	響意	Xiǎngyì	Kōi
Revata	shravaka, monk, arhat	IM DF	Revata	離婆多	Líbōduō	Rihata
Sagara The father of the dragon princess in chapter 12.	dragon king	DF	Sāgara	娑伽羅	Suōqiéluó	Shakara
Saha This world, which is Shakyamuni's buddha land.	buddha land	DF	Sahā	娑婆	Suō pó	Shaba
Sal-Tree King	buddha	DF	Śalendrarāja	娑羅樹王	Suōluóshùwáng	Sharaju-ō
Sandalwood Virtue	buddha	US		栴檀德	Zhān tán dé	Sendantoku
Saving All Worlds from Suffering	buddha	DF	Sarvalokadhātūpadra-vodvegapratyuttīrṇa	度一切世間苦惱	Dùyīqiè shìjiān kūnǎo	Do-issai-seken kunō
Savior of All	brahma king	DF	Sarvasattvatrātar	救一切	Jiùyīqiè	Ku-issai
Seen with Joy	eon	DF	Priyadarśana	喜見	Xǐjiàn	Kiken
Seen with Joy by All the Living	bodhisattva	DF	Sarvasattvapriyadarśana	一切眾生憙見	Yīqiè zhòngshēng xǐjiàn	Issai-shujō-kiken
Shakyamuni Literally, "the sage of the Shakyas," the Shakyas being a clan.	buddha	IM DF US	Śākyamuni	釋迦牟尼	Shìjiāmóuní	Shakamuni
Shariputra In the Lotus Sutra Shariputra is the Buddha's leading disciple. Renowned for being the greatest in wisdom among the disciples, he converses with the Buddha in many sutras.	shravaka, monk	IM DF	Śāriputra	舍利弗	Shèlìfú	Sharihotsu

English	Category	Abbr.	Sanskrit	Chinese	Pinyin	Japanese
Shikhin One of the names of Brahma.	brahma king	DF	Śikhin	尸棄	Shīqì	Shiki
Snatcher of the Spirits of all the Living	ogre	DF	Sarvasattvojohārī	奪一切衆生精氣	Duó yīqiè zhòngshēng jīngqì	Datsu-issai-shujō-shōke
Space Dweller	buddha	DF	Ākāśapratiṣṭhita	虛空住	Xūkōngzhù	Kokūjū
Subhuti One of the Buddha's ten major disciples.	shravaka, monk	IM DF	Subhūti	須菩提	Xūpútí	Shubodai
Sumeru The highest mountain, occupying the center of a world.	mountain	DF	Sumeru	須彌山	Xūmí shān	Shumi-sen
Sumeru Form	buddha	DF	Merukalpa	須彌相	Xūmíxiàng	Shumisō
Sumeru Peak	buddha	DF	Sumerukūṭa	須彌頂	Xūmí dǐng	Shumichō
Sun and Moon Light	buddha	DF	Candrasūryapradīpa	日月燈明	Rìyuèdēngmíng	Nichigatsutōmyō
Sundarananda	shravaka, monk	DF	Sundarananda	孫陀羅難陀	Sūntuóluónántuó	Sondarananda
Superior Medicine	bodhisattva	DF	Bhaiṣajyasamudgata	藥上	Yàoshàng	Yakujō
Superior Practice	bodhisattva	DF	Viśiṣṭacāritra	上行	Shàngxíng	Jōgyō
Svagata	shravaka, monk, arhat	IM DF	Svāgata	莎伽陀	Suōqiétuó	Shakada
Takshaka	dragon king	DF	Takṣaka	德叉迦	Déchājiā	Tokushaka

Name	Category	Sutra	Sanskrit	Chinese	Pinyin	Japanese
Tamalapatra Sandalwood Fragrance	buddha	DF	Tamālapatracandanagandha	多摩羅跋栴檀香	Duōmóluóbá zhāntánxiāng	Tamarabatsu-sendankō
Tamalapatra Spiritually Powerful Sandal Fragrance	buddha	DF	Tamālapatracandanagandhā-bhijña	多摩羅跋栴檀香神通	Duōmóluóbá zhāntánxiāng shéntōng	Tamarabatsu-sendankō-jinzū
Ten Jewels Mountains	mountains	DF		十宝山 / 十寶山	Shíbǎoshān	Jippōsen
Thinking of Buddha	layman	DF	Sugatacetanā	思佛	Sīfó	Shibutsu
Thus Willed	griffin king	DF	Maharddhiprāpta	如意	Rúyì	Nyoi
Trayastrimsha Another name for the Heaven of the Thirty-three Gods, home of Indra.	heaven	DF	Trāyastriṃśa	切利天	Daolì tiān	Tōriten
Treasure Purity	buddha land	DF	Ratnaviśuddhā	宝浄/寶浄	Bǎojìng	Hōjō
Treasure Radiance	eon	DF	Ratnāvabhāsa	宝明/寶明	Bǎomíng	Hōmyō
Treasury of Freedom from Anxiety	bodhisattva	IM		無憂蔵	Wúyōuzàng	Muuzō
Treasury of Great Majesty	bodhisattva	IM		大威徳蔵	Dà wēidé zàng	Daiitokuzō
Treasury of Great Oration	bodhisattva	IM		大辯蔵	Dàbiàn zàng	Daibenzō
Tushita The fourth of the heavens of this world of desire, where Maitreya lives until he comes to this world as its next buddha.	heaven	DF	Tuṣita	兜率天	Dōushuò tiān	Tosotsu-ten

English	Role	Code	Sanskrit	Chinese	Pinyin	Japanese
Udayin	arhat	DF	Udayin	優陀夷	Yōutuóyí	Udai
Undoubting Intention	prince	DF	Vimatisamudghātin	除疑意	Chúyíyì	Jogii
Universal Fragrance	god	DF	Samantagandha	普香	Pǔxiāng	Fukō
Universal Light	buddha	DF	Samantaprabhāsa	普明	Pǔmíng	Fumyō
Universal Purity	heaven	DF	Śubha-kṛtsna	遍淨	Biànjìng	Henjō
Universal Sage	bodhisattva	DF US	Samantabhadra	普賢	Pǔxián	Fugen

Also translated as Universal Worthy, Universally Worthy, Universal Virtue, and so on. I have used "Sage" to attempt to capture the idea that he is both virtuous and wise. He symbolizes religious practice, putting wisdom and compassion into everyday life.

English	Role	Code	Sanskrit	Chinese	Pinyin	Japanese
Unlimited Practice	bodhisattva	DF	Anantacāritra	無邊行	Wúbiānxíng	Muhengyō
Upali	shravaka, monk	IM		優婆離	Yōupólí	Ubari
Upananda	shravaka, monk	IM	Upananda	優婆難陀	Yōupónántuó	Ubananda
Upananda	dragon king	DF	Upananda	跋難陀	Bánántuó	Batsunanda
Upholding the Dharma	chimera king	DF	Dharmadhara	持法	Chífǎ	Jihō
Uruvilva-Kashyapa	shravaka, monk, arhat	IM DF	Uruvilvā-Kāśyapa	優樓頻螺迦葉	Yōulóupínluójiāshě	Urubinra-kashō
Utpalaka	dragon king	DF	Utpalaka	優鉢羅	Yōubōluó	Uhatsura
Vaidehi	queen	DF	Vaidehī	韋提希	Wéitíxī	Idaike

The wife of King Bimbisāra of Magadha and mother of Ajatashatru.

Name	Category	Sutra	Sanskrit	Chinese	Pinyin	Japanese
Vairocana	buddha	US		毘盧蔗那	Pílúzhènà	Biroshana
Said to be another name for Shakyamuni.						
Vaisali	place	US		毘舍離國	Píshèlí guó	Bishari koku
Vaishravana	king of heaven	DF	Vaiśravaṇa	毘沙門天	Píshāmén tiān	Bishamon-ten
One of the four kings of heaven. Also translated into Chinese as 多聞天.						
Vakkula	shravaka, monk	IM		薄拘羅	Bójùluó	Hakura
Valuable Cane	bodhisattva	IM		宝杖/質杖	Bǎozhàng	Hōjō
Varanasi	place	DF	Vārāṇasī	波羅㮈	Bōluónài	Haranai
The present day city of Benares [Varanasi], once a small kingdom west of Magadha. The site of Deer Park, where the Buddha preached his first sermon.						
Vasuki	dragon king	DF	Vāsuki	和修吉	Héxiūjí	Washūkitsu
Vemacitrin	asura king	DF	Vemacitrin	毘摩質多羅	Pímózhíduōluó	Bimashittara
Vilamba	ogre	DF	Vilambā	毘嵐婆	Pílánpó	Biranba
Vimabhara	bodhisattva	IM		毘摩羅	Pímóluó	Bimabāra
This bodhisattva is unknown outside of this text.						
Well Purified	buddha land	DF	Suviśuddhā	善淨	Shànjìng	Zenjō
Well Made	buddha land	DF	Saṃbhavā	好成	Hǎochéng	Kōjō

English	Type	Code	Sanskrit	Chinese	Pinyin	Japanese
Wisdom Blessed by the King of Constellations Called the Sound of Thunder in the Clouds	buddha	DF	Jaladharagarjitaghoṣa-susvaranakṣatrarājasaṃkusumitābhijña	雲雷音宿王華智	Yúnléiyīnsù wáng huázhì	Unrai-onshuku-ōkechi
Wisdom King of the Pure Flower Constellation Literally, perhaps, "Knowledge from the King of Constellations, Pure Flower."	buddha	DF	Kamaladalavimalana-kṣatrarājasaṃkusumitābhijña	淨華宿王智	Jìnghuāsù wáng zhì	Jōkeshukuōchi
Wonderfully Adorned	king	DF	Śubhavyūha-rāja	妙莊嚴王/妙莊嚴王	Miàozhuāngyán wáng	Myōshōgon-ō
Wonderful Dharma	brahma king	DF	Sudharma	妙法	Miàofǎ	Myōhō
Wonderful Dharma	chimera king	DF	Sudharma	妙法	Miàofǎ	Myōhō
Wonderful Joy See Kingdom of Wonderful Joy	buddha land	US				
Wonderful Light	bodhisattva	DF	Varaprabha	妙光	Miàoguāng	Myōkō
Wonderful Voice	bodhisattva	DF	Gadgadasvara	妙音	Miàoyīn	Myō-on
World-Filling Wonderful Sound	eon	DF	Manojñaśabdābhigarjita	妙音徧滿	Miào yīn piānmǎn	Myō-on-hem man
Yashodhara Wife of Shakyamuni and mother of Rahula. She was one of the first Buddhist nuns.	nun	DF	Yaśodharā	耶輸陀羅	Yéshūtuóluó	Yashutara

Glossary of Terms

Term	Sanskrit	Chinese	Pinyin	Japanese
afflictions Also understood to be passions or desires.	kleśa	煩惱	fánnǎo	bonnō
aggregates See five constituent aggregates.				
arhat See worthy of offerings.				
ascetic practices Probably refers to the twelve ascetic practices followed by Indian monks: living in forests or fields, living only on offerings, begging from house to house without discrimination, eating only at one place, eating from only one bowl, not eating after noon, wearing only discarded clothes, wearing only three robes, living in a cemetery, living at the foot of a tree, living in the open air, and sleeping in a sitting position.	dhūta	頭陀	tóutuó	zuda
aspiration for awakening The aspiration to become a buddha.	bodhicitta	菩提心	pútí xīn	bodaishin
assurance of becoming a buddha Sometimes translated as "prediction" or "prophecy," in the Dharma Flower Sutra it certainly is not a prediction in the sense in which weather or the outcome of a game is predicted, and it is not threats spoken on behalf of God as in Old Testament prophecy. It is an assurance of something that will take place eventually.	vyākaraṇa	授記/受記	shòujì	juki
asura A kind of angry godlike being. One of the six states of existence and the ten realms.	asura	阿修羅	āxiūluó	ashura
bimba fruit Fruit of the bimba tree.	bimba	頻婆果	pínpó guǒ	binbaka
bodhi tree The term used for the tree under which the Buddha became awakened.	bodhi dhruma / bodhi vṛkṣa	菩提樹	pútí shù	bodaiju

bodhisattva — *bodhisattva* — 菩薩 — púsà — bosatsu
One who is becoming a buddha, mainly by being a compassionate teacher of Buddha-dharma, and is characterized by having the wisdom to know that one can be saved only by saving others.

brahma king — *brahmadevarāja* — 梵天王 — fàntiān wáng — bonten-ō
A ruler of the Brahma heaven, the lowest of the four heavens above this world of desire in the world of form.

brahman — *brāhman* — 婆羅門 — póluómén — baramon
The clerical and highest caste in the Indian caste system. Also spelled "brahmin."

buddha — *buddha* — 佛 — fó — butsu/hotoke
One who has become fully and completely awakened. An abbreviation of "butsuda" (佛陀), which does not occur in the Lotus Sutra.

buddha-land — *buddha-kṣetra* — 佛土 — fótǔ — butsudo
The realm or home of a buddha.

candala — *caṇḍāla* — 旃陀羅 — zhāntuóluó — sendara
A subgroup of the lowest caste, who handled corpses, slaughtered animals, and did other work associated with death and killing.

centaur — *gandharva* — 乾闥婆 — gāntàpó — kendatsuba
One of the eight mythical beings that protect Buddhism and play musical instruments.

child/children of the Buddha — *buddha-putra* — 佛子 — fózǐ — busshi
In the Dharma Flower Sutra, this term probably always refers to bodhisattvas, as they are created by the Buddha's teachings.

chimera — *kiṃnara* — 緊那羅 — jǐnnàluó — kinnara
One of the eight mythical beings that protect Buddhism, they are skillful in singing and dancing.

complete nirvana — *parinirvāṇa* — 般涅槃 — bān nièpán — hatsunehan
A buddha's death. Also called "nirvana without residue."

Term	Sanskrit	Chinese	Pinyin	Japanese
comprehensive wisdom The wisdom of a buddha, involving knowledge of everything.	vastu-jñāna	一切智	yīqiè zhì	issai-chi
concentration Meditative absorption.	samādhi	定／三昧	dìng/sān mèi	jō/sammai
the devil / devils An evil demon, sometimes rendered in English by the proper name "Mara."	māra	魔	mó	ma
dharma Sometimes translated as "Law," this term has at least four senses: (a) things, all entities, objects of perception or phenomena, (b) Buddhist teaching—words and practices, (c) the truth that is taught, (d) the reality that the truth reveals, that which enables and sustains things in accord with interdependence. In this translation, when it is clear that (a) is meant, "things" is used as the translation.	dharma	法	fǎ	hō
dharma wheel The wheel of the Dharma refers to teaching the Dharma, as such teachings "roll" from one person to another.	dharma cakra	法輪	fǎlún	hōrin
diamond pounder An abbreviation of 金剛杵, a ritual object in esoteric Buddhism symbolizing hardness.	vajra-vara	金剛	jīngāng	kongō
divine faculties See six powers.	abhijñā	神通	shéntōng	jinzū
divine powers Unusual, charismatic power.	ṛddhi-prātihārya	神力	shénlì	jinriki
dragon The Chinese equivalent of the naga, a mythical sea serpent. Not having nagas among their own mythical creatures, Chinese translators turned them into Chinese dragons.	nāga	竜	lóng	ryū

eightfold holy path āryāṣṭāngo mārga/ārya mārga 八聖道/八正道 bā shèngdào/bā zhèngdào hasshōdō

Though we can assume that it is the fourth of the four truths, the eightfold path is not actually mentioned in the Dharma Flower Sutra. It is included here only for reference. The eight parts of the path are right views or understanding, right thinking, right speech, right action, right way of life, right effort, right remembering, and right concentration.

eight (kinds of) guardians of Buddhism aṣṭa-gatyaḥ 八部 bābù hachibu

Gods, dragons, satyrs, centaurs, asuras, griffins, chimeras, and pythons.

eight kinds of liberation aṣṭā-vimokṣa 八解脱 bā jiětuō hachi gedatsu

One version of the eight kinds of liberation or emancipation is liberation from (1) the view that the body is pure, (2) the view that the world is pure, (3) illusions, (4) the view that matter exists, (5) the view that consciousness is limited, (6) the view that things have their own properties, (7) the view that thought exists or thought does not exist, and (8) the view that mentality exists. Another version is liberation from (1) lust for things, (2) external things, (3) illusions, (4) limitations of space, (5) limitations of consciousness, (6) views of substantiality, (7) limitations of thought, and (8) mental activity.

eight kinds of teaching 八重法 bā zhòngfǎ hachi jūhō

We don't know what this term refers to. It occurs only once in the Universal Sage Sutra.

eight precepts 八戒 bājiè hakkai/hachikai

The precepts observed by laypeople on certain days of the month: not killing, not stealing, not engaging in improper sexual behavior, not lying, not using intoxicants, not using cosmetics or personal decorations and avoiding music and dance, not sleeping on a bed, and not eating after noon.

eighteen unique qualities aṣṭādaśāveṇikā buddha-dharmāḥ 十八不共法 shíbā bùgòng fǎ jūhachi-fugū-hō

Features of a Buddha not shared with others, said in the Prajñāpāramitā Sūtra to be: faultlessness in body, eloquence, absence of mental attachments, mental concentration, impartiality, knowledge of all things, untiring ability to lead people, constancy in helping people, consistency with other buddhas, perfect wisdom, complete emancipation from attachments, clarity in insight, consistency in wisdom and action, consistency in wisdom and speech, consistency in wisdom and thought, unrestricted knowledge of the past, unrestricted knowledge of the future, and unrestricted knowledge of the present.

eighty different attractive features aśīty-anuvyañjanāni 八十種好 bāshízhǒng hǎo hachijisshu-gō

Distinctive characteristics of a buddha's body. Some are included among the thirty-two features of a buddha.

elements

See four elements.

TERM	SANSKRIT	CHINESE	PINYIN	JAPANESE
elements of the Way		道品	dàopǐn	dōhon
This is probably a reference to the thirty-seven practices conducive to becoming awakened. It should not be confused with the four elements.				
emancipation	vimokṣā	解脱	jiětuō	gedatsu
Liberation, salvation, especially from suffering.				
entrustment	parindanā	囑累	zhǔlèi	zokurui
Transmission to others.				
eon	kalpa	劫	jié	kō
An indeterminately long age.				
epithets of a buddha				
See ten epithets of a buddha.				
faultless or flawless	anāsrava		wúlòu	muro
Literally, without outflows. Interpreted as pure, undefiled, without illusions, etc.				
five constituent aggregates	pañca-skandha	五蘊	wǔyùn	goun
Elements, literally accumulations, from which all existing things are composed. The five are form or matter, feelings or perceptions, conceptions, impulses or volitions, and consciousness.				
five desires	pañca-kāma	五欲	wǔyù	goyoku
Usually for property or wealth, sex, food and drink, fame, and sleep, but can refer to the desires of the five objects of the senses: forms, sounds, smells, tastes, and tangible objects. The five are six senses (六入 rokunyū or 六根 rokkon), including mind or intellect. There is no clue in the Dharma Flower Sutra as to which version of the five desires is intended, except perhaps for a sentence in chapter 3 where the addition of desire for wealth might lead us to think that the second version is what is intended. The term "six desires" does not occur in the Dharma Flower Sutra.				
five emotions		五情	wǔ qíng	gojō
Probably a reference to the emotions that arise as a consequence of the five senses.				

five irredeemable sins — pañcānantarya — 五無間 — wǔ wújiān — go muken
Probably the same as the five wicked sins.

five kinds of eyes — pañca cakṣūṃṣi — 五眼 — wǔ yǎn — gogen
Usually the five kinds of eyes are given as the physical eyes of those who live on earth, the eyes of gods in heaven, the wisdom eyes of shravakas, the Dharma eye of bodhisattvas, and the Buddha eye, which includes the first four. But in the Universal Sage Sutra it is said that the buddhas all attain the five kinds of eyes.

five obstacles — pañcāvaraṇāni — 五障 — wǔ zhàng — goshō
A woman cannot become a great brahman, an Indra, a Mara, a wheel-rolling king, or a buddha.

five-part Dharma body — pañca-dharma-skandhāḥ — 五分法身 — wǔ fēn fǎshēn — go bunhōshin
Morality, concentration, wisdom, liberation, and knowledge of and insight into liberation.

five powers / five divine powers — 五通/五神通 — wǔ tōng/wǔ shéntōng — gozū/gojinzū
Refers to the first five of the six divine powers.

five precepts — pañca-veramaṇī — 五戒 — wǔ jiè — gokai
Minimal rules for lay devotees: not killing, not stealing, not engaging in improper sexual behavior, not lying, and not using intoxicants.

five states of existence — 五道諸有 — wǔ dào zhūyǒu — rokudō shou
The six states, excluding heavenly beings.

five wicked sins — pañcānantarya — 五逆罪 — wǔ nìzuì — gogyakuzai
Several sets of five especially evil acts can be found. Perhaps the most common is: killing one's father, killing one's mother, killing a saint, injuring a buddha, and causing disharmony among the monks.

flawless
See faultless.

four elements — catvāri mahā-bhūtāni — 四大 — sì dà — shidai
Earth, water, fire, and wind.

TERM	SANSKRIT	CHINESE	PINYIN	JAPANESE
four evil paths The states of purgatory dwellers, hungry spirits (*pretas*), animals, and asuras.		四惡道	sìèdào	shi akudō
four fruits Probably refers to the four kinds of saints in early Buddhism: the stream-enterer, the once-returner, the non-returner, and the arhat.	atvāri- phalāni		sì guǒ	shika
four groups Monks, nuns, laymen, and laywomen.	catasraḥ parṣadaḥ	四衆	sì zhòng	shishu
four kinds of freedom from fear There are varying accounts of the four kinds of freedom both for buddhas and for bodhisattvas. A version for buddhas lists fearlessness in declaring the reality of all things, in claiming that he has extinguished all desire and illusion, in teaching that desire and actions in the past can be obstacles to awakening, and in teaching that one can overcome all suffering by practicing Buddha-dharma.	catvāri vai śaradyāni	四無所畏	sì wúsuǒwèi	shimushoi
four kinds of unobstructed wisdom A complete understanding of the Dharma, a complete grasp of the meanings derived from the Dharma, a complete freedom in being able to express the Dharma in a variety of languages and dialects, and, based on these three, an ability to preach to all people whenever needed.		四無礙智	sì wúài zhì	shi-mugechi
four kings of heaven Protectors of Buddhism in the four directions: east, south, west, and north.	catvāri mahā-rājikāḥ	四天王	sìtiān wáng	shitennō
four modes Emerging, lasting or living, changing, and perishing.	catvāri lakṣaṇāni	四相	sì xiàng	shisō
four social teachings Four ways of winning people over: making gifts, using loving speech, behaving kindly, and doing things together with those one wants to serve.	catvāri saṃgraha-vastūni	四攝法	sì shèfǎ	shishōbō
four truths Often referred to as the four "noble truths," but not in the Lotus Sutra. The truth that life involves suffering, the truth of the cause or origin of suffering, the truth that suffering can be ended, and the truth that the way to end suffering is in the eightfold path.	catvāri ārayasatyāni	四諦/四聖諦	sì shèngdì	shishōtai

English	Definition	Sanskrit	Chinese	Pinyin	Japanese
god	The basic meaning of the Chinese character 天 is "heaven," but it is also used for heavenly beings or gods.	deva	天	tiān	ten
great one	Another term for a bodhisattva and often combined with "bodhisattva." Also sometimes translated as 大士 (great man or hero).	mahāsattva	摩訶薩	móhēsà	makasatsu
Great Vehicle	A movement which began in India around the first century BCE and later spread to China, Vietnam, Korea, and Japan. It also spread to Southeast Asian areas, from which it subsequently disappeared. Many of the main emphases of the Great Vehicle are found in the Dharma Flower Sutra.	Mahāyāna	大乘	dàshéng	daijō
griffin	A kind of mythical bird, regarded as the enemy of nagas or dragons.	garuḍa	迦樓	jiālóu	karura
hero of the world	An epithet for a buddha.	mahāvīra	世雄	shìxióng	seō
highest heaven	Literally, the summit of existence.	bhavāgra	有頂天	yǒudǐngtiān	uchō-ten
hundreds of thousands of billions of revolutions incantation	Probably this incantation can be put to a great many uses.	koṭiśatasaha-srāvartā	百千万億旋陀羅尼	bǎiqiānwànyì xuán tuóluóní	hyakusenman-noku-sen darani
ignorance	Also understood to mean delusion or absence.	avidyā	無明	wúmíng	mumyō
impartial, proper awakening	Awakening proper to a buddha.	anuttara-samyak-saṃbodhi	阿耨多羅三藐三菩提	ānòuduōluó sānmiǎo sānpútí	anokutara-sanmyaku-sanbodai
incantation	Mystical spells, sometimes intelligible, sometimes not. In the Dharma Flower Sutra the term is also used for powers presumably gained from incantations.	dhāraṇī	陀羅尼	tuóluóní	darani

TERM	SANSKRIT	CHINESE	PINYIN	JAPANESE
insight Literally, seeing with knowledge or wisdom, or views based on knowledge or wisdom.	jñāna-darśana	智見	zhìjiàn	chiken
jatika A kind of jasmine.	jāti	闍提	shétí	shadai
jivakajivaka A kind of pheasant.	jīvakajīvaka	命命	mìngmìng	myōmyō
kalavinka A bird with a beautiful voice, said to live in the valleys of the Himalayas.	kalaviṅka	迦陵頻伽	jiālíngpínqié	karyōbinga
kimshuka A precious red stone, perhaps ruby.	kiṃśuka	甄叔迦	zhēnshūjiā	kenshukuka
kovidara A kind of sandalwood tree.	kovidāra	拘鞞陀羅樹	jūbǐtuóluó shù	kubidaraju
kshatriya The second caste in the Indian system, consisting mainly of rulers and warriors.	kṣatriya	剎利	chàlì	setsuri
kumbhanda demons A class of demons with giant testicles.	kumbhāṇḍa	鳩槃荼鬼	jiūpántú guǐ	kuhandaki
kunduruka A kind of frankincense.	kundurūka	薰陸	xūnlù	kunroku
league A yojana supposedly is the distance a royal army could travel in a day. But other sources give longer and shorter estimates for the yojana, some as short as 4.4 miles. In the Dharma Flower Sutra it is difficult to make sense of any consistent rendering. I have chosen the term "league" because it too has no consistent meaning.	yojana	由旬	yóuxún	yujun

lesser teachings — hinayāna — 小乘 — xiǎoshēng — shōjō
The lesser or small vehicle.

lowest purgatory — Avīci — 阿鼻地獄 — Ābí dìyù — abi jigoku
The most terrible of the hot purgatories.

mallika — mallikā — 末利 — mòlì — mari
A kind of jasmine.

mandarava flower — māndārava — 曼陀羅華 — màntuóluó huá — mandara-ke
A red flower that blooms in heaven; also great mandarava flower.

mani — maṇi — 摩尼 — móní — mani
A jewel.

manjushaka flower — mañjūṣaka — 曼殊沙華 — mànshūshāhuā — manjusha-ke
A white flower that blooms in heaven; also great manjushaka flower.

mendicant — śramaṇa — 沙門 — shāmén — shamon
While sometimes used to refer to Buddhist monks and nuns, usually in the Lotus Sutra it refers to all kinds of ascetics, especially non-Buddhist ascetics.

merely formal Dharma — saddharma-pratirūpaka — 像法 — xiàngfǎ — zōbō
The period of the Dharma following the period of true Dharma and traditionally preceding a period of decline of the Dharma. During such a time the Dharma is preached and practiced in a formal way but has no effect on people.

nectar — amṛta — 甘露 — gānlòu — kanro
Often used as a way to describe Buddha-dharma.

nirvana — nirvāṇa — 涅槃 — nièpán — nehan
The goal of extinction, extinction of passions. In the Dharma Flower Sutra nirvana is usually seen as a teaching for shravakas which falls short of the goal of becoming a buddha.

TERM	SANSKRIT	CHINESE	PINYIN	JAPANESE
nirvana without residue Death of a buddha. Also called "nirvana without remainder" and "complete nirvana."		無餘涅槃	wú yú nièpán	muyonehan
noble practices Apparently refers to a variety of religious or moral practices traditionally performed by brahmans, the priestly and highest caste in Indian society.	brahmacaryā	梵行	fànxíng	bongyō
non-returner The third level of attainment of one striving to be an arhat. A non-returner cannot be reborn in the realm of desire.	anāgāmin	阿那含	ānàhán	anagon
novice A novice monk.	śrāmaṇera	沙彌	shāmí	shami
once-returner The second level of attainment, of one striving to be an arhat. A once-returner can be reborn in the realm of desire only once.	sakṛdāgāmin	一来果	yīlái guǒ	ichirai-ka
parjata A kind of flowering tree.	pārjātaka	波利質多羅	bōlìzhíduōluó	harishittara
patala A kind of flowering tree.	pātala	波羅羅	bōluóluó	harara
pishacha demons A kind of goblin.	piśāca	毘舍闍鬼	píshèshéguǐ	pishajaki
place of the Way The place under the bodhi-tree where the Buddha reached supreme awakening, and by extension any place where supreme awakening is reached.	bodhi-maṇḍa	道場	dàochǎng	dōjō
powers of the divine way See six powers.		神通道力	shéntōng dàolì	jinzūdōriki

pratyekabuddha 緣覺 yuánjué engaku
One of the three kinds of saints in the Dharma Flower Sutra, along with shravakas and bodhisattvas. Especially associated with the teaching of twelve causes and conditions. Often regarded as solitary practitioners.

precepts śīla 戒 jiè kai
Rules of moral behavior.

prikka pṛkkā 單力迦 bìlìjiā hitsurika
A kind of fragrant plant.

purgatory nāraka 地獄 dìyù jigoku
Buddhist purgatories, of which there are a great many, are often translated as "hells," but they are not places of everlasting punishment. Rather they are places for purification through punishment; places from which one eventually emerges and that can be visited by bodhisattvas wanting to help people there.

python mahoraga 摩睺羅伽 móhuóluóqié magoraga
A mythical creature with the head of a snake. One of the eight mythical creatures that protect Buddhism.

real Dharma 真實法 zhēnshífǎ shinjitsu hō
True teaching.

realms of thought dhātavaḥ 界 jiè kai
This is probably a reference to the eighteen components of consciousness—the six senses, their six kinds of object, and the resulting six kinds of awareness.

satyr yakṣa 夜叉 yèchā yasha
One of the eight kinds of mythical creatures that protect Buddhism.

seer ṛṣi 仙 xiān sen
In India, a forest dwelling recluse and religious practitioner. In China, usually associated with mountain dwelling religious practitioners.

seven buddhas 七佛 qī fó shichibutsu
The seven buddhas of the past are normally thought to be Vipaśyin, Śikhin, Viśvabhu, Krakucchanda, Kanakamuni, Kāśyapa, and Śākyamuni, but here the text seems to indicate that Śākyamuni is the eighth.

TERM	SANSKRIT	CHINESE	PINYIN	JAPANESE
seven precious materials	sapta ratnāna	七寶	qī bǎo	shippō
Different sutras have somewhat different lists of the seven. This is the list given in chapter 6 of the Dharma Flower Sutra: gold, silver, lapis lazuli, shell, agate, pearl, carnelian/cornelian.				
shravaka	śrāvaka	聲聞	shēngwén	shōmon
A "voice hearer," one who listens to the Buddha. Originally shravakas were the immediate disciples of the Buddha, but the term later came to be used for all those who follow the small vehicle.				
six faculties	ṣaḍ indriyāṇi	六根	liùgēn	rokkon
The six senses: vision, hearing, smell, taste, touch, and intellect, or the six corresponding organs. They are the fifth of the twelve causes and conditions.				
six kinds of teaching		六重法	liù zhòng fǎ	rokujūhō
One source gives the following: using one's body compassionately, speaking compassionately, using one's heart and mind compassionately, evenly sharing what one has been given, single-mindedly living a pure life observing noble practices, and holding correct views leading to nirvana.				
six powers/divine powers	ṣaḍ abhijñāh	六通/六神通	liù tōng/liù shéntōng	rokutsū/rokujinzū
The ability to go anywhere, see anything anywhere, hear anything anywhere, know the thoughts of others, know past lives, and freedom from passions and illusions.				
six practices		六度	liùdù	rokudo
See six transcendental practices.				
six states	ṣaḍ-gati	六趣/六道	liùqù / liùdào	rokushu/rokudō
The six states or paths of existence into which those who are not fully awakened are reborn: purgatory dwellers, hungry spirits (pretas), animals, asuras, humans, and heavenly beings. Sometimes translated as six destinies.				
six transcendental practices	ṣaṭ-pāramitā	六波羅蜜	liù pōluómì	ropparamitsu
Practices which must be followed by someone following the bodhisattva way. They are called "transcendental" because they lead to "the other shore," a metaphor very common in Buddhism but not used in the Dharma Flower Sutra. The six are: generosity (giving, especially in giving alms to monks, or charity), morality (literally, keeping the precepts), patience (patient endurance of hardship); perseverance (diligence, zeal), meditation, and wisdom.				

English	Sanskrit/Pāli	Chinese	Pinyin	Japanese
six ways of trembling and shaking In the Flower Garland Sutra they are given as moving, rocking, gushing, shocking, quivering, and roaring. Another version has moving, rising, springing, trembling, reverberating, and thudding.		六種震動	liùzhǒng zhèndòng	rokushu-shindō
sixty-two wrong views This is a reference to sixty-two types of philosophy in India at the time. Basically they were concerned with whether the self is permanent. Buddhists rejected all these views.	dvāṣaṣṭi-dṛṣṭi	六十二邪見	liùshíèr xiéjiàn	rokujuni-jaken
skillful means Sometimes improperly translated as "expedients" or "expedient means." Also skill in Dharma-sounds incantation.	upāya	方便	fāngbiàn	hōben
small vehicle Used in contrast with "Great Vehicle."	hīnayāna	小乗	xiǎoshèng	shōjō
stream-enterer The first of four stages of the shravaka path, sometimes translated as "stream-winner."	srotāpanna	須陀洹	xutuohuan	shudaon
stupa A repository for crematory remains or relics, especially of the Buddha. It is the most venerated structure in Buddhism.	stūpa	塔	tǎ	tō
sumana A kind of jasmine.	sumanā	須曼那	xūmànnà	shumana
supreme awakening This literally means something like completely and perfectly awakened. It is one of the epithets applied to a buddha.	samyak-saṃbodhi	三藐三菩提	sānmiǎo sānpútí	sammyaku-sambodai
tagara A fragrant tree.	tagara	多伽羅	duōqiéluó	takara/tagara
tala tree A palmlike tree which grows to a height of twenty-five meters.	tāla	多羅樹	duōluóshù	taraju

TERM	SANSKRIT	CHINESE	PINYIN	JAPANESE
tamalapatra A kind of sandalwood tree, the leaf of which is used to make incense.	tamālapatra	多摩羅跋	duōmóluóbá	tamarahatsu
tathagata Frequently used to refer to the Buddha, it is often translated as "Thus Come One." The meaning, however, is obscure.	tathāgata	如来	rúlái	nyorai
ten directions Refers to the four compass points, the four intermediate points, such as northeast, and the up and down directions. But its meaning is basically "in all directions" or "everywhere."	daśa diśaḥ	十方	shífāng	jippō
ten epithets of a buddha These are: tathagata, one worthy of offerings, truly awakened, having clarity and conduct, well gone, understanding the world, unexcelled leader, trainer of men, teacher of heavenly beings and people, and buddha, world-honored one. In some lists the seventh (unexcelled leader) and eighth (trainer of men) are combined into one, and the tenth (buddha, world-honored one) is regarded as two.	arakan/ōgu	十號	shíhào	jūgō
ten evils/ten evil actions Killing, stealing, adultery, lying, immoral speech, slander, equivocation, greed, anger, and false views.		十悪 / 十悪業	shíè/shíèyè	jūakugō
ten powers Powers of a buddha (in chapter 7, powers of Buddha-dharma) are said in the Prajñāpāramitā Sūtra to be: knowing what to do and not to do, knowing the deeds of people and their effects, understanding all kinds of concentration and meditation, knowing the root capacities of people, understanding the ways of thinking of people, knowing the lineage of people, understanding the effects of the actions of people, remembering past lives, knowing when and where people will die and be born, and knowing how to remove faults and flaws.	daśa-balāni	十力	shílì	jūriki
ten realms The six states of existence plus those of shravaka, pratyekabuddha, bodhisattva, and buddha.		十界	shíjiè	jikkai
thirty-three gods The gods who live on the summit of Mount Sumeru.	trāyastriṃśa	三十三天	sānshísān tiān	sanjūsan-ten
thirty-two characteristics Features, often called "marks," of the body of a buddha. See endnote 6 for two such lists.	dvātriṃśan mahā-puruṣalakṣaṇāni	三十二相	sānshíèr xiàng	sanjūni-sō

English	Sanskrit	Pinyin	Chinese	Japanese
this world — The world in which we live, and in which Shakyamuni Buddha teaches, understood to be a place where suffering is prevalent, has to be endured, and can be endured. Thus it is a place where opportunities to follow the bodhisattva way are numerous.	sāha	suō pó	娑婆	shaba
three destinies — The hot purgatory, the bloody purgatory, and the purgatory of swords.	trayo durgatayaḥ	sān tú	三塗	san zu
three evil paths — The states of purgatory dwellers, hungry spirits (pretas), and animals.		sān èdào	三惡道	san-nakudō
threefold refuge — Taking refuge in, or having faith in, the Buddha, the Dharma, and the sangha.	triśaraṇa	sān guī	三歸	san ki
threefold world — Desire, form, and formlessness. Traditionally understood to be the world in which beings subject to rebirth live. Human beings are understood to live primarily in the realm of desire, and thus to be ruled by desire.	trayo dhātavaḥ	sānjiè	三界	sangai
three hindrances — The three kinds of hindrance are said to be those of affliction, including covetousness, anger, ignorance, etc.; those due to past actions; and that of painful retribution, due to being born in this world.	trīṇyāvaraṇāni	sān zhàng	三障	san shō
three kinds of buddha body — Probably the three bodies mentioned here are the physical body, the reward or enjoyment body, and the Dharma body.	trikāya	fó sānzhǒng shēn	仏三種身	butsu sanshu shin
three kinds of knowledge — Seeing anything anywhere, knowing past lives, and eradicating illusions.		sān míng	三明	sanmyō
three kinds of mental stability — Often understood to be three bases of mindfulness.	trīṇi smṛty-upasthānāni	sān niànchù	三念處	san nenjo

Term	Sanskrit	Chinese	Pinyin	Japanese
three kinds of suffering Suffering from inflicted pain, that is, from undesirable causes and conditions, suffering from being deprived of pleasure or loss of something which brings pleasure, and suffering from the impermanence of things.		三苦	sān kǔ	sanku
three poisons greed, anger (or hatred), and folly (or stupidity, delusion).	tri-viṣa / tri-doṣa	三毒	sān dú	san doku
three teachings Probably refers to the three characteristics or marks of Buddha-dharma in Mahayana Buddhism: impermanence, no enduring self, and nirvana is calm and tranquil.	tri-dṛṣṭi-namitta-mudrā	三法	sān fǎ	sanpō/sanhō
three-thousand great thousandfold world A major world system centered around a Mount Sumeru and said to equal a billion small worlds. There are various sizes of the three-thousand thousandfold worlds. Also called "a thousand millionfold world."	trisāhasra-mahāsāhasrāḥ lokadhāyavaḥ	三千大千世界	sānqiān dàqiān shìjiè	sanzen dai sen sekai
three treasures Buddha, Dharma, and sangha/saṃ gha.	triratna / ratna-traya	三寶	sān bǎo	sambō/sanbō
three vehicles The ways, or vehicles, of the shravaka, the pratyekabuddha, and the bodhisattva.	trīṇi yānāni	三乗	sānshèng	sanjō
three worlds The past, present, and future.	traiya-dhvika	三世	sānshì	sanze/sansei
transcendental practices See six transcendental practices.	pāramitās	波羅蜜	bōluómì	haramitsu
true Dharma The period after the death of a buddha when the teachings continue to be both widely observed and effective.	sad-dharma	正法	zhèngfǎ	shōbō

Term	Transliteration	Chinese	Pinyin	Japanese
turushka — A kind of incense.	turuṣka	兜樓婆	dōulóupó	torōba
twelve causes — Short for twelve causes and conditions.		十二緣	shíèr yuán	jūni-en
twelve causes and conditions — Often called the twelve-link, or twelvefold, chain of dependent origination: ignorance, actions, consciousness, name and form, six kinds of sense, contact, sensations, desires, attachments, existence, birth, and old age and death	dvādaśāṅga-pratītya-samutpāda	十二因緣	shíèr yīnyuán	jūni innen
twenty-five states of existence — Includes the four evil paths, the four continents in which people live, the six heavens of the world of desire, the seven heavens of the world of form, and the four heavens of the formless world.		二十五有	èrshíwǔ yǒu	nijūgo-u
two ways — Probably refers to the Great Vehicle and the small vehicle.		二道	èr dào	nidō
udumbara — A flower that blossoms extremely rarely, sometimes said to be only once in three thousand years.	udumbara	優曇華	yōutánhuā	udonge
unexcelled awakening — The highest awakening or enlightenment, one of the terms for the awakening of a buddha.	anuttara-bodhi	無上菩提	wúshàng pútí	mujōbodai
varshika — A kind of aloe used for making lamp oil.	vārṣika	婆利師伽	pólìshījiā	barishika
wheel-turning king — Several kinds of wheel-turning kings are mentioned in the Sutra of Innumerable Meanings, but in the Dharma Flower Sutra itself the term usually is "wheel-turning saintly king."	cakravartin	轉輪王	zhuǎnlún wáng	tenrin-nō
wheel-turning saintly-king — There are several different explanations of the meaning of "wheel" in this expression, but none in the Dharma Flower Sutra.		轉輪聖王	zhuǎnlún shèngwáng	tenrin-jō-ō

Term	Sanskrit	Chinese	Pinyin	Japanese
worthy of offerings	arhat	応供	yìnggòng	ōgu
The literal meaning of "arhat" is "worthy one," meaning someone who is worthy of offerings. It refers to one who has attained the highest stage of awakening for a shravaka.				
wrong views	mithyā-dṛṣṭi	邪見 /邪心	xiéjiàn/xiéxīn	jaken/jashin
Erroneous or incorrect views.				

Bibliography

TRANSLATIONS

The Lotus Sutra. Translated by Burton Watson. New York: Columbia University Press, 1993.

The Lotus Sutra: The Sutra of the Lotus Flower of the Wonderful Dharma. Translated by Senchū Murano. 1974. 2nd edition, Tokyo: Nichiren Shu Shimbun, 1991.

The Lotus Sutra: The White Lotus of the Marvelous Law. Translated by Tsugunari Kubo and Akira Yuyama. Tokyo and Berkeley: Bukkyō Dendō Kyōkai and Numata Center for Buddhist Translation and Research, 1993.

The Lotus of the Wonderful Law or The Lotus Gospel: Saddharma Pundarika Sutra, Miao-fa Lien Hua Ching. Translated by W. E. Soothill. Oxford: Clarendon Press, 1930; Atlantic Highlands, N.J.: Humanities Press, 1987.

Saddharma-Puṇḍarīka or The Lotus of the True Law. Translated by H. Kern (from Sanskrit). Sacred Books of the East, vol. 21. London: Clarendon Press, 1884; New York: Dover, 1963.

Saddharmapuṇḍarīkasūtra: Central Asian Manuscripts: Romanized Text. Edited with introduction by Hirofumi Toda. Tokushima, Japan: Kyoiku Shuppan Center, 1983.

Scripture of the Lotus Blossom of the Fine Dharma (The Lotus Sutra). Translated by Leon Hurvitz. New York: Columbia University Press, 1976.

The Threefold Lotus Sutra: Innumerable Meanings, The Lotus Flower of the Wonderful Law, and Meditation on the Bodhisattva Universal Virtue. Translated by Bunnō Katō et al. 1971. Reprint, Tokyo: Kosei Publishing Co., 1975.

The Wonderful Dharma Lotus Flower Sutra. Buddhist Text Translation Society. 10 volumes. San Francisco: Sino-American Buddhist Association, 1976–82.

Books Primarily on the Lotus Sutra

Davidson, J. Leroy. *The Lotus Sutra in Chinese Art.* New Haven: Yale University Press, 1954.

Dykstra, Yoshiko K. *Miraculous Tales of the Lotus Sutra from Ancient Japan: The Dainihonkoku Hokekyōkenki of Priest Chingen.* Honolulu: University of Hawaii Press, 1983.

Fuss, Michael. *Buddhavacana & Dei Verbum: A Phenomenological & Theological Comparison of Scriptural Inspiration in the Saddharmapundarika Sutra & in the Christian Tradition.* Leiden: E.J. Brill, 1991.

Ikeda, Daisaku. *The Flower of Chinese Buddhism.* New York: Weatherhill, 1986.

Karashima, Seishi. *A Glossary of Dharmarakṣa's Translation of the Lotus Sutra.* Bibliotheca Philologica et Philosophica Buddhica I. Tokyo: The International Research Institute for Advanced Buddhology, Soka University, 1998.

_____. *A Glossary of Kumārajīva's Translation of the Lotus Sutra.* Bibliotheca Philologica et Philosophica Buddhica IV. Tokyo: The International Research Institute for Advanced Buddhology, Soka University, 2001.

Kim, Young-Ho. *Tao-sheng's Commentary on the Lotus Sutra: A Study and Translation.* Albany: SUNY Press, 1990.

Leighton, Taigen Dan. *Visions of Awakening Space and Time: Dōgen and the* Lotus Sutra. Oxford: Oxford University Press, 2007.

Montgomery, Daniel B. *Fire in the Lotus: The Dynamic Buddhism of Nichiren.* London: Mandala, 1991.

Nhat Hanh, Thich. *Opening the Heart of the Cosmos: Insights on the Lotus Sutra.* Berkeley: Parallax, 2003.

Niwano, Nikkyō. *Buddhism for Today: A Modern Interpretation of the Threefold Lotus Sutra.* Tokyo: Kōsei, 1976.

_____. *A Guide to the Threefold Lotus Sutra.* Tokyo: Kōsei, 1981.

Pye, Michael. *Skilful Means: A Concept in Mahayana Buddhism.* London: Duckworth, 1978.

Reeves, Gene, ed. *A Buddhist Kaleidoscope: Essays on the Lotus Sutra.* Tokyo: Kosei Publishing Co., 2002.

Sangharakshita. *The Dream of Cosmic Enlightenment: Parables, Myths, and Symbols of the White Lotus Sutra.* Glasgow: Windhorse, 1993.

Suguro, Shinjo. *Introduction to the Lotus Sutra.* Freemont, Calif.: Jain, 1998.

Tamura, Yoshirō, and Kurata Bunsaku, eds. *Art of the Lotus Sutra.* Tokyo: Kosei Publishing Co., 1987.

Tanabe, George J., Jr., and Willa Jane Tanabe. *The Lotus Sutra in Japanese Culture.* Honolulu: University of Hawaii Press, 1989.

Tanabe, Willa Jane. *Paintings of the Lotus Sutra.* Tokyo: Weatherhill, 1988.

Tanaka, Chigaku. *What Is Nippon Kokutai?* Translated by Satomi Kishio. Tokyo: Shishi-o Bunko, 1937.

"The Twenty-first Century and the Philosophy of the Lotus Sutra." *Journal of Oriental Studies 6.* Tokyo: The Institute of Oriental Philosophy, 1996.

Yuyama, Akira. *A Bibliography of the Sanskrit Texts of the Saddharmapuṇḍarīkasūtra.* Canberra: Australian National University Press, 1970.

_____. *Eugène Burnouf: The Background to His Research into the Lotus Sutra.* Bibliotheca Philologica et Philosophica Buddhica III. Tokyo: The International Research Institute for Advanced Buddhology, Soka University, 2000.

Index

About the Translator

GENE REEVES has been studying, teaching, and writing in Japan for twenty years, primarily on Buddhism and interfaith relations. Now the International Advisor at Rissho Kosei-kai, he is retired from the University of Tsukuba, where he taught for eight years. He is a founder of and serves as the Special Minister for the International Buddhist Congregation in Tokyo. He also serves as the International Advisor to the Niwano Peace Foundation and he is the coordinator of an annual International Seminar on the Lotus Sutra. In the spring of 2008 Reeves was a visiting professor at the University of Peking, Beijing, China.

Reeves has been active in interfaith conversations and organizations: he served as Chair of the Planning Committee for the 1987 Congress of the International Association for Religious Freedom (IARF) at Stanford University; he was one of the founders of the Council for a Parliament of the World's Religions; and he is a member of the Board of the Society for Buddhist Christian Studies. In Japan he has been an advisor to the Japan Liaison Committee of the IARF, a participant in the Religious Summit at Mount Hiei, and in various activities of the World Conference of Religions for Peace. As a Buddhist teacher, he travels frequently to China, Singapore, Taiwan, America, and Europe to give talks at universities and churches, mainly on the Lotus Sutra.

About Wisdom Publications

Wisdom Publications is the leading publisher of classic and contemporary Buddhist books and practical works on mindfulness. To learn more about us or to explore our other books, please visit our website at wisdompubs.org or contact us at the address below.

Wisdom Publications
199 Elm Street
Somerville, MA 02144 USA

We are a 501(c)(3) organization, and donations in support of our mission are tax deductible.

Wisdom Publications is affiliated with the Foundation for the Preservation of the Mahayana Tradition (FPMT).